RAF COLD WAR JET AIRCRAFT
IN PROFILE

RAF COLD WAR JET AIRCRAFT IN PROFILE 2

CHRIS SANDHAM-BAILEY

First published as Cold War Jets in 2016
This edition published in 2022
by Tempest Books
an imprint of Mortons Books Ltd.
Media Centre
Morton Way
Horncastle LN9 6JR
www.mortonsbooks.co.uk
Copyright © Tempest Books, 2022

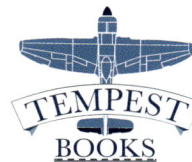

TEMPEST
BOOKS

ISBN 978-1-911658-11-5
Typeset by Jayne Clements (jayne@hinoki.co.uk), Hinoki Design and Typesetting
Printed and bound by Gutenberg Press, Malta

Thanks: I would like to thank a number of people, firstly Dan Sharp and Mortons for supporting this publication. All the hard working volunteers at Bruntingthorpe including the Buccaneer Aviation Group, the Lightning Preservation Group, WT333 and everyone else who keeps these Cold War warriors running. Tangmere, Newark and the East Midlands museums for allowing me access to their collections. John Smith, Phil Willsher, Dave Fleming, Rob Monfea, Joe Warner Cherrie and my long suffering yet understanding family. Lastly Tim Spilsbury and Simon Potter without whom none of this would have been possible.

CONTENTS

INTRODUCTION

Western Europe lived in perpetual fear of attack from the East during the latter half of the 20th century. Countering this threat meant the defences of NATO had to be continually reinforced with the latest technologies — resulting in the cold war arms race.

While it was thought that any actual strike was likely to end in mutually assured destruction, the period would still see intense activity. Ensuring air superiority would be essential since the bombers had to get through with their nuclear payload.

Despite the world teetering on the brink of war, or perhaps because of it, the Royal Air Force and British aviation in general enjoyed a new golden age. The inventions of the 1939-45 war, the jet engine and radar, provided springboards for exciting new projects which were in constant development, the resulting brand new aircraft amazing the crowds at Farnborough's annual SBAC shows.

Glamorous test pilots broke the sound barrier and futuristic aircraft such as the English Electric P.1 and the behemoth that was the Avro 698 mesmerised spectators. Both types went on to become iconic aircraft (the Lightning and Vulcan) that every schoolboy dreamed of one day flying.

As the threat from the USSR and Warsaw Pact nations continued to inform military planning, the roles required of aircraft evolved. Despite the RAF having proven the benefits of operating from temporary airstrips both during the Battle of Britain and as they leapfrogged from airfield to airfield after D-Day, the jets of the post-war period needed hard runways of increasing length to accommodate their greater weight and the distance they required to get airborne.

In later years, both the Jaguar and Harrier were designed to operate in the field should the worst come to the worst and the airfields were lost during a first strike. The Harrier could operate from literally anywhere and the Jaguar was capable of using the autobahns of West Germany.

Bombers which were looking obsolete in their primary role as a nuclear deterrent, due to the submarine fleet taking over that task, were converted to tankers, allowing the RAF to reach any part of the globe; the most famous example being the Black Buck raids when the Victor tanker fleet helped Vulcan bombers reach the Falkland Islands.

While there was never a direct conflict between East and West there were many proxy wars where the RAF and British-designed aircraft were involved. The possibility of a 'domino effect', where one nation after another fell to communism, was a constant worry in the Far East and while it was not involved in the Vietnam War the RAF had a presence in the region for many years.

The RAF was, however, used during the Malayan Emergency and was a permanent presence in Singapore, where types such as the Meteor and Javelin were based at one time or another.

In the Middle East, several RAF types saw action during the Suez Crisis. The RAF Luqa, Malta, and RAF Akrotiri, Cyprus, bases hosted everything from Venoms to Valiants while British and French forces attempted to retake the canal and topple Nasser, the Egyptian president.

Further south at RAF Khormaksar, the RAF saw prolonged action while trying to protect the sovereignty of Aden against various guerrilla groups, eventually pulling out in 1967.

During the 1970s the RAF retained a sizable presence in West Germany and fighters remained on standby in the UK for Quick Reaction Alert to intercept Soviet aircraft that probed British airspace, something that has continued into the 21st century.

As mentioned, the RAF also played a vital role during the Falklands War in 1982, with Harriers being a key component of the expeditionary force. The following decade saw the end of the cold war but the jets built as a result of it continued to be used during the Gulf War and later in the Balkans.

The soaring cost of combat aircraft has resulted in an ongoing reduction in the size of air forces around the globe and the threats to peace in the early 21st century are no longer as clear cut as they were during the cold war when it was the East versus the West. This, combined with the ever-increasing use of drones, means we are unlikely to ever again see an RAF as large or impressive as it was during the cold war.

There is no official consensus on when the cold war started and ended but it is generally agreed that it covered a period from around 1947 to 1991, so all the main front line jets used by the RAF during this time have been included here. Some early and post-cold war schemes have been included too, due to their significance in relation to the type.

There are some notable types absent that provided a vital role and have their own aficionados, including the Phantom, the Nimrod and the Tornado which was a result of the cold war but continued in service long afterwards. Other absent jets include the Provost, Gnat and Hawk, these three being used as trainers by the RAF. The aircraft featured have been limited to the front line British-built fighters and bombers active during the 'hottest' parts of the cold war.

Although the Jaguar was an Anglo-French collaboration and the second generation Harriers were largely American in design, they were still derivatives of the original Hawker P.1127.

Chris Sandham-Bailey

GLOSTER METEOR

The Meteor was the first and only Allied jet to see active service during the Second World War but its career was dominated by service during the cold war. Squadrons were based in Germany as the Iron Curtain descended and remained there into the mid-1950s. The type continued to fly with the RAF in secondary roles for many years and was widely exported.

With the successful early flights of the experimental Gloster E.28/39, which proved Frank Whittle's new turbojet engine, it was evident that the future of combat and aviation lay with the new form of propulsion. At this stage the output of the engines was insufficient for a single unit to power a fighter on its own so specification F.9/40 called for two engines and armament of four 20mm Hispano cannon (originally six were intended but the weight proved too great). Having already worked closely with Whittle's company Power Jets, Gloster was the logical choice for the design. An initial order was placed for 12 aircraft and eight prototypes were eventually built, DG202-DG209.

The jet engine's enormous potential was recognised by the Minister of Aircraft Production, Lord Beaverbrook, and Gloster was instructed to concentrate on the new Twin Engined Whittle Fighter. Informally the project was known as Rampage, then it became Thunderbolt, but with the P-47 in service the name Meteor was eventually settled on to avoid confusion.

Design and construction were relatively straightforward with the only radical departure from previous aircraft being the engines — the layout chosen was analogous to that of the existing Westland Whirlwind, which had nose-mounted cannon and wing-mounted engines. Resources were scarce in 1941 so the Meteor was

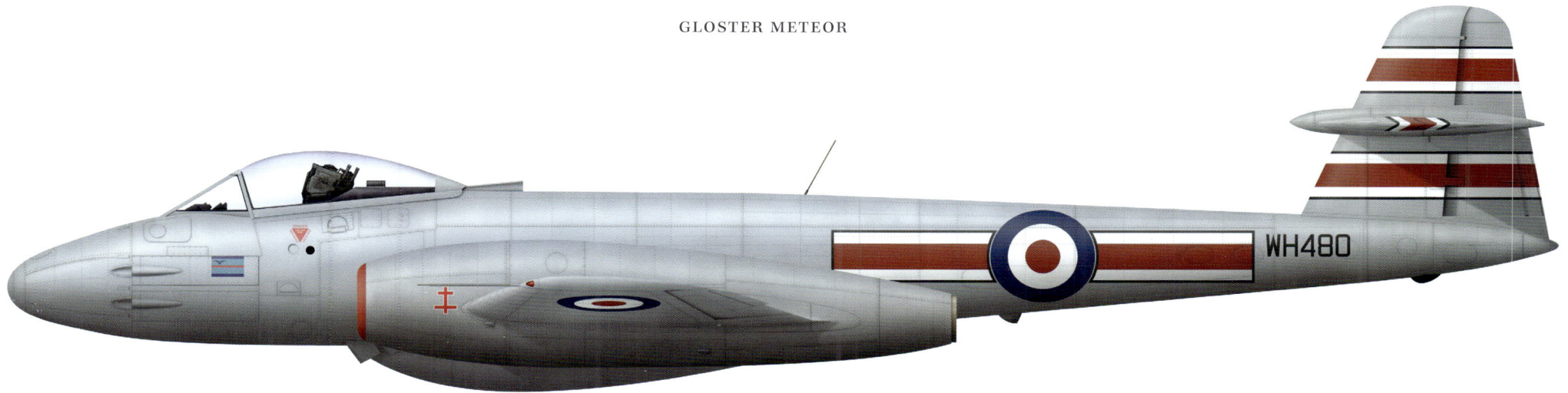

METEOR F.8 WH480 41 SQUADRON

Delivered in January 1952, WH480 served exclusively with 41 Squadron until scrapped in January 1958. The aircraft
initially wore bands on its tail but these were later replaced with the fin flash. Finished in all over aluminium.

designed to make the most of existing machinery and minimal tooling was required for many of its parts.

The first Meteor to fly was the fifth prototype, DG206, on March 5, 1943, at RAF Cranwell. Early testing was beset with complications, two of the prototypes being written off and a third severely damaged.

One major delay was a breakdown in relations between Power Jets and Rover, the latter having been tasked with production of the early engines. In an effort to resolve the difficulties Rolls-Royce was appointed to the project, beginning the company's association with jet engines. 616 South Yorkshire Squadron was the first to convert to the new jet. Initially two flights retained the Spitfire VII and only the third was equipped with the Meteor F.1, the first pilots

beginning their conversion course on June 6, 1944. The squadron was to receive its first Meteors a month later.

The biggest change for many fighter pilots was the two engines, but the slower acceleration and higher top speed also took some getting used to. Concern that the Germans may be able to reverse engineer the Meteor meant that operations were initially limited to flights over UK soil, 616 Sqn being tasked with intercepting V-1 flying bombs.

By the end of the year the more powerful F.3 began to filter through and in February 1945 a flight of four Meteors was based at Melsbroek, Belgium. Most Allied troops had never encountered the Meteor and it was not uncommon for it to be mistaken for the

METEOR F.1 EE222 616 SQUADRON

Written off following a forced landing due to lack of fuel on August 29, 1944, EE222 is thought to have been flown by Wg Cdr A. McDowell of 616 Squadron. Finished in dark green, dark sea grey camouflage with medium sea grey underside and sky band.

Me 262. To remedy this, the Meteors each received an all over white-wash. The F.3 served with 15 squadrons and 210 were constructed.

Further developments saw the introduction of the F.4 which had a more powerful engine, the Rolls-Royce Derwent 5 which was itself a scaled version of the new Rolls-Royce Nene. Extended intakes also allowed for a higher top speed and much greater rate of climb.

The F.4 was found to be a lot more manoeuvrable and amenable to aerobatics, even being able to execute them with only one engine, an indication of the swift progress made. Rapid advancements by Gloster's competitors meant that subsequent iterations had to be radically overhauled to keep up. This led to the F.8 — the final

single seat fighter version of the Meteor.

Initially, experienced piston-engine fighter pilots were given a cursory tour of the cockpit and a copy of the pilot notes then told to get on with it. However, it soon became apparent that pilots found the change to flying jets a considerable challenge. So Specification T.1/47 outlined the need for a dual control jet trainer to reduce the number of accidents caused by unfamiliarity. F.4 G-AKPK had already been used as a company demonstrator and was selected for conversion.

The fuselage was extended to accommodate the pupil and the aircraft (now designated T.7) flew in this configuration for the first time on March 19, 1948. Another advantage of the lengthening

METEOR F.3 EE239 616 SQUADRON

Towards the end of the war, four Meteor F.3s — including EE239 of 616 Squadron — were painted all over White
to identify them as non-hostile and help Allied troops become familiar with the new fighter.

was an improvement in directional stability. For many years the T.7 was the first experience of jet flight an RAF pilot would have.

Following the war, the RAF needed a replacement for the Mosquito night fighter which would be capable of matching the new jet bombers for speed; this ultimately led to the Gloster Javelin but until then an interim solution was required. Airborne interception relied on a radar operator guiding the pilot on to the intruder so the logical basis for a Meteor night fighter was the T.7.

Despite sounding simple the development and introduction of the NF.11 was a protracted affair. With the company's resources already heavily committed to the production of the single seat fighters, the programme was subcontracted to Armstrong Whitworth

at Coventry. A number of changes had a substantial impact on the aircraft, radar equipment increasing its weight and requiring both a greater wingspan and the more powerful Derwent 8 engines. The 20mm Hispano cannon were moved into the wing, the nose now containing the radar and a new feature for the Meteor, a pressurised cockpit.

The NF.11 entered service with the RAF when WD599 was delivered to 29 Sqn at RAF Tangmere on August 20, 1951. Before the month was out, a further seven had been delivered. The next version of the Meteor to enter service was the NF.13 (before the NF.12). This was a tropicalised version of the NF.11 with the introduction of air conditioning. It was to serve in Egypt with 39 Sqn and 219 Sqn.

Development of the NF.12 was more complex than the straightforward alterations made to the NF.13. Externally, it received aerodynamic improvements to the tail and nose, the latter being the result of the larger American APS-57 radar. The canopy and other features remained largely unchanged.

The final iteration of the Meteor was the NF.14 which was a refined version of the NF.12. A new canopy with improved all round vision was added. It also saw a further extension of the nose to accommodate the APQ-4 radar. Many airframes went on to see a second life in a range of roles, some being converted to drones, others being used as target tugs. Along with newly built aircraft a lot of ex-RAF Meteors were exported to the 17 countries which flew the type. It was the very first operational jet produced by the Allies and almost 4000 were built.

Gloster Meteor

VARIANT	LENGTH	SPAN	HEIGHT	ENGINE
F MK.I	41FT 5IN/12.62M	43FT/13.11M	13FT/3.96M	2 X WELLAND
F MK.II	41FT 5IN/12.62M	44FT 3IN/13.49M	13FT/3.96M	2 X GOBLIN
F MK.III	41FT 5IN /12.62M	43FT/13.11M	13FT/3.96M	2 X DERWENT 1
F MK.4	41FT/12.50M	43FT/13.11M	13FT/3.96M	2 X DERWENT 5
T MK.7	43FT 6IN/13.26M	37FT 2.5IN/11.34M	13FT/3.96M	2 X DERWENT 8
F MK.8	44FT 7IN/13.59M	37FT 2.5IN/11.34M	13FT/3.96M	2 X DERWENT 8
FR MK.9	44FT 7IN/13.59M	37FT 2.5IN/11.34M	13FT/3.96M	2 X DERWENT 8
PR MK.10	44FT 3IN/13.49M	43FT/13.11M	13FT/3.96M	2 X DERWENT 8
NF MK.11	48FT 6IN/14.78M	43FT/13.11M	13FT 11IN/4.24M	2 X DERWENT 8
NF MK.12	49FT 11IN/15.21M	43FT/13.11M	13FT 11IN/4.24M	2 X DERWENT 9
NF MK.13	48FT 6IN/14.78M	43FT/13.11M	13FT 11IN/4.24M	2 X DERWENT 8
NF MK.14	51FT 4IN/15.63M	43FT/13.11M	13FT 11IN/4.24M	2 X DERWENT 9

METEOR F.4 VT282 74 SQUADRON

Delivered to 74 Squadron at RAF Horsham St Faith in October 1948, F.4 VT282 served during the early 1950s. It was converted to a U.15 drone in 1956 and shot down on September 8, 1960, off the coast of Malta while part of 728B NAS. All over aluminium.

METEOR F.4 RA444 257 SQUADRON

Based at RAF Odiham, 257 Squadron's RA444 was the first jet to land in Dublin—for a demonstration to the Irish Air Corps during May 1948. The squadron logo was worn on the nose.

METEOR F.8 VZ440 43 SQUADRON

This was the first Meteor delivered to 43 Squadron in August 1949, it was then allocated to 12 MU where it was scrapped in August 1959. WA829 at Tangmere Museum has been painted up to represent VZ440.

METEOR F.8 WA923 63 SQUADRON

Wearing all camouflage on the upper surface with a distinctive check pattern on the fuselage and wing tips, WA923 was delivered to 63 Squadron in November 1950 and scrapped in February 1958. Dark green, dark sea grey upper surfaces and light aircraft grey underside.

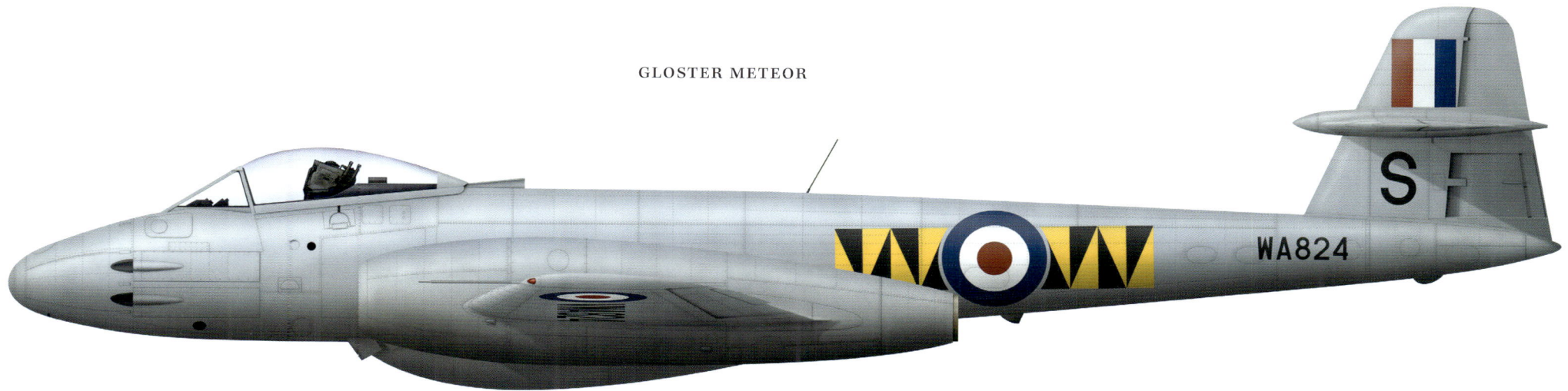

METEOR F.8 WA824 74 SQUADRON

Having already operated earlier marks of Meteor, 74 Squadron converted to the F.8 while at RAF Horsham
St Faith in October 1950. Until 1956 the aircraft were finished in aluminium, then they were repainted in
camouflage. WA824 appeared as part of a squadron display at the Paris Air Show in June 1956.

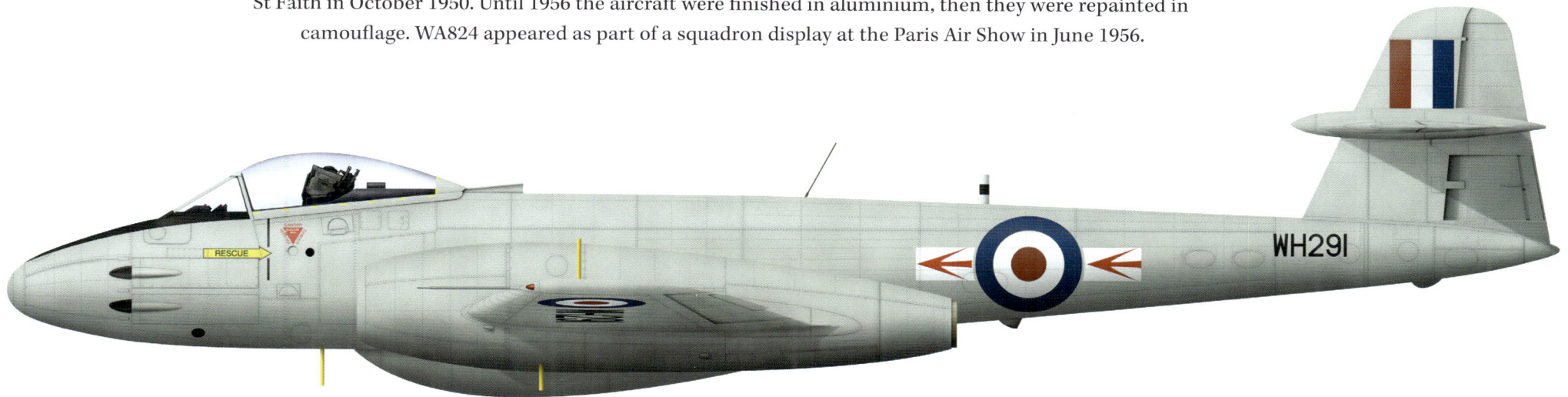

METEOR F.8 WH291 79 SQUADRON

WH291 was delivered to 257 Squadron in November 1951. Following a wheels-up landing, it was eventually allocated to 229
OCU at Chivenor and painted in 79 Squadron (shadow unit) markings and all over light aircraft grey during late 1970.

METEOR F.8 WH301 609 SQUADRON

Currently on display at the RAF Museum, Hendon WH301 served with 609 Sqn and later 85 Sqn. Still wearing these markings when it was acquired by the museum, it was repainted in its original markings in 1989.

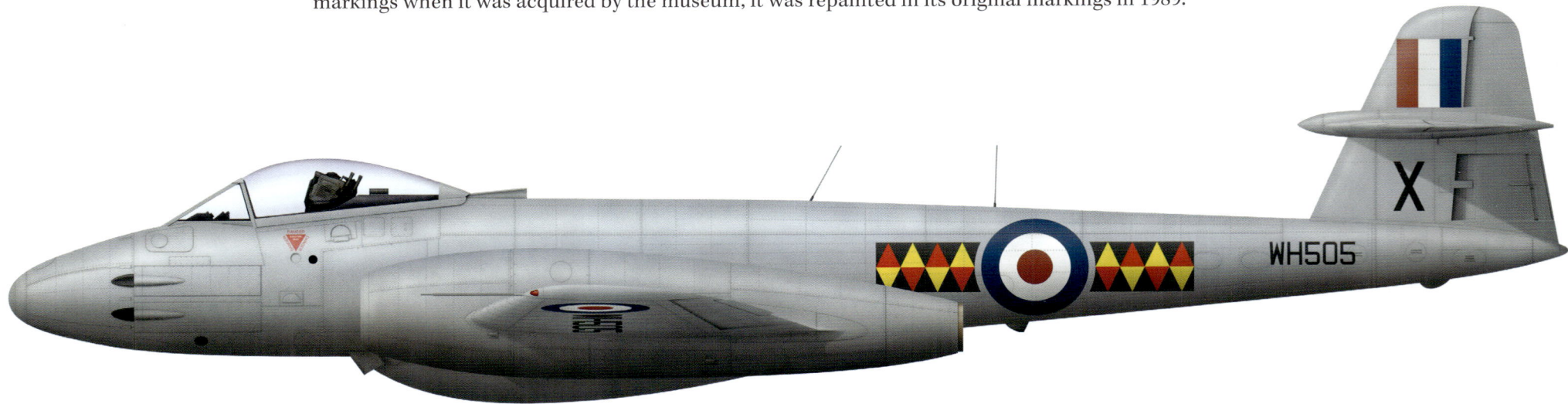

METEOR F.8 WH505 611 SQUADRON

Flown by the leader of 611 Squadron during 1952, WH505 was later converted into a U.16 drone and written off on September 27, 1962.

METEOR T.7 WH127 610 SQUADRON

Based at RAF Hooton Park, 610 Squadron was equipped with the Meteor F.4 and F.8 but also had some trainers including WH127. Following disbandment in 1957, the aircraft was allocated to a training unit and struck off in October 1963.

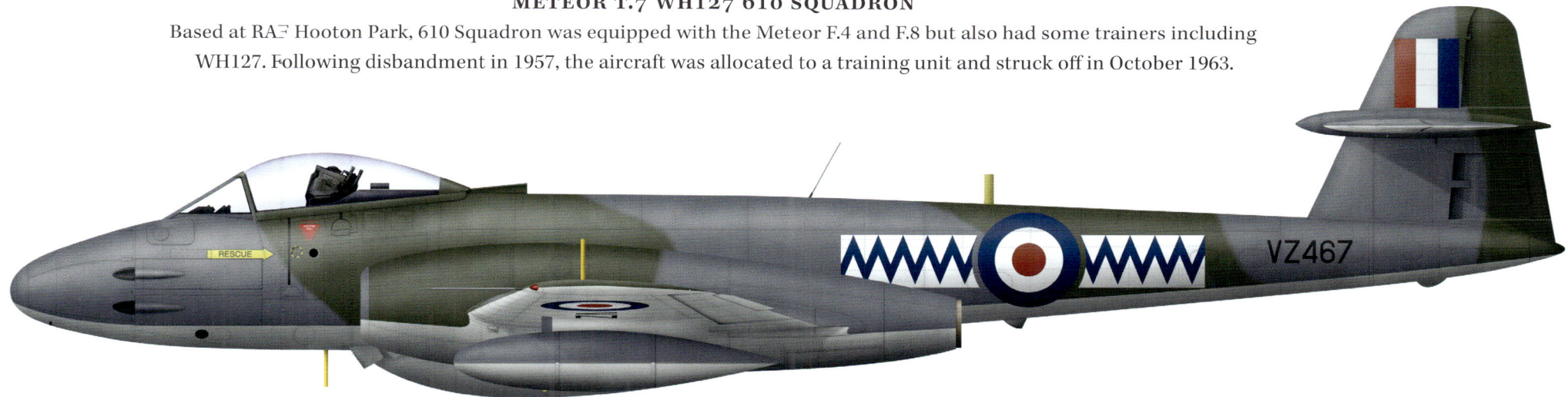

METEOR F.8 VZ467 615 SURREY SQUADRON

Based at 1 TWU RAF Brawdy, VZ467 'Winston' was supposedly painted in 615 Squadron colours for an intended flypast for the 100th anniversary of Sir Winston Churchill's birth in 1970. The scheme was retained until it was retired. Now in Australia as A77-851 and the only airworthy F.8.

METEOR T.7 WF778 613 SQUADRON
Despite 613 Sqn being a Vampire unit, WF778 was kept on strength between April 1951 and February 1957 for pilot assessment.

METEOR T.7 WA669 CENTRAL FLYING SCHOOL VINTAGE PAIR
WA669 was one of two T.7s flown by CFS pilots with Vampire XH304 from the formation of the Vintage Pair display team in 1971. WA669 and XH304 were involved in a mid-air collision on May 25, 1986, at RAF Mildenhall. All over light aircraft grey with Day-Glo bands.

METEOR T.7 WF791

Delivered to the RAF in March 1951, the aircraft was displayed by the CFS first as part of the Vintage
Pair and latterly as a solo display until it was written off at Coventry on May 30, 1988.

METEOR NF.14 WS800 60 SQUADRON

Based at RAF Tengah, Singapore, 60 Sqn received NF.12s and NF.14s between October 1959 and February
1960. WS800 was one of the first two to arrive and was flown by the squadron CO.

METEOR NF.14 WS841 HMT 264 SQUADRON

The squadron replaced their Mosquitos with the NF.11 in 1951 and latterly the NF.14 during
1954 until disbanded. WS841 is notable for having an all-black tail.

METEOR NF.11 WM293 68 SQUADRON

Wearing 68 Squadron colours on its tail in place of the fin flash, WM293 was flown by the CO while based at RAF Wahn, West Germany.

METEOR NF.14 WS729 25 SQUADRON

25 Squadron operated a mix of NF.12s and NF.14s from March 1954 until June 1958. WS729 was delivered
new to the squadron as part of the conversion process and scrapped in January 1961.

METEOR NF.13 WM317 39 SQUADRON

Wearing the black and yellow identification markings of the Suez Crisis, 39 Squadron's aircraft
were based at RAF Luqa, Malta, but were also at RAF Nicosia during the crisis.

METEOR D.16 WK800

WK800 was constructed as an F.8 and served with the Royal Australian Air Force as A77-876, including time in Korea with 77 Squadron. It returned to the UK in 1971. Reverting to the WK800 serial, it was converted to the D.16 drone configuration and operated at Llanbedr. Painted in gloss red and yellow.

METEOR NF.11 WM145 29 SQUADRON

29 Squadron became the first jet night fighter squadron when they took delivery of Meteor NF.11s in August 1952, replacing their night fighter Mosquitos. The squadron was using WM145 while based at RAF Tangmere in the mid-1950s.

GLOSTER METEOR

METEOR NF.11 WD794 96 SQUADRON

The squadron was re-formed at RAF Ahlhorn, Germany in November 1952 with Meteor NF.11s, including WD794. They continued to operate Meteors until the start of 1969 when they were scheduled for conversion to the Javelin and renumbered as 3 Squadron.

METEOR NF.14 WS788 152 SQUADRON

WS788 was issued to 152 Squadron at RAF Wattisham in July 1954. It was later damaged and became RAF Leeming's gate guardian for several years. It was acquired by Yorkshire Aviation Museum in 1991.

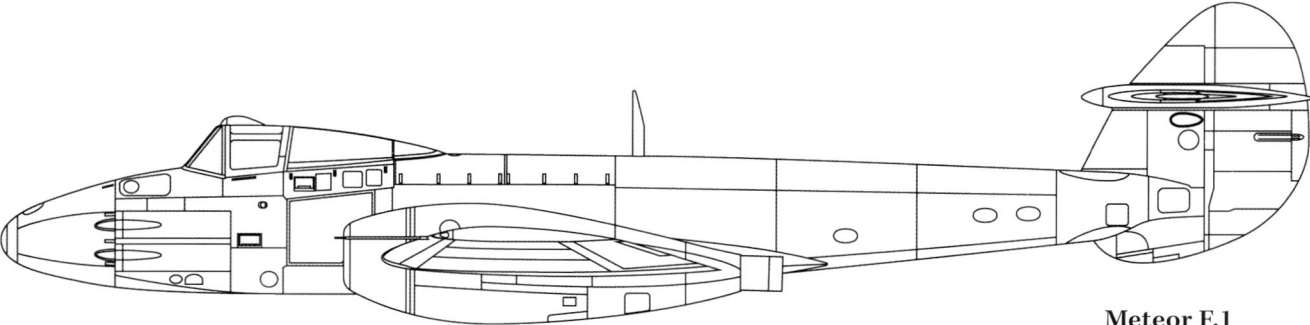

Meteor F.1

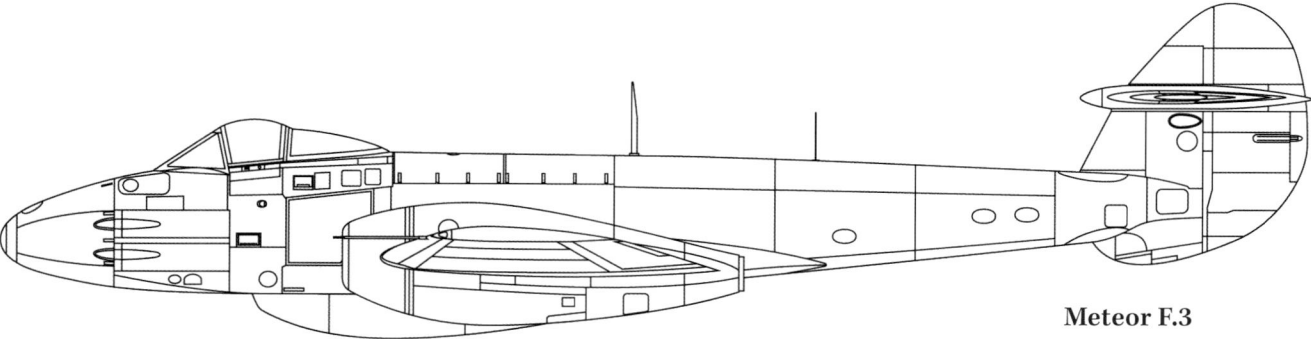

Meteor F.3

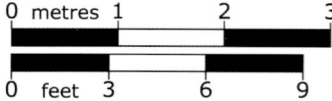

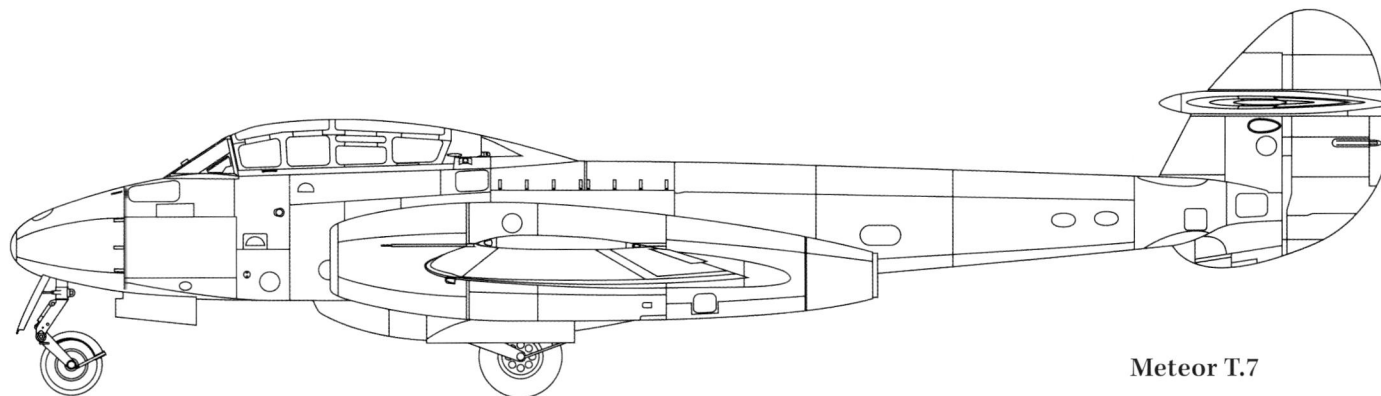

Meteor T.7

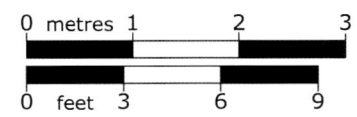

0 metres 1   2   3

0 feet 3   6   9

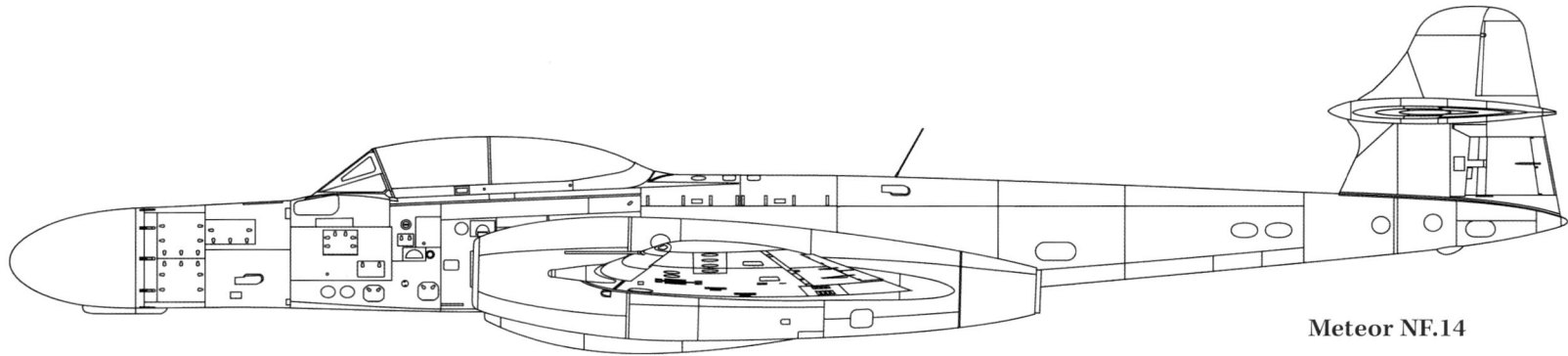

Meteor NF.14

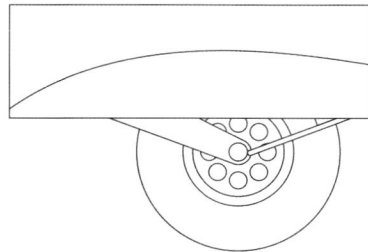

Main wheel

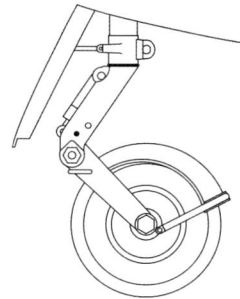

Nose wheel

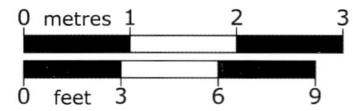

0 metres 1 2 3

0 feet 3 6 9

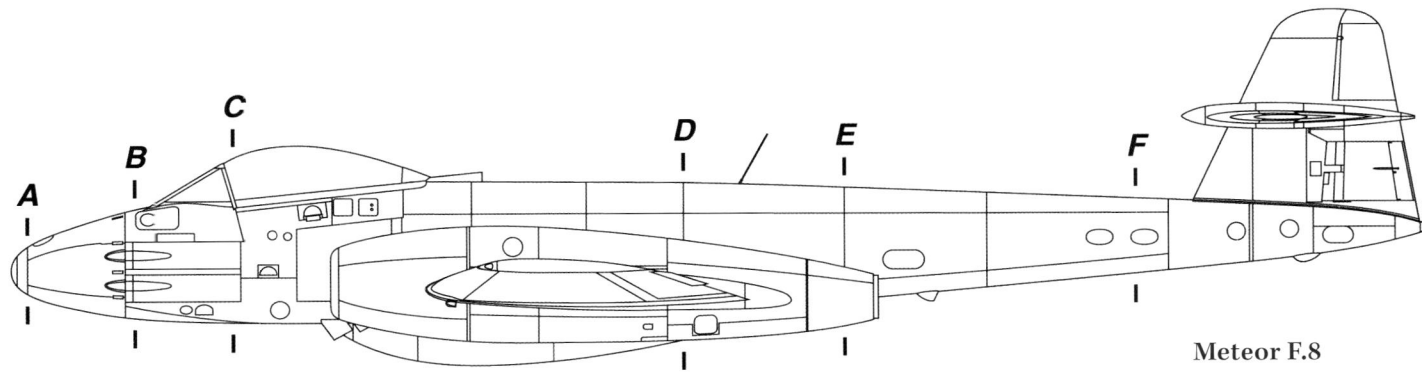

A B C D E F

Meteor F.8

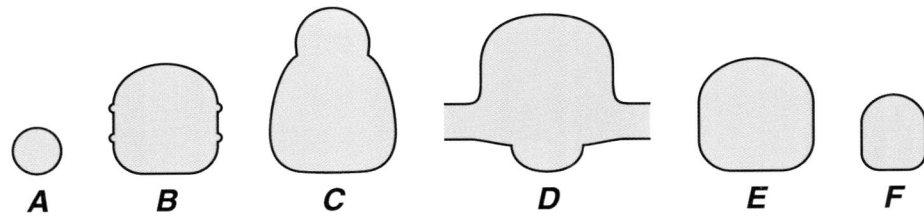

A B C D E F

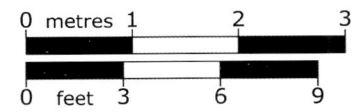

0 metres 1 2 3

0 feet 3 6 9

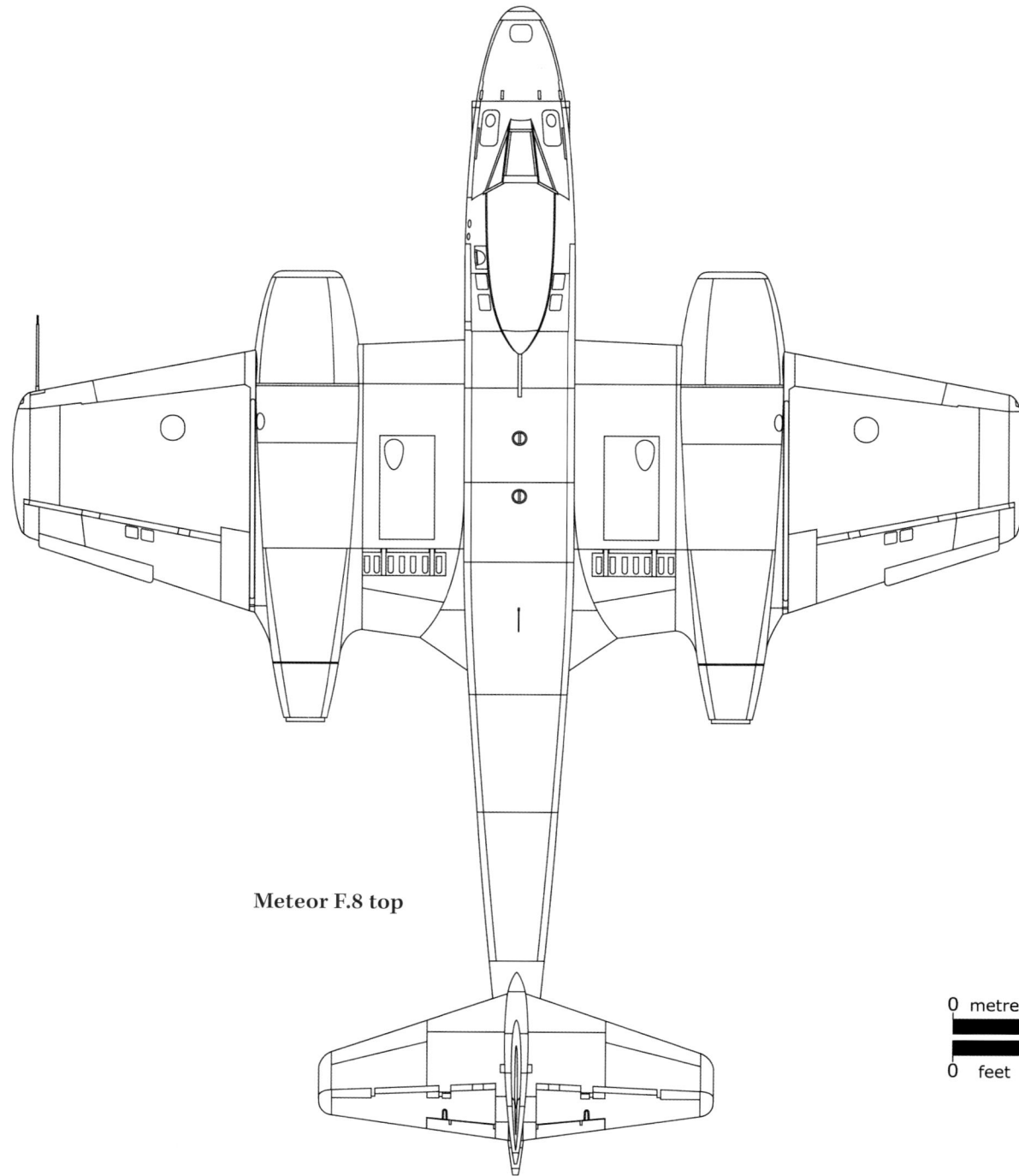

Meteor F.8 top

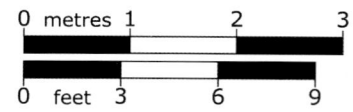

VAMPIRE T.11 XH304
This aircraft was with one of two Meteor T.7s as the RAF Vintage Pair but was involved in a fatal mid-air collision
with Meteor WA669 on May 25, 1986, at RAF Mildenhall. All over light aircraft grey with yellow bands.

Crab' took its official first flight from Hatfield on September 20, 1943. Some minor issues became apparent during the 30 minute flight but these were not insurmountable.

Given the threat posed by the Messerschmitt Me 262 and continued delays at Gloster. the third prototype, MP838, was delivered to Farnborough for testing and evaluation in March 1944. It soon became clear that the Spider Crab was going to be a success and the Air Ministry placed an order for 120 examples on May 13, 1944. The most visible change to the aircraft from prototype to production model was a reduction in the height of the tail, the top being squared off. The tail shape reverted to a more familiar de Havilland silhouette with the FB.5.

247 (China British) Squadron was the first to convert to the Vampire, as it was now known, during March and April 1946. As with the Meteor, no trainer jets existed so pilots had to convert from the Hawker Tempest with no prior experience of the speeds and differences in acceleration that the Goblin provided. By the autumn, 54 Sqn and 130 Sqn were also operational Vampire squadrons, both with the Vampire F.1. The F.1 may have been a well-designed aeroplane but it also had limitations, so work commenced on the F.2 and F.3. The F.2 never entered service but instead was used to explore the use of the Rolls-Royce Nene engine in the Vampire airframe; the aircraft involved were TG276, TG280 and TX807. The F.3, however, was built in significant numbers and served with several frontline squadrons.

A number of improvements were made but the biggest was to

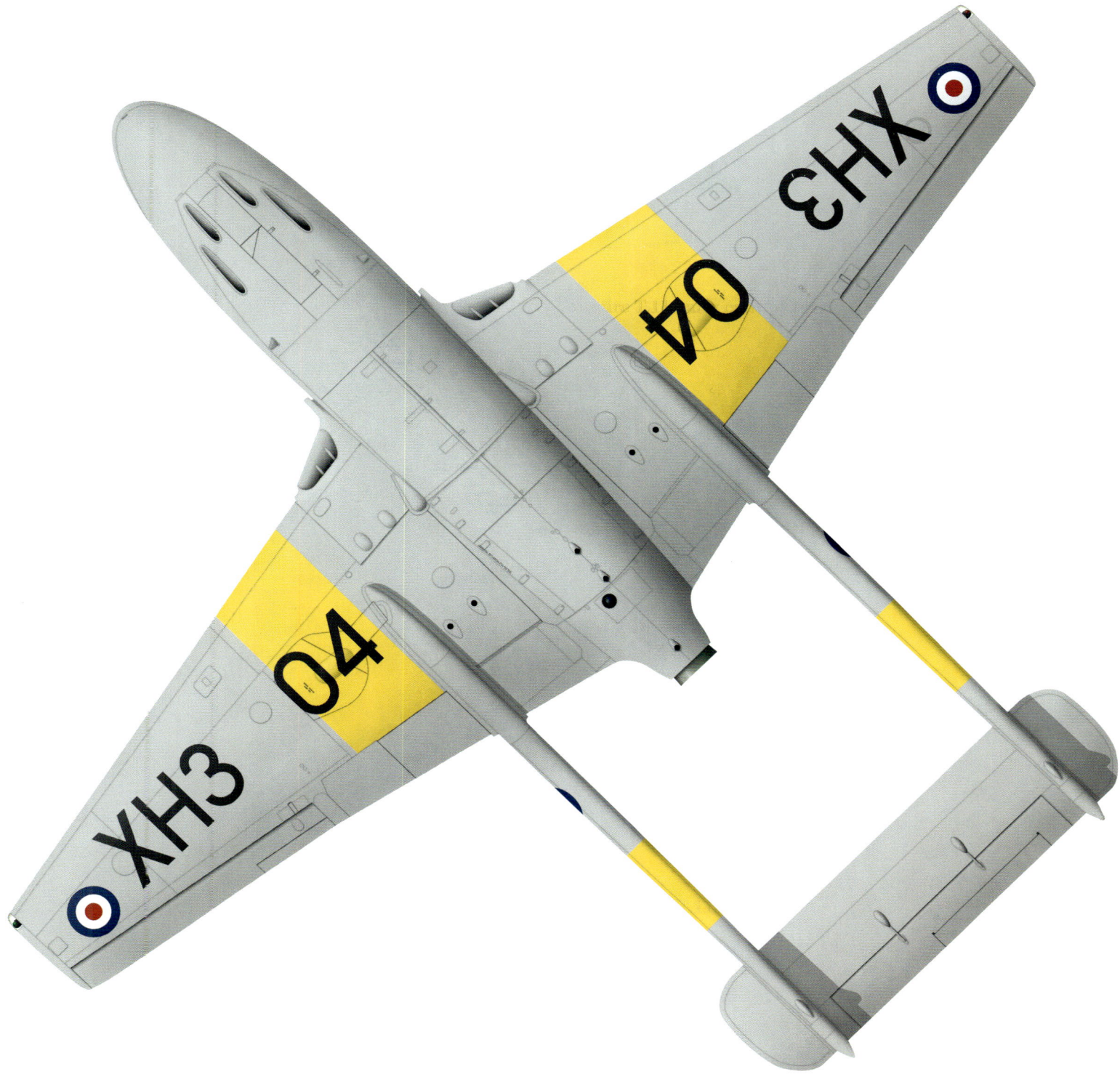

VAMPIRE FB.3 VF335

Finished in all over aluminium and wearing unusual post-war roundels and fin flash when first delivered to the
RAF in June 1947, Vampire F.3 VF335 soon received more conventional markings and served with 54 Squadron,
604 Squadron and 602 Squadron. Having only served for six years it was retired in September 1953.

increase fuel capacity and therefore range. Vampires were already configured to carry slipper tanks similar to those carried by the Mosquito but the internal capacity jumped from 202 gallons to 330 gallons. The F.3 also received a revised tail in a similar style to the original Spider Crab but with a smaller surface area. The changes also meant that orders placed for the F.1 were switched to the F.3 model (a total of 138 being built). 54 Sqn were the first to replace the F.1 when they received the new type in April 1948. Its tenure with the RAF may have been short but many F.3s would later enjoy long careers with overseas air forces.

With the Meteor becoming the interceptor of choice, the role of the Vampire would evolve with the next iteration of the type. As the Tempests began showing their age, a replacement ground-attack aircraft was required. To pre-empt this, de Havilland had produced a report on the suitability of the Vampire for that role in December 1946.

Having not been initially developed for low-level combat, it was anticipated that there would be some shortcomings in the FB.4, but de Havilland decided to go ahead with it. To deal with the increased loads resulting from underslung ordinance, the wing was strengthened and provision for extra hardpoints was made.

There were several issues and delays with the development so orders from both the RAF and the French were cancelled. The RAF still required a Tempest replacement however, so the FB.5 carried on where the FB.4 left off. The new specification, however, called for an ejector seat. Due to the limited size of the cockpit this was to prove too problematic at the time and was omitted from the FB.5. With over 900 being built, the FB.5 can be considered a successful

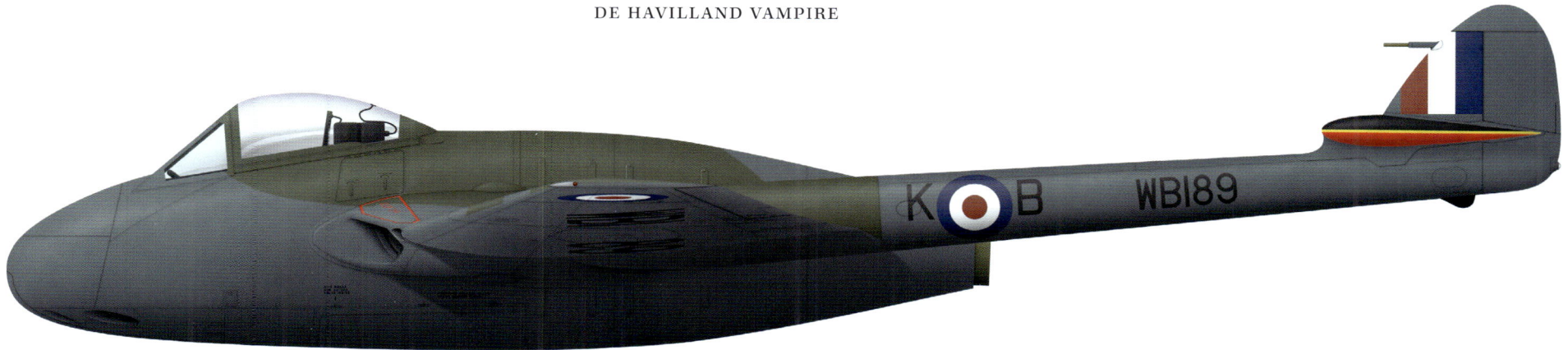

VAMPIRE FB.5 WB189 4 SQUADRON

Having flown with 92 Squadron, WB189 was allocated to 4 Squadron while at RAF Jever, Germany, in October 1952 where it was flown by Fg Off E. Lack in late 1952. Later it went to 226 Squadron and was struck off charge in June 1958. Thought to be painted in ocean, dark green.

variant but there were still improvements to make. With the cold war escalating, the RAF continued to build its presence in West Germany. When the FB.5s arrived they were in all over aluminium but by 1951 had been painted in camouflage.

Even though the FB.5 proved to be a very capable aircraft, operational experience highlighted certain missing features. In particular, having been designed for the European theatre, the Vampire struggled with conditions in the Middle East. The biggest issue was the lack of air conditioning which caused severe problems for the pilot.

In addition, windscreens cracked in the heat and engine thrust was reduced in extreme temperatures. The Goblin was modified to cope with the conditions and following several experiments the Godfrey Cold Air Unit was fitted. This required modifications to the intake and wing root on the starboard side. It was also retrofitted to many FB.5s.

Nearly 350 FB.9s were built, not as many as with earlier models but still a significant number and the type went on to see active service in both Africa and the Far East, performing admirably in the ground support role for which it was intended.

Due in part to the delays to the Meteor programme, and as the result of a private initiative by de Havilland, the Vampire NF.10 two-seater night fighter was created. Using knowledge gained from the Mosquito and perhaps conveniently having an almost identical fuselage diameter, it was decided to position the crew side by side. The nose was extended to house the same AI Mk.10 radar that the Mosquito had used and flying controls were relocated.

These changes caused problems with stability that were solved by altering the tail section yet again and extending the tailplane beyond the booms. The height was also increased. It may have only served for a few years (July 1951 to September 1959) before being replaced by the Meteor NF.11 but it plugged a critical gap in RAF capability.

The Vampire was the first jet many pilots encountered and just like the Meteor converting to the type involved a steep learning curve. Having already embarked on the two-seater NF.10, the basic layout was already in place for a Vampire trainer. De Havilland's resources were already stretched by the demand for single-seat Vampires so the job of creating the T.11 was allocated to the Airspeed company. Anticipating the need for weapons training, the basic configuration of the fighter variants was retained. There were some alterations to the NF.10 cockpit however, since it was rather cramped. By lowering the canopy side rails, sufficient width was created to make it possible to sit the pupil and instructor right next to each other (in both

the Mosquito and NF.10 they had been staggered).

With a layout that allowed the pupil to visually follow the movements of the instructor, the Vampire can be considered a more practical layout than the Meteor T.7 and this arrangement was repeated in later trainers such as the Hunter and Lightning. The Vampire T.11 had a long career with the CFS and most front line squadrons had at least one on strength to be used for instrument ratings, ongoing training and as the squadron hack.

A navalised version of the Vampire was produced as were several export variants, some being constructed by overseas companies. The Vampire was yet another first generation jet that had a long and varied service life around the globe and was an essential aircraft during the early years of the cold war.

De Havilland Vampire

VARIANT	LENGTH	SPAN	HEIGHT	ENGINE
F.1	30FT 9IN/9.37M	40FT/12.19M	8FT 10IN/2.69M	GOBLIN 2
F.3	30FT 9IN/9.37M	40FT/12.19M	8FT 10IN/2.69M	GOBLIN 2
F.5	30FT 9IN/9.37M	38FT 11.58M	8FT 10IN/2.69M	GOBLIN 2
FB.9	30FT 9IN/9.37M	38FT 11.58M	8FT 10IN/2.69M	GOBLIN 2
NF.10	34FT 7IN/10.54M	38FT 11.58M	6FT 7IN/2M	GOBLIN 3
T.11	34FT 7IN/10.54M	38FT 11.58M	6FT 7IN/2M	GOBLIN 3

VAMPIRE FB.5 VZ233 73 SQUADRON

73 Squadron converted to the Vampire in July 1948, receiving the FB.1 which was soon replaced with
later versions. The unit flew Vampires until October 1954 when these was superseded by Venoms. This
is how FB.5 VZ233 appeared in October 1950 when en route to Malta for exercises.

VAMPIRE FB.5 WA331 112 SQUADRON

112 Squadron's tenure with the Vampire was short. They re-formed at RAF Fassberg in May 1951 with the FB.5 and converted to the
Sabre in January 1954. Vampires were initially in NMF with the distinctive tail but were repainted in camouflage with a sharkmouth.

VAMPIRE FB.5 VX474 118 SQUADRON

Based at RAF Fassberg, the 118 Squadron Vampires received a temporary high visibility yellow scheme
over dark sea grey, dark green with PRU blue underside for Exercise Cornet, which involved 2000 aircraft
from nine nations during August 1953. The scheme was removed shortly afterwards.

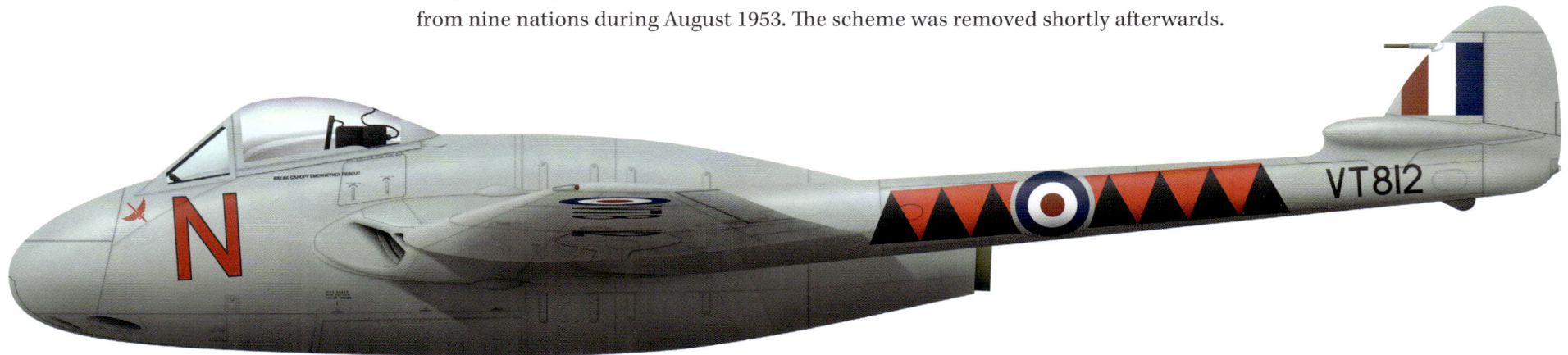

VAMPIRE FB.3 VT812

Vampire F.3 VT812 originally served with 32 Squadron in Cyprus, followed by a brief spell with 614 Squadron. It was
then with 601 Squadron from January 1952 until April when it suffered severe damage. Following repair it was with 602
Squadron and was eventually acquired by the RAF Museum where its 602 Squadron markings were repainted.

VAMPIRE FB.5 WA442 185 SQUADRON

185 Squadron operated the Vampire for less than two years. It was re-formed at Hal-Far, Malta, on September 15, 1951, with the FB.5. After a few weeks in Cyprus the squadron was disbanded during October 1952 in Iraq.

VAMPIRE FB.9 WG888 60 SQUADRON

During the Malayan Emergency in 1950, 60 Squadron received a mix of FB.5s and FB.9s. These replaced the unit's Spitfire Mk.XVIIs and were used in the ground-attack role. Among them was WG888.

VAMPIRE FB.9 WR120 213 SQUADRON

213 Squadron was already at Deversoir, Egypt, when it received the FB.5 in 1949 but by the time of the Suez Crisis it had upgraded to the FB.9. The CO's aircraft, WR120, had a distinctive scheme with a Black nose and tail.

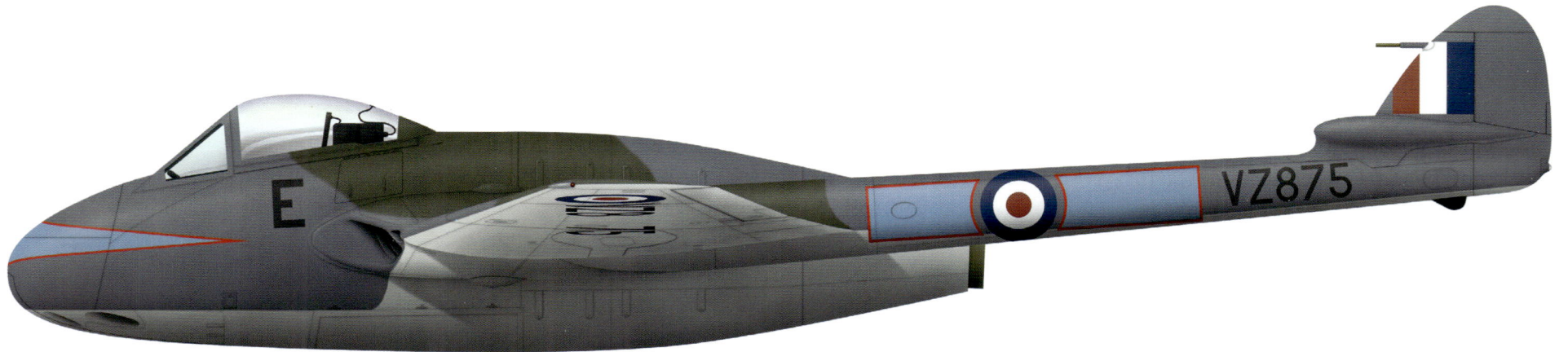

VAMPIRE FB.5 VZ875 605 SQUADRON

605 Squadron replaced its Vampire F.1s with FB.5s in April 1951. These were retained until the squadron was disbanded in March 1957. Dark green and dark sea grey camouflage and aluminium underside.

VAMPIRE FB.9 WR139 20 SQUADRON

While flying Vampire WR183 Flt Sgt Roland 'Sam' Hughes encountered something on July 30, 1952, over West Germany that could not be explained. Following this the ground crew painted a flying saucer on his latest Vampire, WR139. Dark green, dark sea grey camouflage with light aircraft grey underside.

VAMPIRE FB.9 WR128 502 SQUADRON

The first (and only) jet aircraft operated by 502 Squadron was the Vampire, converting to the FB.5 and FB.9 in January 1951. WR128 is notable due to the unusually high demarcation line on the fuselage.

VAMPIRE FB.9 WR257 613 SQUADRON

WR257 was the only FB.9 on squadron strength, 613 Squadron primarily using the FB.5. This aircraft
was flown by the CO Sqn Ldr Jack Wales between June 1954 and December 1956.

VAMPIRE T.11 WZ518 OLDENBURG

A rare camouflaged T.11 with dark green, dark sea grey camouflage and aluminium undersides, WZ518
has the 14 Squadron marking on its nose and was used by RAF Oldenburg station flight.

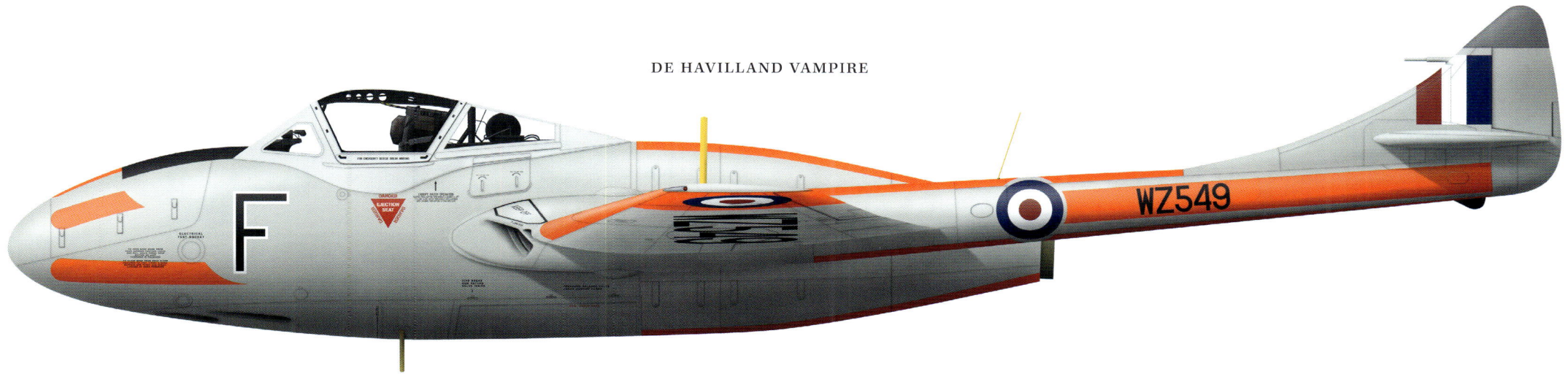

VAMPIRE T.11 WZ549

Built at Broughton in April 1953, serving with 8 and 1 FTS, WZ549 was assigned to the Central Air Traffic Control
School, RAF Shawbury in November 1964 where it was finished in light aircraft grey with Day-Glo bands. It was sent
to RAF Coningsby in 1970 as an instructional airframe. Currently owned by the Ulster Aviation Society.

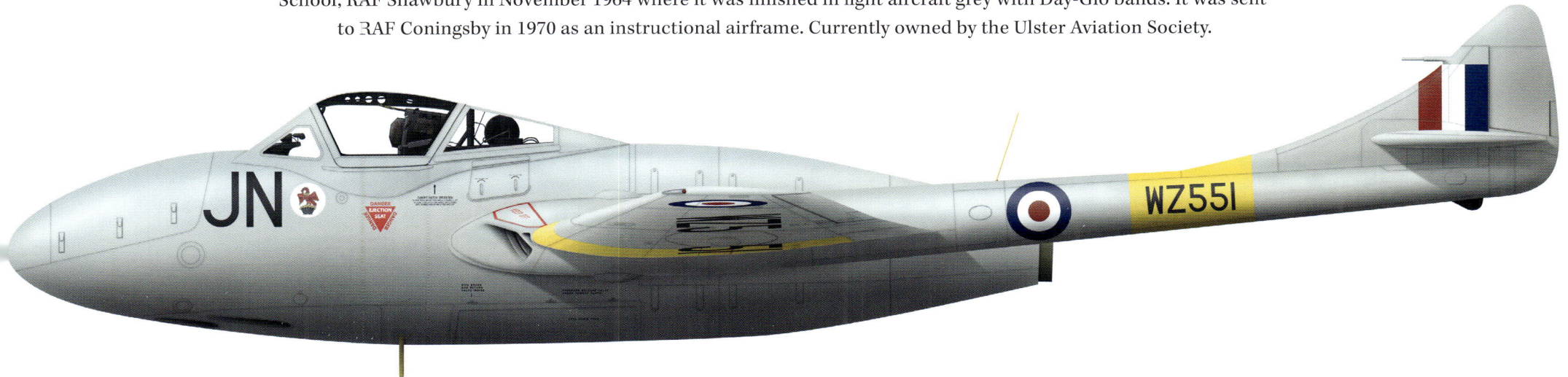

VAMPIRE T.11 WZ551 CFS

Allocated to the Central Flying School, Little Rissington during the mid-1950s, WZ551 was
later sent to 19 MU, Saint Athan, being struck off charge on July 23, 1963.

VAMPIRE T.11 WZ421 62 SQUADRON

Delivered to the RAF on September 3, 1952, and operated by 62 Squadron between 1957 and 1959, T.11 WZ421 was sold for scrap in June 1960.

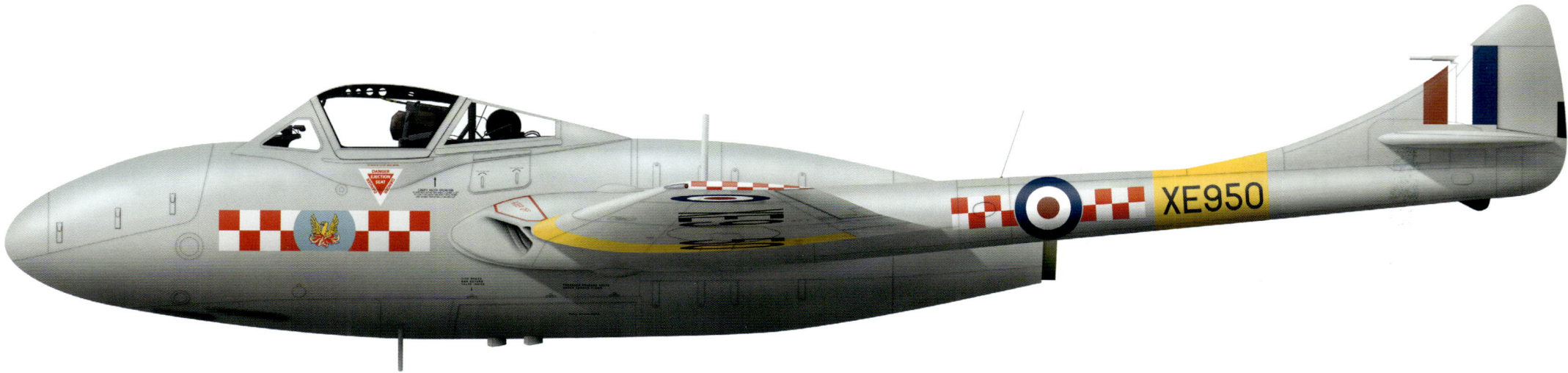

VAMPIRE T.11 XE950 56 SQUADRON

Entering service on April 13, 1955, and displayed in 56 Squadron markings, T.11 XE950
is currently owned by Ailes Anciennes Toulouse museum, France.

VAMPIRE T.11 XE982

XE982 was damaged beyond repair when WL505 taxied into it on the dispersal at RAF Cranwell. WL505 was only slightly damaged. Last reported (in 2020) to be in storage at Tetbury, Gloucestershire.

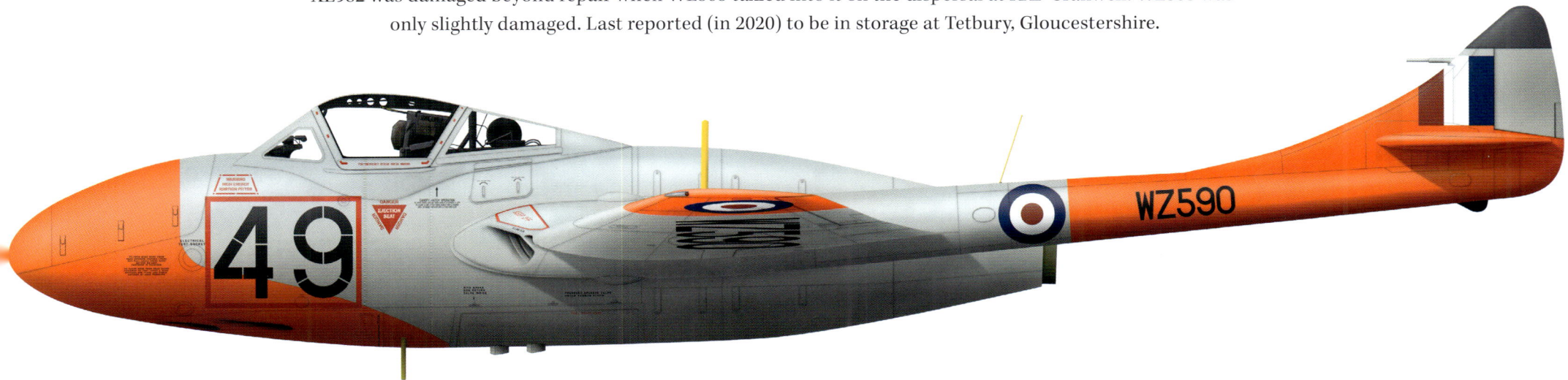

VAMPIRE T.11 WZ590 5 FLYING TRAINING SCHOOL

T.11 WZ590 was delivered in November 1953. Between November 1959 and March 1962 it served with No.5 FTS, RAF Oakington, before being transferred to No.8 FTS at RAF Swinderby. Subsequently acquired by the Imperial War Museum in 1973.

VAMPIRE FB.1 VF279 3 SQUADRON

Delivered to the RAF on September 13, 1946, VF279 was immediately allocated to 3 Squadron at RAF Gütersloh
and remained on strength for several years. It later served with 605 Squadron and while with 208 Advanced Flying
School at RAF Merryfield, Somerset, it flew into the ground out of cloud on September 25, 1952.

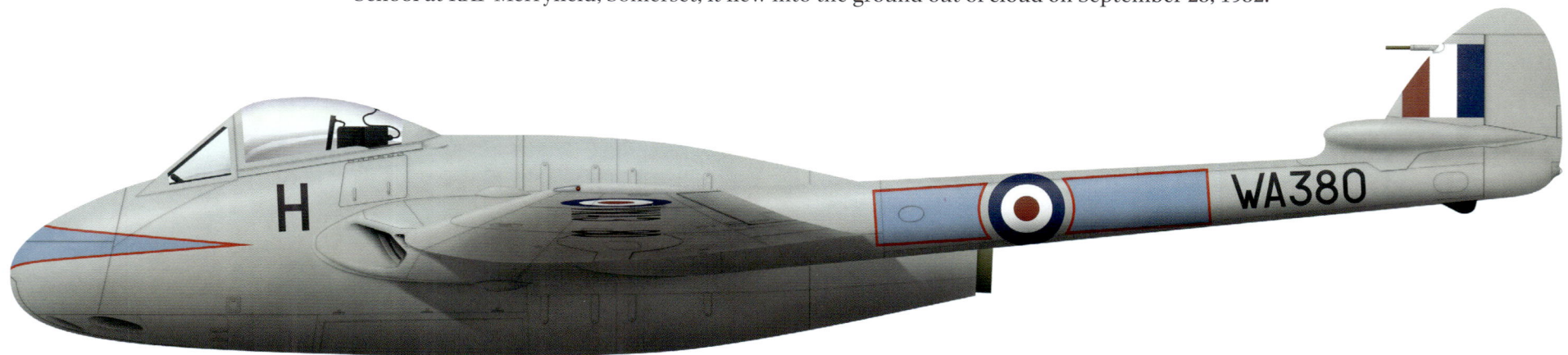

VAMPIRE FB.5 WA380 605 COUNTY OF WARWICK SQUADRON

Delivered to the RAF in April 1951, WA380 was briefly operated by 605 Squadron before being passed to 118 Squadron
in West Germany. It entered a spin and crashed, killing the pilot, P/O Smith, on December 21, 1953.

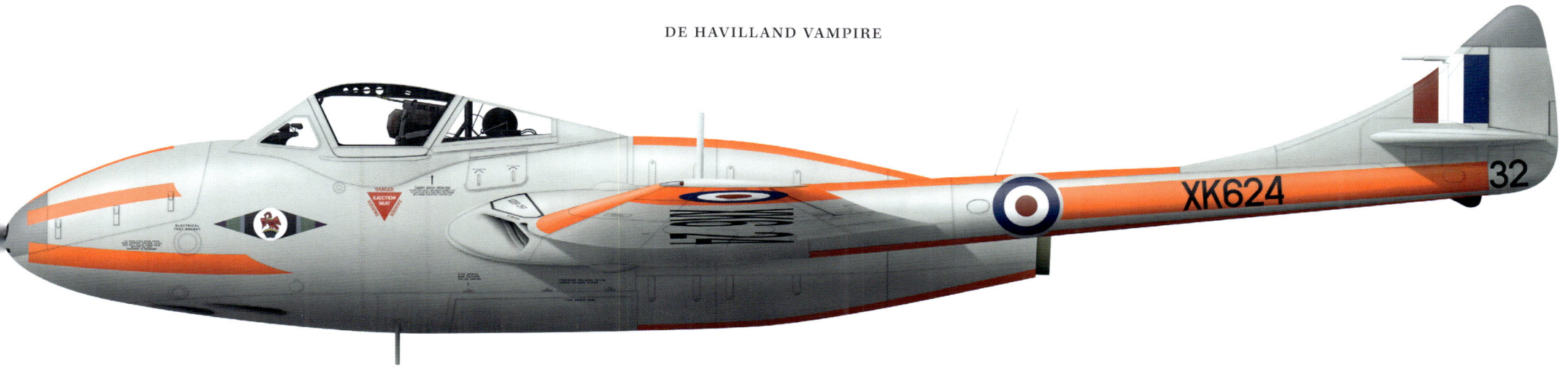

VAMPIRE T.11 XK624 CENTRAL FLYING SCHOOL

For many years XK624 was based at Little Rissington and by the time it was retired from service in December 1971 the paint had weathered considerably. It was later acquired by the Norfolk and Suffolk Aviation Museum.

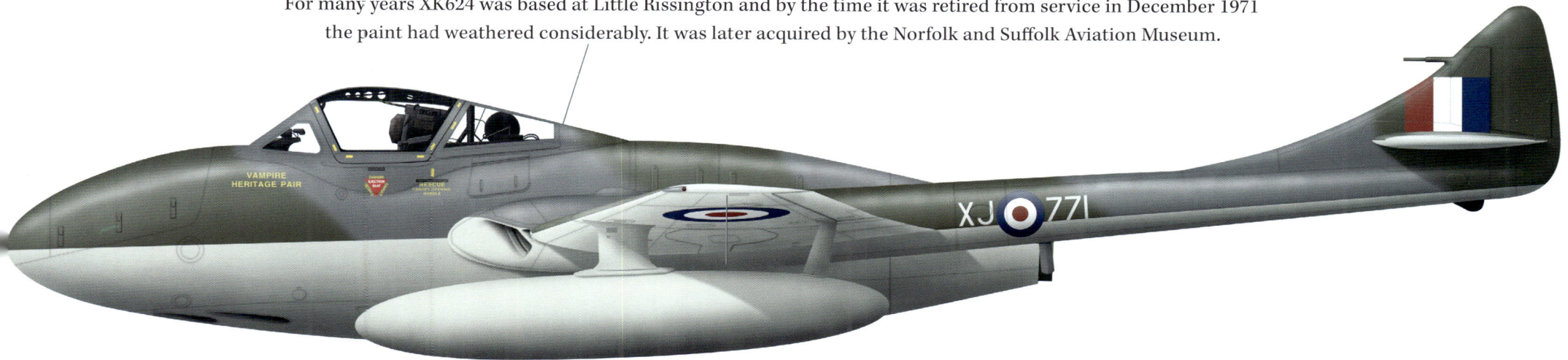

VAMPIRE T.55 U-1215

Originally built as a T.55 for the Swiss Air Force, this aircraft was flown in fictitious RAF markings between 1991 and 2016 with the code XJ771 — which has never been allocated officially. Subsequently sold to the Royal Jordanian Historic Flight and repainted.

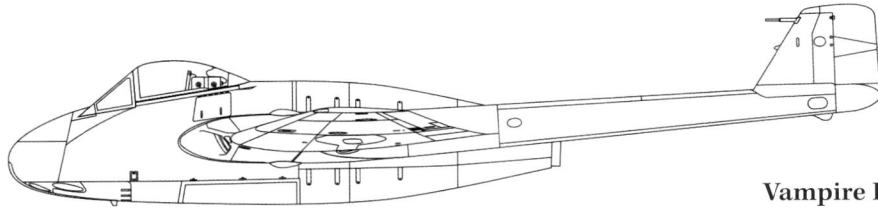

Vampire FB.1

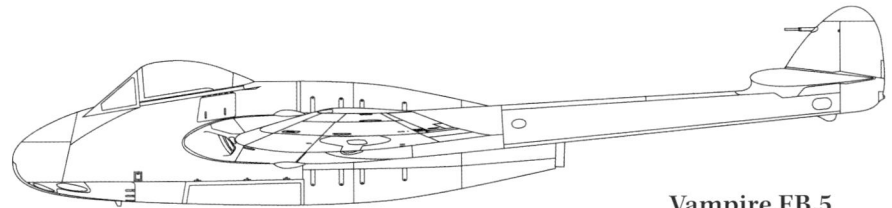

Vampire FB.5

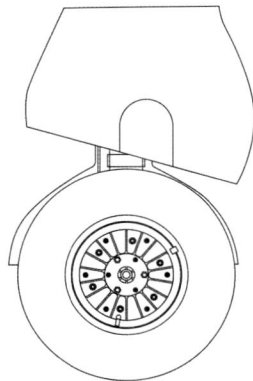

Main wheel

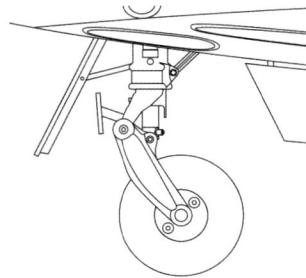

Nose wheel

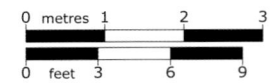

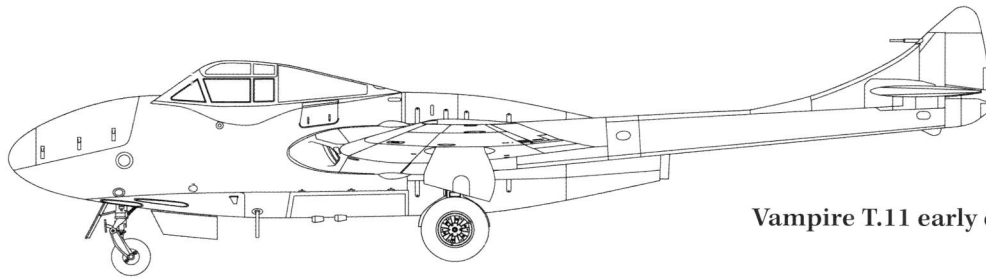

Vampire T.11 early canopy

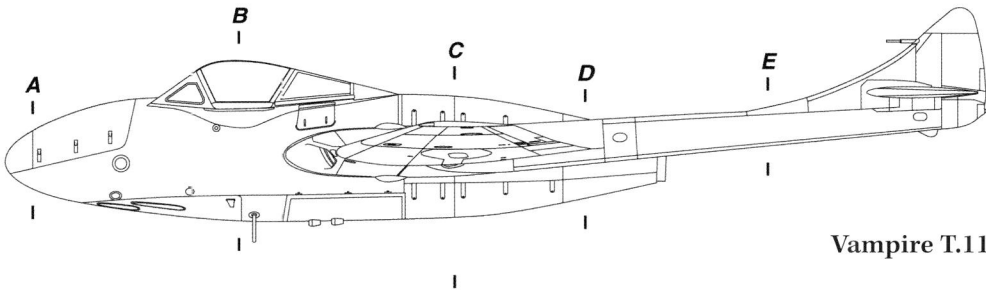

A

B

Vampire T.11

A

B

C

D

E

C

D

E

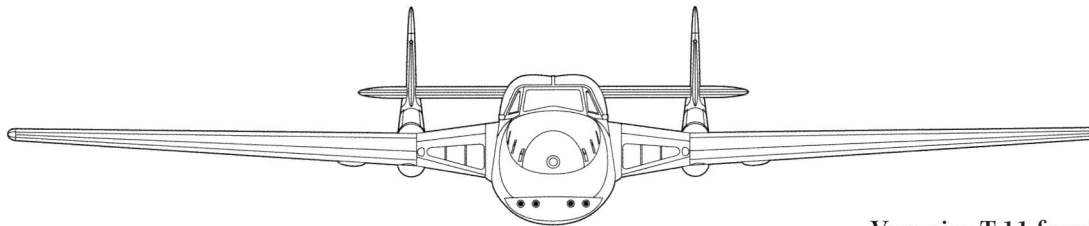

Vampire T.11 front

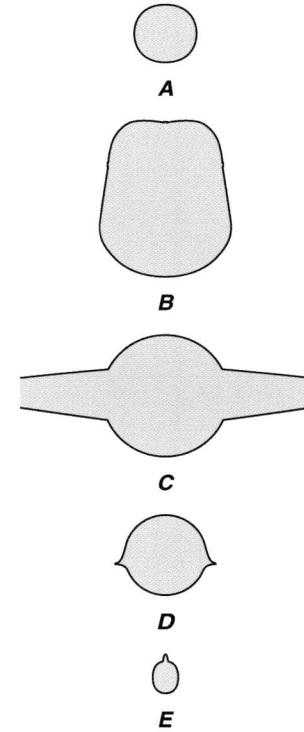

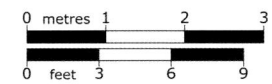

0 metres 1 2 3

0 feet 3 6 9

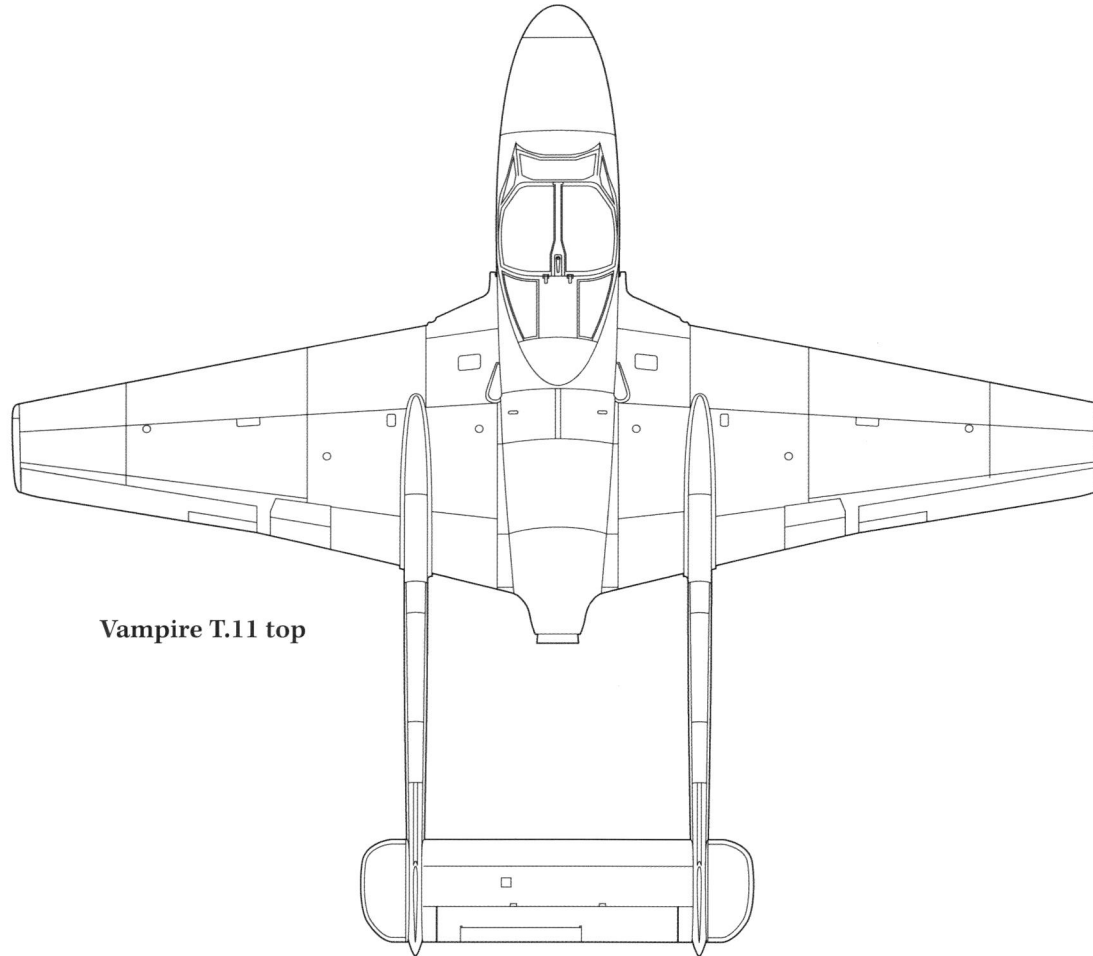

Vampire T.11 top

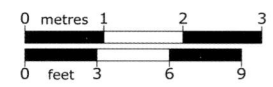

0 metres 1 2 3

0 feet 3 6 9

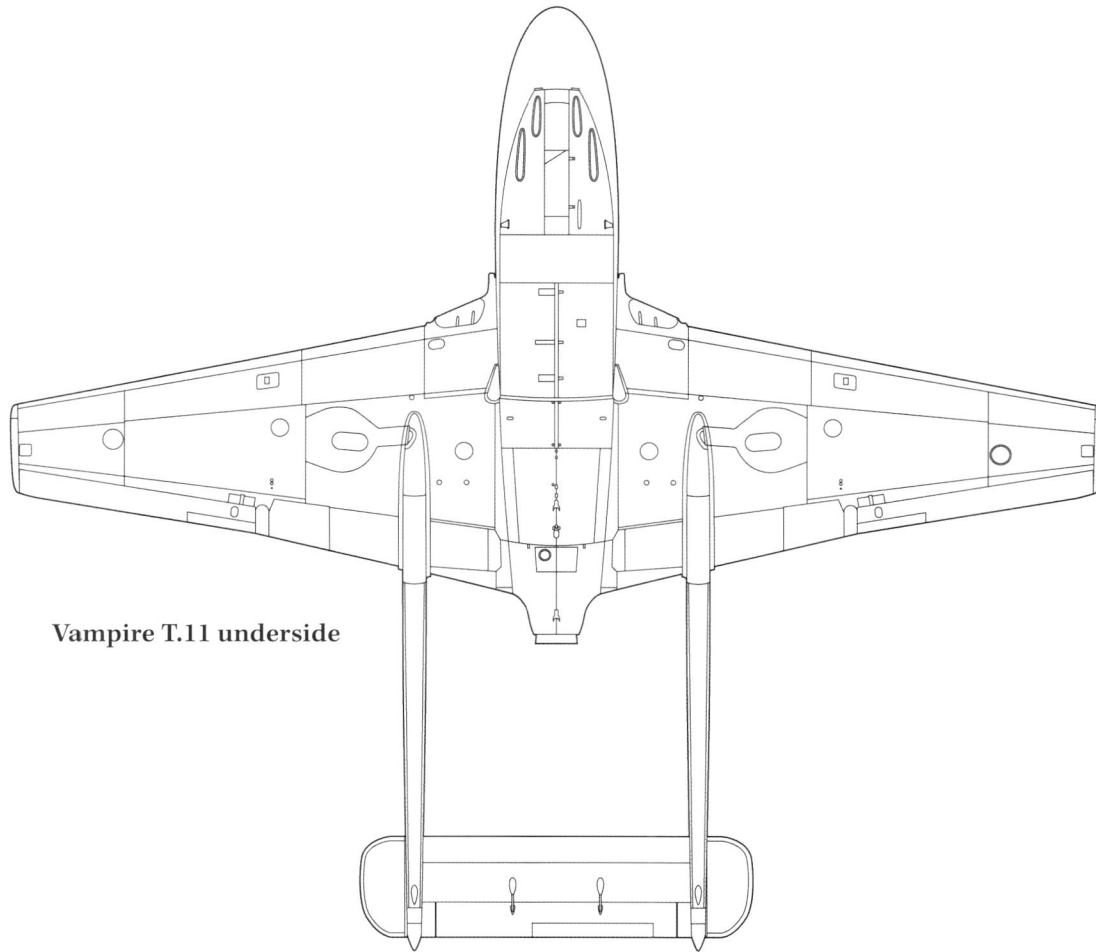

Vampire T.11 underside

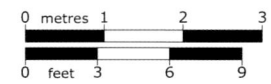

0 metres 1 2 3

0 feet 3 6 9

DE HAVILLAND VENOM

To the uninitiated the Venom is just a souped-up derivative of the Vampire and an aircraft that filled a gap while other types were in development. This may have been true with the original version but it fails to take account of the improvements and capabilities of later versions or the admiration and affection in which the aircraft is held by the pilots and crew who worked on it.

A key factor in the birth of the Venom was its power plant. The Vampire's Goblin engine delivered up to 3500lb of thrust, but research suggested that alterations and scaling up could increase this significantly.

The new engine, named the Ghost, could produce 5000lb of thrust, a significant improvement on the original. It was intended to install the engine in a modified Vampire and de Havilland issued a proposal outlining the replacement of the Vampire with the more powerful version.

The Vampire F.8 (as it was initially named) would have a thinner wing and the fuselage was lengthened to accommodate the engine.

The fuselage section would remain wooden, like that of the earlier Vampires, making it the last RAF fighter to be built in such a way.

Early in 1949, two FB.5 airframes were removed from the production line at Preston and allocated to the F.8 programme. These airframes, VV612 and VV613, were delivered to the Hatfield factory in February 1949 and work commenced on their conversion. Work continued over the summer, during which time development of the Ghost continued, the engine being tested in a converted Avro Lancastrian test bed.

VV612 had been completed by September and on September 2 it took to the air for the first time with John Derry at the controls.

VENOM NF.2A WL872 219 SQUADRON

219 Squadron was a night fighter unit in the post-war years, first with the Mosquito and later with the Meteor. In 1955
it was re-formed at RAF Driffield with the Venom but this only lasted two years before it was disbanded.

It was only four days later that the aircraft put in an appearance at the SBAC show at Farnborough.

Following Derry's display, Specification F.15/49 was issued – written specifically for the thin-wing Vampire. Further to the proposed improvements to the FB.5, the addition of wingtip tanks was called for to increase range and the booms were significantly strengthened. Provision was also made to carry stores under the wings.

Shortly after this, the new name was revealed. It had become apparent that the F.8 would be significantly different to the FB.5/9, in effect replacing the Vampire with a new aircraft, and the decision was taken to redesignate the type as the DH.112 Venom. Flight trials commenced soon after and continued throughout the following year, primarily being conducted by Derry and John Wilson but also by A&AEE.

Handling was found to be heavier than the Vampire and the rate of roll was considered very poor. Wing fences were also required to mitigate the potential to stall during landing approaches and the tailplane was extended beyond the booms. The airbrakes were also found to have negligible effect.

The majority of these issues were entirely resolved and the rest satisfactorily corrected, however. There was also research into using reheat on the Venom which produced positive results – but the idea was abandoned due to costs.

WE255 was the first production Venom FB.1 to roll off the production line and was delivered to A&AEE to confirm that the alterations had improved the handling of the aircraft. WE225 was not alone as several more of the early production aircraft were used for testing and evaluation. This revealed a weakness in the

VENOM FB.1 WE283 11 SQUADRON
Based at RAF Wunstorf, West Germany, 11 Squadron converted to the Venom in 1952. WE283
is painted in dark green, dark sea grey camouflage with PRU blue underside.

wing spar and the aircraft was limited to 6g manoeuvres – quite a hindrance when comparable aircraft were cleared to 10g.

The Venom entered service with 11 Squadron, based at RAF Wunstorf, West Germany, in August 1952 and during the following months a programme of upgrades was rolled out to strengthen the offending spars.

The 2nd Tactical Air Force in West Germany continued to be the focus of Venom deliveries, to 5 and 226 Squadrons also in 123 Wing. These were followed by deliveries to 14, 98 and 118 Squadrons in 121 Wing at RAF Fassberg, West Germany, replacing their Vampires.

Finally, in 1954, the squadrons of 139 Wing converted to the Venom and by this stage the FB.4 was also being produced. The aircraft also replaced the Vampire in both the Middle East and Far East, seeing action in both theatres of operation. However, the

single seat variant never saw service with a UK-based squadron.

In the Middle East, 6, 8 and 249 Squadrons were involved in the Suez Crisis, the FB.4s flying 390 sorties during the period and being supported by the Royal Navy's Sea Venoms. Missions ranged from attacking convoys to destroying gun positions.

Further south and around the same time, 8 Squadron based at RAF Khormaksar, Aden, had their Vampires replaced with Venoms and continued their peacekeeping duties in the region.

Venoms also found their way to the Far East to replace the Vampires operating in the region. 28 Squadron was based at RAF Kai Tak, Hong Kong, and maintained a presence in the colony. Venoms were also involved in the ongoing Malayan Emergency, 60 Squadron working with the Venoms of 14 Squadron RNZAF to carry out strikes on communist guerrillas. The squadron did get

VENOM FB.1 WR354 32 SQUADRON
Posted to the Middle East during the Second World War, 32 Squadron remained there
until 1957 and was based at RAF Amman, Jordan, during 1955.

some respite from operations when some of the Venoms undertook a tour of the Far East as an aerobatic team.

For the tour, the aircraft were painted all over white with red tanks and rudders. Like many other Venom squadrons, their time operating the type was rather short and added up to a total of three years for the FB.1 and a further two years with the FB.4 until the Venoms were swapped for Meteor night fighters.

With the Vampire NF.10 already under development, de Havilland proposed to the Air Ministry a Ghost 103-powered version and despite a muted official response the company went ahead with modifying a Vampire NF.10 to accept the engine and Venom wings.

This was a straightforward affair with only minor alterations to the wings required. Prototype G-5-3 did retain the distinctive Vampire boom and tail but the nose was extended to accommodate

the AI Mk.10 radar system. The prototype flew for the first time on August 22, 1950, from Hatfield.

Official interest was only piqued when delays to the Gloster Javelin became apparent and the Government bought the Venom NF – the prototype receiving the serial WP227. Just over three years after its first flight the production model entered service with 23 Squadron, based at RAF Coltishall. Four were delivered on November 23, 1953. The squadron already had a reputation as a night fighter unit so it was a logical decision to equip it with the Venom.

With the improved NF.2A being worked on, 23 Squadron was the only RAF unit to fly the NF.2. And even they started converting to the NF.2A in August 1954.

The Venom NF.2A featured a number of improvements to the basic design including a revision of the tail, improved visibility with a new canopy and minor internal upgrades. This version went on to serve with several squadrons, though just like other variants its time in service was rather short.

This was due in part to the introduction of the final version to be operated by the RAF, the NF.3. It was seen as a competitor to the Meteor NF.11 and was a considerable improvement on the NF.2A. The Ghost 104 was capable of producing 4950lb of thrust and the AI Mk.21 had double the range of the Mk.10, reaching up to 20 miles. The radome was also altered to allow for easier access to the equipment.

Powered flying controls were introduced and further changes were made to the tail. Not only did it replace the NF.2A with existing Venom squadrons but went on to equip yet more squadrons, a total of 129 NF.3s being built. It was the same old story however – with newer aircraft coming into service the life of the NF.3 was short, with some being scrapped only three years after coming off the production line.

Like later versions of the Meteor and Vampire, the Venom was an interim aircraft that evolved and adapted to new technology as it became available. The RAF saw a high turnover of jets in the postwar years and the Venom was a victim of this, but just like other de Havilland aircraft the design did find longevity in exports and with the Royal Navy in the carrier based all-weather fighter configuration.

De Havilland Venom

VARIANT	LENGTH	SPAN	HEIGHT	ENGINE
V	31FT 10IN/9.7M	41FT 8IN/12.7M	6FT 2IN/1.88M	GHOST 103
FB.4	31FT 10IN/9.7M	41FT 8IN/12.7M	6FT 2IN/1.88M	GHOST 103
NF.2	33FT 10IN/10.31M	42FT 11IN/13.08M	7FT 7IN/2.31M	GHOST 103
NF.3	36FT 7IN/11.15M	42FT 11IN/13.08M	6FT 6IN/1.98M	GHOST 104

VENOM FB.1 WE388 118 SQUADRON

Part of the Fassberg Wing, 118 Squadron Venoms had black lightning bolts on the nose and tip tanks along with the aircraft code letter.

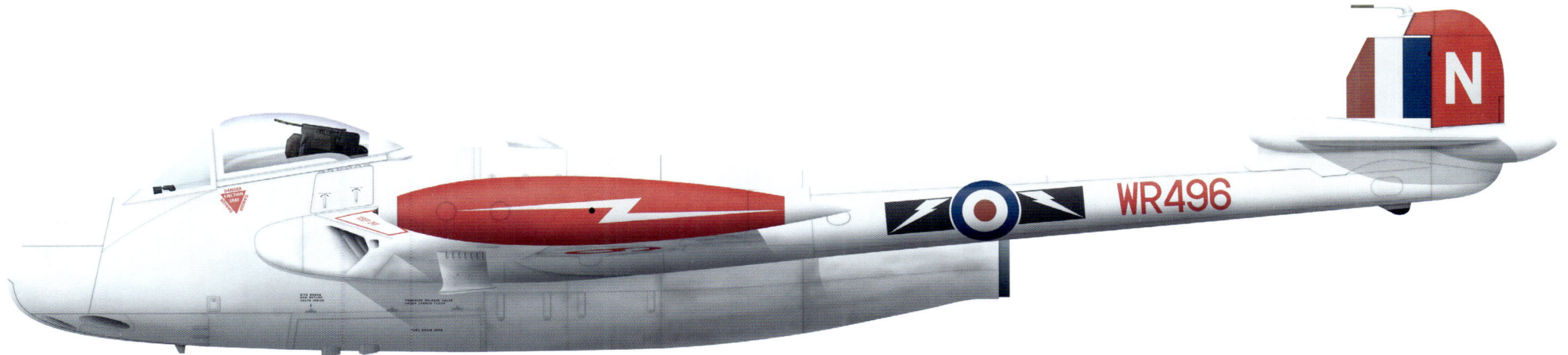

VENOM FB.4 WR496 60 SQUADRON

While continuing to operate out of RAF Tengah, Singapore, most of the squadron aircraft retained standard camouflage with black tanks. But in December 1957 the squadron's aerobatic team painted their Venoms white.

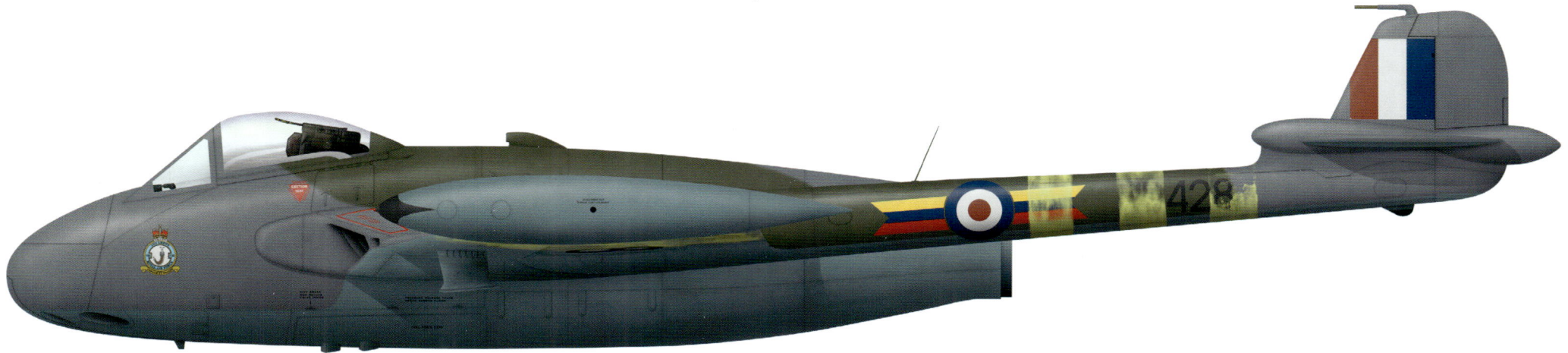

VENOM FB.4 WR428 8 SQUADRON

During the Suez Crisis, 8 Squadron flew from RAF Akrotiri, Cyprus and had temporary bands applied. These were supposed to be yellow but due to a paint shortage on the base it was mixed with cream.

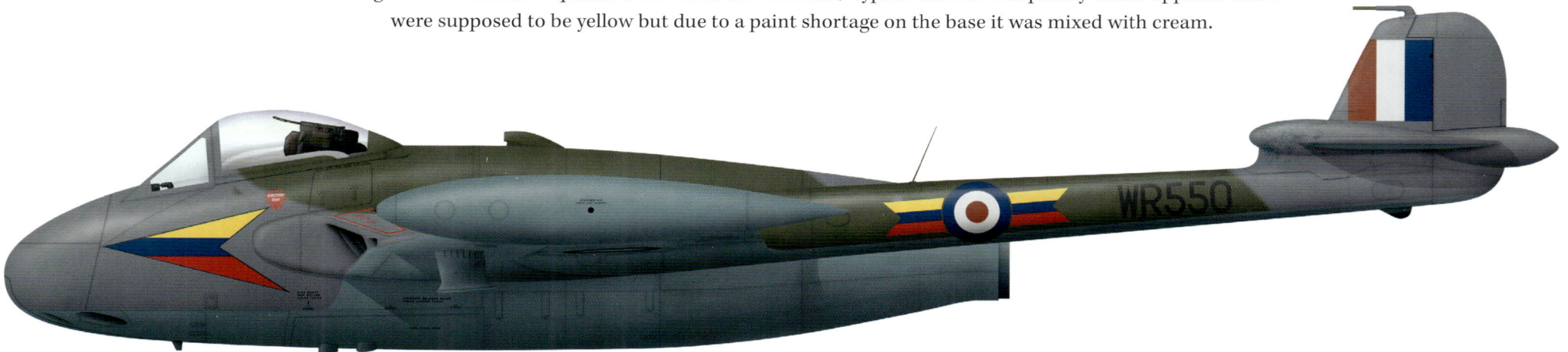

VENOM FB.4 WR550 8 SQUADRON

Based at RAF Khormaksar, Aden, WR550 made a forced landing as a result of a ricochet which wrote off the aircraft on August 22, 1957. The pilot, Flt Lt Dave Foster, was uninjured.

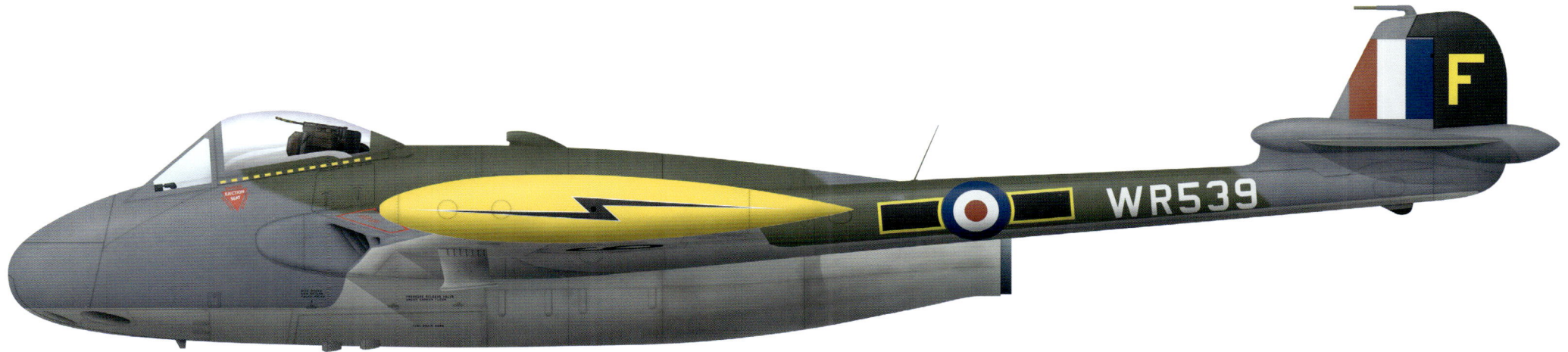

VENOM FB.4 WR539 28 SQUADRON
After 28 Squadron retired the Venom at Kai Tak, Hong Kong, WR539 remained on display for several years as the gate guardian. It was acquired by the de Havilland Museum in 1992 and has since been partially restored.

VENOM FB.4 WR419 208 SQUADRON
208 Squadron operated from a number of bases in the Middle East and parts of Africa, training in Kenya while flying the Venom during the late 1950s.

VENOM NF.2A WR794 33 SQUADRON

Finished in dark sea grey, dark green camouflage with medium grey undersides, 33 Squadron
operated this NF.2A while based at RAF Driffield during the mid-1950s.

VENOM NF.2A WL841 253 SQUADRON

Having been disbanded in 1947, 253 Squadron was re-formed to fly the Venom NF.2/2A for two years from
1955 until 1957 before being disbanded again. It was based at RAF Waterbeach during this time.

VENOM NF.3 WX853 23 SQUADRON

23 Squadron previously operated the Vampire NF.10 and the Venom NF.2 before replacing them with the NF.3 in 1957. WX853 later became the gate guardian at RAF Debden.

VENOM FB.4 WE474 94 SQUADRON

Several aerobatic teams were formed by the Venom squadrons of West Germany but 94 Squadron were selected to represent 2TAF. The tanks were NMF with red bands.

VENOM NF.3 WX841 141 SQUADRON

141 Squadron operated the Venom for two years before converting to the Javelin in 1957. They would become a Bloodhound squadron in 1959.

VENOM NF.3 WX794 151 SQUADRON

151 Squadron was equipped with several night fighters during the post-war years including, for 20 months, the Venom.

VENOM FB.1 WE281

This aircraft was displayed by de Havilland at the annual SBAC show held at Farnborough in September 1952. It was not delivered to the RAF until August 11, 1953. On March 23, 1954, while serving with 118 Squadron in West Germany, it crashed into the ground during a simulated attack on an army convoy. The pilot did not survive. The demarcation line of the lower surfaces was much higher than it would appear on later aircraft.

VENOM FB.1 WE253 JUBILEE RACE

WE253 was due to compete in the Jubilee Trophy air race scheduled for June 26, 1956, hence the race number. However, poor weather at Hatfield led to the race being cancelled. The aircraft was finished in overall aluminium paint.

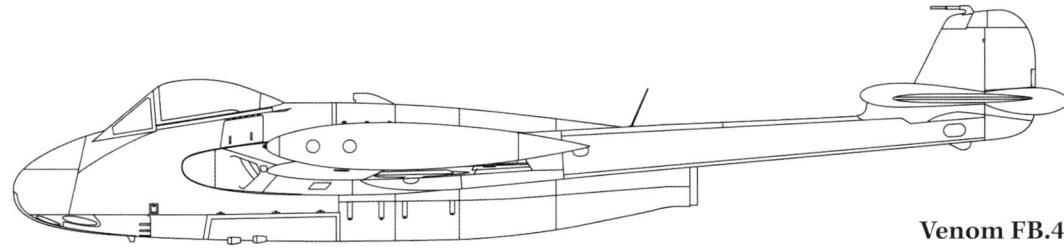

Venom FB.4

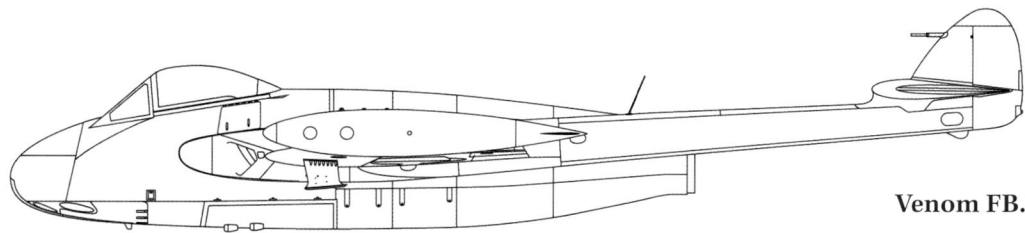

Venom FB.1

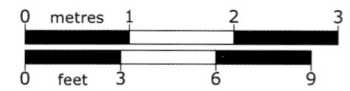

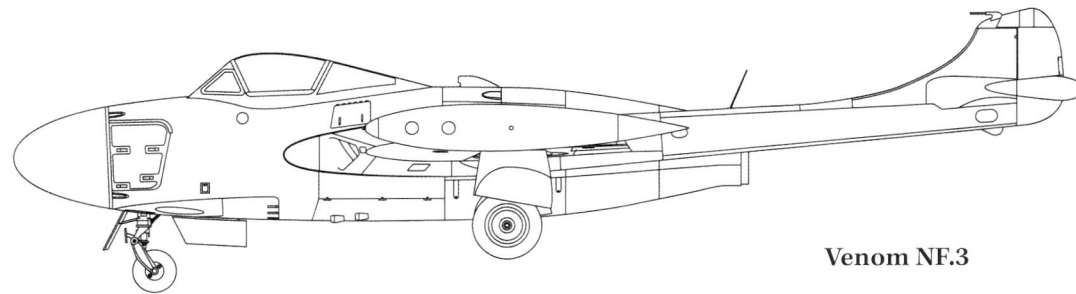

Venom NF.3

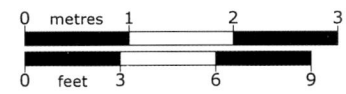

0 metres 1 2 3

0 feet 3 6 9

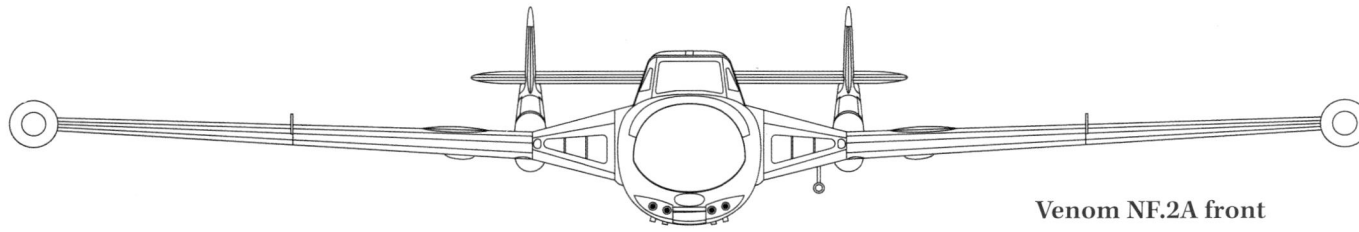

Venom NF.2A front

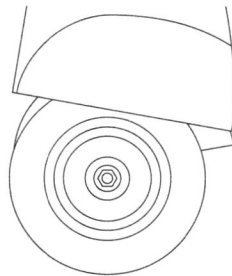

Main wheel

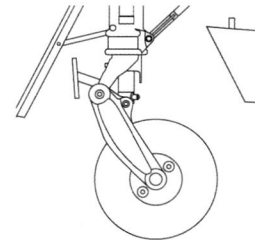

Nose wheel

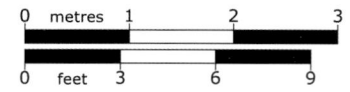

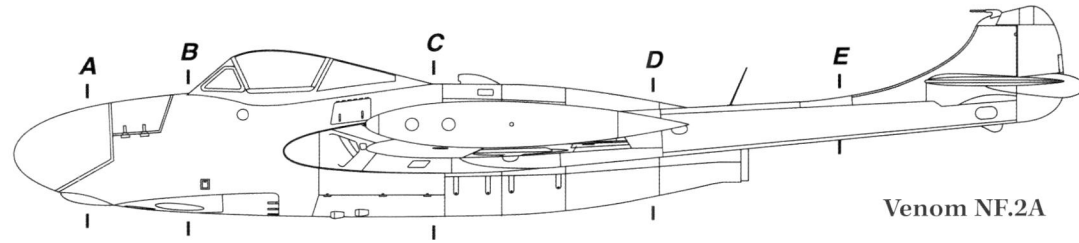

Venom NF.2A

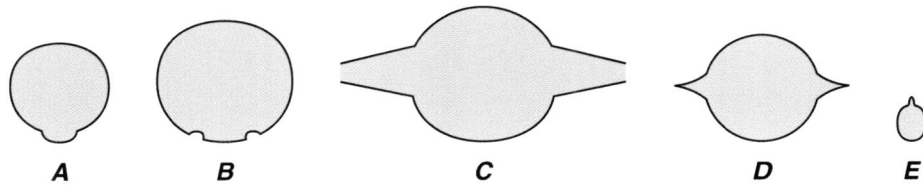

A   B   C   D   E

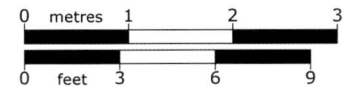

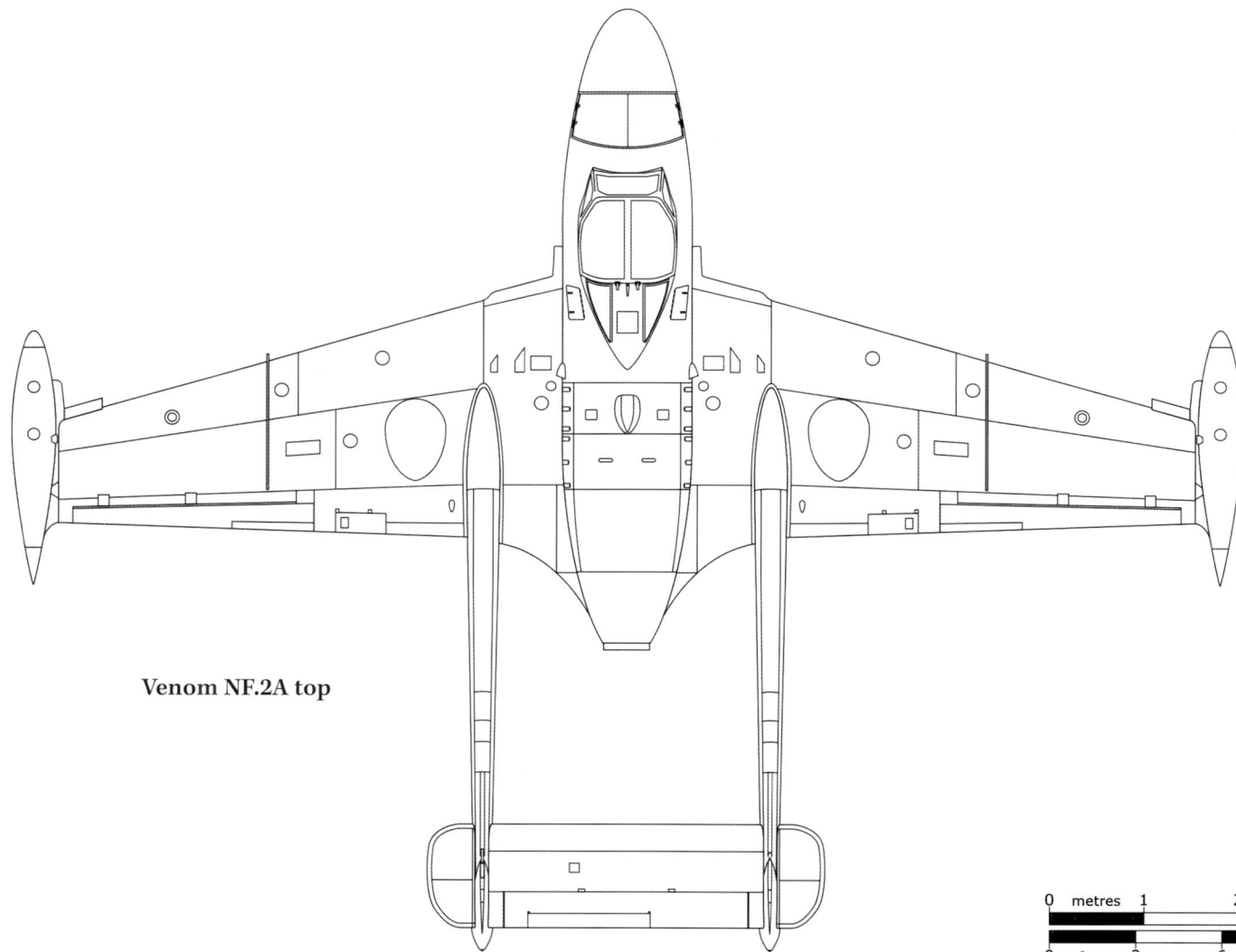

Venom NF.2A top

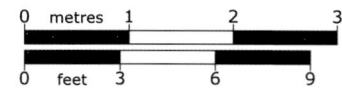

0 metres 1 2 3

0 feet 3 6 9

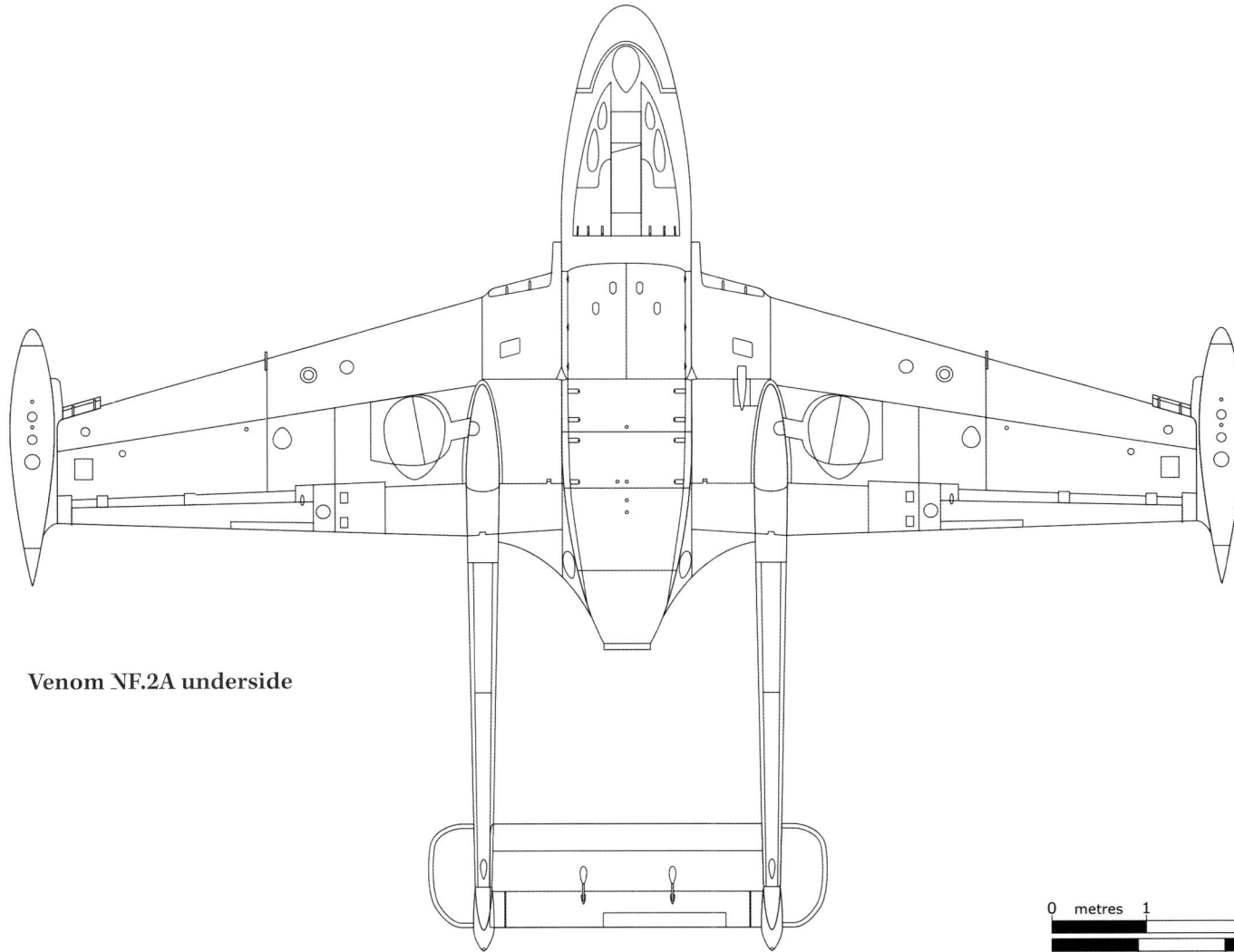

Venom NF.2A underside

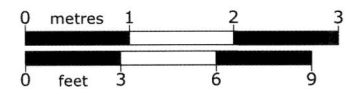

0 metres 1 2 3

0 feet 3 6 9

ENGLISH ELECTRIC CANBERRA

The Canberra's simple design and longevity make it a remarkable jet. First conceived of during the Second World War, when the Lancaster was the mainstay of Bomber Command, the Canberra was a huge leap forward in technology with a much smaller crew, greater range, higher climb rate and considerably higher speed than its prop-driven predecessors. The foresight of lead designer W. E. W. Petter and his team at English Electric was impressive, creating an aircraft that first flew only a few years after the war but carried on well into the 21st century.

With the development of the jet engine and the success of the Meteor fighter it was apparent that a replacement for the high-altitude bomber version of the Mosquito would be required. This resulted in Specification B.1/44 being issued by the Air Ministry, asking for a high-altitude twin-engine jet bomber which could fly at 530mph while still being manoeuvrable at low level. This piqued the interest of Westland designer Petter, who began working on concepts and gained the support of the company. Early drawings showed a nose intake and the two engines inside the fuselage.

The engine position was then shifted to the wing roots and eventually they were to be mounted in the wings. While Petter was away on leave, however, Westland decided to proceed with the Wyvern naval fighter rather than his bomber. This ultimately led to the designer leaving for English Electric — even though Westland was his family's company — where his ideas would be realised.

With other companies focusing on larger bomber designs, which would eventually become the V force, English Electric was left with no competition for Petter's twin-engine bomber and work began

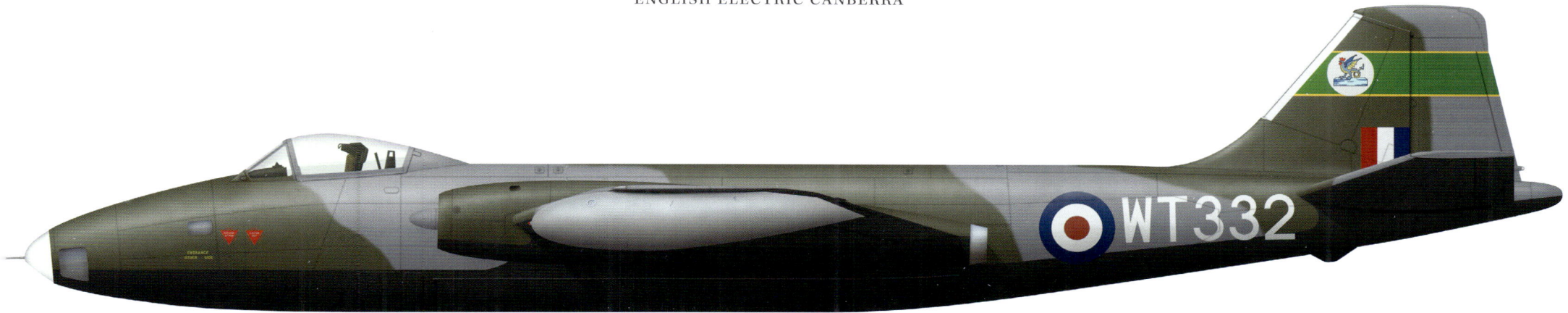

CANBERRA B(I)8 WT332 3 SQUADRON

3 Squadron operated Canberras in West Germany for just over a decade from 1961 before replacing
them with the Harrier GR.1. Finished in dark green, dark sea grey with a black underside.

in 1945. Heavily swept wings were a feature of the early designs but with the thrust available from the early Rolls-Royce jet engines, compressibility was not considered an issue and a similar wing form to that of the Meteor was chosen.

Work progressed at a steady pace and by May 1949 the new bomber was ready for flight testing. With Wg Cdr Roland Beamont at the controls, VN799 undertook several high-speed taxi runs and a first short hop on May 9, 1949. Following more hops to test flight controls, VN799 lifted off from Warton on Friday, May 13. It was not the most auspicious day but the flight was considered a success. The only significant changes made were to the rudder and the dorsal fillet, which was removed.

By September the Canberra was ready for public display and painted in a high gloss cerulean blue. At Farnborough it is reported to have stolen the show with Beamont putting on a stunning performance every day which included a variety of high- and low-speed passes, dramatic climbs and rolls.

A further three prototypes (VN813, VN828 and VN850), designated B.1, were constructed and used for ongoing development trials of the type. The original intention was for the Canberra to bomb from altitude by radar, but the equipment available at the time turned out to be too bulky for the aircraft so changes had to be made to accommodate a third crew member for visual bomb aiming duties.

A transparent nosecone was added and the resulting aircraft, the B.2, would become the most successful Canberra variant. A total of 416 were delivered to the RAF commencing on May 25, 1951, with delivery of WD936 to 101 Sqn at RAF Binbrook, where it replaced the Avro Lincoln.

CANBERRA B(I)8 WT333

Originally built as a B(I)8, WT333 had a modified B.2 nose fitted in 1972 for trials. For several years it flew with a mixed scheme before being repainted in Raspberry Ripple in 1978. Upon retirement it was delivered to Bruntingthorpe, Leicestershire, in January 1995.

To cope with the order, half of production was subcontracted to Avro, Handley Page and Short Brothers, helping to keep these companies active while they developed their V bombers. The B.2 squadrons operated across the globe, detachments from several of them participating in the Suez Crisis.

Based at Tengah, B.2s flew regular sorties against insurgents during the Malaya Emergency. As well as tours to the Far East and Africa, there was a constant Canberra presence in Germany for many years throughout the cold war and the type was a regular fixture at RAF Akrotiri in Cyprus.

One derivative of the B.2 was the T.4. The Canberra may have had few vices but there was still a need for a dual control version due to the high number of B.2s entering service and the consequent need for conversion of bomber pilots from piston to jet engines.

Two seats were fitted in WM467 with no external redesign and the aircraft first flew on June 12, 1952. Delivery to 231 OCU began in September 1953. Deliveries continued until 1955 by which time 66 had been produced. A further 17 B.2s were also converted to the T.4 configuration.

Prior to the T.4's delivery, it was evident that mistakes arising from the power and acceleration of the jet engine, a common problem during the early days of conversion to jets, combined with a somewhat laid back approach to training, had resulted in a number of Canberra accidents in either poor weather or at night by pilots who had few hours on the type.

A revised training programme was introduced alongside the T.4, which led to a considerable reduction in accidents.

Only one B.5 was built, VX185, but it was a very successful and

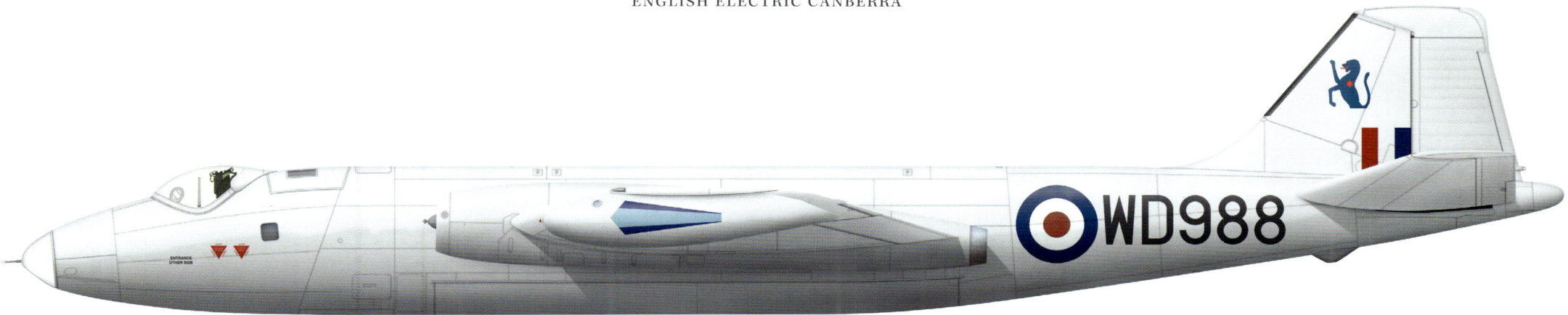

CANBERRA B.2 WD988 75 SQUADRON

While at El Adem in 1958 WD988 was painted in a trial all over white scheme, standard national markings and squadron on the tail.

active aeroplane. Key changes included leading edge fuel tanks, upgraded radar, improved low level handling, Avon Mk 109 RA7 engines and a new Dunlop anti-skid braking system. During range trials it became apparent at Warton that the ultimate trial would be to cross the Atlantic and return. This eventful double Atlantic Flight took place on August 25, 1952. Four hours and 34 minutes after leaving Aldergrove, VX185 touched down at Gander, Newfoundland. Following a service and refuelling it was time to return to the UK. The whole trip took 10 hours and three minutes, despite an extended turnaround, and became a media sensation.

The Canberra was also given a night interdiction role, with the B.6 being developed for that purpose. Based closely on the B.2 but with the enhancements of the B.5, only 20 were built. One squadron also saw their B.6s fitted with a ventral gun pack and underwing pylons.

The type's career was short-lived due to the introduction of the

B.8. This variant was designed with flexibility in mind, its roles including high-altitude bomber, long-range interdictor, nuclear delivery system, low level operations and target marking.

To achieve all this the front of the Canberra saw a significant redesign with a narrower yet raised fighter style canopy for improved visibility. The seat for the bomb aimer/navigator was moved into the nose. Like the B.6, it had provision for a gun pack and its underwing pylons that could carry a 1000lb bomb, Matra rocket launcher or 37 Sneb 2in rockets. Only 57 were built but many went on to see a second life on the export market.

The Mk.8 was the last Canberra bomber but it was by no means the end of the Canberra. Even as the B.2 was being developed, a photo reconnaissance Canberra was also being worked on. The B.2 forward fuselage was extended to accommodate an extra fuel tank, cameras and flares.

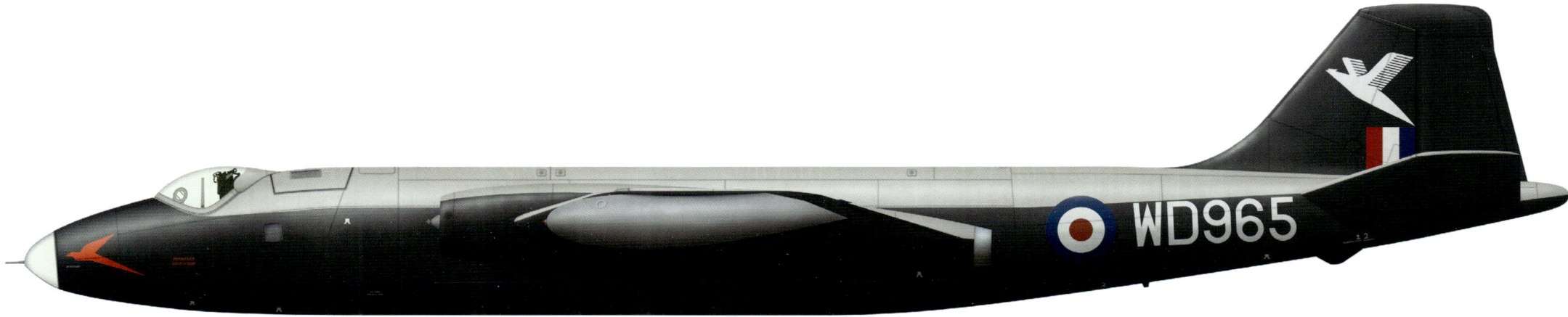

CANBERRA B.2 WD965 10 SQUADRON

Early Canberras were painted in the Medium Altitude Night Bomber scheme which consisted of gloss black underside and medium sea grey upper surface. The 10 Squadron aircraft were later repainted in camouflage.

Testing of the prototype, VX181, revealed extensive vibrations however—not a good thing for high-altitude photography. Investigations indicated that the issue was being caused by a combination of the new split flaps and extended fuselage. Despite increases to the weight of the tab and elevator mass balances, the problem was never fully cured for the PR.3 and only 35 were completed.

Nevertheless, the PR.3 it was still considered a success by the RAF and English Electric began work on the PR.7, utilising the new features that had been introduced in the Mk.5 and Mk.6 but with a PR.3 fuselage. The improved performance evidently endeared the type to the RAF with 74 being produced in three batches.

Canberra trials had already reached 54,000ft but the requirement for the new PR.9 was to exceed 60,000ft. Due to a revised nose causing an increase in drag, the PR.9 prototype failed to reach this by 200ft. Even though the prototype retained the B.2 style canopy, production versions had the newer B.8 style configuration. The most notable visual change compared to other British versions of the Canberra was the increased wingspan—this being necessary to cope with the thinner air at high altitude.

The standard span was 63ft 11½in (19.5m) whereas the PR.9 had a span of 67ft 11½in (20.7m). With 32 PR.9s built, the first was delivered to the RAF in September 1958 and the type was eventually retired in 2006 when 39 Sqn conducted the last sortie on July 28. One PR.9, XH143, is still believed to be airworthy.

While the PR.9 was the last variant off the production line for the RAF, 23 having been built, many went on to receive modifications

CANBERRA B.2 WF890 SWIFTER FLIGHT

Operation Swifter was set up to investigate high-speed low level flights for the TSR2 and Buccaneer programmes. A dedicated flight was established for this, which included WF890.

and upgrades to extend their service life. Variants included the U.10 and U.14 which were unmanned types converted from B.2s and used for weapon trials. The T.17 also evolved from the B.2, its most distinctive feature being the addition to the extended nose which housed electronic countermeasures systems and provided ECM training. Serving with both the RAF and Royal Navy yet more B.2s were converted for target tug duties, replacing the ageing Meteors.

Over 70 years later, the Canberra is still undertaking operational flights with NASA albeit in the heavily modified WB-57F configuration. It would still be recognised by W E W Petter, however. It is a testament to the robust yet flexible design that more than 1350 were built including 403 B-57s.

The type served with 17 different air forces and with 61 RAF squadrons, finally being retired 55 years after entering service. Involved in several conflicts around the world, the Canberra demonstrated its excellent qualities itself again and again. It proved that despite being the first British jet bomber the design was exceptional and it outlasted many of its successors.

English Electric Canberra

VARIANT	LENGTH	SPAN	HEIGHT	ENGINE
B.1	65FT 6IN/19.96M	63FT 11.5IN/19.49M	15FT 8IN/4.78M	2 X AVON RA.2 OR NENE RNE.2
B.2	65FT 6IN/19.96M	63FT 11.5IN/19.49M	15FT 8IN/4.78M	2 X AVON RA.3 MK.101
PR.3	66FT 8IN/20.32M	63FT 11.5IN/19.49M	15FT 8IN/4.78M	2 X AVON RA.3 MK.101
T.4	65FT 6IN/19.96M	63FT 11.5IN/19.49M	15FT 8IN/4.78M	2 X AVON RA.3 MK.101
B.5	65FT 6IN/19.96M	63FT 11.5IN/19.49M	15FT 8IN/4.78M	2 X AVON RA.7 MK.109
B(I).6	65FT 6IN/19.96M	63FT 11.5IN/19.49M	15FT 8IN/4.78M	2 X AVON RA.7 MK.109
PR.7	66FT 8IN/20.32M	63FT 11.5IN/19.49M	15FT 8IN/4.78M	2 X AVON RA.7 MK.109
B(I).8	65FT 6IN/19.96M	63FT 11.5IN/19.49M	15FT 8IN/4.78M	2 X AVON RA.7 MK.109
PR.9	66FT 8IN/20.32M	67FT 10.5IN/20.69M	15FT 8IN/4.78M	2 X AVON RA.24 MK.206
U.10	65FT 6IN/19.96M	63FT 11.5IN/19.49M	15FT 8IN/4.78M	2 X AVON RA.7 MK.109
B.15	65FT 6IN/19.96M	63FT 11.5IN/19.49M	15FT 8IN/4.78M	2 X AVON RA.7 MK.109
B.16	65FT 6IN/19.96M	63FT 11.5IN/19.49M	15FT 8IN/4.78M	2 X AVON RA.7 MK.109
T.17	67FT 3IN/20.50M	63FT 11.5IN/19.49M	15FT 8IN/4.78M	2 X AVON RA.3 MK.102

CANBERRA B.2 WH649 139 SQUADRON

WH649 wears a less well known scheme of light slate grey and medium sea grey upper surface with
PRU blue underside. 139 Squadron eventually replaced the Canberra with the Victor.

CANBERRA B.2 WH668 10 SQUADRON

WH668 had an interesting scheme with the tanks and engine pods finished in aluminium. 10 Squadron only
operated the Canberra for four years but during that time the aircraft were involved in the Suez Crisis.

CANBERRA B.2 WH725 50 SQUADRON

Based at RAF Binbrook and later RAF Upwood, 50 Squadron converted to the Canberra in August 1952. WH725 was not delivered until May 1953. It is preserved at IWM Duxford and the stripes have since been removed.

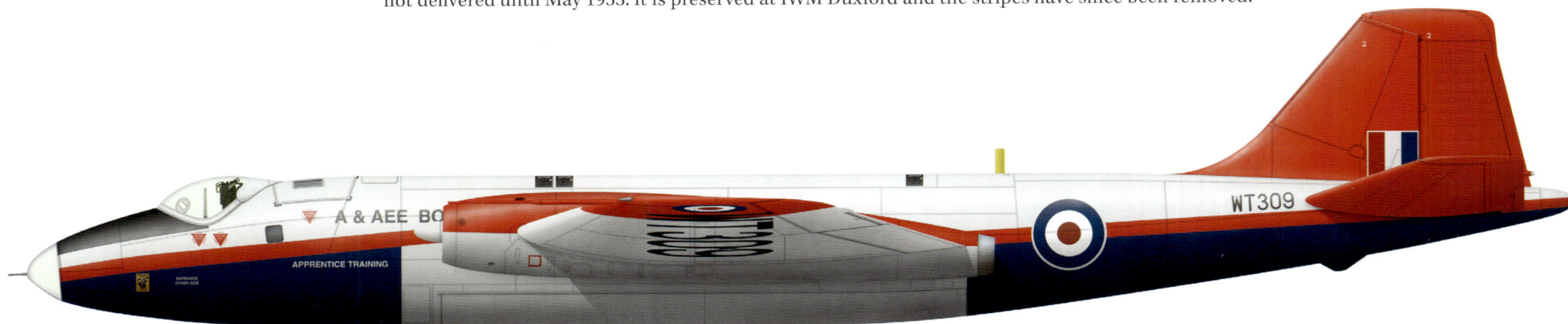

CANBERRA B(I)6 WT309 A&AEE

Unlike the other B(I)6 built, WT309 never entered squadron service. Instead it was allocated to A&AEE, Farnborough and became part of Weapons Flight. During the mid-1980s it was retired and eventually scrapped. Finished in standard Raspberry Ripple.

CANBERRA B.2 WJ567 85 SQUADRON

Having had a colourful career, WJ567 was used as a target by 85 Squadron and painted in light aircraft grey with Day-Glo bands during 1974.

CANBERRA B.2 WJ611 101 SQUADRON

101 Squadron was the first to fly the Canberra in 1951 at RAF Binbrook. WJ611 had minimal markings
and just a flash on the nose outlined in black. WJ611 is finished in all over aluminium.

CANBERRA B.2 WJ614 6 SQUADRON

Wearing the squadron band on the tail and the 'flying can opener' on the tip tank is 6 Squadron's WJ614. It has a white tail and all over aluminium. Later converted to TT.18 configuration and used by the Royal Navy.

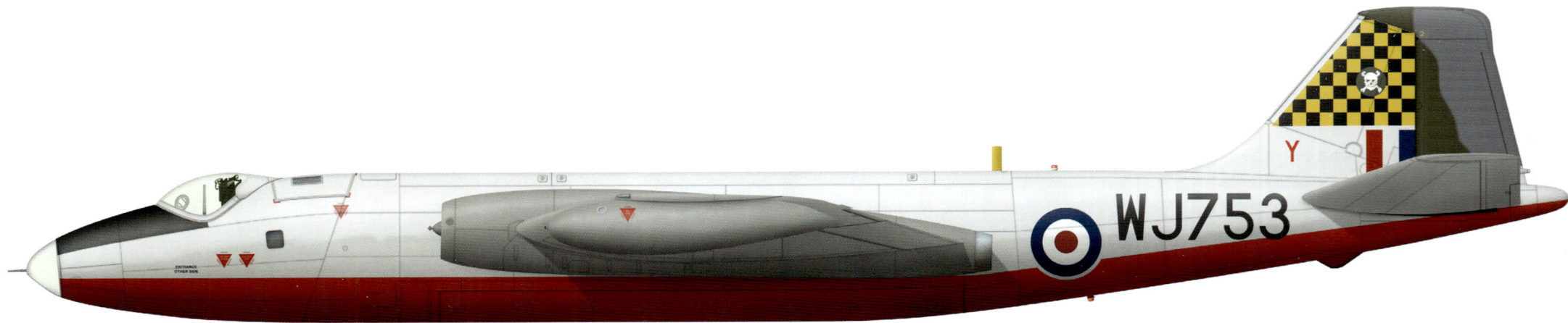

CANBERRA WJ753 100 SQUADRON

Originally delivered to the RAF in 1954, WJ753 was with 100 Sqn when it was written off in 1978. It was painted in white and red but had been fitted with a replacement camouflaged rudder in 1975.

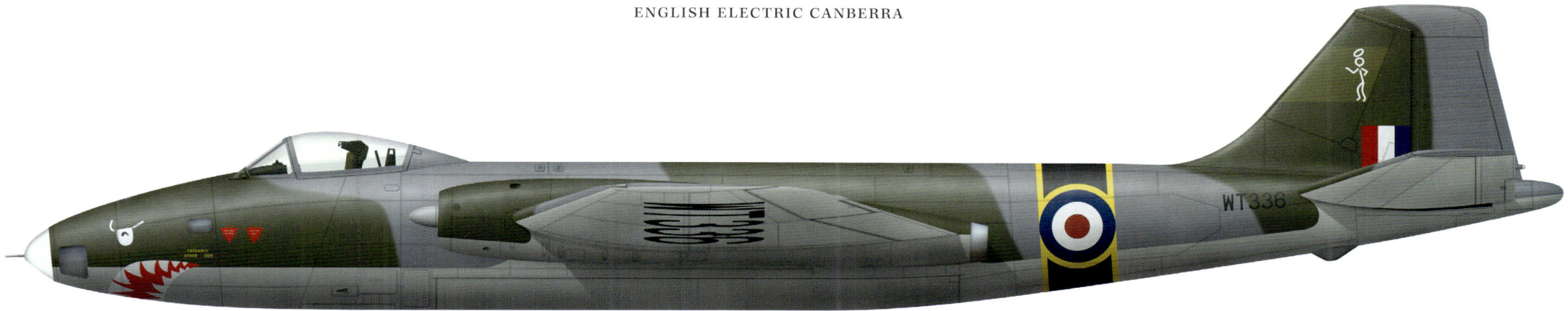

CANBERRA B(I)8 WT336 16 SQUADRON

During the early 1970s, while based at RAF Laarbruch, West Germany, 16 Squadron tended to apply shark mouths to its aircraft. They were also adorned with the Saint on the tail, a tradition that has carried on with subsequent aircraft.

CANBERRA T.4 WT480 102 SQUADRON

WT480 was used during 1955 and 1956 as a Training and Checkflight Aircraft by RAF Gütersloh. At the time 102 Squadron was part of 551 Wing and the wing badge was worn on the nose.

CANBERRA T.17 WJ607 360 SQUADRON

360 Squadron was a Joint Electronic Warfare Trials and Training Force which operated the T.17—a heavily modified B.2. The initial scheme was dark sea grey and dark green over light aircraft grey.

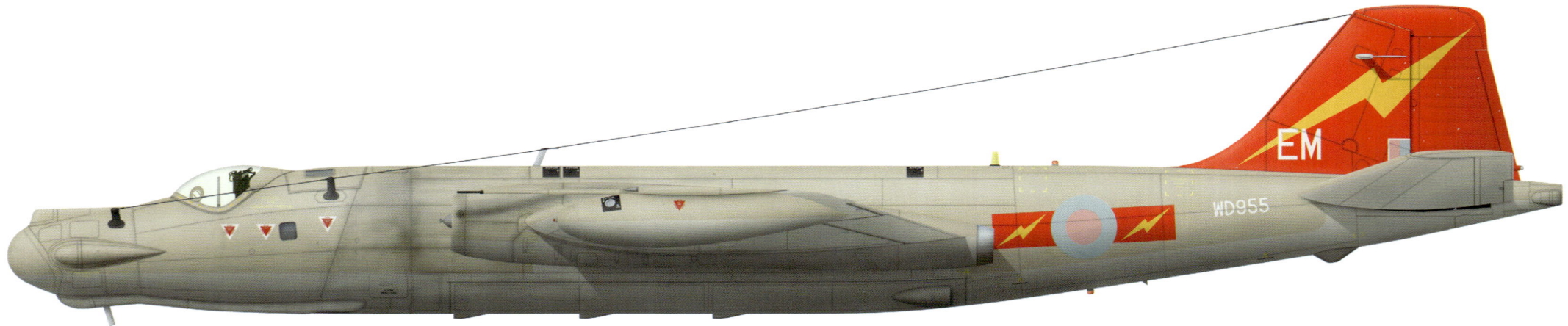

CANBERRA T.17 WD955 360 SQUADRON

360 Squadron aircraft were later completely repainted in camouflage grey upper surface and light aircraft grey underside with a red tail.

ROYAL AIR FORCE SIGNALS COMMAND
WJ681

CANBERRA B.2 WJ681 98 SQUADRON

245 Squadron was renumbered to 98 Squadron on April 19, 1963, and used the Canberra for radar calibration. The first Canberras to serve with the unit, including WJ681, were bare metal with Day-Glo markings but later wore a variety of paint schemes.

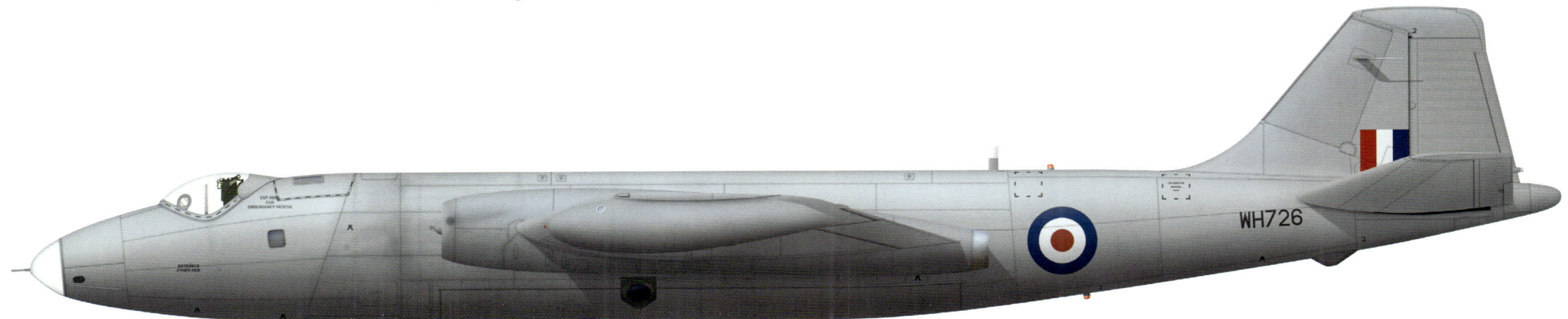

WH726

CANBERRA B.2 WH726 540 SQUADRON

During 1953, WH726 was modified to carry a 240in Robin camera and take photographs of military installations within East Germany at an altitude of 48,000ft. It may also have carried out reconnaissance flights over the USSR.

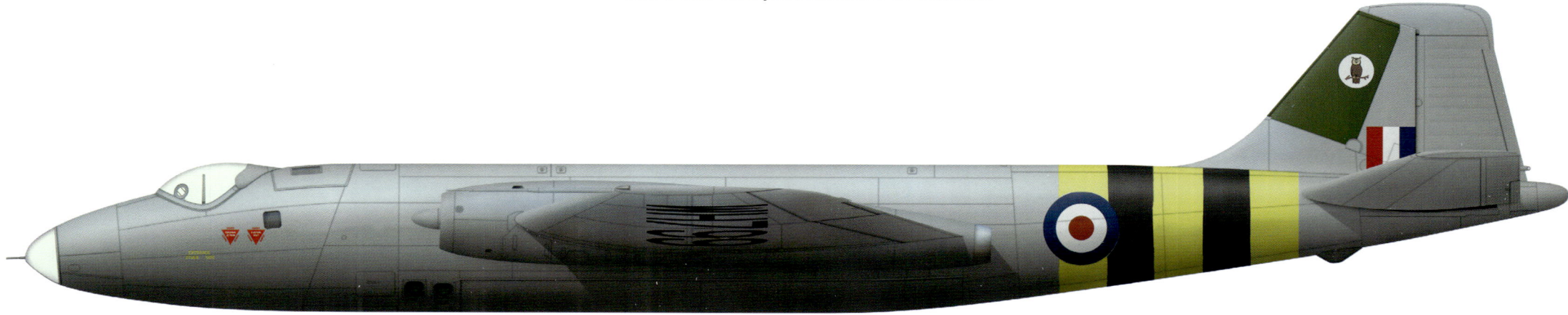

CANBERRA PR.7 WH799 58 SQUADRON

58 Squadron was posted to RAF Akrotiri prior to the Suez crisis. On November 6, 1956, WH799 took off to monitor the Syrian Air Force. It was intercepted by two Meteor NF.13s and shot down. Navigator FO R. Urquhart-Pullen was killed but the other two crew, pilot Flt Lt Hunter and Flt Lt Small, survived.

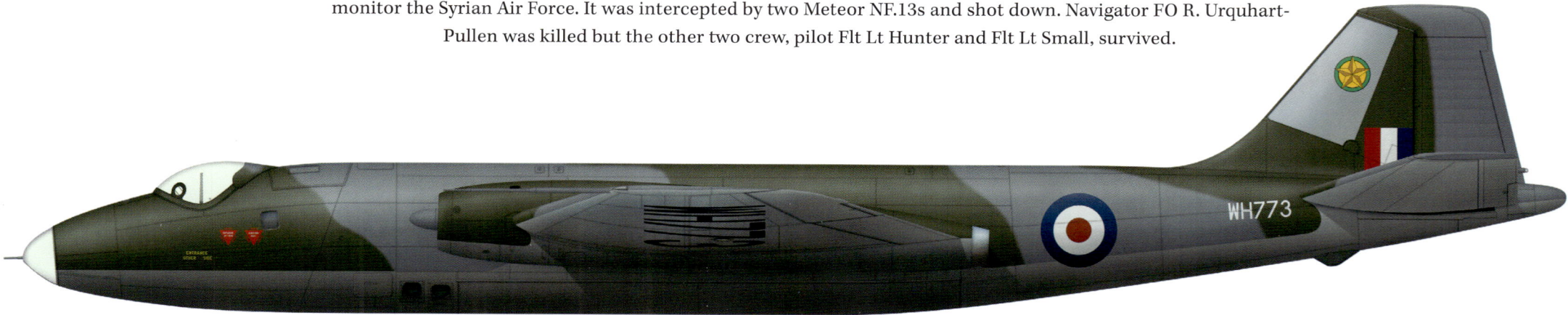

CANBERRA PR.7 WH773 31 SQUADRON

Having served with 540, 80 and 82 Squadrons based in the UK, WH773 was transferred to 31 Squadron based at RAF Laarbruch, Germany, where it was used for low level tactical reconnaissance flights. It then served with several more squadrons around Europe before its eventual retirement in 1981.

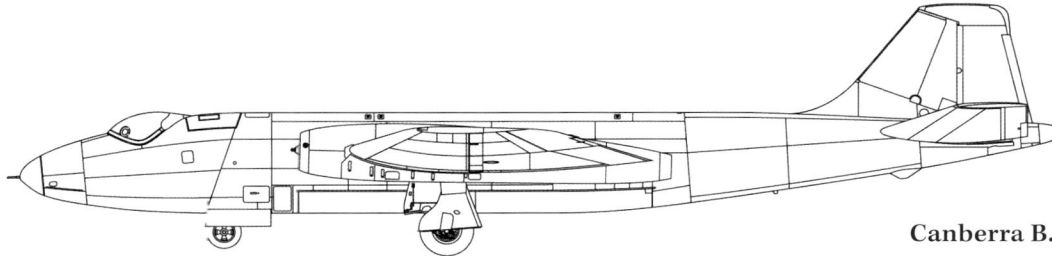

Canberra B.2

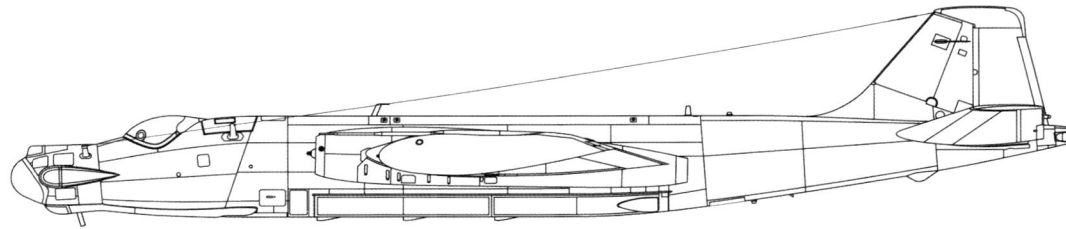

Canberra T.17

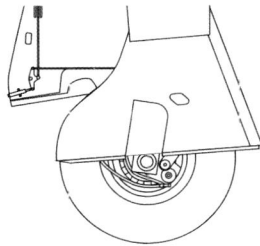

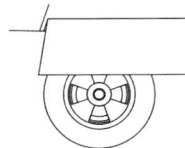

Main wheel **Nose wheel**

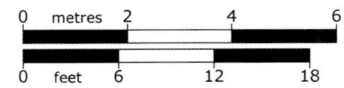

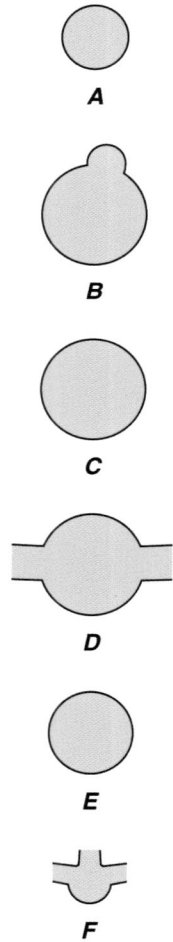

A

B

C

D

E

F

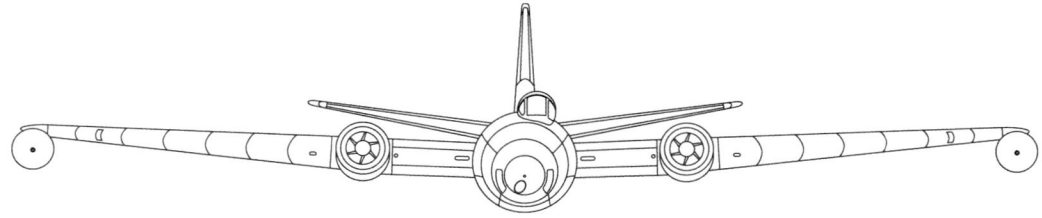

Canberra B.8 front

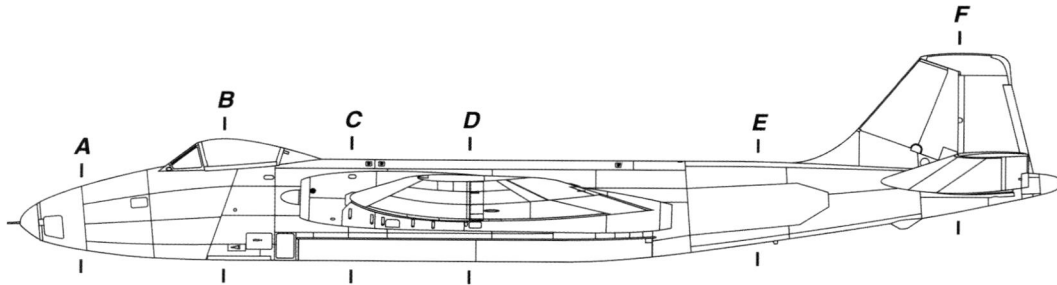

A B C D E F

Canberra B.8

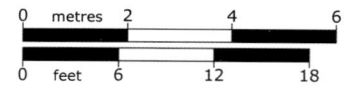

| 0 | metres | 2 | 4 | 6 |

| 0 | feet | 6 | 12 | 18 |

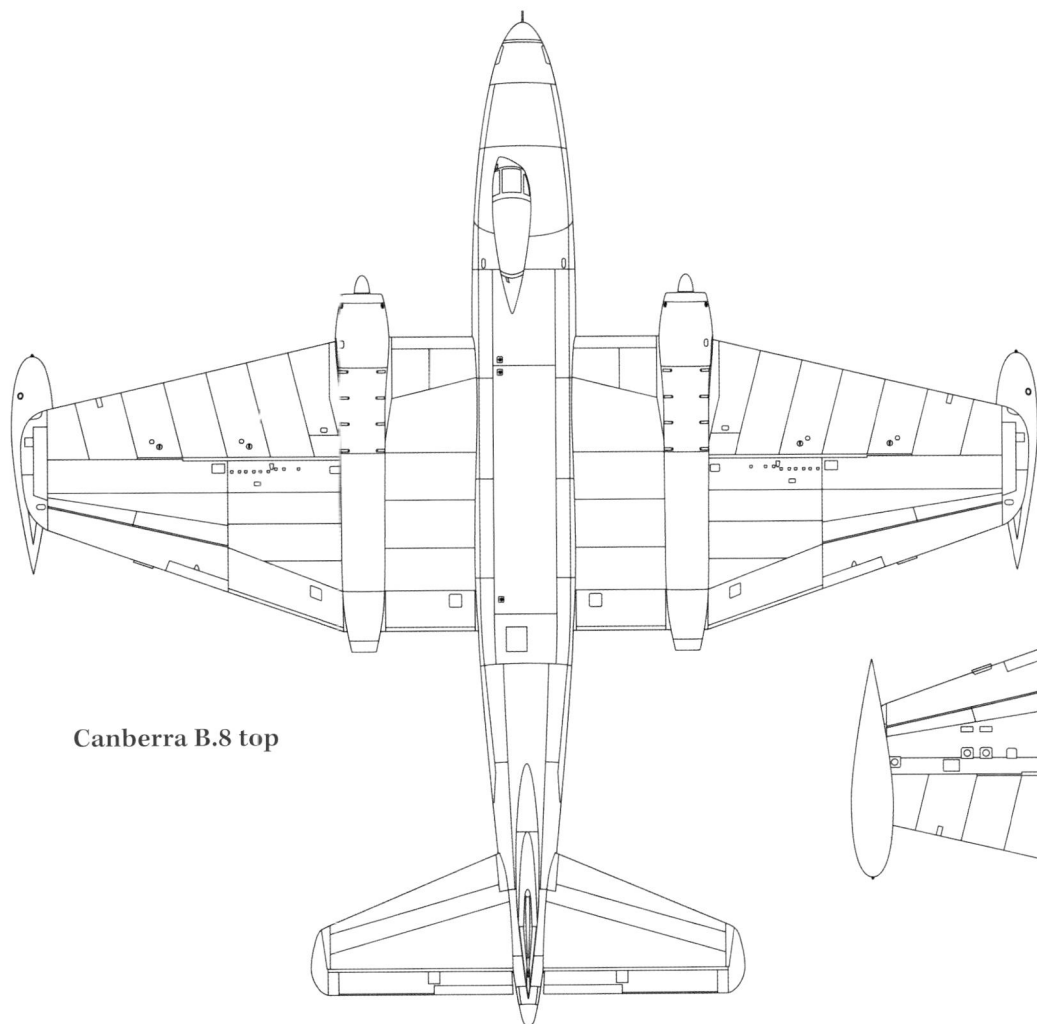

Canberra B.8 top

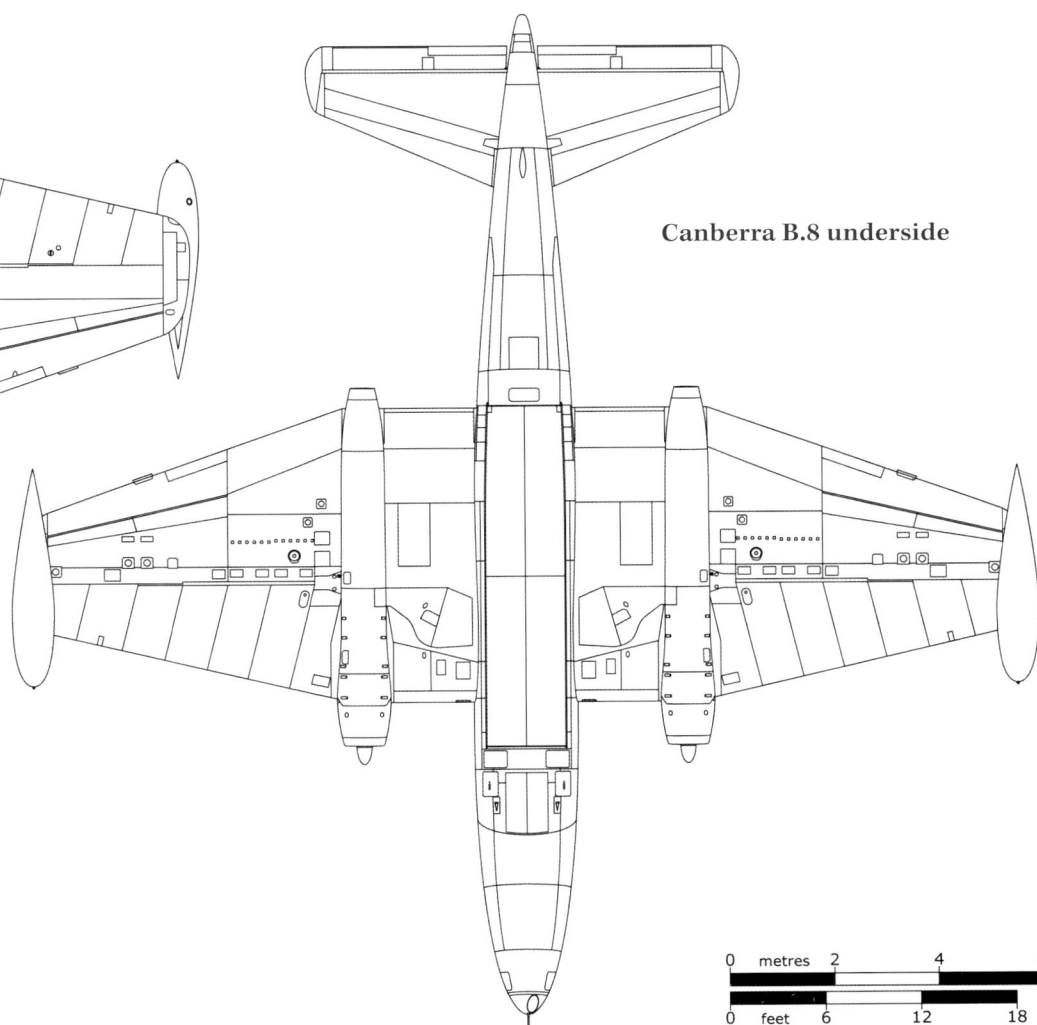

Canberra B.8 underside

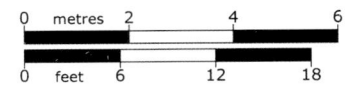

0 metres 2   4   6

0 feet 6   12   18

SUPERMARINE SWIFT

In a roundabout way the Swift was part of the Spitfire linage but without the pedigree or reputation. The Spitfire had evolved into the Spiteful, which was the basis for the Attacker and that in turn became the foundation for the Swift. The hindering effect of trying to reuse older airframes combined with stiff competition from the Hawker Hunter meant the Swift gained a poor reputation and had only a brief service life, despite holding the world speed record for a short time.

Supermarine's Swift resulted from the company's research into swept wing jets and the RAF's need for a fast new day interceptor/fighter. Having already produced the Attacker, the firm was contracted to explore high-speed flight.

A test aircraft was created by fitting wings with a 40° sweep-back to an Attacker fuselage. Known as the Supermarine 510, VV106 first flew in December 1948 and was used for flight testing. Even at this stage it was unofficially being called the Swift, a name that would stick.

Running concurrently with this at Hawker was the Hunter. The Ministry of Supply wanted to ensure that at least one of the two aircraft succeeded for the sake of Britain's air defence.

VV106 was joined by a second experimental aircraft in 1950. VV119 featured a number of design improvements including a longer nose, revised tail, a change in the undercarriage configuration and the installation of a Nene engine. As the programme progressed there were ongoing alterations as test results came in and the aircraft was now visually more akin to what would become the Swift F.1 than the Attacker.

As tensions rose in Europe and the conflict in Korea escalated,

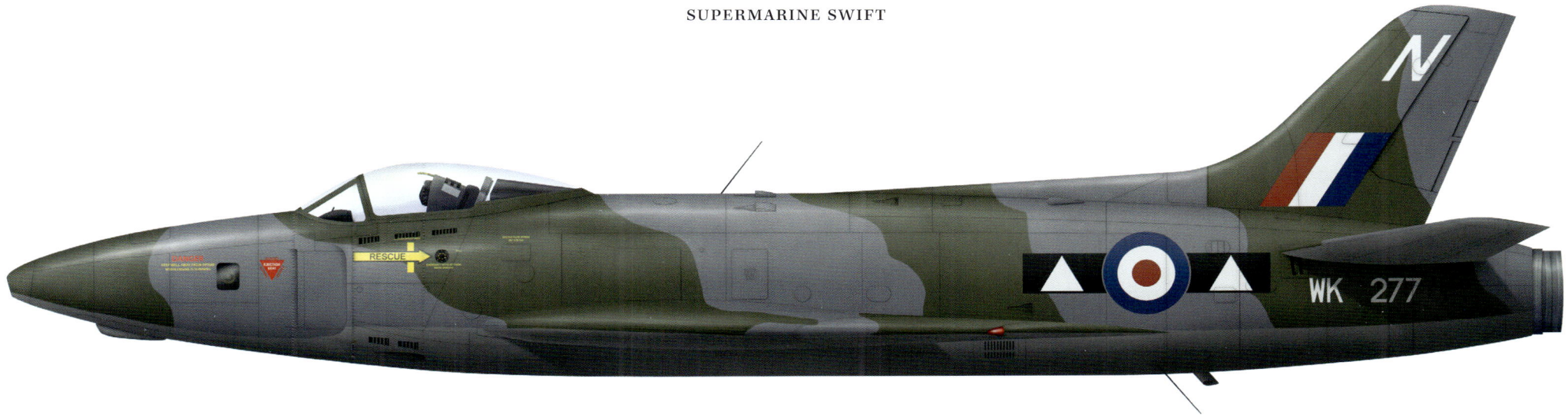

SWIFT FR.5 WK277 2 SQUADRON

WK277 was originally designated an F.4 during construction but upgraded to FR.5 configuration. It served with 2 Squadron between 1959 and 1961. It was then retired and used as a ground trainer at RAF Cosford. It is currently on display at Newark Air Museum.

the need for a jet fighter to counter the communist air forces became increasingly urgent. Consequently, the development of the Swift had to be progressed as rapidly as possible. It was hoped that the Swift would start entering service by October 1952 and an order for 150 was placed.

WJ960 was the first of the pre-production prototypes and differed little from the final iteration of VV119. The wings had a slight curve and the ailerons had been enlarged but it was not yet the final package.

The second pre-production WJ965 prototype was much closer to the F.1 however; the fin had been enlarged, the layout and size of the cockpit revised and the fuel capacity increased. It flew for the first time on July 14, 1952, and two years later succeeded in breaking

the sound barrier with David Morgan, one of Supermarine's test pilots, at the controls.

By August 1952 the first F.1 had been completed and WK194 flew on the 25th. It spent much of its career with A&AEE at Boscombe Down before being used as a ground trainer and later scrapped. Several other early production F.1s were used for a variety of testing and development roles. Some, such as WK198 and WK200, were used as the basis for later variants – the F.4 and F.5 respectively. It was only from WK205 onwards that the aircraft served with front line squadrons.

56 Squadron received their first F.1 on February 20, 1954, when it was escorted by a pair of Meteors to RAF Waterbeach. Initially the Swift was welcomed by its pilots, who had been used to the

SWIFT F.1 WK207 56 SQUADRON
Early Swifts were delivered and flew in NMF. 56 Squadron applied the squadron bars and code letter to the tail of WK207.

already dated Meteor. Before the end of the month the squadron received three more and a conversion programme was initiated. During this period the Swift began earning notoriety, several aircraft being lost during the spring with serviceability or lack of it being a major factor.

Before a single F.1 had entered service however, work had commenced on subsequent variants of the Swift. The F.2 had provision for extra guns in the lower fuselage, although this led to stability issues, and the F.3 was fitted with reheat. Despite this, no F.3 ever entered service, the entire run being relegated to the ignominious role of instructional airframes.

WK198 was used as the basis for the F.4 variant and was used by Supermarine to break the world speed record, which had previously been gained by Neville Duke in Hawker Hunter WB188 on September 7, 1953.

Later in the month WK198, by now painted light blue, was dispatched to Libya for another attempt. Based at Idris Airfield, the team had everything in place and ready by September 25. Following four runs, an average speed of 735.7 mph was officially recorded. WB188 survived and is currently at Brooklands.

It was becoming clear with the introduction of the Hunter and comparable US aircraft, that the Swift was struggling. It lacked the performance and handling that a dedicated fighter required. At the same time, the reconnaissance version of the Meteor was looking antiquated and in need of replacement. The Swift seemed like a potential candidate.

Testing of an F.4 by A&AEE indicated that many of the type's earlier handling issues had been resolved and it was recommended that the Swift be considered for conversion. The FR.5 received a revised nose which would house three oblique cameras. It could call upon reheat should it need extra speed but the detrimental effect this would have on range was a problem. To increase endurance, provision was made to fit a belly tank but at the cost of some speed. The aircraft also retained two Aden cannon.

2 and 79 Squadrons, both based in West Germany were selected to operate the type and deliveries commenced in mid-1956. The FR.5 performed the task admirably and was far more suited to the reconnaissance role than as a fighter, flying with the two squadrons for five years until the much more capable Hunter FR.10 was ready.

During this transition period, on December 30, 1960, 79 Squadron was disbanded. Many elements were taken over by a re-formed 4 Squadron, including the remaining Swifts – two of which briefly wore both 79 and 4 Squadron markings.

Two final variants of the Swift were developed. Only one PR.6 was built and even then the project was cancelled before construction

was completed. The F.7 was intended to intercept bombers and carry four AAMs, the Fireflash and later Firestreak. It also featured a revised canopy, the Avon 116 engine and a new nose which would accommodate the Ekco radar used by the Fireflash. In total 14 were completed and all were used in testing by the Guided Weapons Development Squadron at RAF Valley.

The F.7 was eventually replaced by the Javelin in 1958. Only 197 Swifts were built, far fewer than any other post-war RAF fighter, but the pace of technological advancement combined with the number of jets being commissioned by the Ministry of Supply during the cold war arms race meant that some would just not be as successful as others and the Swift was one such aircraft.

Much that was learnt from the Swift went into the final Supermarine aircraft, the Scimitar, and despite the low numbers built several airframes have survived at museums around the country.

Supermarine Swift

VARIANT	LENGTH	SPAN	HEIGHT	ENGINE
F.1	41FT 5.5IN/12.66M	32FT 4IN/9.86M	12FT 6IN/3.81M	AVON RA.7
F.2	41FT 5.5IN/12.66M	32FT 4IN/9.86M	12FT 6IN/3.81M	AVON RA.7
F.4	41FT 5.5IN/12.66M	32FT 4IN/9.86M	12FT 6IN/3.81M	AVON RA.7R
F.5	42FT 3IN/12.88M	32FT 4IN/9.86M	13FT 6IN/4.11M	AVON 114
F.7	43FT 9IN/13.34M	35FT/10.67M	13FT 6IN/4.11M	AVON 116

SWIFT F.1 WK239 56 SQUADRON

By the summer of 1954, Swifts being delivered to 56 Squadron had the upper surface painted in
dark sea grey and dark green camouflage, the underside was aluminium. WK239 ended up being
used in nuclear tests at Woomera. It survived, only to be scrapped in Australia.

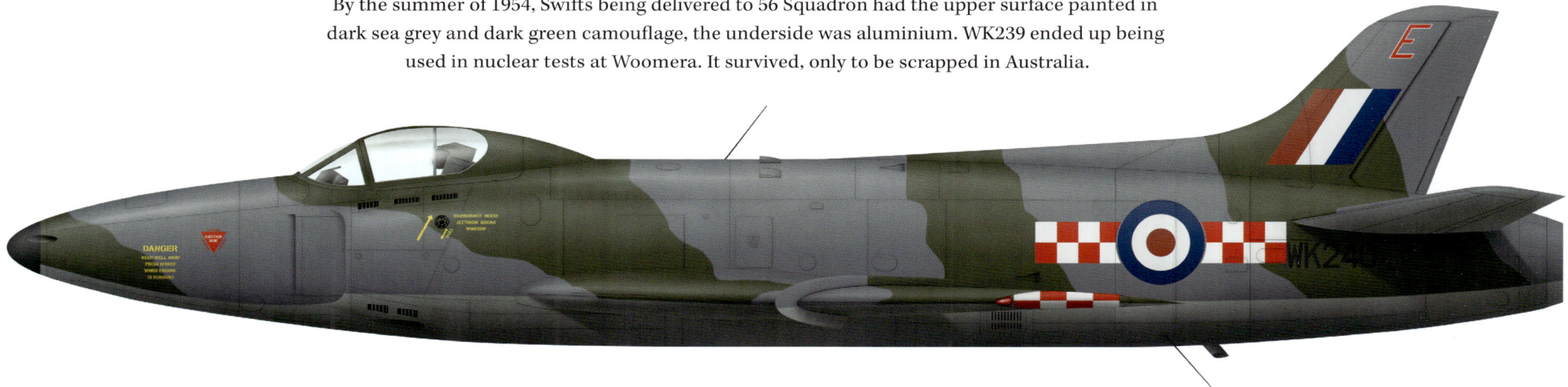

SWIFT F.2 WK240 56 SQUADRON

WK240 served with 56 Squadron for just over a year before being used for maintenance training. The
squadron bar and aircraft code letter had been applied by the time it was photographed.

SWIFT F.3 WK264 15 MAINTENANCE UNIT

Several F.3s never made it to a front line squadron, instead they ended up at maintenance units, such as 15 MU based at RAF Wroughton, and were used as ground trainers at various RAF bases. Having been delivered in January 1956, WK264 was scrapped two years later.

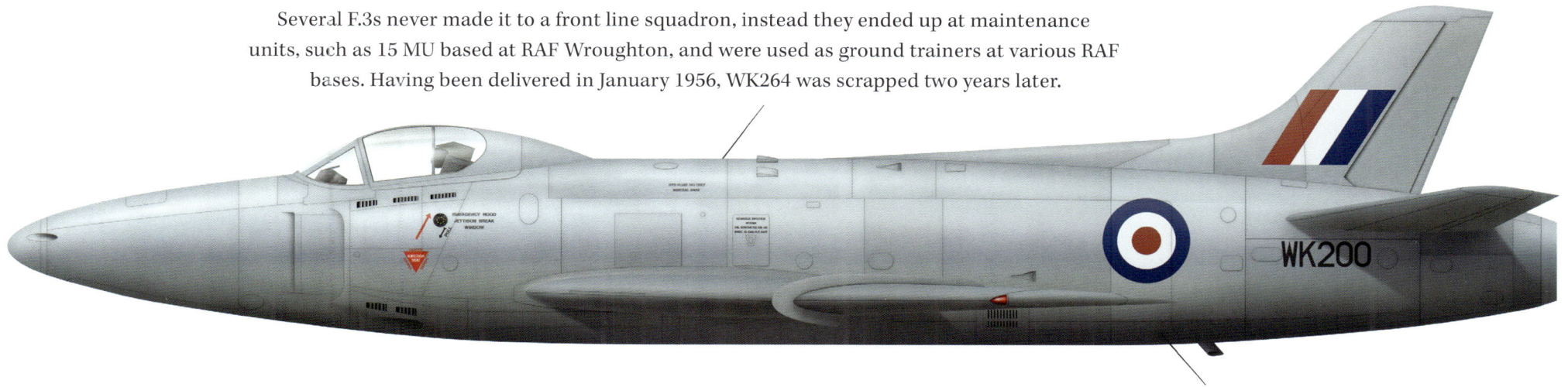

SWIFT F.1 WK200 A&AEE

This aircraft was built as an F.1 but was then converted to become the prototype FR.5. Trials commenced at Boscombe Down in July 1953 but on May 10, 1955, its engine disintegrated while taxiing. Compressor blade shards pierced its fuel lines and started a fire. The pilot escaped unhurt and the unrepaired wreck was scrapped in October 1955.

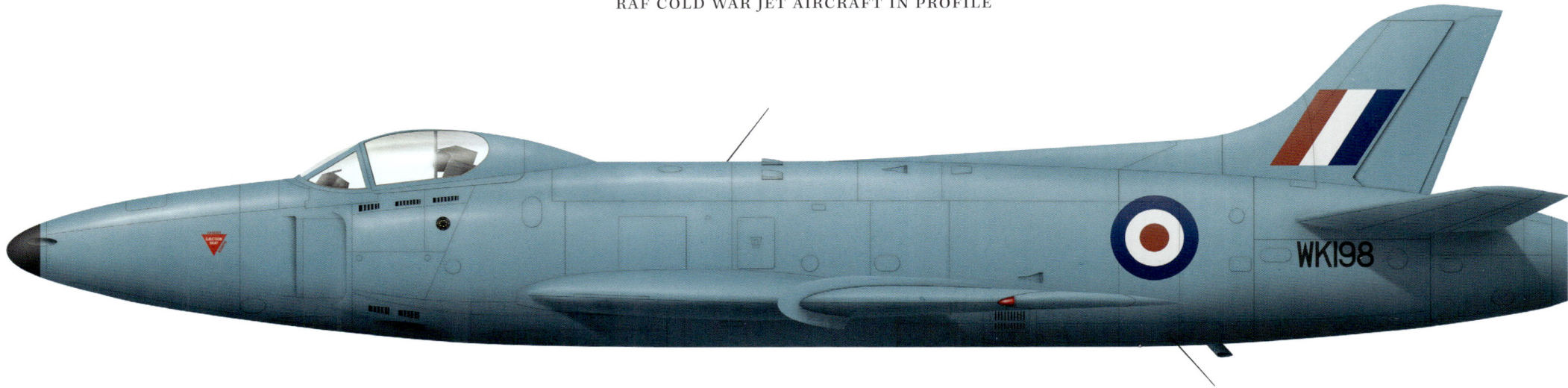

SWIFT F.4 WK198

Like WK200, WK198 was built as an F.1 but then converted into a prototype—this time for the F.4 configuration.
It was painted Light Blue when it broke the world speed record in Libya on September 25, 1953.

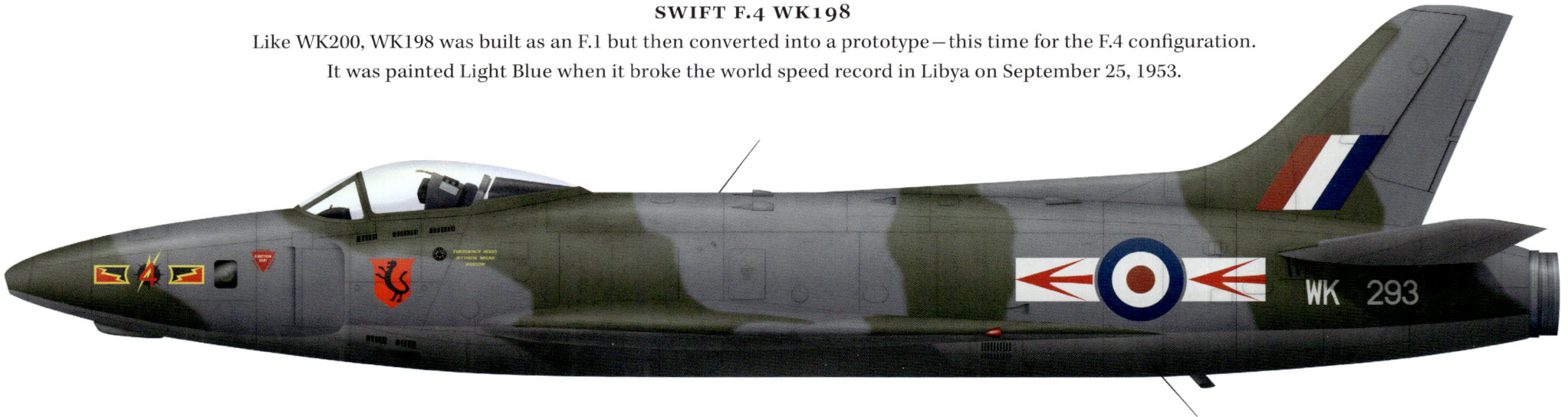

SWIFT FR.5 WK293 4/79 SQUADRON

For a very brief period, 4 Squadron operated the Swift when 79 Squadron was renumbered on January 1, 1961, hence
the dual squadron markings on WK293. However, 4 Squadron quickly returned to operating the Hunter.

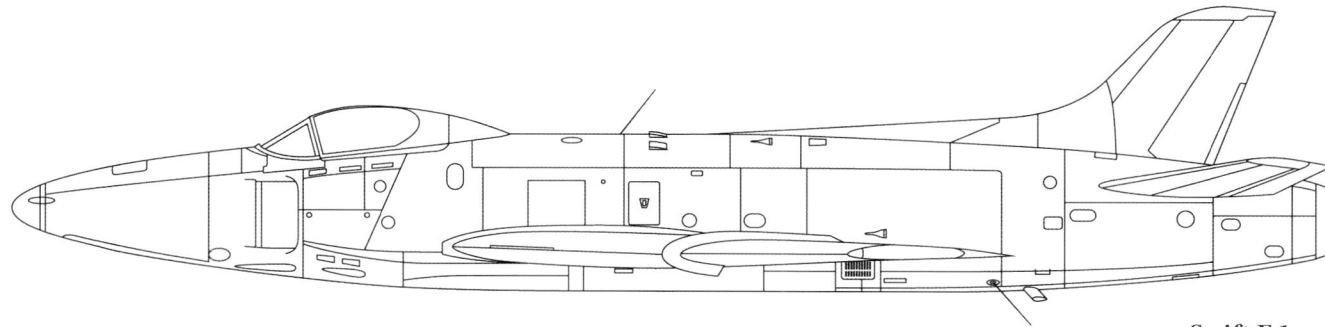

Swift F.1

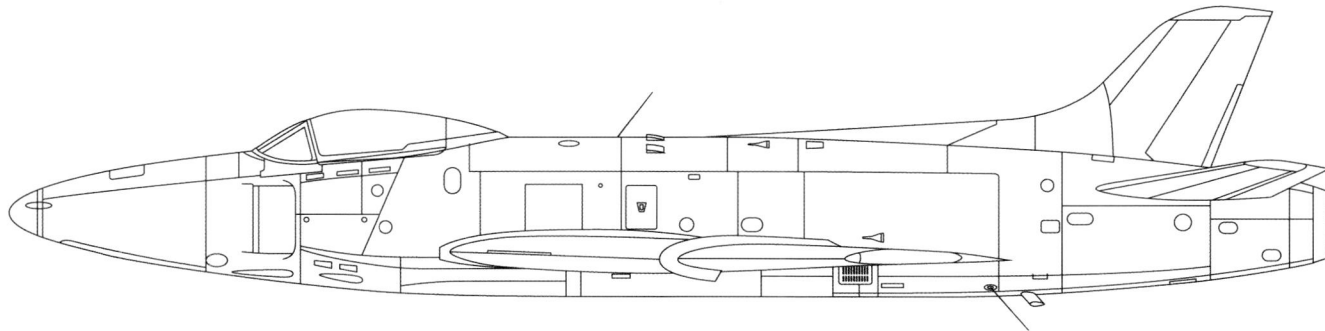

Swift F.3

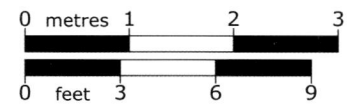

Swift FR.5 with tank

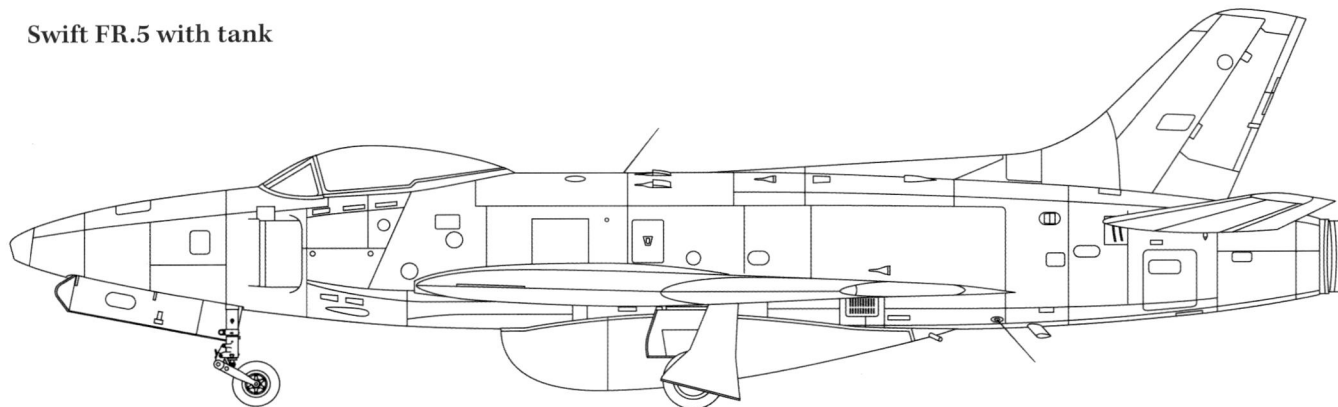

Swift FR.5 front

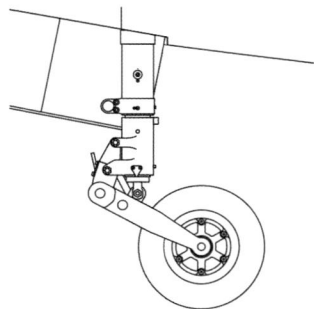

Nose wheel

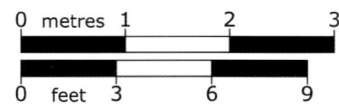

0 metres 1   2   3

0 feet 3   6   9

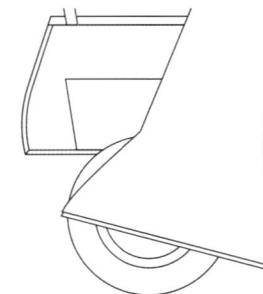

Main wheel

Swift FR.5

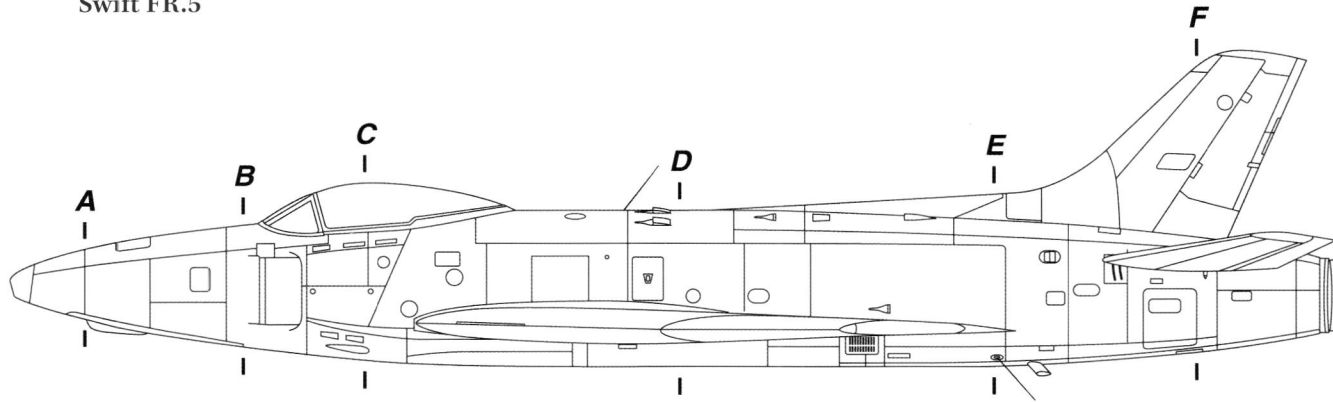

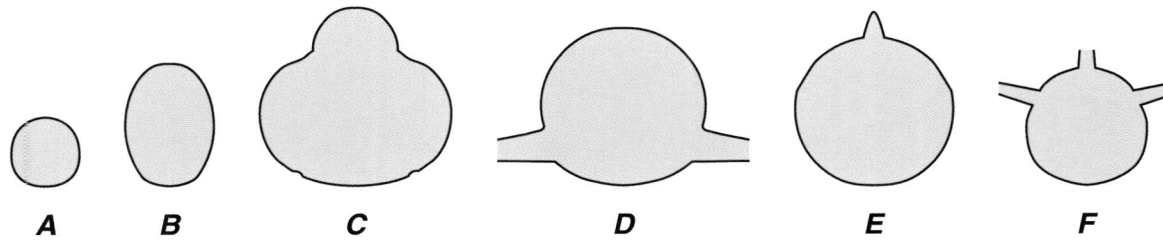

A   B   C   D   E   F

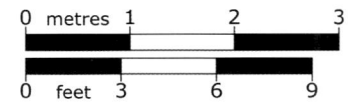

0   metres   1   2   3

0   feet   3   6   9

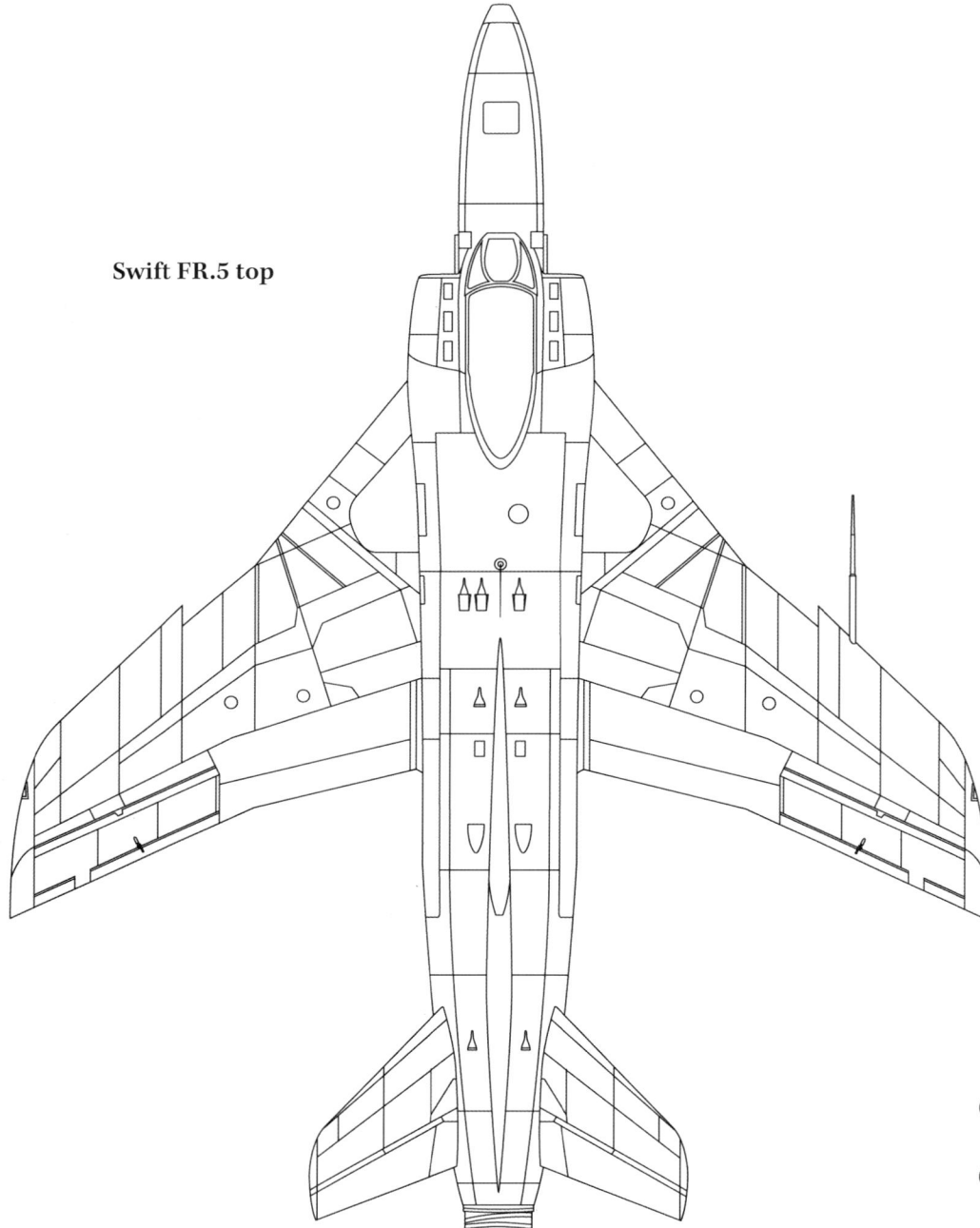

Swift FR.5 top

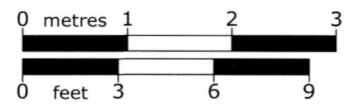

Swift FR.5 underside

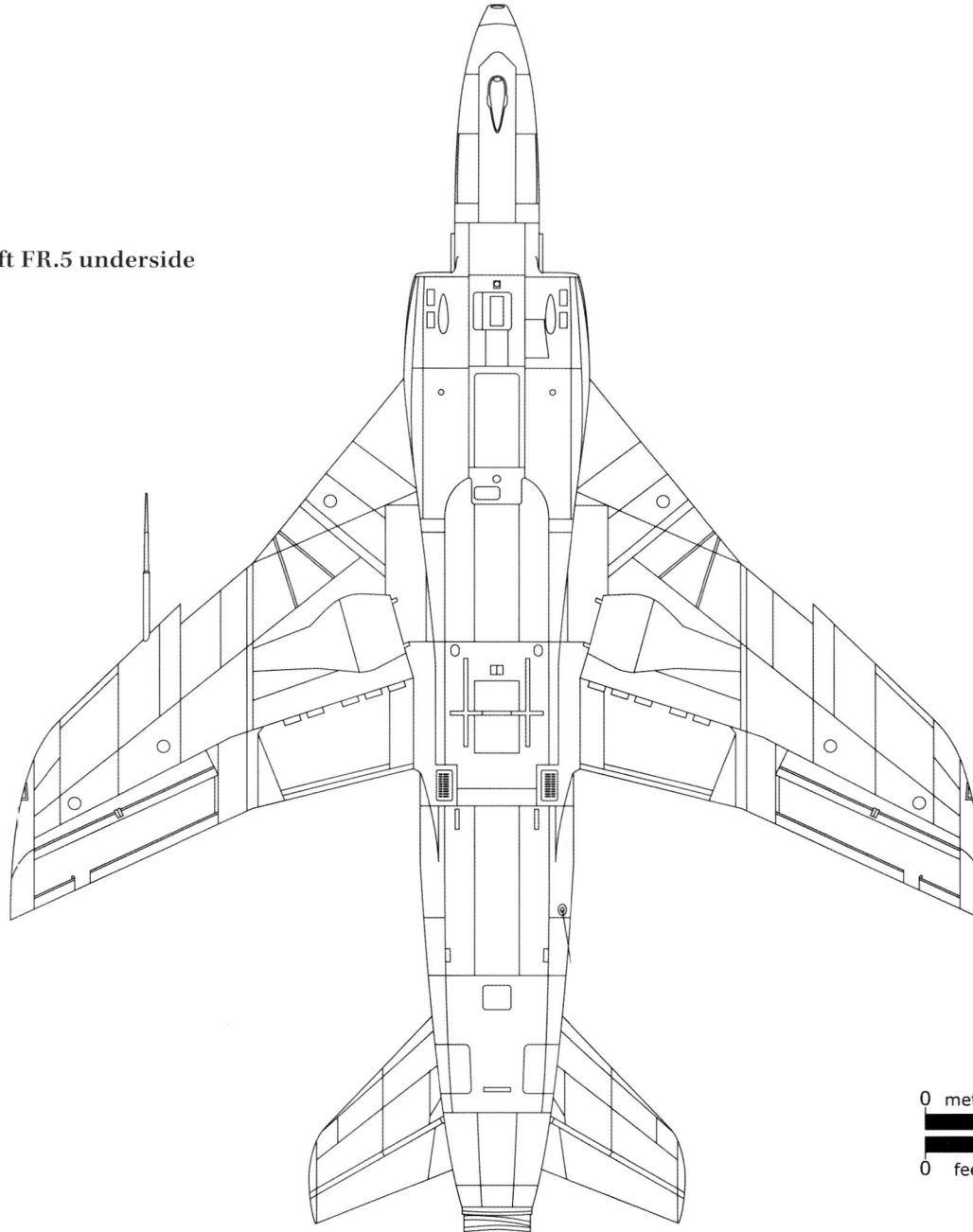

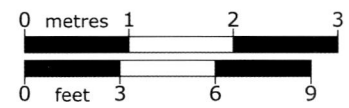

0 metres 1 2 3

0 feet 3 6 9

HAWKER HUNTER

With clean and elegant lines, the Hawker Hunter certainly epitomises the old adage 'if it looks right it will fly right'. Like other early post-war jets, the Hunter has certainly earned its reputation as a robust yet versatile aircraft — remaining in military service for 60 years, flying with 22 air forces and engaging in conflicts across the globe. Many still fly today in the fleets of private companies. Others are owned by individuals and can be regularly seen at air shows.

During the early post-war years the consensus was that bombers would fly at high altitude to avoid ground based defences. Countering this threat meant a fighter interceptor was required that could reach the bombers. Specifications F.43/46 and F.44/46 were issued in January 1947 and called for day and night fighters that could climb to an altitude of 45,000ft/13,717m in under six minutes while being able to fly at 629mph (Mach 0.953). With other companies tied up developing the V Force aircraft, Hawker was approached to submit a proposal.

The company had already begun exploring swept wing performance using the P.1052 prototype — a Sea Hawk fuselage fitted with swept wings which would became the foundation for the Hunter. The first example, VX272, remained largely unchanged but following test flights the second (VX279) saw extensive modifications to the tail, bringing it closer to the Hunter shape. As a result of these changes it was redesignated the P.1081.

Hawker's direct response to the specification was the P.1067, which used the new Rolls-Royce AJ.65 engine, soon to be renamed Avon. Early sketches had the intake in the nose along the lines of the F-86 Sabre and MiG-15 plus a T-tail similar to that of the

HUNTER FGA.9 XF442 1 SQUADRON

In protest against RAF cuts and the lack of recognition for the 50th anniversary of the RAF, Alan Pollock flew XF442 through the spans of Tower Bridge on April 5, 1968, having beat up Parliament. He was later officially discharged on medical grounds, avoiding a court martial which may have won Pollock public support and proven embarrassing for the Government.

Javelin. The tail position was soon lowered and the intakes moved to the wing roots, echoing the Sea Hawk. These refinements led to a revision of the original specification, which had cited a high tail and nose intake as requirements.

As the design process continued, the Government placed an order for three prototypes. Through constant testing, the shape of the P.1067 evolved so that by the time the first prototype (WB188) took to the air on July 20, 1951, it was visually almost identical to the Hunter F.1. The second prototype (WB195) didn't fly until a year later but was fitted with four 30mm Aden cannon and a gunsight. One notable issue with the prototypes was elevator flutter which caused heavy vibration when the aircraft was diving. The issue

having been resolved, WB195 exceeded Mach 1 for the first time during a shallow dive on June 24, 1952.

Such was the confidence in the new Hunter that orders for production aircraft were placed before WB188 had flown. The order was for both the Avon-powered F.1 and the Sapphire-powered F.2. Early F.1s used for trials and evaluation highlighted issues such as engine surges and even flame outs caused by the firing of the guns. An interim solution was to reduce fuel flow to the engine with the F.1 and F.2.

The problem was subsequently resolved entirely with changes introduced with the F.4. Endurance remained very low however, with flying time being as little as 40 minutes under certain

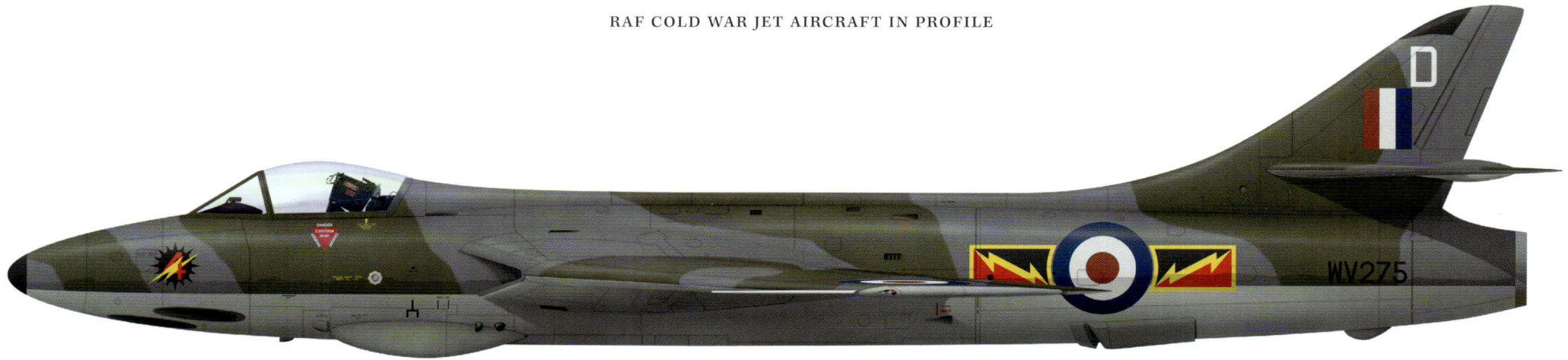

HUNTER F.4 WV275 4 SQUADRON

F.4 WV275 served with 4 Squadron from July 1955 until March 1957 when it was allocated to 111
Squadron. Painted in dark green, dark sea grey with light aircraft grey underside.

circumstances due to a 330 gallon/1500 litre fuel tank capacity. The prototypes and early production Hunters also lacked an adequate air brake; following experiments on WB188 a single ventral air brake was considered the best solution and this was introduced in time to be fitted to the 12th production Hunter.

43 Squadron was the first unit to receive the Hunter F.1, in July 1954. Prior to this, early deliveries had been made to the Central Fighter Establishment so that operational trials could be conducted before the type entered service. In quick succession 222 Squadron, 54 Squadron and 247 Squadron converted to the type, with 229 and 233 Operational Conversion Units also being set up.

Despite its early teething problems, the Hunter was very popular with pilots. The only F.3 was the modified prototype WB188, which was adapted for attempts on the world speed record by Neville

Duke. Painted in high gloss red and fitted with an aerodynamic nose cone, it managed to briefly hold the record until it was broken by a Supermarine Swift the following month.

The F.4 saw the introduction of the more powerful Avon RA.21 113 in the F.4. It was also found that spent casings and links from firing the aircraft's cannon caused damage to the fuselage, the light weight stopping them falling away quickly enough. The solution was to collect them in pods that are a distinctive feature of the Hunter. The F.4 also saw the introduction of wing pylons for external fuel tanks to overcome the limited range.

Small fuel tanks were also added to the wing leading edges, increasing internal capacity to 414 gallons. F.4 squadrons were first deployed to West Germany when 98 Squadron formed at RAF Jever in April 1955. Other West Germany based squadrons

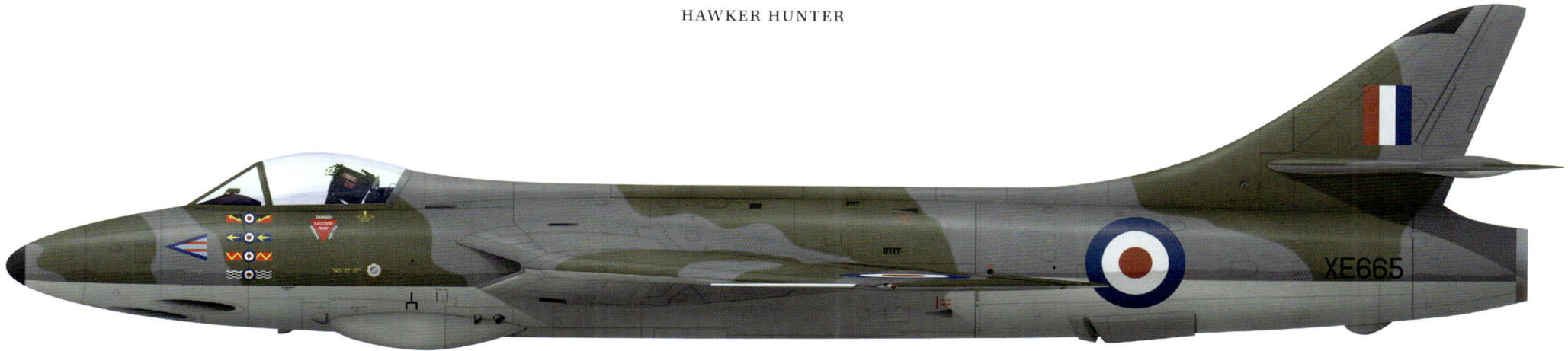

HUNTER F.4 XE665 122 WING

Flown by Wing Commander Cyril S. John 'Hammer' West of 122 Wing, XE665 has the pennant and bars of the four squadrons (4 Squadron, 93 Squadron, 98 Squadron and 118 Squadron). It was based at Jever during the mid-1950s.

subsequently replaced the F.1 with the F.4. Externally there was no difference between the Hawker-built F.4 and the Armstrong Whitworth-built F.5, but the latter was fitted with the Sapphire 101 instead of the Avon.

The F.5s of 1 and 34 Squadrons were the first Hunters to see action when they became embroiled in the Suez Crisis. These were painted in black and yellow identification stripes on the fuselage and wings. Providing cover for the bombers and later airfield air defence, they never actually had any aerial encounters with Egyptian forces.

The Hunter F.6 saw the introduction of the more powerful 200 series Avon engines, requiring a redesigned tail pipe to cope with the increase in power. The wing leading edge was redesigned and a second pylon was added outboard of the existing one. This allowed for a further increase in fuel capacity both internally and

externally if a second pair of external tanks were fitted. Alternatively, the pylons could be used to carry a range of ordnance from rockets to bombs, all these changes to the wing being known as Mod 228. There was also a revision of the starter system with the old cartridge type being replaced with the AVPIN system.

Many F.6s were also later upgraded to FGA.9 spec. The F.6 was phased in during 1956, with 19 Squadron being the first to receive it. But as a fighter-interceptor the Hunter's days were already numbered; the English Electric Lightning could easily outperform it and began replacing it during 1961.

Construction of new airframes may have ceased but the Hunter's development was not yet at an end. In terms of performance, the Venom was showing its age and a replacement for the ground-attack role was necessary.

HUNTER F.5 WP130 34 SQUADRON

34 Squadron were based at Cyprus in late 1956 to support operations during the Suez Crisis. Identification markings were hastily applied in black and yellow bands on the fuselage and wings, as seen on WP130.

Converting existing Hunters for ground-attack proved both viable and cost effective, with aircraft upgraded to FGA.9 standard receiving the more powerful and reliable Avon 207 engine, strengthened wings to carry heavier weapon loads and outer pylons fitted with explosive bolts should they need to be ejected in an emergency.

The cockpit also received air conditioning for tropical operations. The conversion proved to be fortuitous when Hunter FGA.9s of 208 Squadron relocated from Kenya to Aden in 1961 and were operated in close support of British ground forces. As the conflict grew, more Hunter squadrons were posted to RAF Khormaksar. It also drew in other RAF units and the Fleet Air Arm.

FGA.9s also saw active service in the Far East; following the re-forming of 20 Squadron at RAF Tengah, Singapore, in 1961, the squadron's Hunters were required to initially defend the border against Indonesian forces opposed to the formation of Malaysia. The squadron continued to support British forces until the eventual pull-out in 1970. Hunters configured for the ground-attack role also served with several foreign air forces, further proving the success of the type.

In keeping with the need to train pilots, a two-seater version of the Hunter was developed by Hawker when an order was placed in 1954. The originally intended tandem configuration was rejected following wind tunnel tests and the side-by-side layout already seen in the Vampire was selected, this in spite of the original concerns that a less streamlined profile would result in a loss of performance.

With a wider forward section the fairing aft of the cockpit saw several modifications before being finalised in 1965. The sliding canopy was also exchanged for a wider hinged version. The tail saw the addition of a braking parachute and slightly modified tailpipe. This feature was included in the FGA.9 and retrofitted to many older fighters.

Fifty-five T.7s were ordered initially but 10 of these were built as the navalised T.8. In addition, the F.4's design made converting it into a T.7 relatively straightforward. The T.7 eventually entered service with 229 OCU at RAF Chivenor in 1958 and went on to equip numerous front line squadrons, remaining in service with the RAF for many years.

With nearly 2000 Hunters being built and exported to 21 nations, many are still flying around the world – testament to the sheer quality of possibly the most successful of Britain's post-war military jets.

Hawker Hunter

VARIANT	LENGTH	SPAN	HEIGHT	ENGINE
P.1067	45FT 11IN/14M	33FT 8IN/10.26M	13FT 2IN/4.01M	AVON 103
F.1	45FT 11IN/14M	33FT 8IN/10.26M	13FT 2IN/4.01M	AVON 113
F.2	45FT 11IN/14M	33FT 8IN/10.26M	13FT 2IN/4.01M	SAPPHIRE 101
F.3	45FT 11IN/14M	33FT 8IN/10.26M	13FT 2IN/4.01M	AVON 115
F.4	45FT 11IN/14M	33FT 8IN/10.26M	13FT 2IN/4.01M	AVON 113 OR 121
F.5	45FT 11IN/14M	33FT 8IN/10.26M	13FT 2IN/4.01M	SAPPHIRE 101
F.6	45FT 11IN/14M	33FT 8IN/10.26M	13FT 2IN/4.01M	AVON 203
T.7	48FT 10IN/14.88M	33FT 8IN/10.26M	13FT 2IN/4.01M	SEVERAL AVON VARIANTS
T.8	48FT 10IN/14.88M	33FT 8IN/10.26M	13FT 2IN/4.01M	SEVERAL AVON VARIANTS
FGA.9	45FT 11IN/14M	33FT 8IN/10.26M	13FT 2IN/4.01M	AVON 207
FR.10	46FT 1IN/14.05M	33FT 8IN/10.26M	13FT 2IN/4.01M	AVON 207
GA.11	45FT 11IN/14M	33FT 8IN/10.26M	13FT 2IN/4.01M	AVON 121

HUNTER F.6 XF382 234 SQUADRON
Like 63 Sqn, 234 Sqn was a shadow squadron that made up 229 OCU. It flew the Hunter from 1958 until 1992.

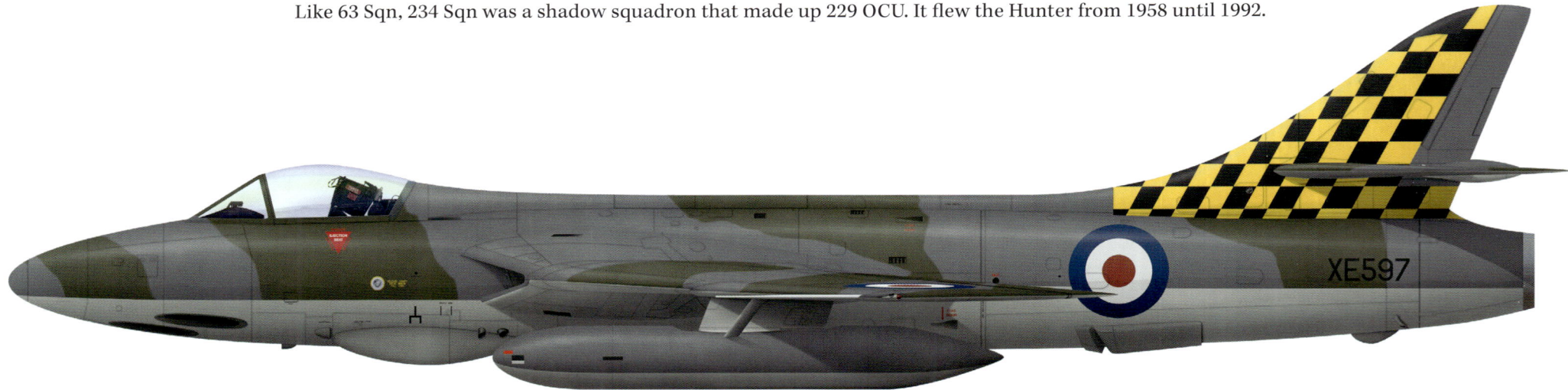

HUNTER F.6 XE597 63 SQUADRON
As a shadow unit for 229 OCU, 63 Sqn operated the Hunter from 1956 until 1992 when it was disbanded.

HUNTER F.4 XF319 112 SQUADRON

112 Sqn was the only F.4 unit to have the sharkmouth, while based at Bruggen in 1957. Pictured is F.4 XF319.

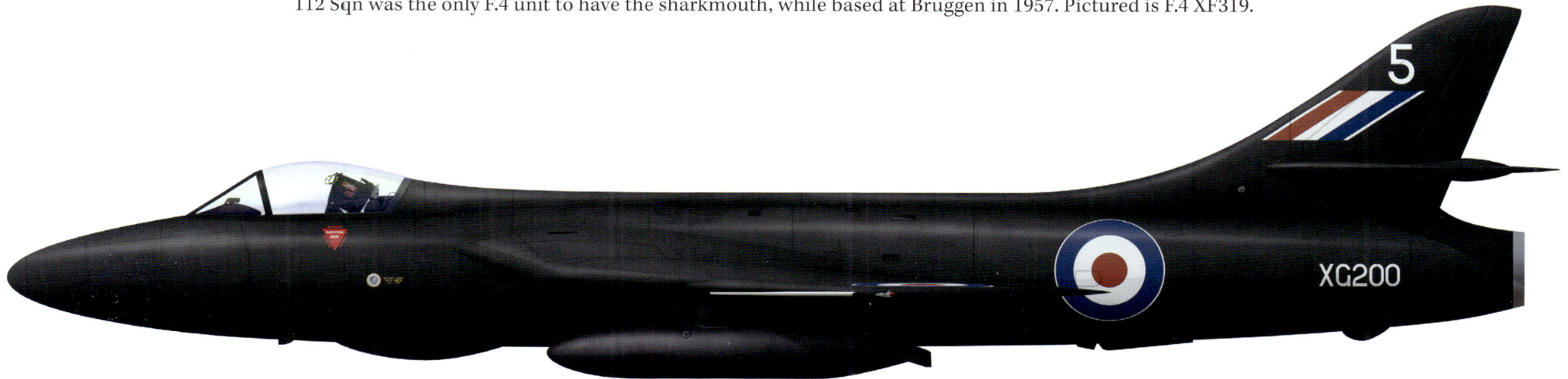

HUNTER F.6 XG200 111 SQUADRON

During the late 1950s the official display team of the RAF was 111 Squadron's Black Arrows. They hold the record for looping in formation, with 22 aircraft in 1958. The aircraft, like XG200, were all painted in gloss black.

HUNTER F.6 XG225 92 SQUADRON
The Blue Diamonds team was formed in 1960 by 92 Sqn using Hunters painted in aircraft blue.
During 1961 and 1962 they were the official aerobatic team representing the RAF.

HUNTER FGA.9 XF418 1TWU
The Tactical Weapons Unit painted some Hunters in high visibility markings including XG225 which had
a Yellow tail, wingtips and spine and XF418 which was Red. These were worn during 1979.

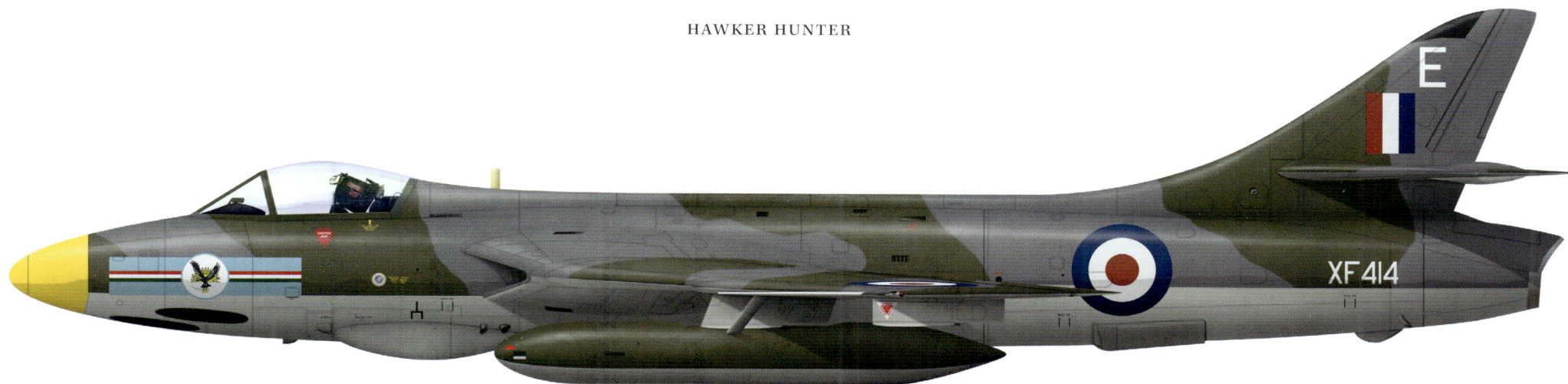

HUNTER FGA.9 XF414 20 SQUADRON

Based at Tengah, Singapore, 20 Squadron operated its Hunters from 1960 until 1970 when it was re-
formed in Germany with the Harrier. XF414's nose is painted yellow for exercises.

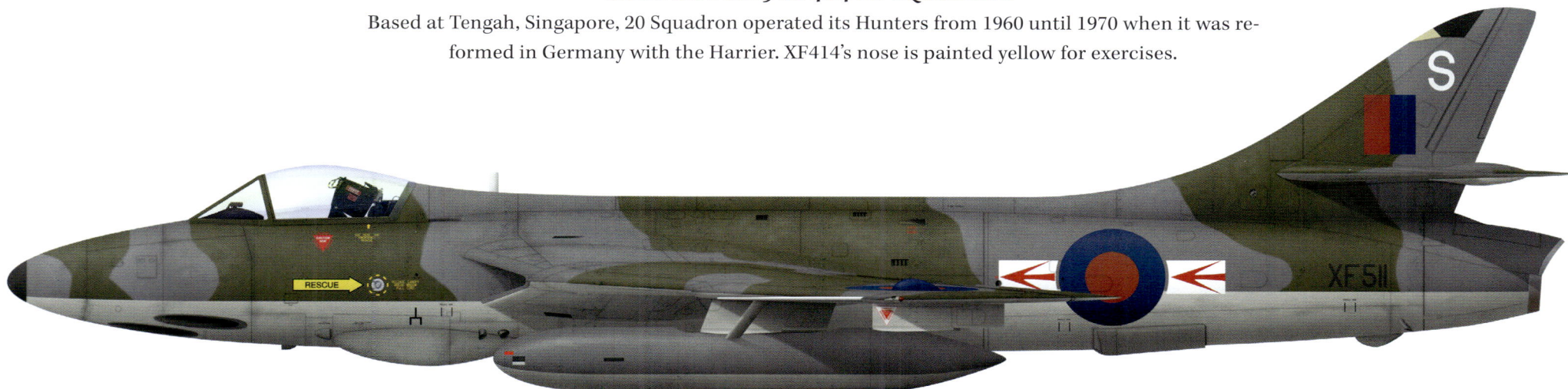

HUNTER FGA.9 XF511 229 OCU

XF511 was photographed at RAF Chivenor in 1974 when 229 OCU had relocated to RAF Brawdy.

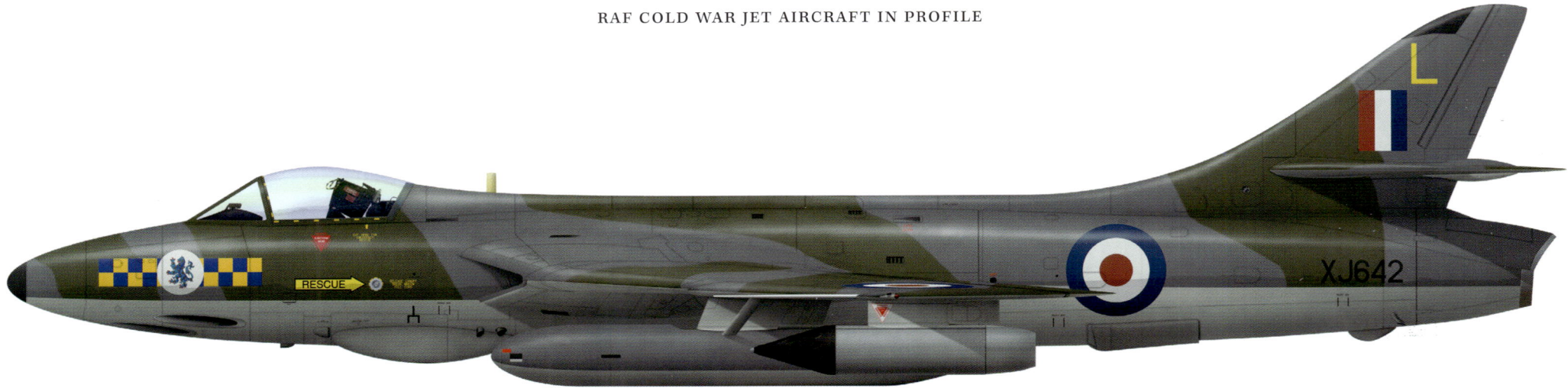

HUNTER FGA.9 XJ642 54 SQUADRON

54 Squadron operated several variants of the Hunter, including the FGA.9, from 1955 to 1969 while based at RAF West Raynham. XJ642 is depicted as it appeared in the late 1960s.

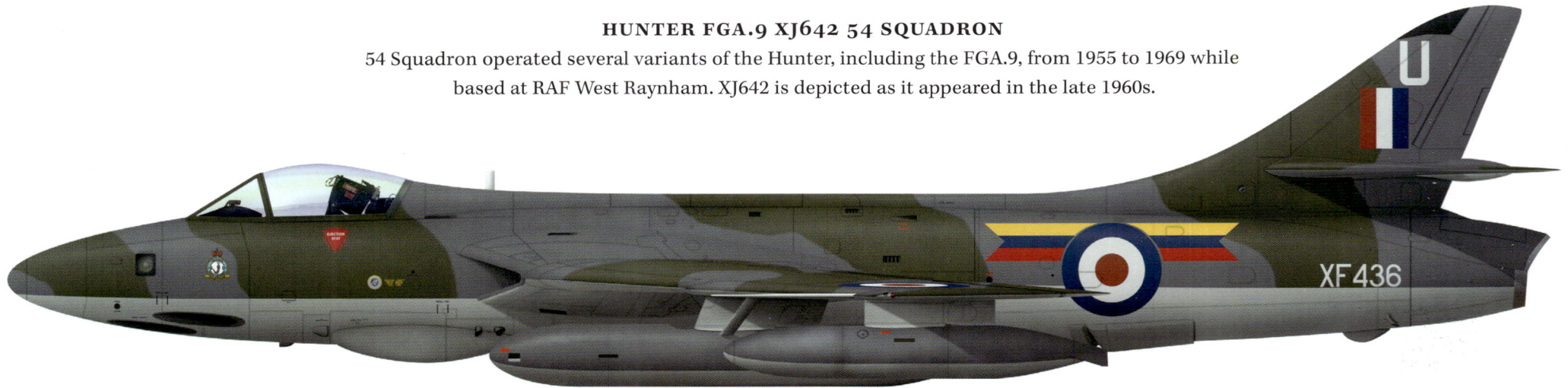

HUNTER FR.10 XF436 8 SQUADRON

The squadron was based at RAF Khormaksar following the Second World War until 1967, mainly operating the FGA.9 but B flight had four FR.10s on strength from 1961.

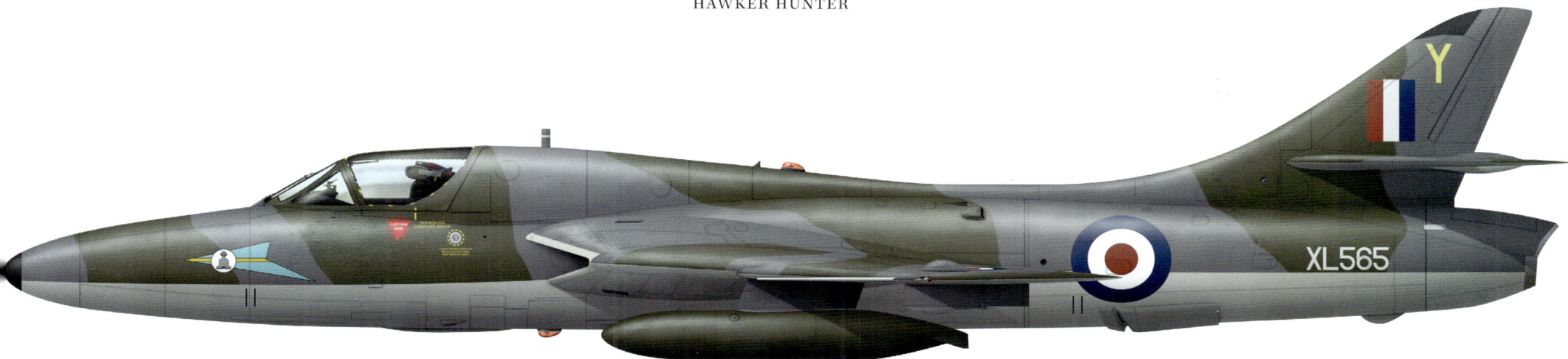

HUNTER T.7 XL565 208 SQUADRON

Wearing 208 Squadron markings, XL565 was allocated to 1417 Flight – a reconnaissance unit based at RAF Khormksar, which took over duties from 8 Sqn. The flight consisted of five FR.10s and the single T.7.

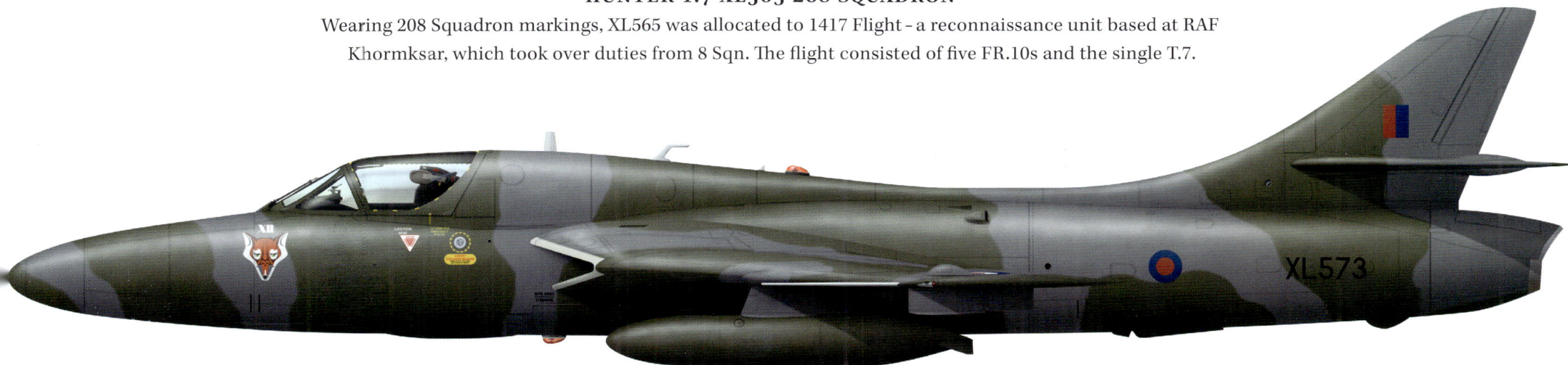

HUNTER T.7 XL573 12 SQUADRON

While flying the Buccaneer, the squadron retained the Hunter for a range of duties during the 1980s. XL573 continued flying until 2015 and now resides undercover at the South Wales Aviation Museum.

HUNTER T.7 XL620 74 SQUADRON
The squadron replaced its Meteors with Hunter F.4s and F.6s in 1957 but also had XL620 for a brief period from 1959
to 1960 for training and familiarisation purposes. Painted in all over aluminium with yellow band.

HUNTER T.7 XL621 4 FLYING TRAINING SCHOOL
XL621 received high visibility markings – a white tail, spine and wing tips along with red tanks – while serving with 4 FTS during 1973.

HAWKER HUNTER T.7 WV383 DRA

Originally built as a F.4, WV383 was converted to T.7 configuration following an accident in 1955. It was allocated to RAE Farnborough in 1971 and flown until 1998 in Raspberry Ripple, red, white and Oxford blue. Currently on display at Farnborough Air Sciences Trust museum.

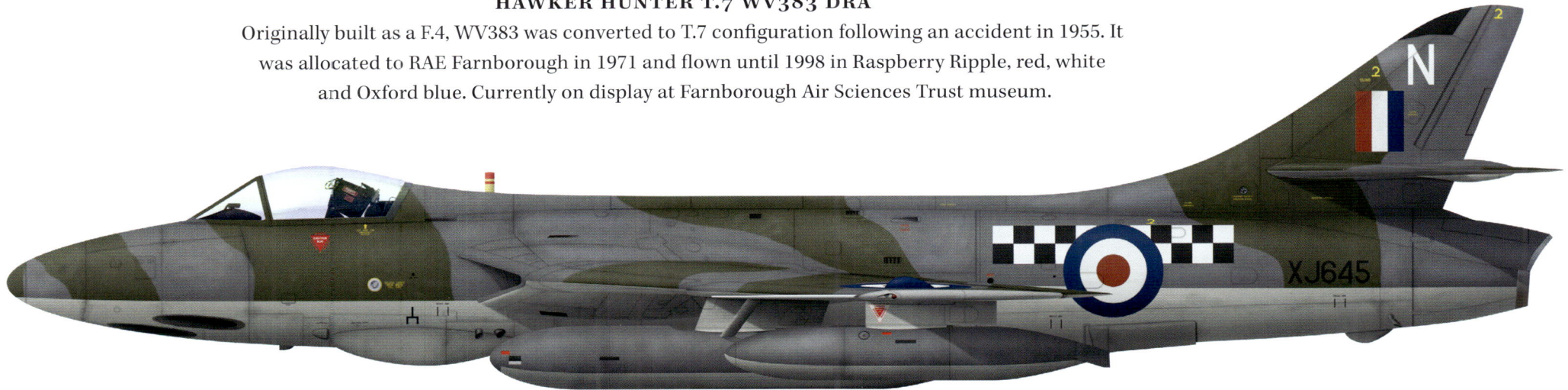

HUNTER FGA.9 XJ645 43 SQUADRON

The first squadron to fly the Hunter, 43 Squadron, converted to the FGA.9 in 1960 and was based at RAF Khormaksar, Aden, from 1963 until 1967.

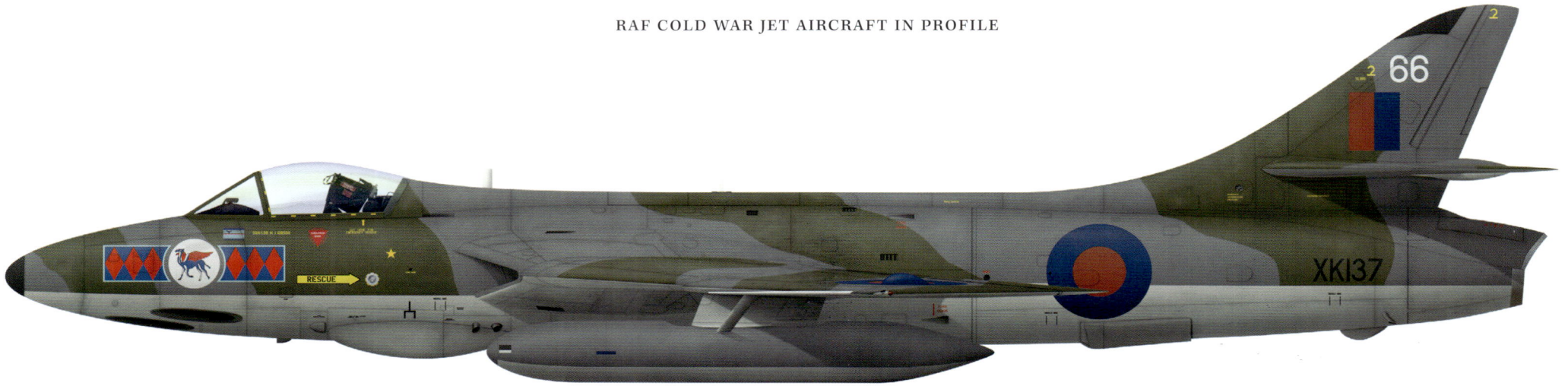

HUNTER FGA.9 XK137 45 SQUADRON

45 Squadron operated as a Hunter ground-attack training unit between August 1972 and July 1976. Due to their age and role, the aircraft had become heavily weathered by the time the squadron retired them.

HUNTER T.7 XL623 54 SQUADRON

During the 1960s, 54 Squadron operated the Hunter F.1 and FGA.9, retaining some trainers including XL623. The aircraft was eventually purchased by Woking Council and for several years was displayed on a pole in the centre of town. Over time it began to suffer fatigue and was eventually removed and donated to the Hawker Association for restoration.

HUNTER T.7 XL609 56 SQUADRON

Despite being a Lightning unit during the 60s, 56 Squadron also kept a couple of Hunters on strength including XL609. In keeping with the Lightnings, these were painted in all over aluminium. The majority of XL609 was later scrapped but the nose section was preserved.

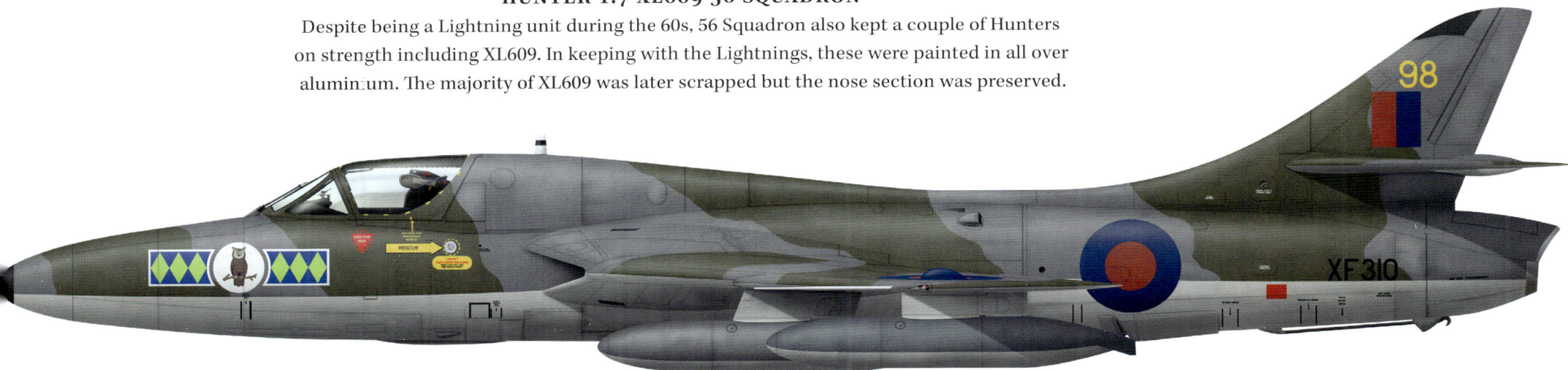

HUNTER T.7 XF310 58 SQUADRON

Built as an F.4, XF310 was converted to a T.7 before entering service in May 1959. It was first allocated to 20 Squadron at Tengah. It then served with the RN, followed by a period with 45 Squadron, then to 58 Squadron — a Hunter ground-attack training unit. The aircraft later served with FRADU before being sold to a collector in Australia.

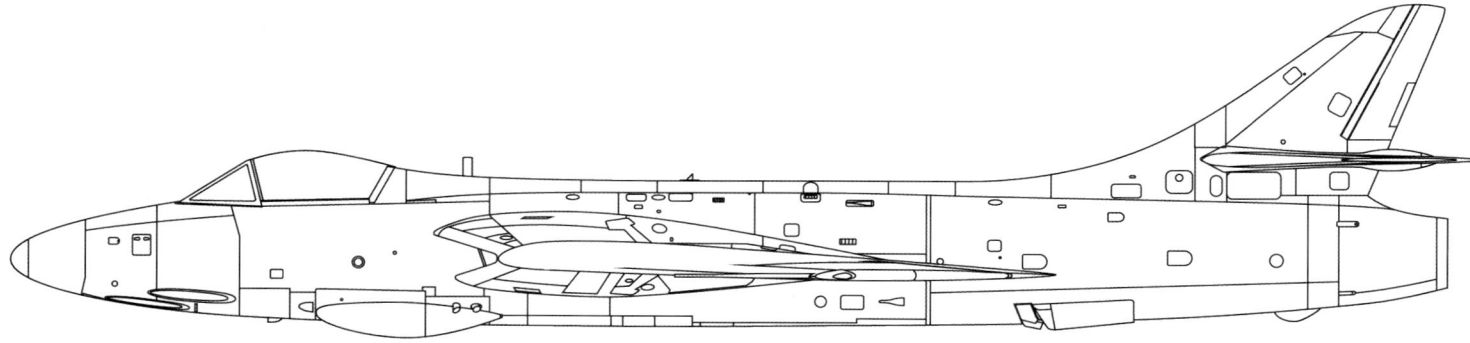

Hawker F.4

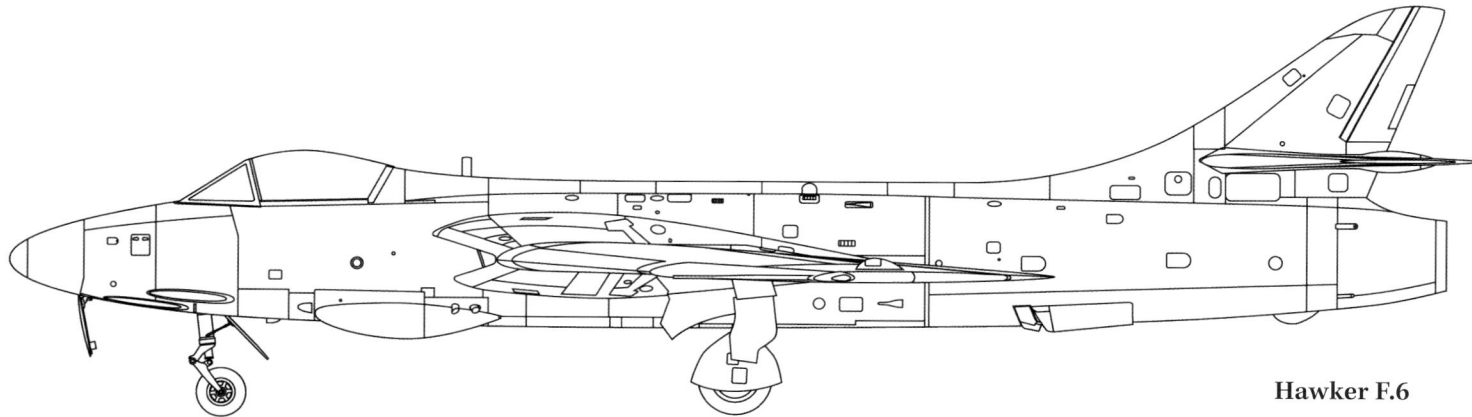

Hawker F.6

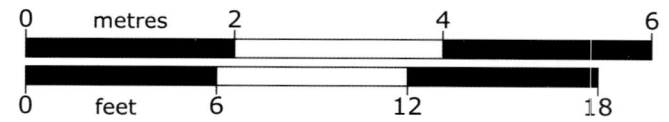

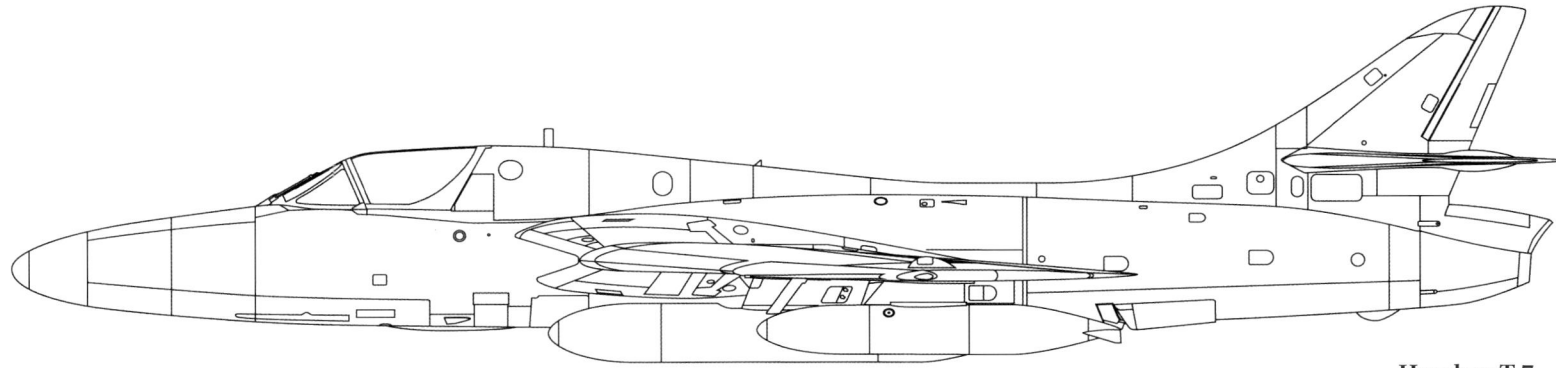

Hawker T.7

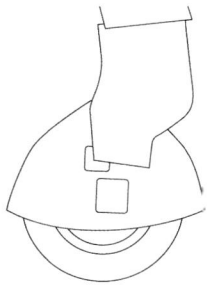

Main wheel

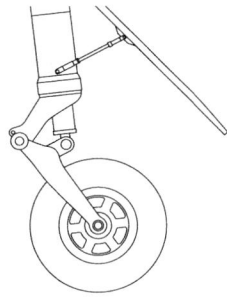

Nose wheel

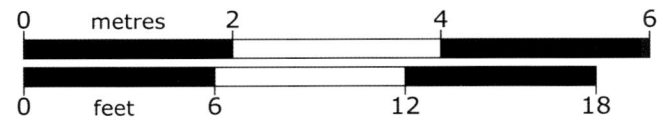

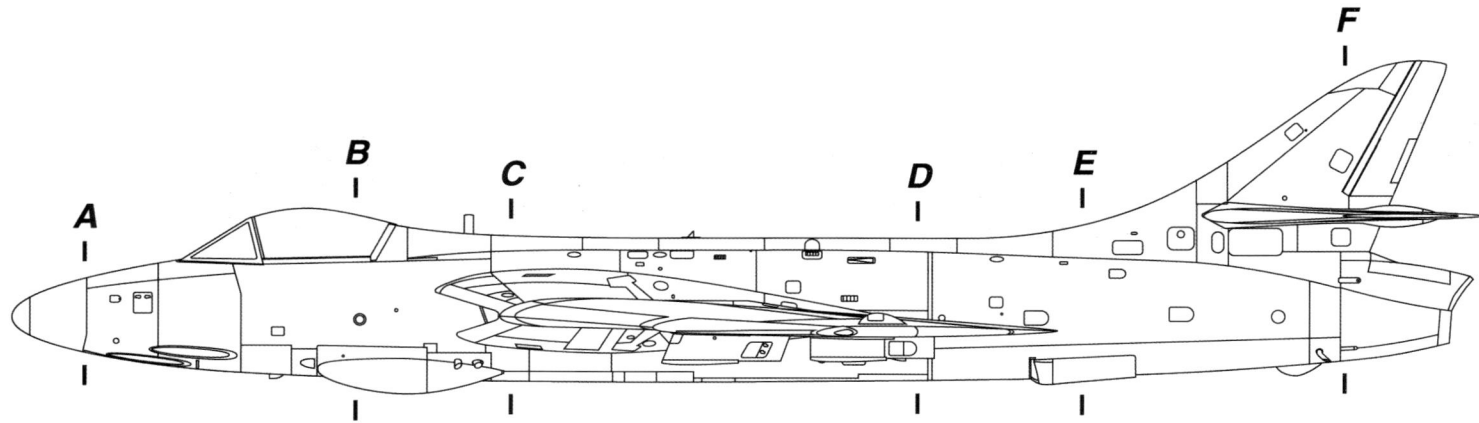

Hawker FGA.9

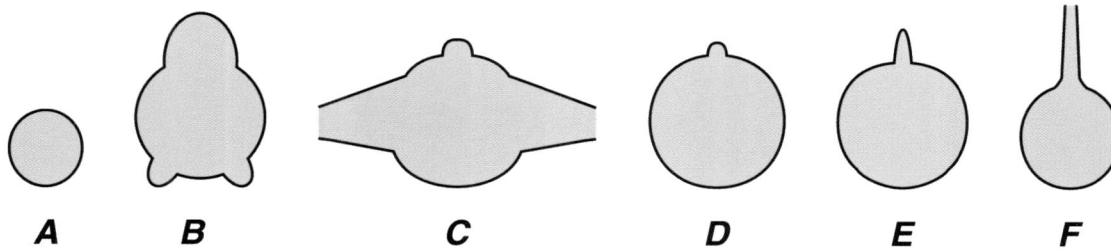

A   B   C   D   E   F

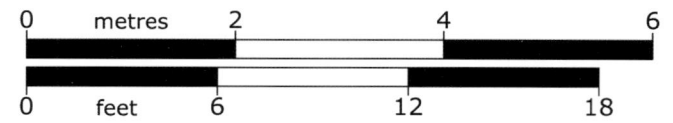

| 0 | metres | 2 | 4 | 6 |

| 0 | feet | 6 | 12 | 18 |

Hawker FGA.9 underside

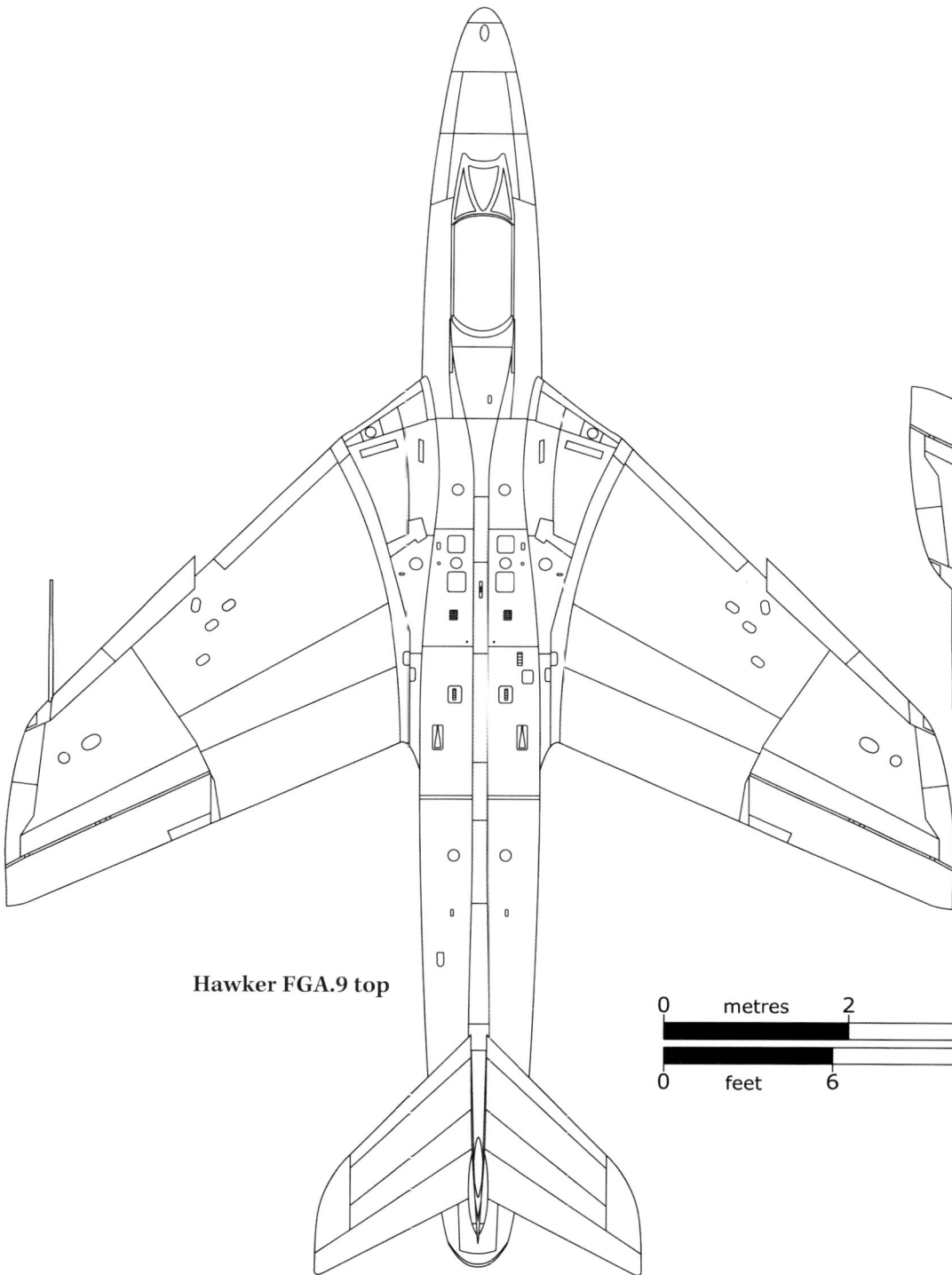

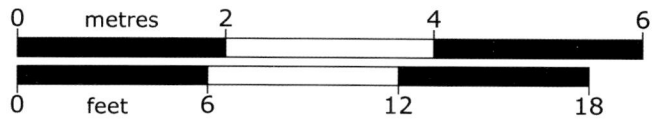

Hawker FGA.9 top

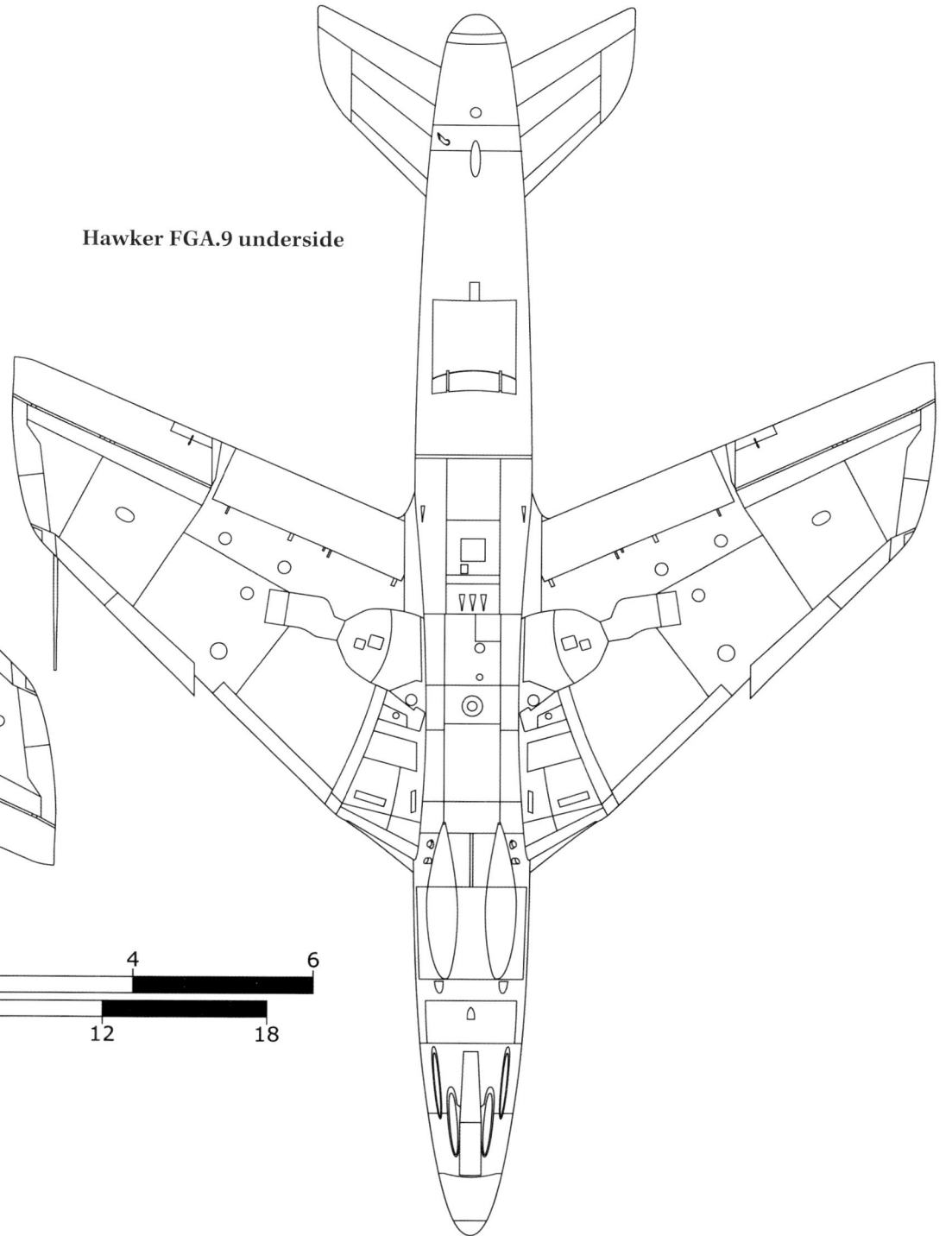

0 metres 2 4 6

0 feet 6 12 18

VICKERS VALIANT

The Vickers Valiant lives in the shadow of the more successful V bombers – the Victor and Vulcan. Perhaps this is because the type was only in service for a decade, whereas the Victor and Vulcan flew for far longer and became indelibly marked on the public consciousness. Despite being side-lined, the Valiant was an essential part of Bomber Command during the late 1950s while the other V bombers were being phased in, taking on the role of nuclear deterrent for Britain as cold war tensions rose.

Following the Second World War, Bomber Command's heavies, the Avro Lincoln and B-29 Washington, were considered obsolete due to the jet engine and the Canberra had yet to enter service. In addition the Canberra was seen as a tactical bomber, with new heavy bombers needed for the strategic role. The devastating potential of atomic bombs had been well proven and the RAF now needed a method of delivering them. This would lead to four different bombers being developed and three entering service.

The first specification issued, B.14/46, was for a direct Lincoln replacement and was intended to cover the Shorts S.A.4 Sperrin.

The Sperrin was designed to accommodate the Blue Danube bomb and was viewed as insurance should the more complex Avro and Handley Page designs already in the works fail to meet expectations.

Shortly after this, Specification B.35/46 was issued for a bomber that could fly at Mach 0.9-1.0 and altitudes above 50,000ft. Alongside the two other firms' more radical designs, Vickers tendered a six-engined high-altitude bomber design that was considered more aerodynamically conventional. Again, there was a pressing need for at least one of the designs to succeed. However, all three were accepted by the Air Ministry — only the Sperrin failing to make the cut.

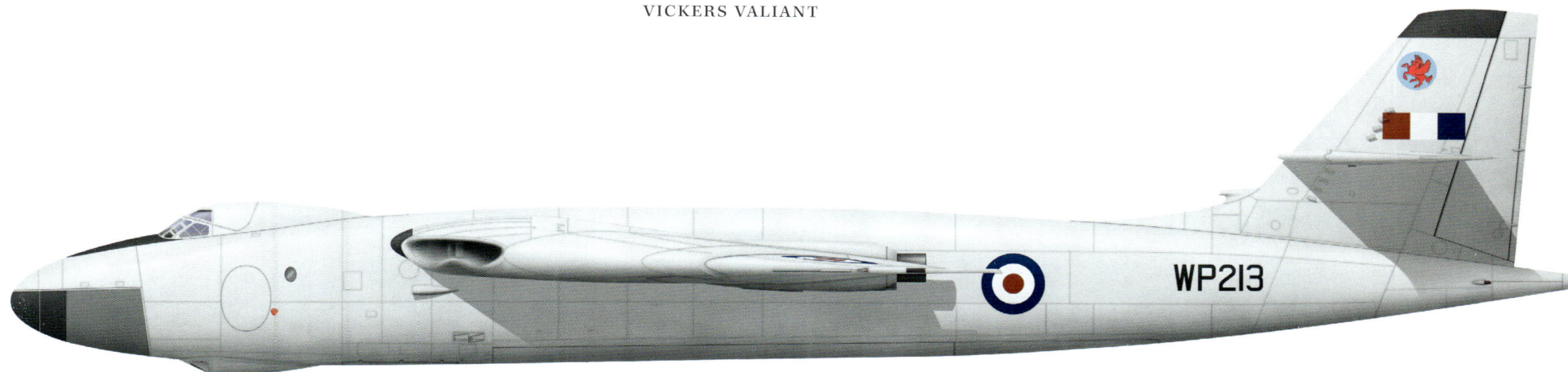

VALIANT B.1 WP213 18 SQUADRON
Having already served with 138 and 199 Squadrons, WP213 was with 18 Squadron from 1958 until 1962
after which it was retired. Finished in gloss white but wearing standard national markings.

The Vickers design was soon revised to incorporate four Avons or Sapphires mounted in the swept wing. The issue of range was considered critical and the company thought that the most practical and flexible solution was external tanks.

Vickers Type 660, WB210, fitted with Rolls-Royce RA.3 Avon engines, was the first prototype completed. Progress was rapid and it first flew from Wisley on May 18, 1951, rather than January 1952 as originally expected. At the controls was Joseph 'Mutt' Summers (who had previously taken the first Spitfire prototype, K5054, on its maiden flight) and Gabe 'Jock' Bryce was in the co-pilot's seat.

The five minute flight was uneventful, the most noteworthy aspect being the grass runway used for both take-off and landing. The aircraft left rather large ruts and a tarmac runway was laid very soon after at Wisley.

WB210 was lost on January 12, 1952, when a failed relight during a series of engine shutdowns and relights in mid-air led to a build-up of leaked fuel near the tailpipes on the starboard side. Once it had ignited, the fire burned through a main fuel pipe before it was noticed by the crew. As he jumped from the burning aircraft, the co-pilot, Sqn Ldr Brian Foster, hit the tail and later succumbed to his injuries. The rest of the crew survived.

With the completion of the second prototype drawing near, the loss of WB210 did not cause a major disruption to the development of the Valiant. Although it was originally intended to use Sapphires, the new aircraft, WB215, was fitted with Avon RA.7s instead. These required a greater airflow and the intakes were modified from the elegant narrow slot sported by WB210 to something that looked more like a pair of spectacles.

VALIANT B.(K).1 XD875 138 SQUADRON

XD875 was flown by 138 Squadron during 1961/1962, having originally been delivered to 207 Squadron. It was subsequently written off at RAF Bruntingthorpe in November 1962. At the time of writing the cockpit was on loan to Morayvia at Kinloss, Scotland.

Despite the revision, it was discovered that the shape could cause the engines to flame out. Experimentation with modifications to the intake using putty and fabric eventually produced a form which allowed for smooth airflow. The trials continued with a thorough testing programme, including detailed examination of the flight envelope and bombing systems.

WJ954 was the third Valiant completed. It was the only B.2 built and was used to explore the type's potential. It was proposed that the B.2 would have a crew of just two, 20% greater range and a higher cruising speed thanks to the inclusion of Conway engines. Its primary role was as a target indicator but it was also to fulfil a secondary role in photo reconnaissance.

By the time WJ954 flew on September 4, 1953, these roles were deemed unnecessary for the Valiant and the order was cancelled.

In an all over gloss black, it did however support the development of the B.1. Following a landing accident, WJ954 was transported to Foulness in 1958 where it was unceremoniously destroyed during tests to determine the effect of various projectiles on an airframe.

The Valiant which entered service differed very little from the second prototype. There were some internal differences and the Avon RA.14 was fitted in place of the RA.7 but it was essentially the same. In order to train crews who had previously flown the Lancaster and Lincoln, 232 Operational Conversion Unit was formed at RAF Gaydon in 1954. It also catered for ground crew and engineers, introducing them to the new technology.

Due to the costs of the new aircraft and the responsibility involved in potentially carrying out a nuclear strike, V force crews had to meet certain criteria. Early captains had to have a minimum

VALIANT B.1 WB215

The second prototype built, WB215 went through several modifications during testing. Following the completion of tests it was delivered to the RAF and eventually retired in February 1961. Finished in natural metal.

of 1750 hours in the position on other types, to have completed a full tour on the Canberra and preferably to have experience of a four-engined post-war 'heavy'.

Second pilots also had to have completed a Canberra tour and have a minimum of 700 hours as captain. While there were later changes to the requirement for piston-engine experience, the high standards were continued and applied to the selection process for Victor and Vulcan crews.

138 Squadron became the first official Valiant squadron, forming on January 1, 1955. That summer the unit was relocated to Wittering where the RAF already had nuclear stockpiles. Wittering was a key V force base during the cold war, with Victor and Vulcan squadrons subsequently being based there. 138 Squadron went on to fly the first Valiants to the Far East during a tour in 1958.

As more aircraft rolled off the production line and crews were trained, nine additional Valiant squadrons were formed over the next two years. These included C Flight of 199 Squadron (the other flights operating the Canberra) where it was used for ECM training. 1321 Flight was also re-formed for the explicit purpose of undertaking Blue Danube trials with the Valiant. Based at Wittering, it used Orford Ness for dummy drops and ranges at Maralinga, Australia and Christmas Island for nuclear testing.

Trials were completed in March 1956 and the flight was integrated into 138 Squadron. Not long after the Valiant squadrons had formed, they were involved in the Suez Crisis. 138, 148, 207 and 214 Squadrons sent a total of 24 Valiants to RAF Luqa, Malta, to support the British operation.

Range was not an issue for the type and bombing commenced on

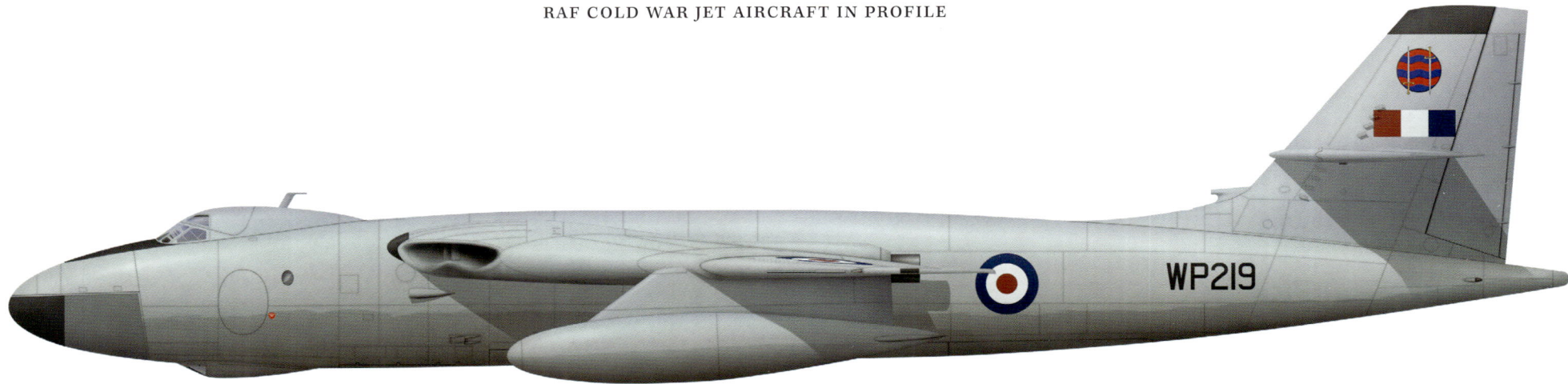

VALIANT B.(PR).1 199 SQUADRON WP219
199 Squadron only operated the Valiant for a short period during 1957/58, concurrently with
the Canberra in the ECM role. The unit was disbanded on December 15, 1958.

October 31, 1956, the target being Almaza Airfield. As the campaign continued, 49 sorties were flown by the Valiants. The bomber could undertake a secondary role if fitted with a photographic pack in the bomb bay and several aircraft were adapted to accommodate this equipment. Two B(PR).1s of 543 Squadron were put to good use after British Honduras suffered a severe hurricane.

Based at Jamaica, they were used to assess the damage and support the aid operation. Just like the other V bombers, Valiants were also adapted to fly as tankers. Unlike the others, however, the conversion for the Valiant was simple. As with the PR pack, a unit encompassing a fuel tank and drogue could be fitted in the bomb bay. The B.2, WJ954, was the first to receive this conversion and was used for trials in 1953 not long after its first flight. So successful was the refuelling that Valiants were involved in the first long range refuelling exercise when they supported four Javelins sent to reinforce British operations in the Far East during October 1960.

These roles, while valuable and making good use of the Valiant, were not the primary roles for which it was commissioned. The Valiant was designed as a nuclear deterrent and it did drop many live bombs during tests. Valiant WZ366 dropped the first British atomic bomb (a Blue Danube) at Marlinga, Australia, on October 11, 1956. Valiants continued to be involved in the atomic warfare programme for several years, ranging from further live tests to aerodynamic trials involving the Blue Steel missile.

Following the shooting down of a U2 by a Soviet SAM in 1960, there was a radical change to bombing methods. Prior to this event, bombers were considered safely out of range of any threat at high altitude. Now, in order to evade enemy defences, a switch to low

VALIANT B.1 WP204 A&AEE
This aircraft was only flown by A&AEE and was used in a number of testing roles, including Blue Steel trials
where dummy bombs were fitted. It was later assigned as a ground trainer at Woodbridge.

level was made. This put a lot more stress on the airframe however, due to the denser air low down and the more extreme manoeuvres required when following the terrain.

These stresses and strains revealed an inherent weakness in the construction of the Valiant and during 1964 several suffered cracks in the rear wing spar. Despite some repairs to aircraft, the fleet was grounded and by January 1965 the Ministry of Defence had decided it was too costly to repair the aircraft. With the Victors

and Vulcans still in service, the Valiant was considered surplus to requirements.

While it may have been runner-up to the Vulcan and Victor, during almost 10 years of service the Valiant fulfilled a wide range of roles from being a test bed for the Pegasus engine, which ended up in the Harrier, to being at the forefront of the atomic age. Despite such a vital contribution only one complete Valiant survives at RAF Cosford.

Vickers Valiant

VARIANT	LENGTH	SPAN	HEIGHT	ENGINE
B.1	108FT 3IN/32.99M	114FT 4IN/34.85M	32FT 2IN/9.8M	AVON RA.14 OR RA.28
B.2	112FT 9IN/34.37M	114FT 4IN/34.85M	32FT 2IN/9.8M	AVON RA.14

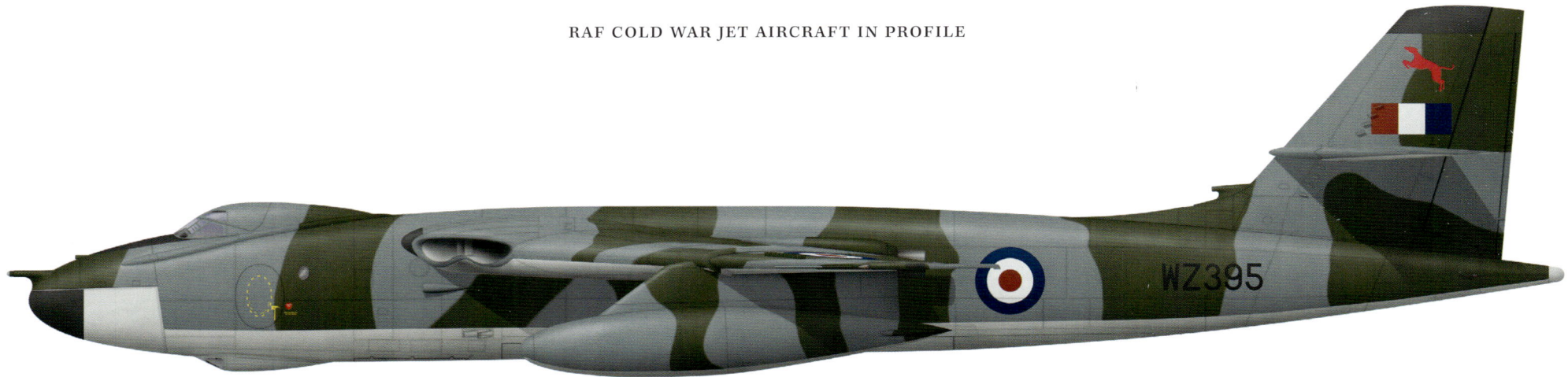

VALIANT B.(K).1 WZ395 49 SQUADRON

While with 214 Squadron, WZ395 was involved in the Suez Crisis. It was later allocated to 49 Squadron where it was painted in camouflage, medium sea grey and dark green upper surface, lower surfaces remained gloss white.

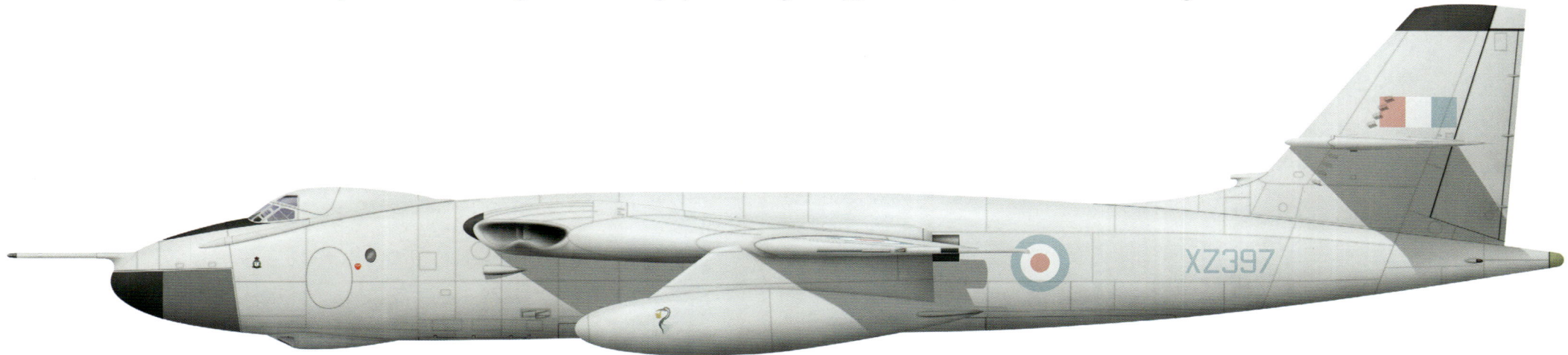

VALIANT B.PR(K).1 WZ397 543 SQUADRON

Involved in the Suez Crisis while it was with 214 Squadron, WZ397 was transferred to 543 Squadron in 1957. Finished in gloss white with the squadron crest on the nose and badge applied to the tanks.

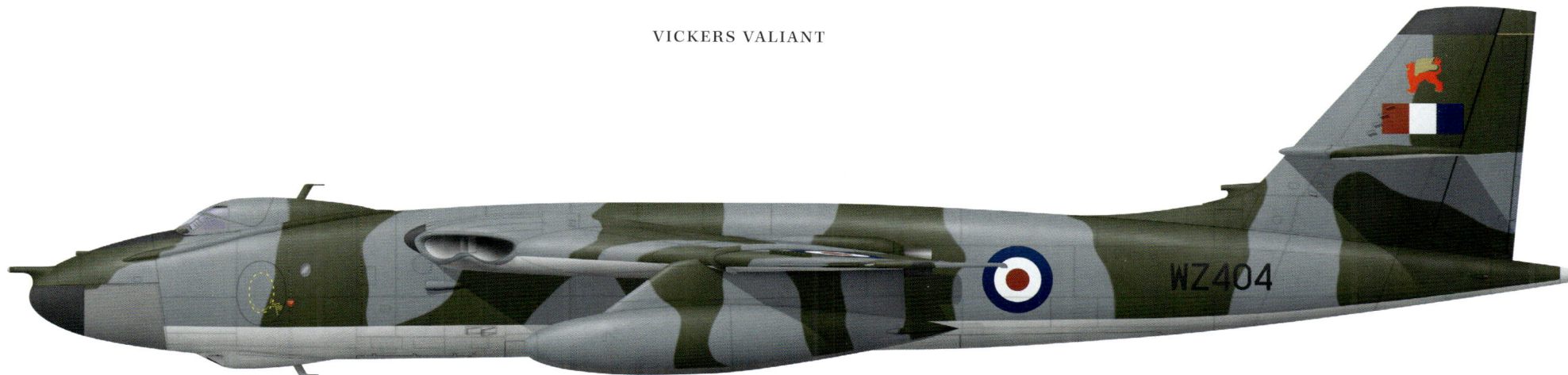

VALIANT B.(K).1 WZ404 207 SQUADRON

Wearing the late camouflage scheme, WZ404 was delivered to 230 OCU in July 1956 but shortly afterwards
was allocated to 207 Squadron where it remained until struck off charge in March 1965.

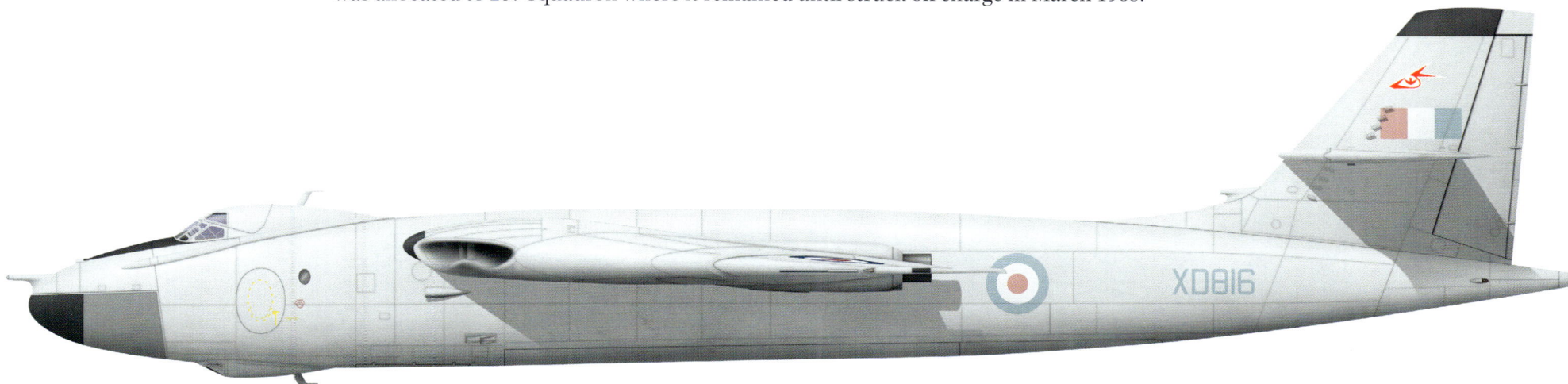

VALIANT B.(K).1 XD816 214 SQUADRON

One of the Valiants supplied by 148 Squadron during the Suez Crisis, XD816 later served with 214
Squadron. The nose section has been preserved at Brooklands Museum, Surrey.

VALIANT B.1 XD826 7 SQUADRON

Delivered in January 1957 to 7 Squadron with national markings and the squadron badge applied to the tail,
XD826 went on to serve with several other squadrons. The nose was retained as a ground trainer.

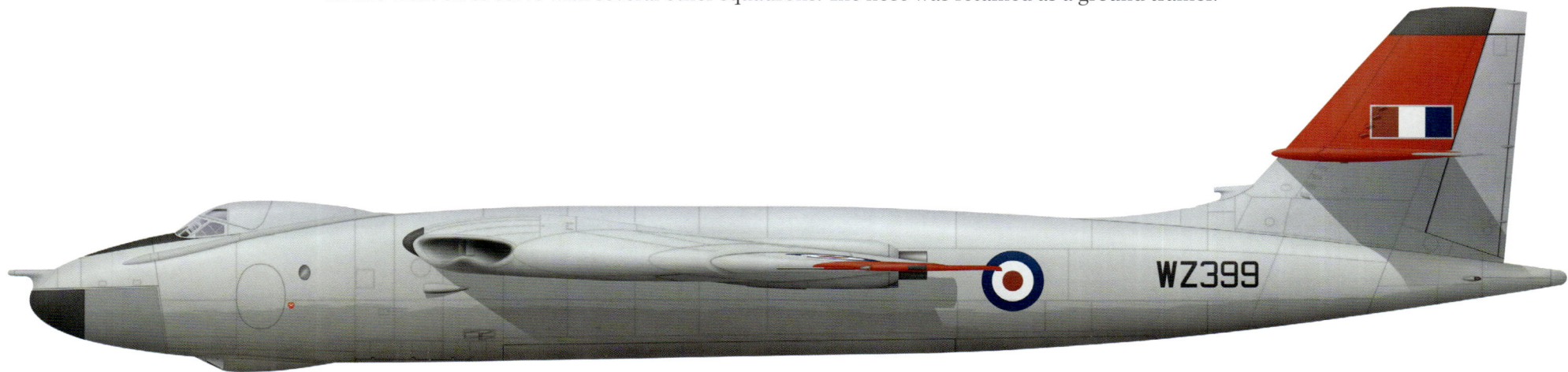

VALIANT B.PR(K).1 WZ399 543 SQUADRON

WZ399 served exclusively with 543 Squadron until it crashed during take-off from Offutt AFB, Nebraska, on March
11, 1961, due to the pitot tube icing over. Red panels were applied for high visibility during arctic operations.

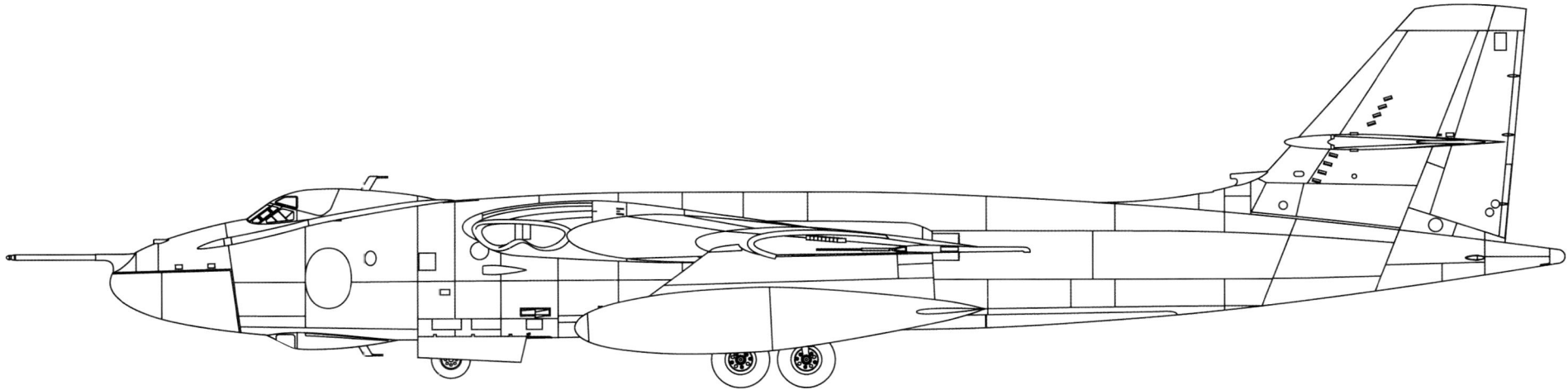

Valiant B.1

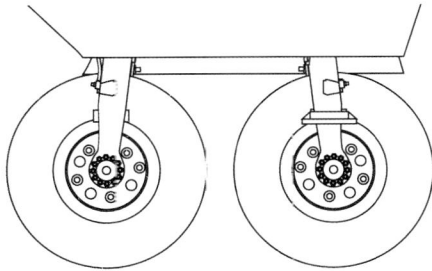

Main wheel

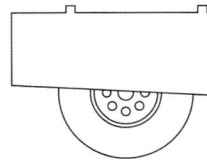

Nose wheel

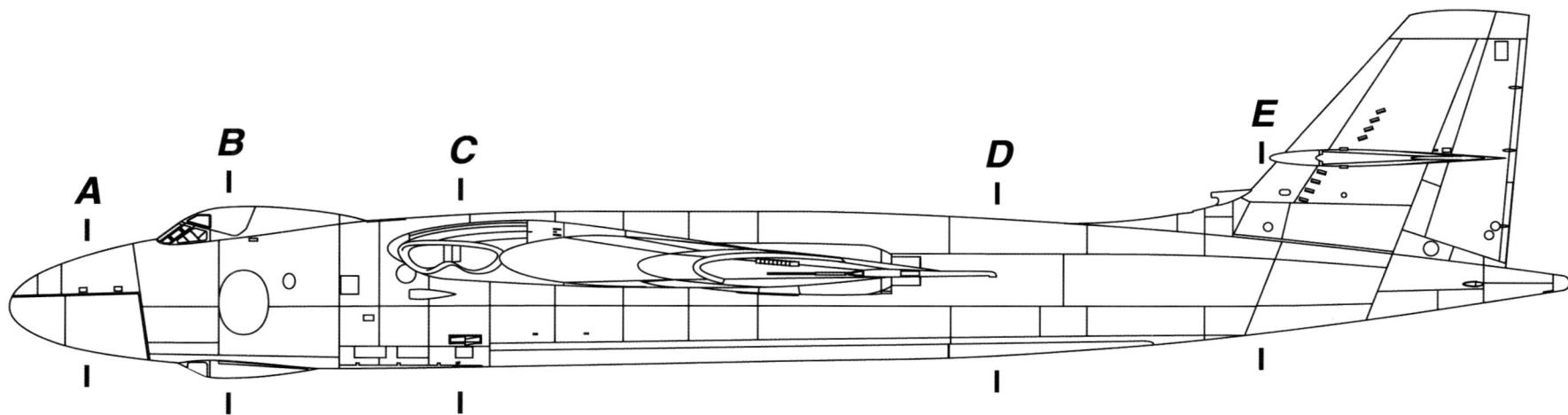

A   B   C   D   E

Valiant B.1

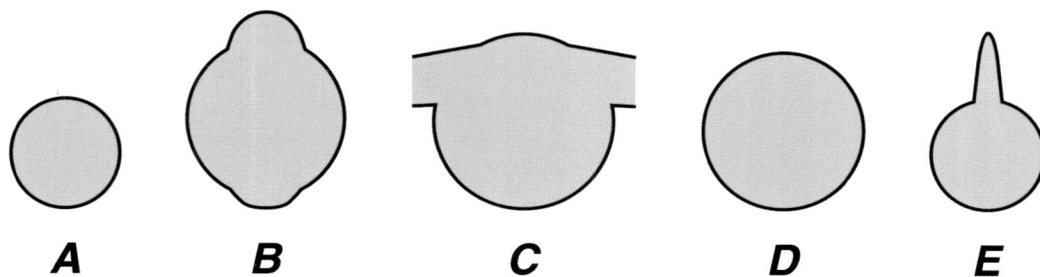

A   B   C   D   E

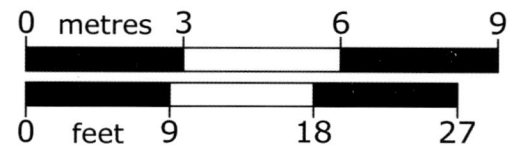

0   metres   3   6   9

0   feet   9   18   27

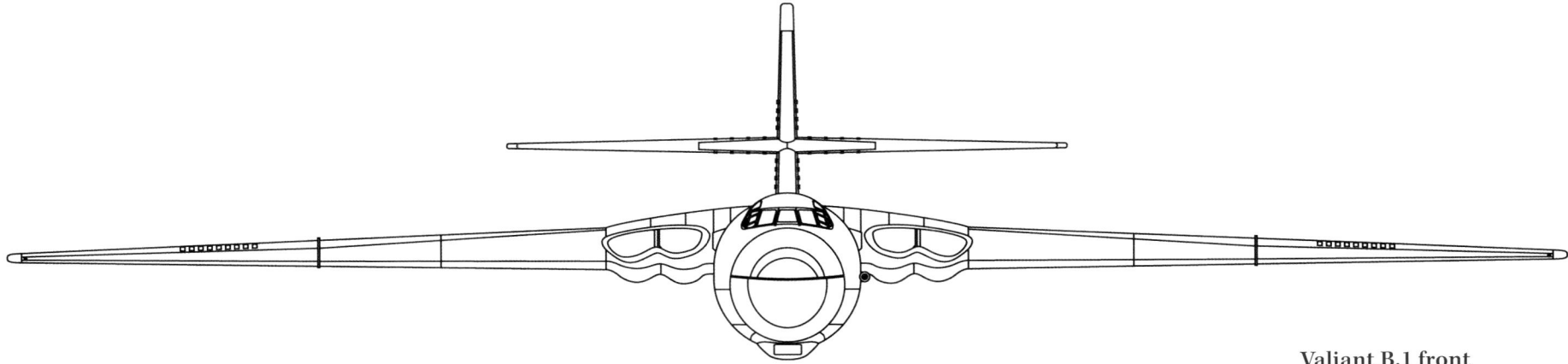

Valiant B.1 front

0 metres 3   6   9

0 feet 9   18   27

Valiant B.1 top

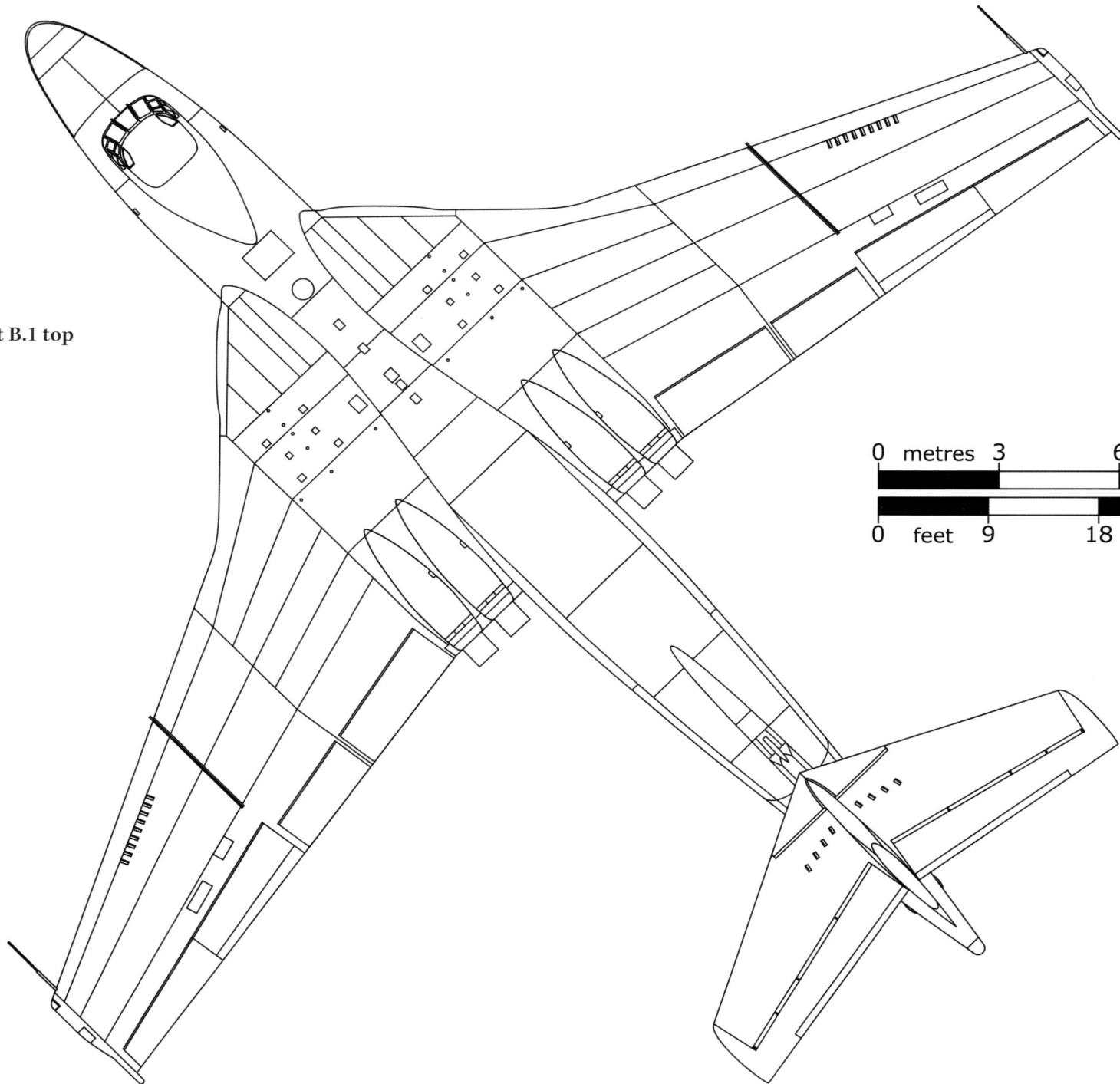

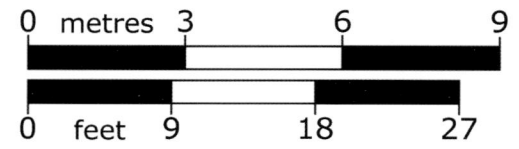

| 0 | metres | 3 | | 6 | | 9 |

| 0 | feet | 9 | | 18 | | 27 |

Valiant B.1 underside

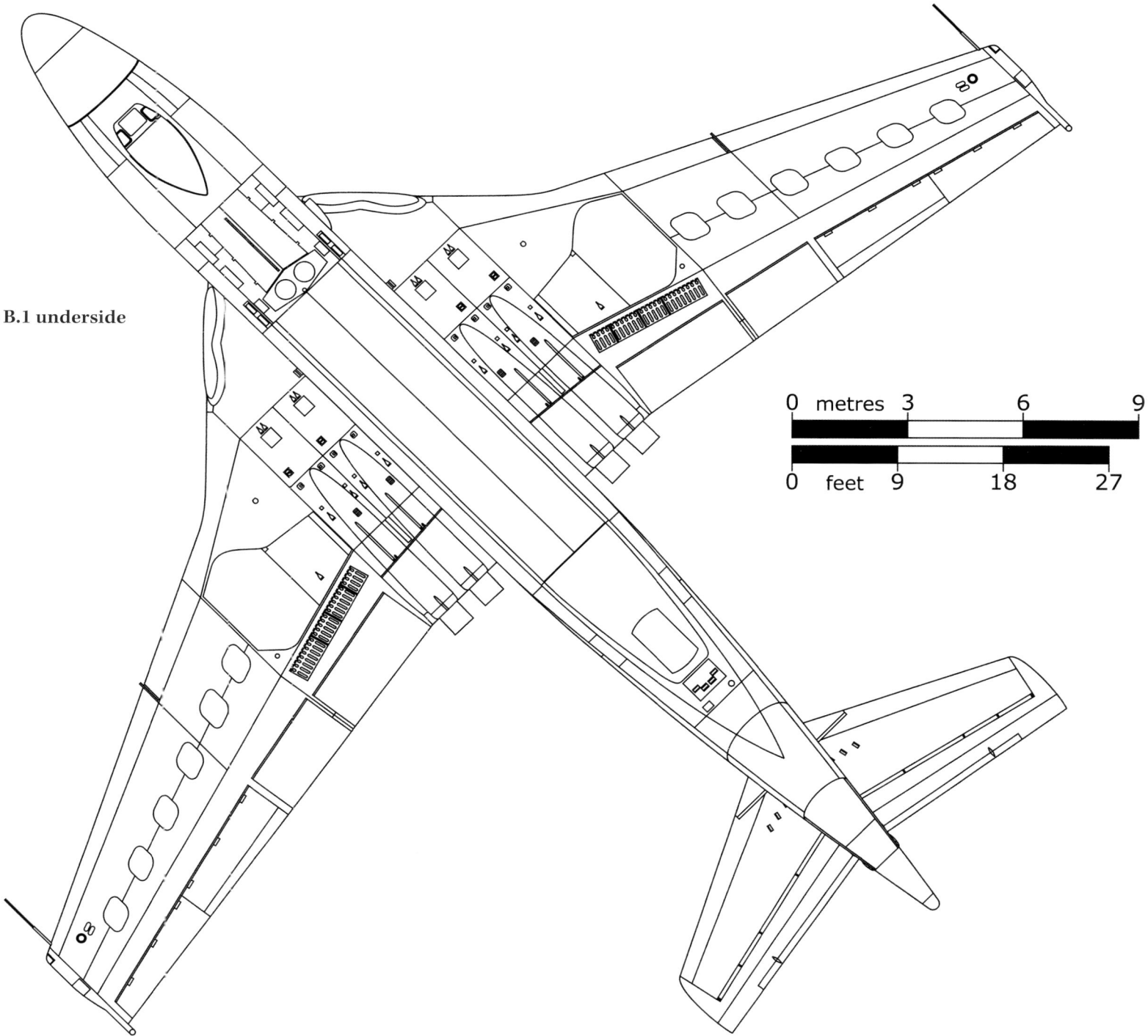

0 metres 3 6 9

0 feet 9 18 27

GLOSTER JAVELIN

The Javelin is one of the forgotten warriors of the cold war. A total of 436 were built but it only remained in front line service for 12 years and just a single example continued to fly until 1975. Yet the Javelin represented a big step up from the Vampires and Meteors it replaced, and the addition of Firestreak missiles and Sapphire engines made later variants formidable all-weather fighters.

The order for the aircraft that would eventually become the Javelin was issued when de Havilland Mosquitoes were still employed as night fighters with several squadrons. With jet engine development advancing rapidly, it was clear that a much more capable replacement would be required.

The short term solution was to adapt Meteors and Vampires for the role but a dedicated aircraft would still be needed. With this in mind, specifications F.43/46 and F.44/46 were issued for a day and night fighter respectively; subsequent specifications would be issued but these were to lay the foundation for what would eventually be the Javelin.

Early concepts involved modifications to Gloster's existing Meteor design but these slowly evolved into a delta wing aircraft with a delta tail unit too, and the engines were moved into the fuselage. Even during the early stages of the project the Armstrong Siddeley Sapphire was the preferred power choice.

There was considerable indecision at the Ministry of Supply over the preferred armament however. At one stage it was thought that no guns should be fitted, with the fighter relying wholly on the Red Hawk AAM. Once an official order had been raised for the type, work commenced on the Gloster GA.5 and WD804 took to the air on November 26, 1951, with Gloster chief

JAVELIN FAW.9 XH903 33 SQUADRON

Originally built as a FAW.7 in 1954, XH903 was upgraded to FAW.9 standard and returned to 33 Squadron in January 1961. It was then loaned to 29 Squadron before being eventually struck off charge on December 2, 1967. It is now in the Jet Age Museum collection.

test pilot William Arthur 'Bill' Waterton at the controls.

Early flights highlighted a number of issues with the design, such as buffeting and vibration arising from the exhaust. These issues were overcome with a pen nib style fairing that was fitted to early variants. There was also a significant setback to the testing programme on June 29, 1952, when severe flutter caused the elevators to detach during the aircraft's 99th flight.

Waterton attempted a landing at Boscombe Down and got the aircraft onto the ground using the tailplane trimmer for pitch control. It was necessary to land at a much higher speed than the undercarriage had been designed to withstand however and it collapsed, putting the aircraft onto its belly. The prototype skidded

to a halt but the port undercarriage had punctured a fuel tank and a fire ensued which eventually destroyed it. Waterton escaped unharmed and managed to rescue the flight data – a feat for which he received the George Medal.

The loss of WD804 did not deter the Ministry and the aircraft was selected to go into production, an order for 200 being placed.

The DH.110, which was a direct competitor, was dropped but interest had been shown by the Royal Navy and it ended up in service as the Sea Vixen. The 'Javelin' name was selected for the GA.5 in August 1952, in preference to the alternative – 'Spearhead'.

More prototypes were constructed so that testing could continue and WD808 took to the air on August 20, 1952. As the programme

JAVELIN FAW.2 XA778

XA778 did not see front line service but was passed straight to the Aircraft Armament & Experimental Establishment
at RAF Boscombe Down. It was used for FAW.7 tests and as a pace aircraft for air speed calibration trials with other
aircraft. Originally all over high gloss it became heavily weathered. Eventually it was replaced by XH897.

continued, numerous revisions and alterations were made. For example, a bulge was required in the canopy to accommodate the crew and their helmets comfortably, and from the fifth prototype it was also split into two, replacing the original single unit.

As with the Vulcan delta bomber, a straight leading edge to the Javelin's wings resulted in high-speed, high altitude handling issues. The solution for both aircraft was to introduce a kink and in the case of the Javelin the outer leading edge saw a reduction in the angle of sweepback.

Series production of the FAW.1 was progressing well by the summer of 1954 and the first Mk.I, XA544, flew on July 22, 1954.

However, it was not until February 24, 1956, following RAF trials, that a Javelin finally reached a front line squadron – 46 Squadron receiving XA570 at RAF Odiham. The factory was producing 4.5 Javelins per month on average so a steady stream of aircraft went to both 46 Squadron and 87 Squadron at RAF Bruggen, West Germany.

To complement the FAW.1, the FAW.2 also went into service. The differences between the two were minor, the most significant being the replacement of the AI.Mk.17 S-band radar with the American APQ.43 (AI.Mk.22) radar. This necessitated a slight enlargement to the radome and revised access, which was now hinged. These changes led to some delays in production and the type did not

JAVELIN FAW.4 XA632 11 SQUADRON

This aircraft was first delivered to 11 Squadron in March 1956 while at RAF Geilenkirchen, West Germany, and flown as 'A'. At this time the squadron decorated the tail code with their colours instead of the squadron badge which replaced it. XA632 was retired and stored at RAF Shawbury in August 1962.

enter service until May 1957, being received primarily by 46 Squadron with some ending up in West Germany.

The next variant to roll off the production line was the radar-less T.3 trainer. Taking the radar's hefty weight out of the aircraft's nose caused a shift in the centre of gravity, which required a fuselage extension to correct. The conversion to dual controls, however, was relatively straightforward and the T.3 also featured a new all-moving tailplane.

Most of the 22 T.3s built found their way into squadron service at some stage but the primary user was 228 OCU, based at RAF Leeming. On September 19, 1955, the first FAW.4 flew – XA629. It was based on the FAW.1, with the same radar, but had the all-moving tail from the T.3. Vortex generators were also fitted to the wing and another feature appreciated by pilots was a stall warning device which allowed for more extreme manoeuvres to be executed in confidence.

Provision to fix ventral tanks was introduced too, doubling flying time from 45 minutes to one hour 30 minutes – though they naturally had a detrimental effect on the performance. The FAW.4 had a slower climb rate than the FAW.1 and the flying controls were heavier, increasing the rate of pilot fatigue, but even with these limitations Mach 1.04 could be reached in a shallow dive.

A total of 50 were built, the construction split between the

RAF COLD WAR JET AIRCRAFT IN PROFILE

JAVELIN FAW.5 XA654 72 SQUADRON

XA654 was first operated by 23 Squadron before being passed on to 72 Squadron, while they were based at RAF
Leconfield. The aircraft remained on strength until the squadron was temporarily disbanded in June 1961.

Gloster factory and Armstrong Whitworth, Baginton. They served with eight fighter squadrons.

An increase in the internal fuel was sufficient to warrant a new variant number despite no other significant changes to the basic FAW.4 and the FAW.5 was built in slightly larger numbers, with a total of 64 being produced, manufacturing duties again being divided between Gloster and Armstrong Whitworth.

Another variant, the FAW.6, was created by mating the revised wing to a FAW.2 fuselage, retaining the AI.22 radar. Only 33 of these were built. With the introduction of the uprated Sapphire SA7, the FAW.7 came into being. The new engines were 32% more powerful and required a fuselage extension to accommodate them.

Thanks to some excellent foresight the original design anticipated this and repositioning the engines required minimal structural revision. The improvements meant that even with ventral tanks fitted the FAW.7 could out-climb the FAW.4 and 5. Early FAW.7s coming off the line retained the distinctive pen nib tail but extending the whole section was a considerably simpler solution. Landing earlier Javelins in the rain had been a problem for pilots in the past – despite the Javelin supposedly being an all-weather fighter – so a revised rain dispersal system was also fitted to the FAW.7's windscreen.

Further modifications allowed either four 100 gallon external tanks or Firestreak AAMs to be fitted to the underwing pylons. The

JAVELIN FAW.4 XA723 11 SQUADRON

This aircraft was flown to Canada in 1957 for cold weather trials. It reached the Central Experimental
and Proving Establishment facility at RCAF Namao in Alberta after travelling from Goose Bay, to an RCAF
base near Quebec, then to Uplands, Ottowa. The CEPE badge appears on its engine nacelle.

missile system had yet to be completed as production commenced and as a result it had to be retrofitted to the first 30 FAW.7s – a revised control panel being installed to incorporate the fire control system needed to operate Firestreak. So successful was this iteration of the Javelin that 142 were built.

The last version was the FAW.8 which saw the introduction of reheat to the Sapphire SA7 and an increase in thrust by a further 12%. This alteration was the most noticeable external change to the Javelin, with the system extending the external tailpipes, which included the reheat pipes. There were alterations to the leading edge as well. The improvement in performance was such that 116

FAW.7s were later upgraded (including the wing modification) to FAW.8 standard and redesignated FAW.9.

The FAW.8 had the same radar as the Mk.2 and Mk.6 – the AI.22. An initial order for 60 FAW.8s was placed but the order for the last 13 was rescinded, these airframes, at various stages of construction, being used for spares.

Javelins were operated by the RAF throughout the world in various hotspots and were a constant presence in West Germany. During the Malayan crisis of 1964, a 60 Squadron Javelin forced an Indonesian C-130 to crash, this being the type's only air-to-air victory.

As the squadron pulled out, several Javelins were left as instructional airframes and had their national markings painted over. For many years the Javelin also defended British airspace from Soviet probes and remained on constant alert until it was replaced by the much more powerful Lightning. As the type was phased out, a single Javelin FAW.9, XH897, continued to fly. Operated by the RAE, it wore a high visibility red and white scheme. But even this was eventually retired to IWM Duxford on January 24, 1975.

As the first dedicated all-weather jet fighter, and given the success of other British jets, it might be expected that the Javelin found air forces across the globe eager to buy it, but this was not the case. Interest was expressed by Austria and Belgium, but with a plethora of other jets now in production and development - some of which were much more flexible in other roles - no sales materialised.

During its time in service, the Javelin was respected and appreciated by its pilots and did what was required so no more could be asked.

Gloster Javelin

VARIANT	LENGTH	SPAN	HEIGHT	ENGINE
FAW.1	56FT 3IN/17.15M	52FT/15.85M	16FT/4.88M	2 X SAPPHIRE 6
FAW.2	56FT 3IN/17.15M	52FT/15.85M	16FT/4.88M	2 X SAPPHIRE 6
T.3	59FT 11IN/18.26M	52FT/15.85M	16FT/4.88M	2 X SAPPHIRE 6
FAW.4	56FT 3IN/17.15M	52FT/15.85M	16FT/4.88M	2 X SAPPHIRE 6
FAW.5	56FT 3IN/17.15M	52FT/15.85M	16FT/4.88M	2 X SAPPHIRE 6
FAW.6	56FT 3IN/17.15M	52FT/15.85M	16FT/4.88M	2 X SAPPHIRE 6
FAW.7	56FT 3IN/17.15M	52FT/15.85M	16FT/4.88M	2 X SAPPHIRE 7
FAW.8	56FT 3IN/17.15M	52FT/15.85M	16FT/4.88M	2 X SAPPHIRE 7R
FAW.9	56FT 9IN/17.15M	52FT/15.85M	16FT/4.88M	2 X SAPPHIRE 7R

JAVELIN FAW.4 XA730 23 SQUADRON

Operated by 23 Squadron, based at RAF Horsham-Saint Faith, XA730 wore the early simple
squadron badge in solid red on the tail. The aircraft later served with 72 Squadron.

JAVELIN FAW.4 XA638 3 SQUADRON

A 3 Squadron Javelin that was based at RAF Geilenkirchen, West Germany, with the code J on the
tail. XA638 had served with both 141 and 41 Squadrons prior to 3 Squadron. After only a little more than
three years in service it was retired in January 1961 and scrapped the following year.

JAVELIN FAW.4 XA639 141 SQUADRON

The last aircraft operated by 141 Squadron was the Javelin (it later became a Bloodhound unit), while based at RAF Horsham-Saint Faith. XA639 went on to fly with 41 and 87 Squadrons.

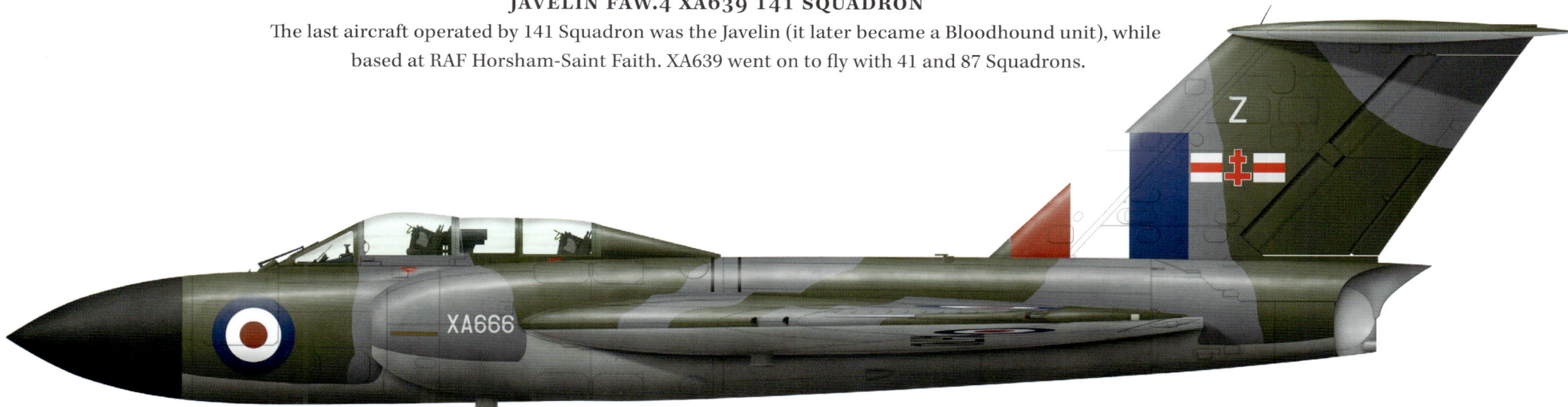

JAVELIN FAW.5 XA666 41 SQUADRON

While primarily operating first the Javelin FAW.4 and later FAW.8, 41 Squadron did have other types including XA666 which was first used by 228 Operational Conversion Unit. Following a period with 41 Squadron, while at RAF Coltishall, it was then passed on to 5 Squadron.

JAVELIN FAW.5 XH710 151 SQUADRON
XH710 was delivered to RAF Turnhouse on May 16, 1957, pending the arrival of 151 Squadron
for conversion to the type. It received the letter Y before the squadron moved to RAF
Leuchars that October. XH710 was retired in 1961 and scrapped two years later.

JAVELIN FAW.7 XH835 33 SQUADRON
Flown by 33 Squadron's commanding officer, Wing Commander N. Poole, XH835 carries his initials. It was on
squadron strength while based at RAF Middleton Saint George, County Durham between 1958 and 1962.

JAVELIN FAW.7 XH789 64 SQUADRON

64 Squadron received its Javelins in September 1958 while at Duxford and operated the FAW.7 and FAW.9 until disbanding in June 1967 at RAF Tengah. XH789, flown by Flt Lt Grindley, with Sgt S. Sanders as navigator, was written off after a hydraulic failure caused it to overshoot the runway at RAF Akrotiri, Cyprus, on July 30, 1959.

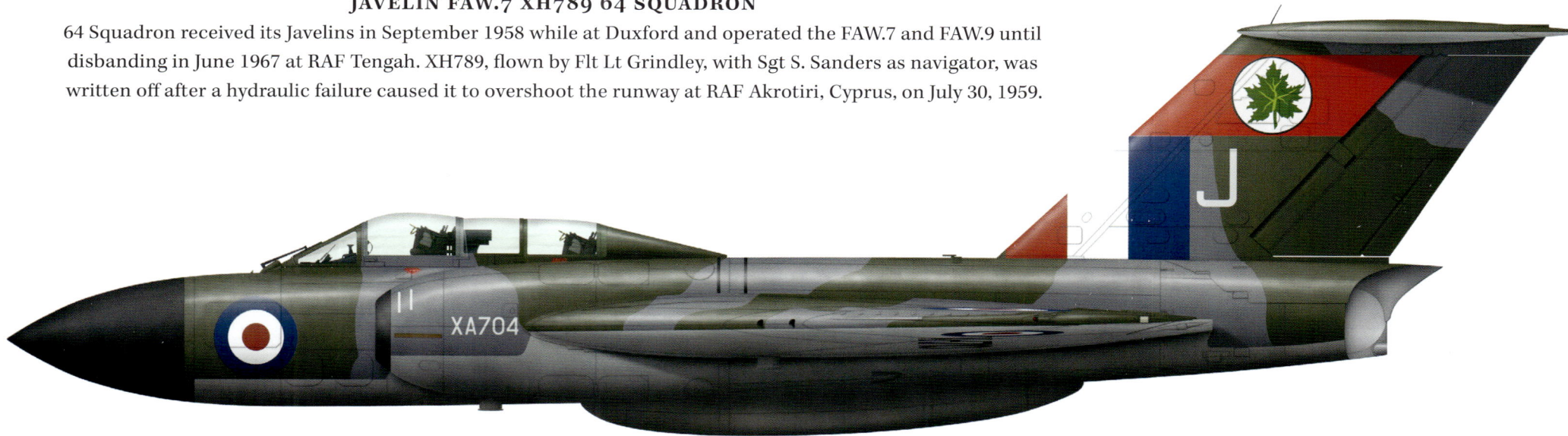

JAVELIN FAW.5 XA704 5 SQUADRON

A 5 Squadron Javelin based at Laarbruck, West Germany, 1962, XA704 was delivered on July 24, 1957.
Having served with the squadron as 'J' for five years it was retired and scrapped in 1965.

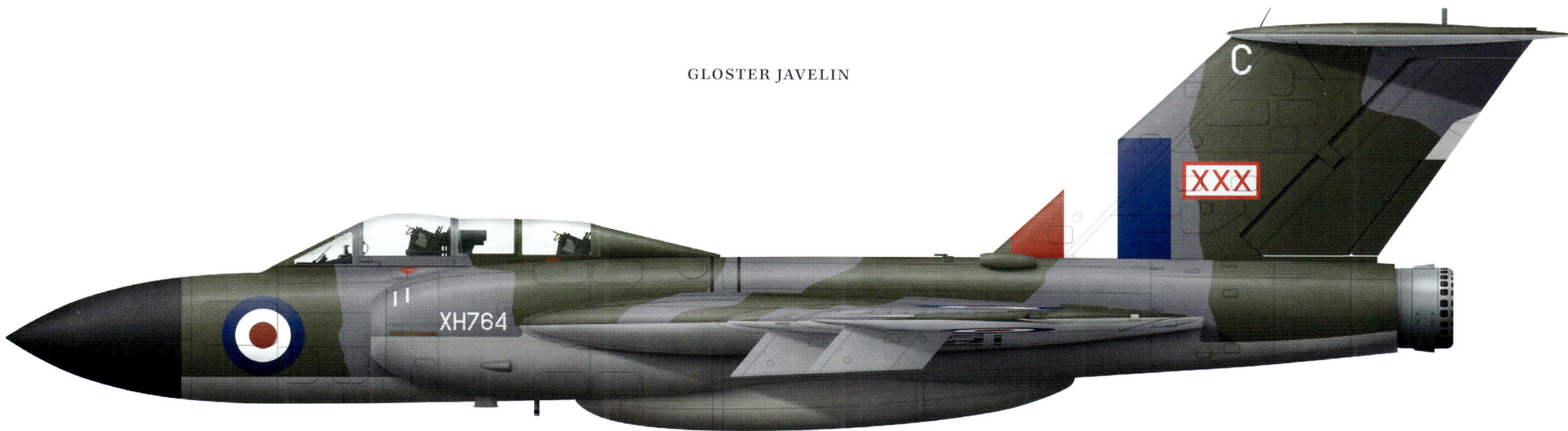

JAVELIN FAW.9 XH764 29 SQUADRON

XH764 was flown by 29 Squadron, which converted to the Javelin in 1957 and operated the type for a decade. Having been retired, XH764 was on a ferry flight pending disposal when it suffered a heavy landing at RAF Manston and was written off. Later it became the gate guardian at RAF Manston before being scrapped in 1990. While on display it was painted to represent XA639 of 87 Squadron.

JAVELIN FAW.9 XH721 60 SQUADRON

Delivered as a FAW.7, XH721 served with 33 Squadron. Upgraded to FAW.9 standard, it was transferred to 60 Squadron, based at RAF Tengah, Singapore. There it wore the initials of the unit's CO, Wing Commander Michael H. Miller, on its tail. It would never return home – being scrapped in Singapore.

JAVELIN FAW.9 XH885 23 SQUADRON

23 Squadron Javelin with long range refuelling probe fitted while on detachment to Luqa, Malta. XH885
was written off following a fire during start-up at RAF Tengah, Singapore, on November 15, 1966.

JAVELIN FAW.9 XH897

Following retirement from front line service, XH897 was retained for testing purposes as a replacement
for XA778 at the A&AEE. The standard camouflage scheme was replaced with this high visibility scheme.
On January 24, 1975, it was finally retired to IWM Duxford where it is still on display.

JAVELIN FAW.9 XH768 11 SQUADRON

Originally constructed as a FAW.7 but converted to FAW.9 standard before delivery to the RAF, XH768 first served with 25 Squadron with the code E. It was then transferred to 11 Squadron at RAF Geilenkirchen, West Germany, and retained the tail code. Following a period with 29 Squadron it was used as a ground trainer. It is currently on display at the Parco Temetico Dell'Aviazione, Cerbaiola, Italy, wearing the code XH707.

JAVELIN FAW.9 XH880 25 SQUADRON

Converted from a FAW.7 to FAW.9 before delivery, XH880 served with 25 Squadron as the commanding officer's personal aircraft, bearing the initials of Wg Cdr Jim Walton. Later transferred to 11 Squadron it was eventually used for spares at RAF Seletar, Singapore, in 1967.

JAVELIN FAW.9 XH898 228 OCU

The personal aircraft of 228 Operation Conversion Unit's CO, Sqn Ldr George H. Beaton while at RAF Leuchars, this is the only Javelin to have flown in a natural metal finish. XH898 entered service as a FAW.7 but was upgraded while with 25 Squadron. 228 OCU received the aircraft in May 1966 and flew it until it was retired eight months later.

JAVELIN FAW.2 XA778

XA778 (see earlier) as it appeared in its original overall high gloss, prior to weathering.

Javelin FAW.5

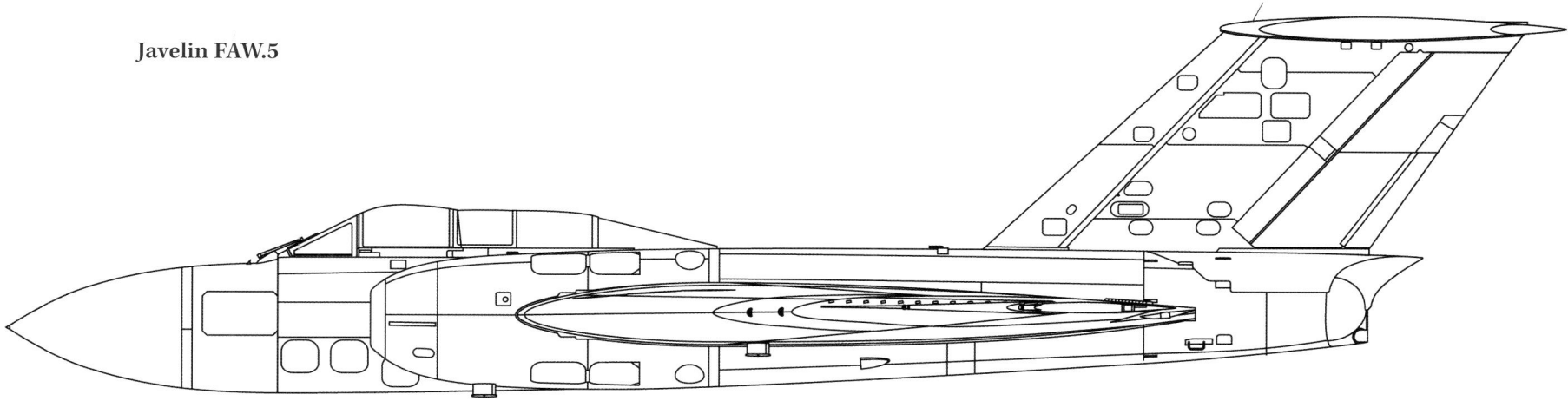

Javelin FAW.7

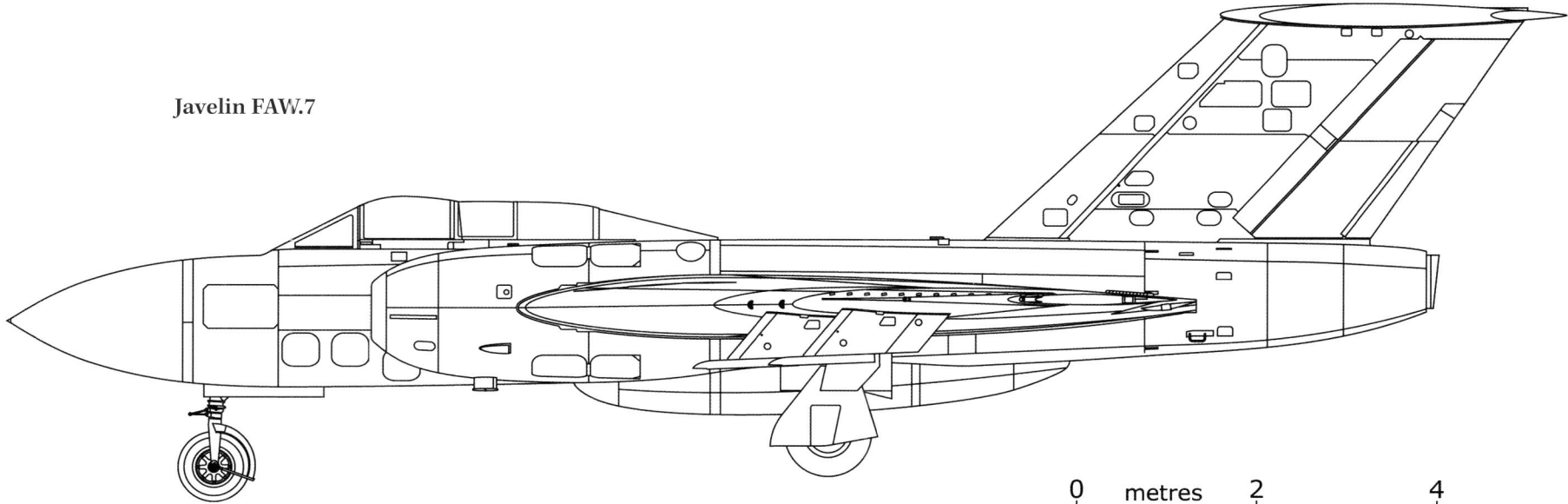

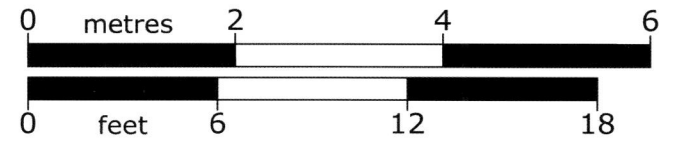

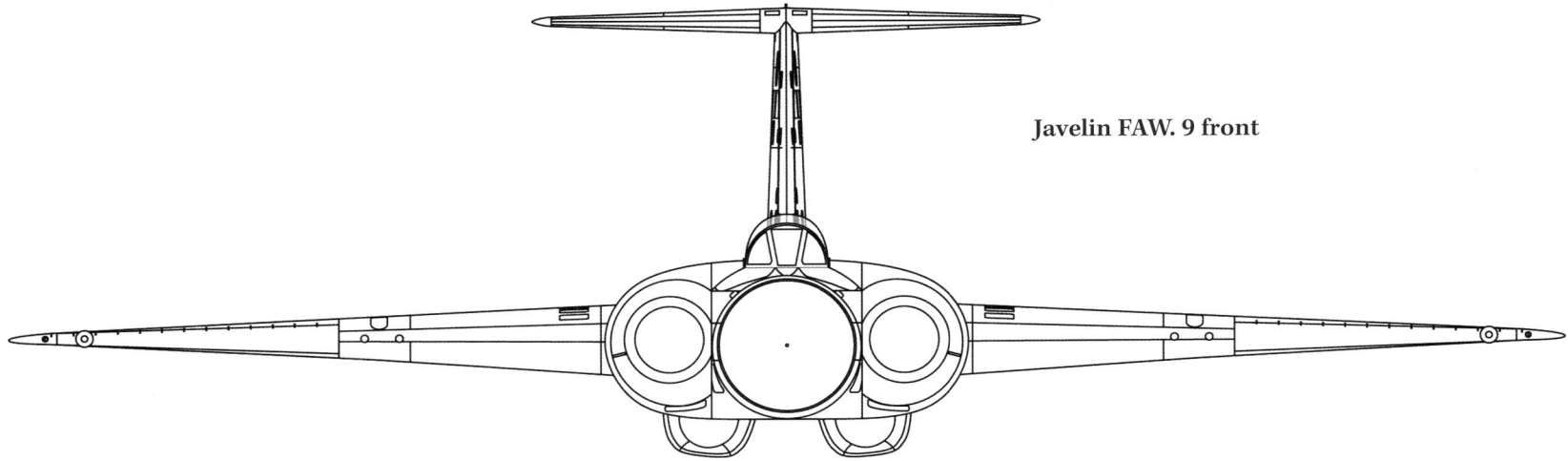

Javelin FAW. 9 front

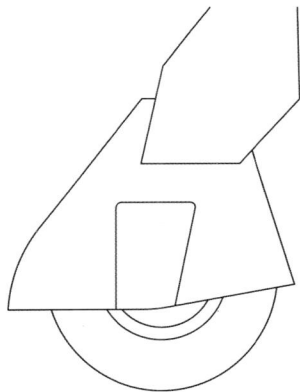

Main wheel

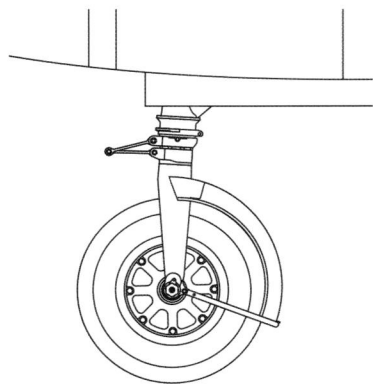

Nose wheel

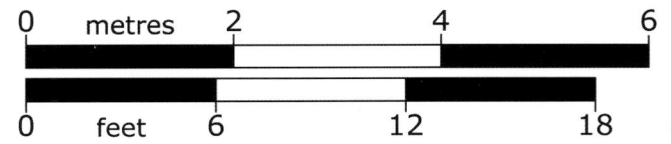

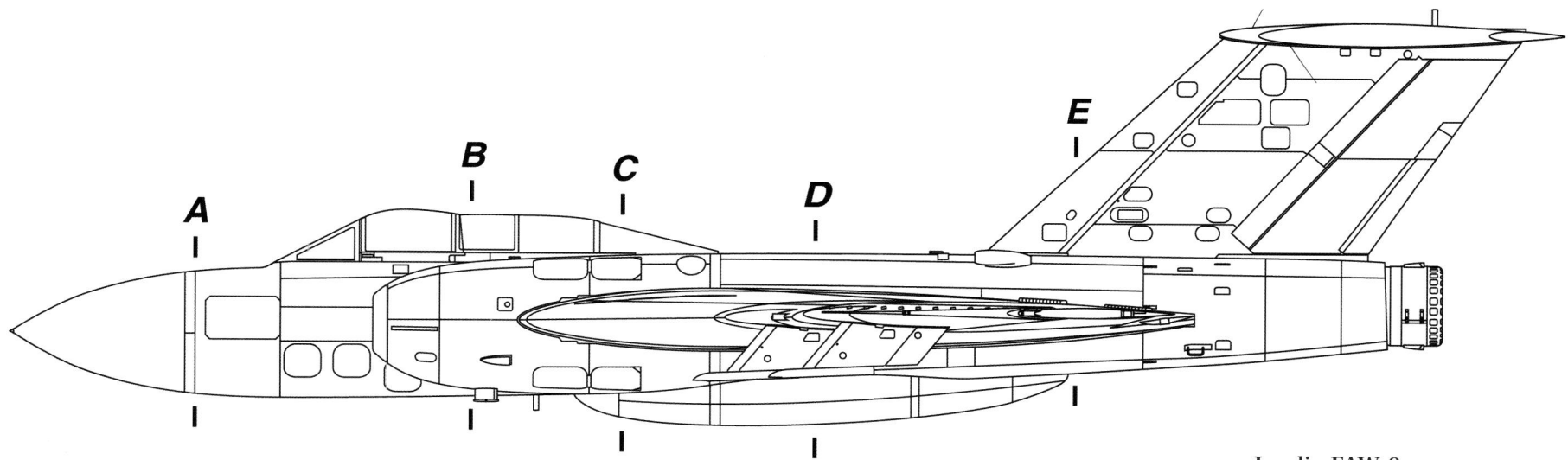

A

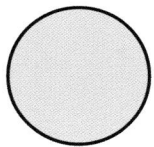

Javelin FAW. 9

C

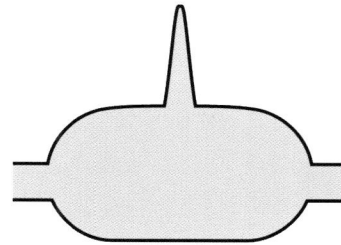

E

B

D

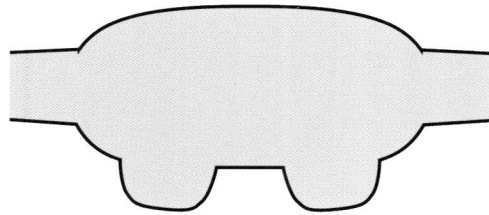

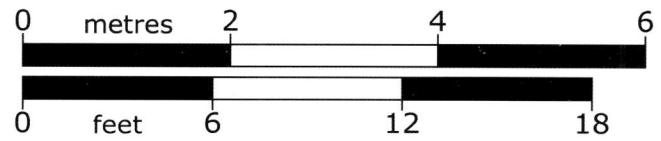

| 0 | metres | 2 | 4 | 6 |
| 0 | feet | 6 | 12 | 18 |

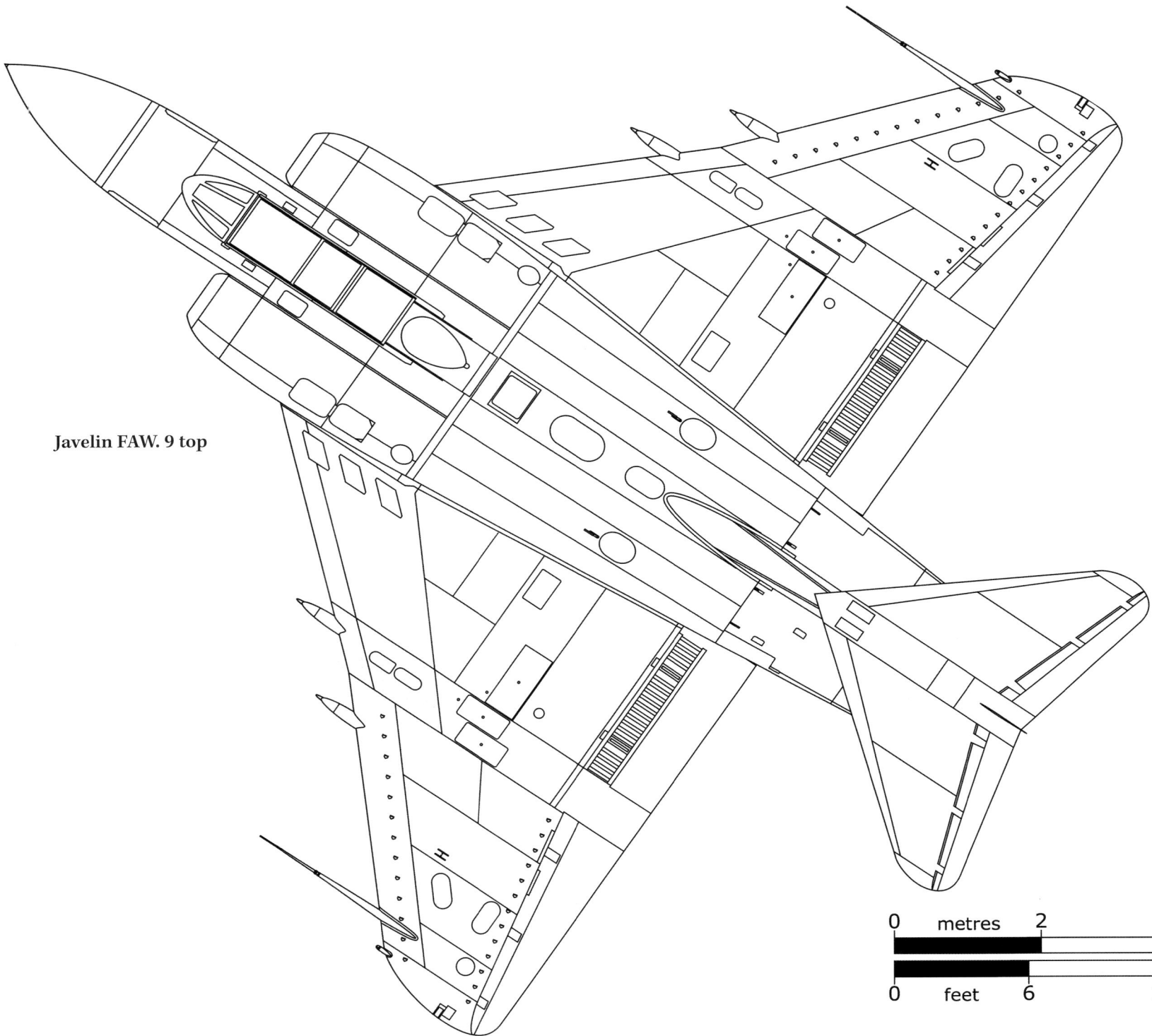

Javelin FAW. 9 top

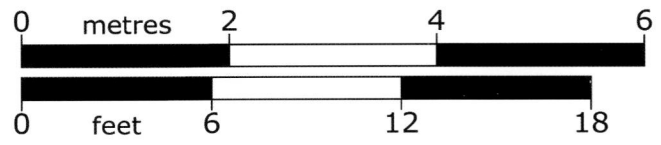

0 metres 2 4 6

0 feet 6 12 18

Javelin FAW. 9 underside

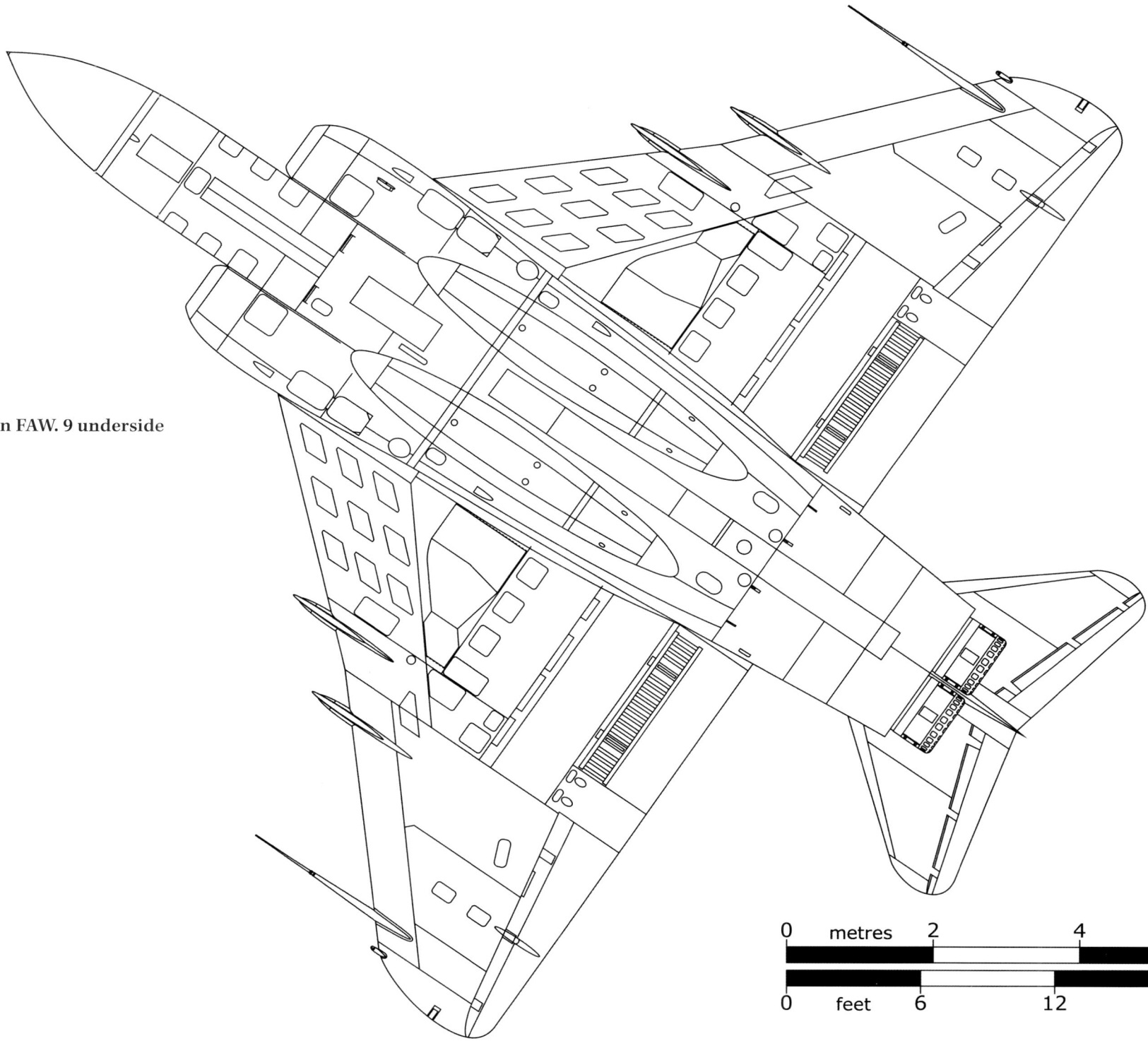

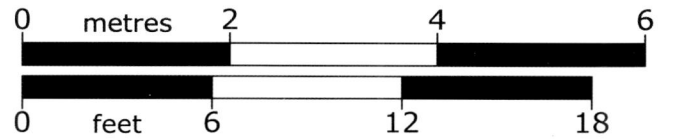

0 metres 2 4 6

0 feet 6 12 18

HANDLEY PAGE VICTOR

The Vulcan may have beaten the Victor into the air by four months but the Victor remained in service for nearly a decade longer in the secondary role of tanker, in which guise it made a valuable contribution during two conflicts. Like the Vulcan, the Victor was way ahead of its time in terms of design and expectations of performance, the low crescent wings and smooth intakes giving it a futuristic look even in the 21st century.

Details of Specification B.35/46 have been covered in the Valiant section and Handley Page's proposal was the HP.80. The specification had been anticipated by Sir Frederick Handley Page in 1945 when he became aware of the contract issued to English Electric for a jet-propelled bomber (the Canberra). He instructed the design team at Handley Page to start investigating both a twin-engined bomber and a larger four-engined type. Research by company aerodynamicist Dr Gustav Lachmann suggested that a swept crescent style wing would be suitable for the near Mach speeds the HP.80 would reach.

Much of the research that led to the HP.80 came from the HP.75 Manx experimental tailless aircraft which had been built by subcontractor Dart Aircraft. It was commissioned in 1937 and delivered in 1939 but did not fly until June 11, 1943, due to issues with structure, weight and the rapid deterioration of the wing structures. However, when it did eventually fly the research gathered convinced the Handley Page design team that scaling up the concept would be feasible and it was fed into the HP.80 programme.

Another research aircraft, the HP.88 was then built under contract by Blackburn to generate more data. Consisting of a Supermarine Attacker fuselage with new wings similar to those intended for the HP.80, it was unfortunately destroyed only 36 days after its first flight.

VICTOR B.2 XL233 WITTERING WING

This aircraft was operated by Wittering Wing until it was converted to a tanker in 1970, going on to serve with 232 OCU and 55 Squadron. It was painted in standard RAF camouflage of dark green and medium sea grey upper surfaces and white undersides. The Wittering Wing shield was on the nose.

The form of the HP.80's wings may have been advanced but many other aspects of the design were conventional; the fuel tanks were fitted into the wings and the weapons bay, with space for a 10,000lb atomic bomb, was in the centre of the fuselage.

A pressurised compartment in the nose accommodated the crew of five — pilot, co-pilot, navigator/plotter, navigator/radar operator and radio/electronic countermeasures operator. Only the two pilots had the luxury of an ejection seat, the three other crew having to bail out via the door in the event of an emergency. The door was at least fitted with a cover to protect them as they entered the slipstream.

Work on the first HP.80, WB771, was progressing at a steady pace by May 1952 and thoughts turned to its debut flight. The facilities at Radlett airfield, Hertfordshire, were deemed unsatisfactory by the Ministry of Supply and it was therefore ordered that the aircraft should be moved to Boscombe Down, where the 10,000ft runway would allow ample space for the untested bomber.

Moving such a large aircraft along the ground — even in sections — meant the roads along the route had to be specially modified. Once everything was settled at Boscombe Down, work commenced on putting WB771 back together and completing it. There was added pressure because Handley Page was still competing with Avro at this stage and was uncertain whether the Victor would win the contest for orders.

Delays to the project meant that the aircraft did not even get to taxi until the week before Christmas but on Christmas Eve Handley Page's chief test pilot, Squadron Leader Hedley George Hazelden, was finally able to fly it. With Ian Bennett as the flight test observer, Hazelden took WB771 on a couple of circuits, landing on the second one for what was an uneventful yet successful first flight. As the New Year arrived it was officially announced that the HP.80 would henceforth be known as the Victor in keeping with the preference for the new bombers to be named with a V.

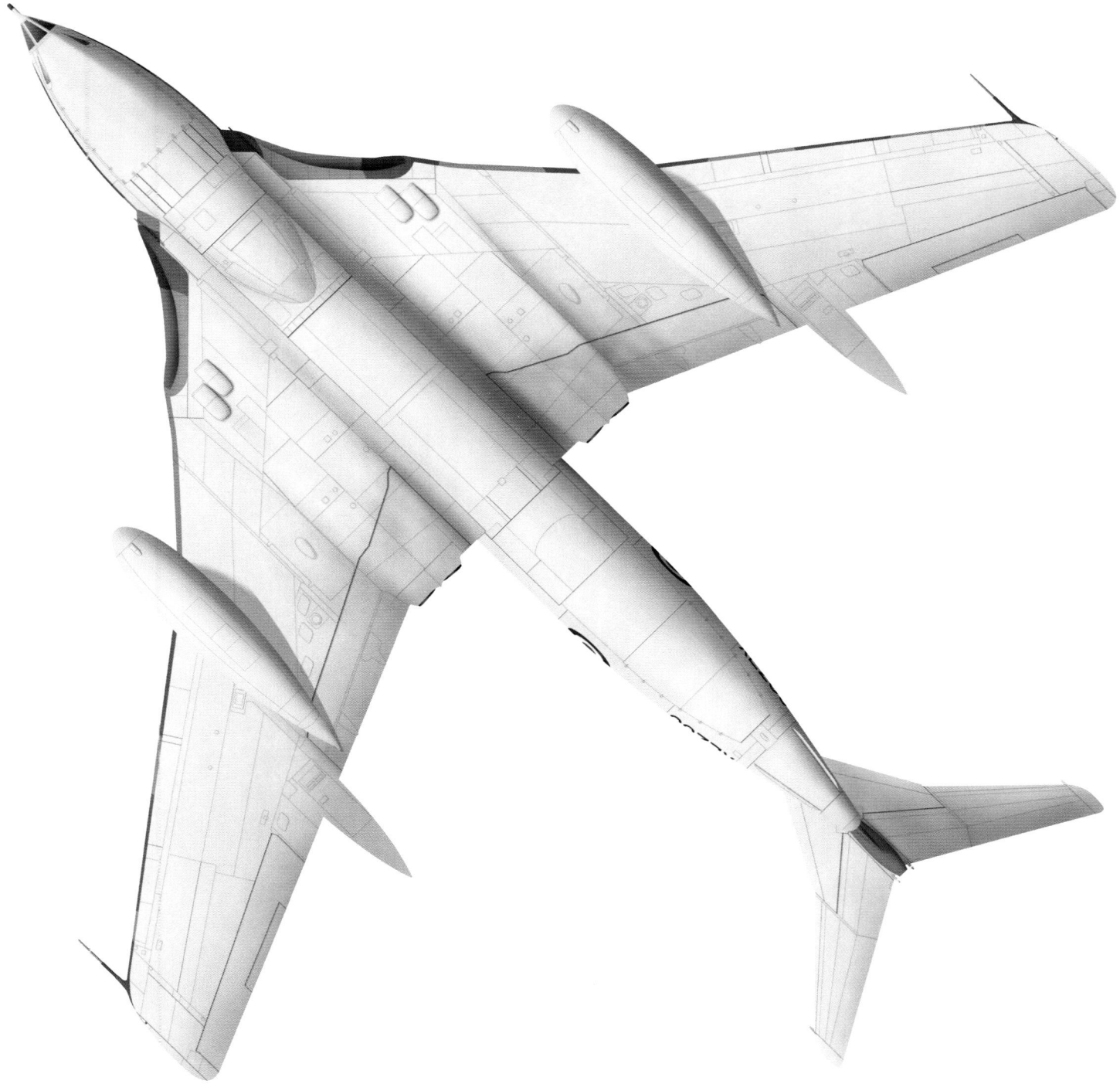

VICTOR PROTOTYPE WB771

The first prototype Victor originally wore an all over aluminium finish. It was repainted for the 1953 SBAC Show
in matt black with red trim on the fuselage and with the wings and tail remaining in aluminium.

Early trials showed some issues with the undercarriage system. The system stopping the wheels from spinning once they were retracted remained locked on one occasion — causing all 16 of the main wheel tyres to burst upon touchdown. Subsequent flights raised yet more issues but fitting cameras into the undercarriage bays enabled the engineers to quickly identify the problems and deal with them.

When it first flew, WB771 was finished in an overall aluminium and light grey finish but by the time of the SBAC show at Farnborough in 1953 it was wearing a very distinctive scheme of a black fuselage with a red cheat line running the length of the fuselage. The wings and tail retained the aluminium scheme.

Testing continued at a steady pace until the aircraft reached Mach 0.98 during one high-speed test, causing damage to the skin of the tail. To keep up the testing programme, WB771 was given the tail of the second prototype WB775 — which had been nearing completion — and flying continued smoothly until July 14, 1954, when it was called upon to undertake speed calibration tests at Cranfield.

At the controls was Ronald Ecclestone, Hazelden having a prior engagement that day. As he began a second pass of the airfield at speed the tailplane detached from the fin, causing the aircraft to descend at speed into the runway and disintegrate. None of the five crew survived.

Two months later, WB775 was ready to fly and testing resumed. Having completed the trials satisfactorily by the following March, it was delivered to A&AEE for testing by the RAF.

By this time an order had been placed for the B.1, which only had minor differences to the second prototype. The first production Victor, XA917, flew on February 1, 1956. Unlike subsequent B.1s, XA917 was destined for A&AEE where it remained until suffering a crash landing at Radlett in January 1964. Rolls-Royce's Avon engine

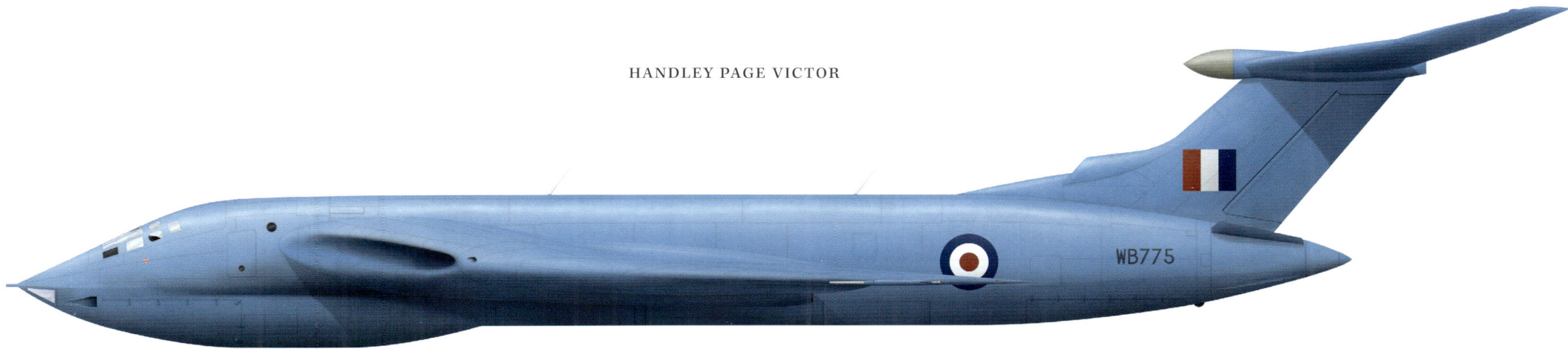

VICTOR PROTOTYPE WB775

The second prototype was painted in cerulean blue for the SBAC Show in 1955. Following trials, the aircraft was transferred to Proof & Experimental Establishment at Foulness in 1961.

had originally been proposed for the Victor but by the time the B.1 flew it was fitted with four Armstrong Siddeley Sapphire ASSa seven engines.

232 Operational Conversion Unit received XA931 on November 28, 1957. By now all Victors coming off the production line were finished in all over white but with standard national markings. It was not until later that the markings were toned down. 232 OCU, based at RAF Gaydon, already had several Valiants and these were allocated to B Squadron, making way for the Victors to form A Squadron.

By April 18 the following year, 10 Squadron was re-formed at RAF Cottesmore as the first operational Victor unit. This was slightly marred by the fact that there were only two aircraft on strength. A further six were delivered over the remainder of the year. During September, 10 Squadron was joined by 15 Squadron.

A great deal more had been learnt about the Victor by now and advances in electronic counter measures had been made — so an upgrade programme was initiated for the existing B.1s and those still in production were built as B.1As. The same ECM features were also fitted to the Vulcan fleet at this time. In-flight refuelling equipment was also fitted during the upgrade, though for some reason the probe was not added.

Units receiving fresh Victor deliveries now included 10 Squadron, 15 Squadron, 55 Squadron, 57 Squadron, 100 Squadron, 139 (Jamaica) Squadron, 214 Squadron, 543 Squadron and 232 OCU. The last of the 50 Mark 1s was delivered to the Honington Wing on March 3, 1961.

Once again advances in Soviet SAM technology forced the pace of aircraft design in the UK. The Victor B.2 was conceived in the belief that altitude would still allow bombers to evade missiles. Initially, it was proposed that the wing would be redesigned and six Sapphire ASSa.9 engines would be fitted, the engine being

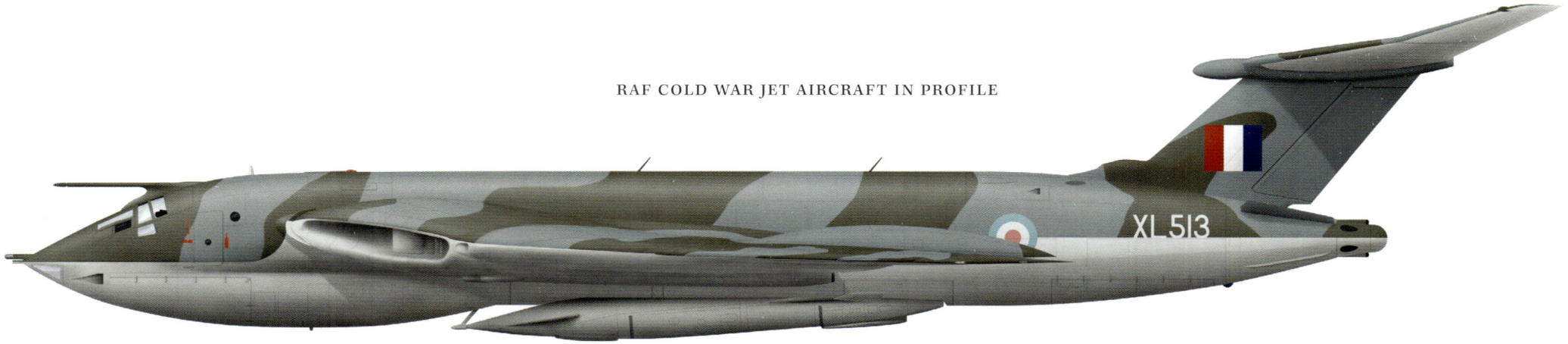

VICTOR B.2R XL513 139 SQUADRON

XL513 was used for camouflage trials, being the first Victor to wear such a scheme. Unlike all other camouflaged Victors, this aircraft was painted in NATO green (ref No. 409) and NATO grey (ref No. 407). It also retained the anti-flash roundel on the fuselage. The aircraft crashed on take-off at RAF Marham in 1976 due to a bird strike.

developed for an aerodynamically refined Javelin variant, known literally as the Thin Wing Javelin. With the cancellation of that project however, Handley Page had to opt for the Rolls-Royce Conway R.Co.11 to supply the extra power required.

The Victor had been designed to carry Britain's nuclear weapons: Blue Danube, Yellow Sun and later the Blue Steel stand-off missile, which due to the size and the low clearance of the Victor bomb bay made loading a challenge. Blue Steel also had reliability issues and was only seen as a short term nuclear deterrent. The Victor's days as a nuclear bomber were clearly numbered but its service life was extended with the retirement of the Valiant fleet and the need for a replacement tanker however.

Naturally, if the Valiant could do it so could the Victor and the type was converted. Trials began in 1964 when XA918 was adapted and tested for suitability. By May 1965, six had been successfully converted, two drogues fitted to the wings and a third in the fuselage. 55 Squadron became a combined bomber and tanker squadron at RAF Marham, this henceforth being the home of the Victor tanker fleet for many years.

As the Mk.Is came to the end of their flying hours they were replaced with the B.2s. By now the nuclear bomber concept was becoming obsolete and the role of nuclear deterrent was taken over by the Royal Navy's submarine fleet. During the Falklands War of 1982, the tanker fleet was required to undertake the longest mission involving refuelling ever contemplated and the planning required was extensive.

To stop the Argentines basing their fast jets at Port Stanley, the runway needed to be taken out of the equation. The Vulcan was chosen for the job but it would need to make an 8000 mile journey and for this 11 tankers were required. Several of the Victors used were just to refuel other Victors and give them the range to refuel the Vulcans. A total of five raids were flown, two more were planned but aborted, one due to weather and the other due to a fault with the tankers.

Victors were also involved in Operation Granby and Desert Storm during 1990/1991 when 10 Victors were painted in a hemp scheme and sent to the Gulf region. The original plan was only to support RAF Jaguars and Tornado F.3s, VC10s refuelling the Tornado GR.1s. However, they ended up refuelling Canadian, French, USN and USAF aircraft as well.

Only two years later, on October 15, 1993, the last Victor unit, 55 Squadron, was disbanded and the aircraft dispersed to museums or scrapped.

The Victor was a highly flexible aircraft, which explains its remarkable longevity. Adapting it to new roles saved money and at one stage it was even considered as a troop transporter — with transport pods fitted under the wings and a third in the bomb bay. Perhaps fortunately for the troops, this concept never made it off the drawing board.

Like so many other Cold War aircraft, several examples are preserved and two are still regularly taxied, XL231 Lusty Lindy at the Yorkshire Air Museum, Elvington, and XM715 Teasin' Tina at Bruntingthorpe, the latter having made the last unofficial flight of a Victor when a miscommunication led to an inadvertent short hop during a high-speed run on May 3, 2009.

Handley Page Victor

VARIANT	LENGTH	SPAN	HEIGHT	ENGINE
HP.80	111FT 7IN/34.01M	110FT/33.53M	26FT 10.5IN	4 X SAPPHIRE 101
B.1	114FT 11IN/35.05M	110FT/33.53M	28FT 1.5IN/8.57M	4 X SAPPHIRE SA.7
B.1A	114FT 11IN/35.05M	110FT/33.53M	28FT 1.5IN/8.57M	4 X SAPPHIRE SA.7
K.1	114FT 11IN/35.05M	110FT/33.53M	28FT 1.5IN/8.57M	4 X SAPPHIRE SA.7
B.2	114FT 11IN/35.05M	120FT/36.58M	28FT 1.5IN/8.57M	4 X CONWAY RCO.11
B.2RS	114FT 11IN/35.05M	120FT/36.58M	28FT 1.5IN/8.57M	4 X CONWAY RCO.11
B(SR).2	114FT 11IN/35.05M	120FT/36.58M	28FT 1.5IN/8.57M	4 X CONWAY RCO.11
K.2	114FT 11IN/35.05M	117FT/35.66M	28FT 1.5IN/8.57M	4 X CONWAY RCO.11

VICTOR K.2 XH669

XH669, piloted by Flt Lt Steve Biglands, was originally intended to fly the longest section in support of the Vulcan during the first Black Buck mission. However, the aircraft's probe broke during refuelling and XL189 flown by Sqn Ldr Bob Tuxford had to fly the final leg.

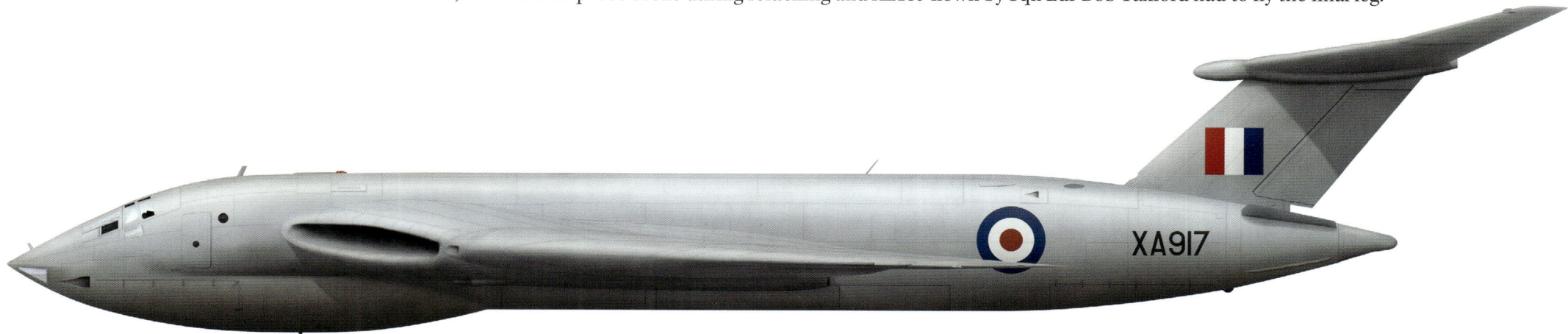

VICTOR B.1 XA917 A&AEE

All the early Victors including XA917, the first production aircraft, were painted initially in all over aluminium with standard RAF markings and serial.

VICTOR K.2 XL161 55 SQUADRON

Seen here in typical K.2 tanker configuration with tanks and high visibility markings on the refuelling pods and wings, XL161 was transferred to RAF Lyneham and was used as a ground trainer from 1993 to 1995.

VICTOR K.2 XL189 57 SQUADRON

Having been upgraded to B.2R standard, XL189 was then converted to a tanker in 1970 and served with 232 OCU, 55 & 57 squadrons. In 1986 it became a ground trainer at RAF Waddington.

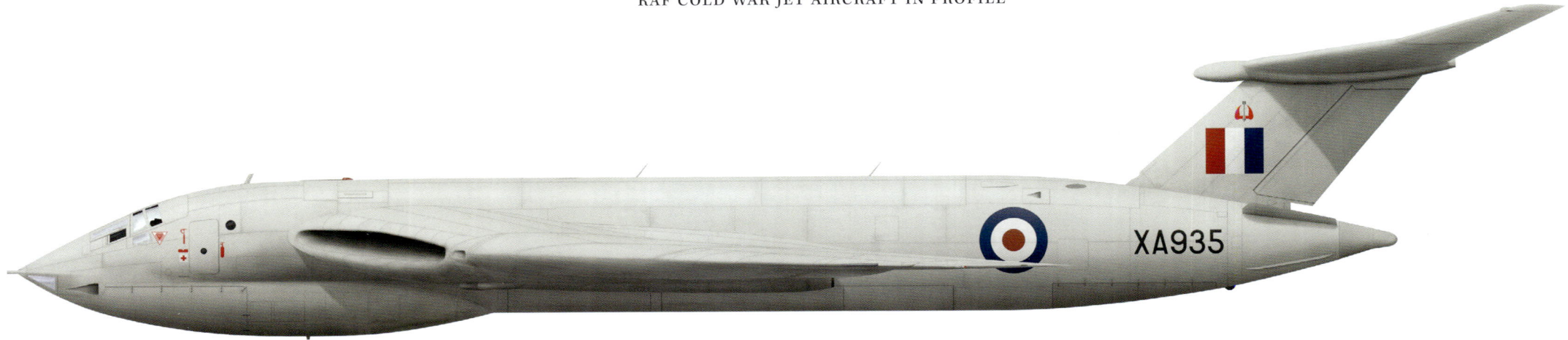

VICTOR B.1 XA935 10 SQUADRON

Painted in Anti Flash White but retaining the high visibility markings, XA935 is typical of the original B.1 scheme worn by the Victors. The aircraft also served with 15 Sqn and 232 OCU. It was put in storage in June 1964 and officially struck off charge in 1974.

VICTOR K.2 XL232

XL232 had a varied career, serving first as a B.2, then being converted to B.2R and eventually to a K.2. Having served with most of Victor units it was eventually lost during a ground fire following an engine explosion at RAF Marham in 1982

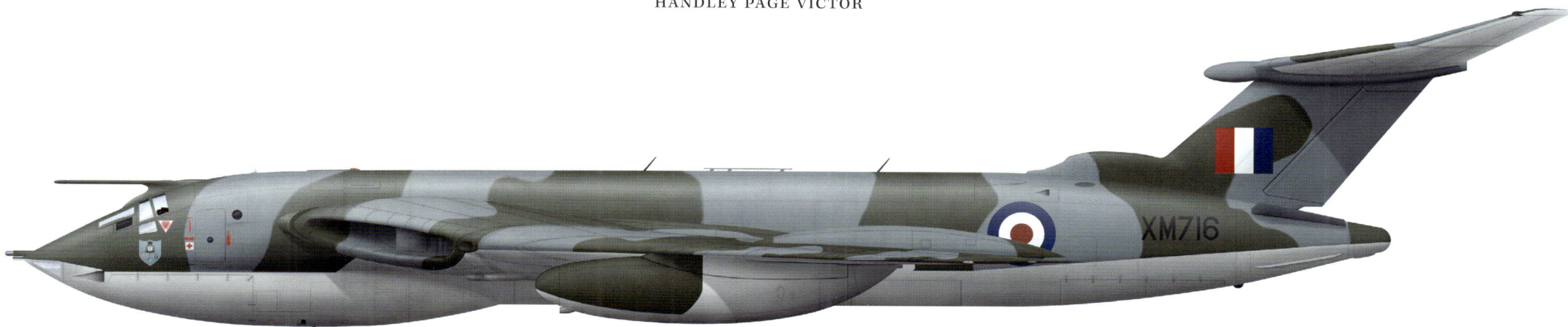

VICTOR SR.2 XM716 139 SQUADRON

Converted into an SR.2 in 1964, XM716 served with 543 Sqn. The tail broke off in mid-air on June 29, 1966, and the aircraft was lost with all crew

VICTOR K.2 XL231 57 SQUADRON

Entering service as a B.2 with 139 Sqn in 1962, the aircraft saw action with Operation Granby and
was eventually acquired by Yorkshire Air Museum where it is currently preserved.

Victor B.1

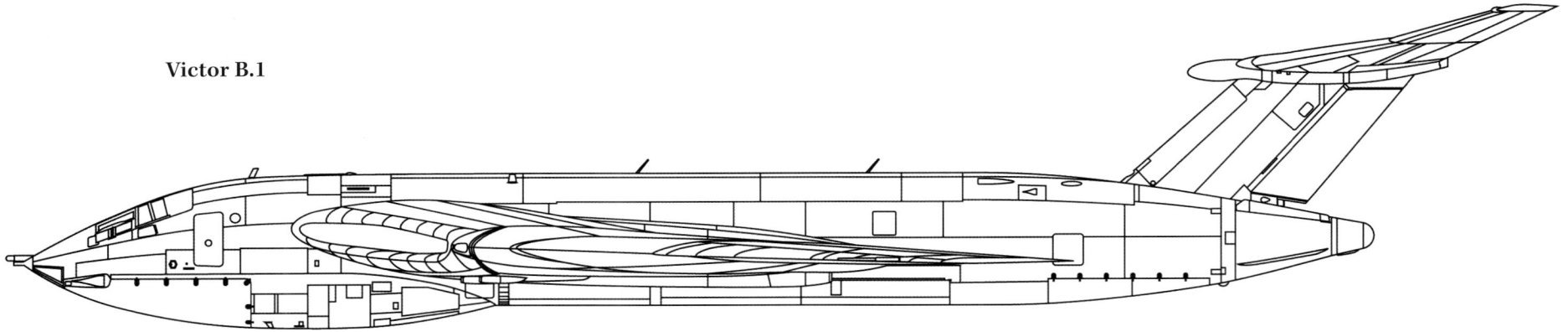

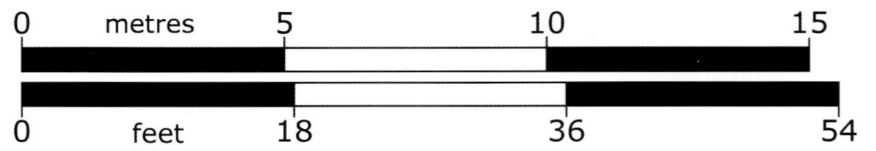

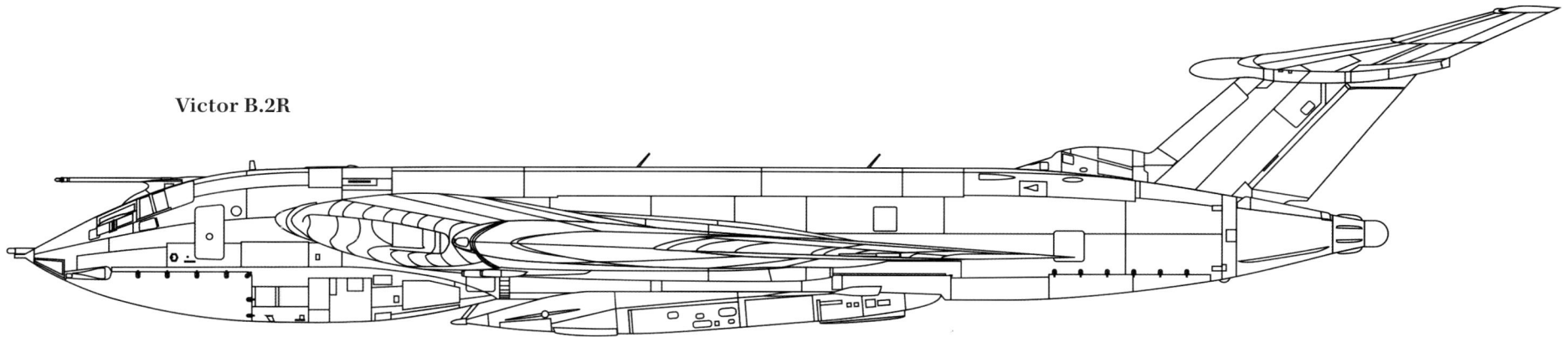

Victor B.2R

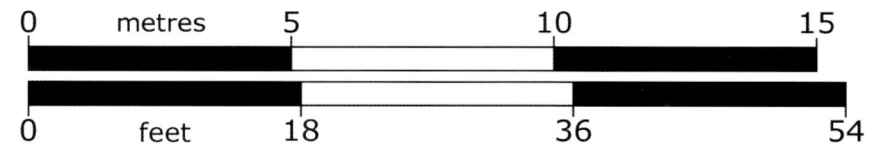

| 0 | metres | 5 | 10 | 15 |

| 0 | feet | 18 | 36 | 54 |

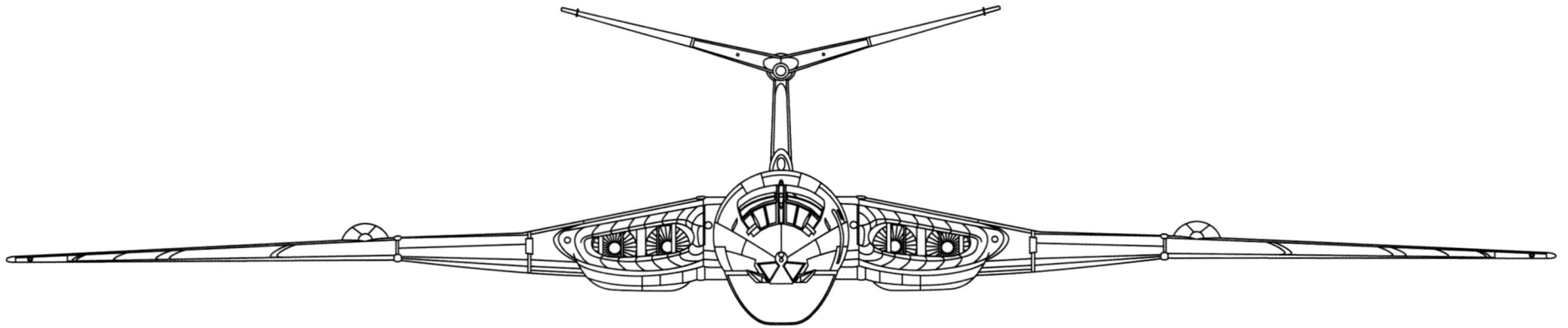

Victor B.1 front

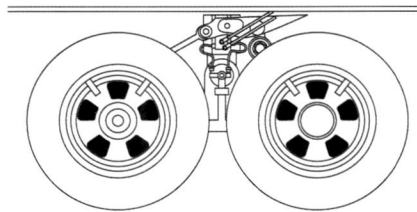

Main wheel

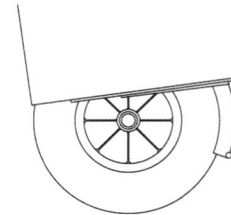

Nose wheel

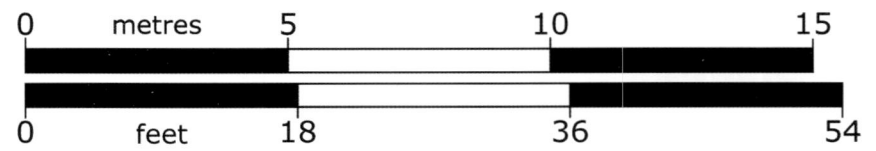

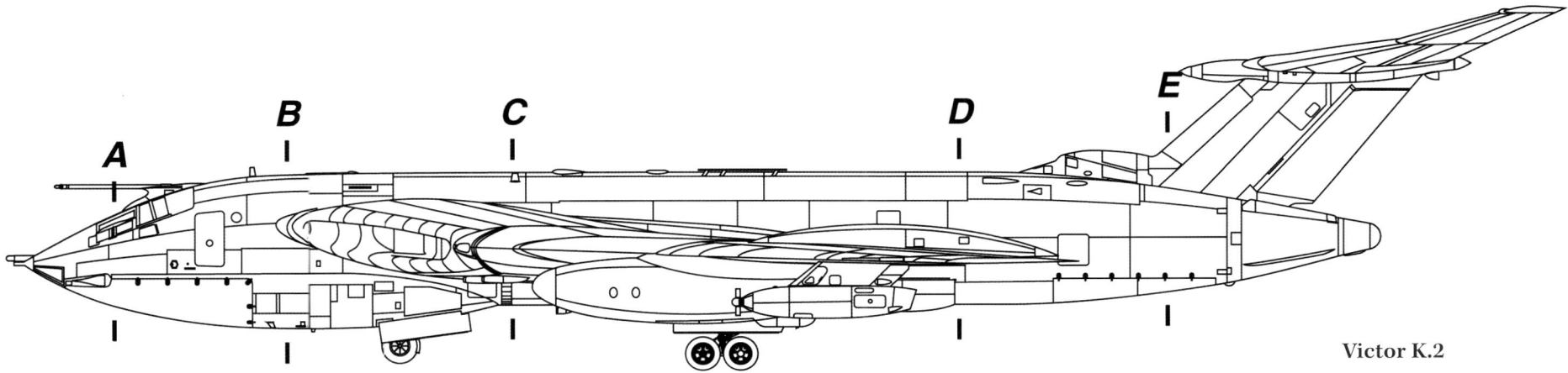

Victor K.2

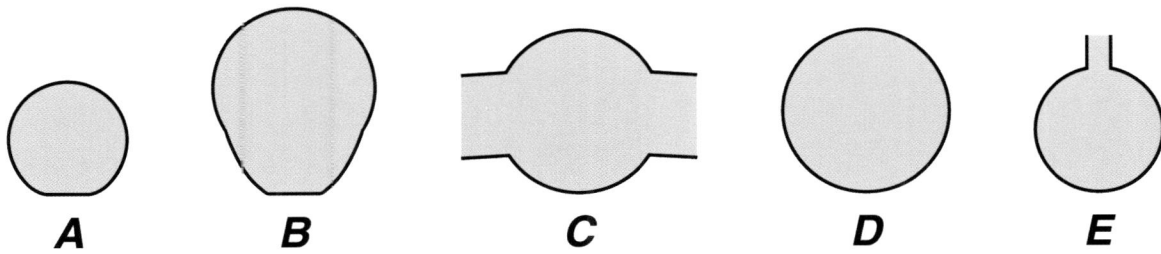

A   B   C   D   E

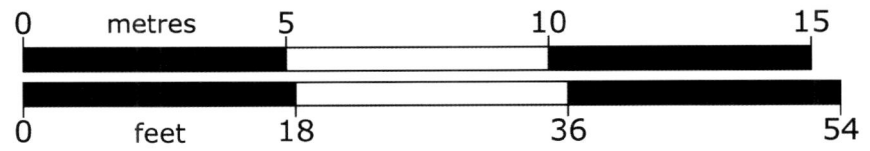

| 0 | metres | 5 | | 10 | | 15 |
| 0 | feet | 18 | | 36 | | 54 |

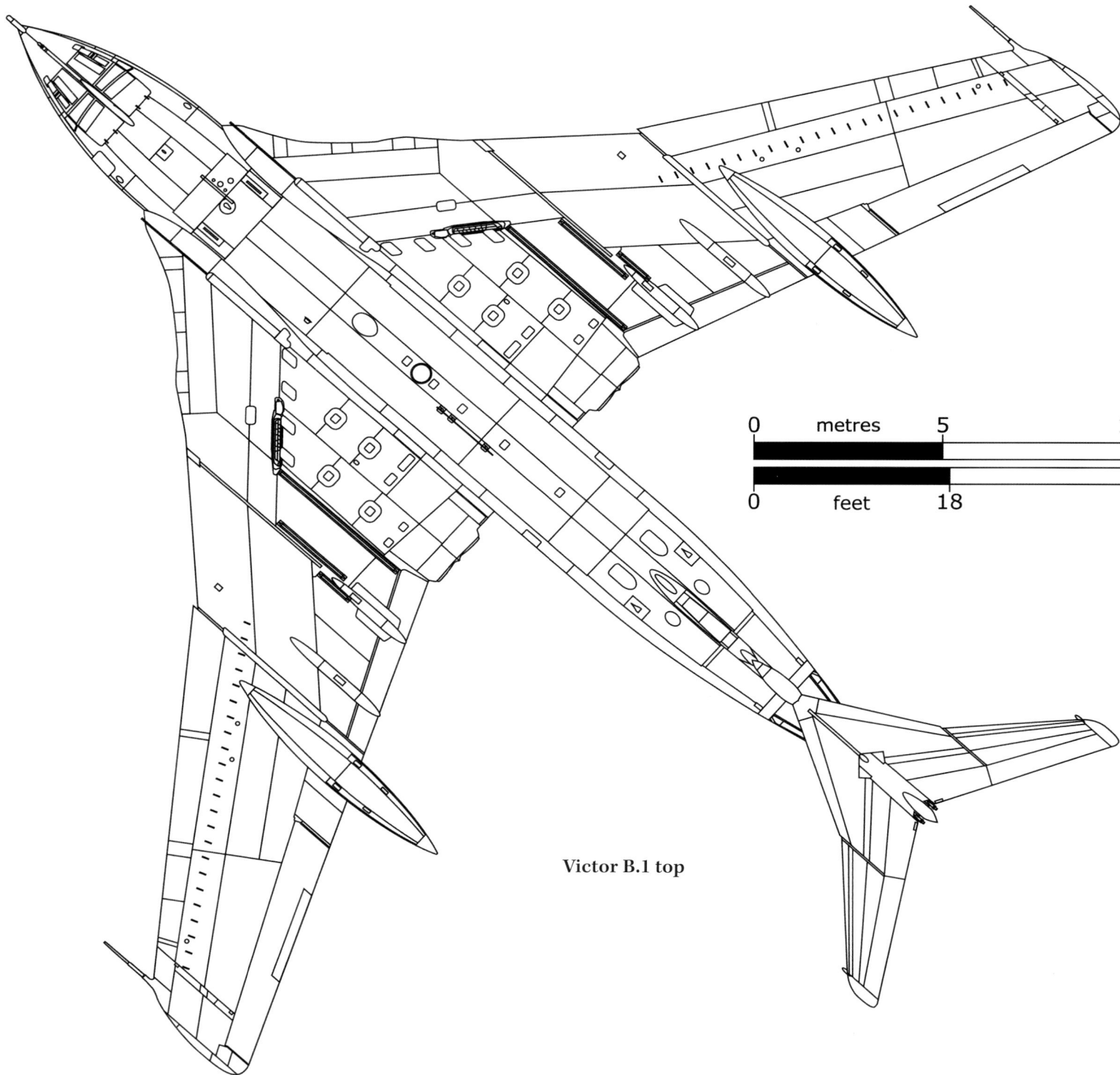

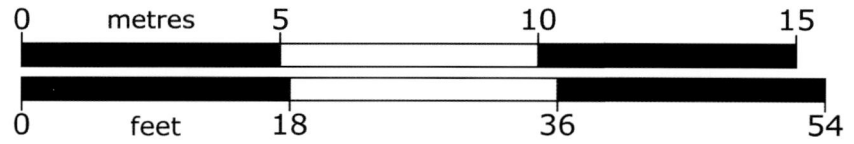

Victor B.1 top

| 0 | metres | 5 | 10 | 15 |

| 0 | feet | 18 | 36 | 54 |

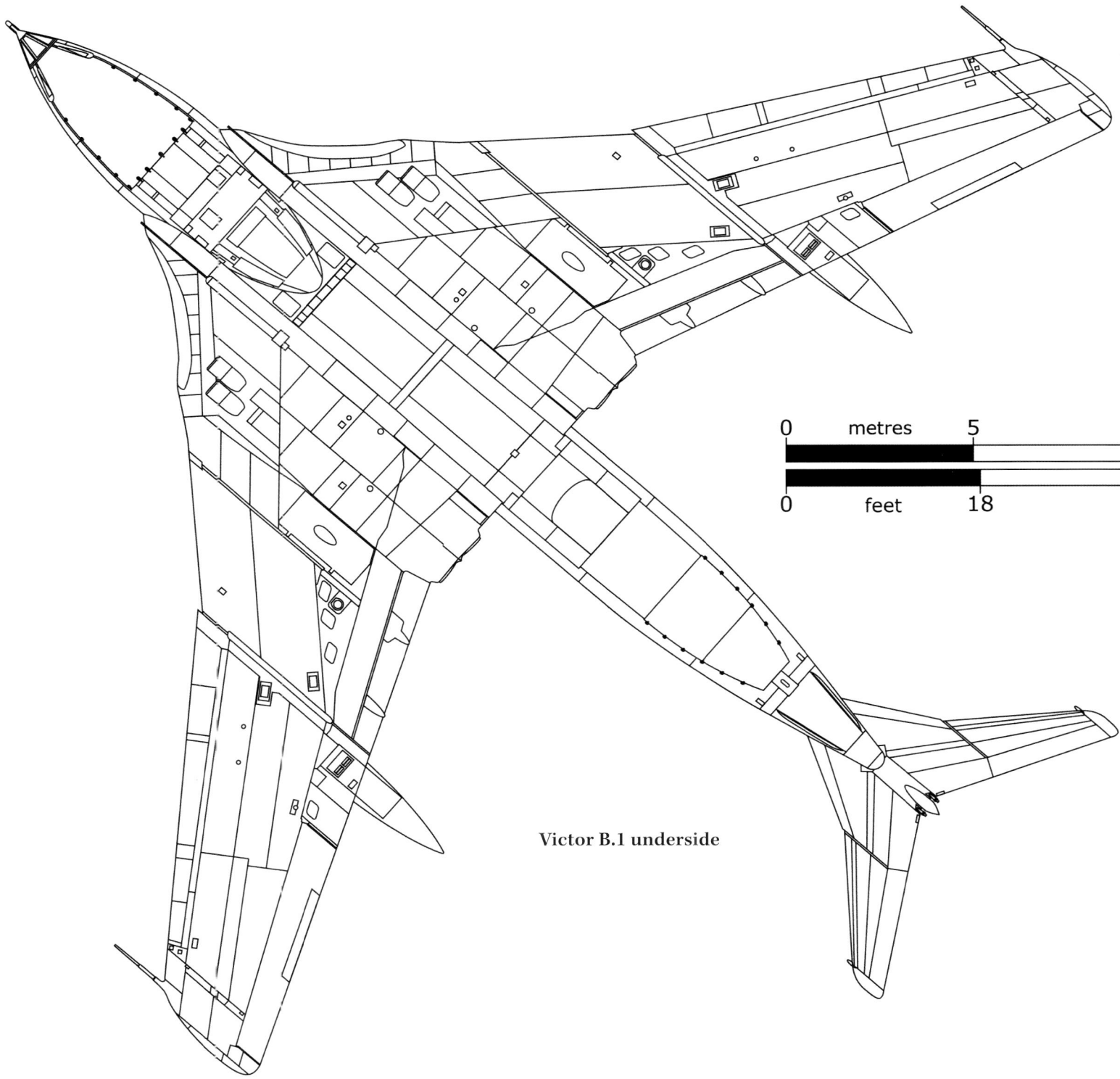

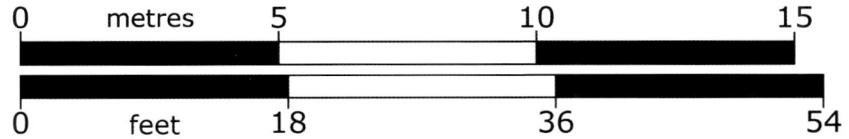

Victor B.1 underside

| 0 | metres | 5 | 10 | 15 |

| 0 | feet | 18 | 36 | 54 |

AVRO VULCAN

The triangular behemoth that is the Avro Vulcan flew for the last time 63 years after it first took to the skies. During that time it became a symbol of the cold war — yet it only saw action bombing a tiny airfield on an island in the South Atlantic during the twilight years of its military service. Despite being considerably larger and more powerful than the Avro Lancaster, only 11 years separated their first flights. The Vulcan represented a quantum leap in bombers and it never failed to impress when seen in flight.

I n working out their answer to Specification B.35/46, Roy Chadwick and the design team at Avro were already aware of the research conducted by Professor Alexander Lippisch into delta wing designs in Germany during the Second World War and it was this which influenced even the early sketches for the Avro 698.

With no experience of delta wing aircraft and the 698 being such a massive undertaking, one-third scale versions were constructed to explore flight characteristics under the 707 programme.

The information gathered from the 707s and aerodynamic testing at RAE Farnborough led to extensive alterations to the 698 and

a three-month delay to construction. The Valiant had first flown in 1951 but there was a race between Handley Page and Avro to see who could get their bomber airborne first, the prototype Valiant having been transported to Boscombe Down for reassembly in anticipation of flight testing. At this stage both companies believed that only one of the two bombers would enter service — so there was considerable pressure within Avro to get the prototype into the air.

With the parts having been transported from the factory in Manchester to nearby Woodford and rapidly assembled, it was on August 30, 1952, that after one high-speed taxi Roly Falk opened

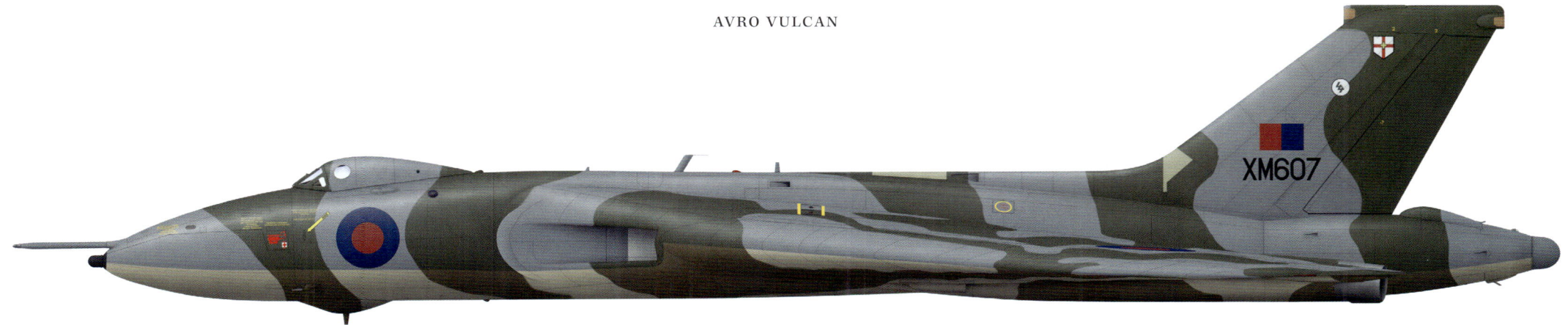

VULCAN B.2 XM607 44 SQUADRON

During the Red Flag '77 exercises at Nellis AFB, Nevada, XM607 had an experimental desert camouflage applied
of light stone and dark earth, the upper surfaces were dark green and medium sea grey. XM607 went on to be used
in the first of the Black Buck missions to bomb the runway at Port Stanley during the Falklands War.

up the four Rolls-Royce Avon RA.3s and lifted VX770 off for the first time. The test flight was slightly marred by a warning light that indicated the undercarriage had failed to retract, however. A hastily scrambled Vampire and Avro 707 performed a quick visual inspection and confirmed that it had indeed retracted — but they did discover that the rear undercarriage fairings had become detached due to wing flex, which had not been anticipated.

Faulk later claimed that the massive aircraft was easier to handle than an Avro Anson. VX770 was subsequently upgraded to the more powerful Armstrong Siddeley Saphire ASSs.6, the Avons only being an underpowered interim engine.

Trials showed that the straight wing leading edge caused buffeting at high altitude, which would result in a lack of accuracy during bombing runs. Therefore a kink in the leading edge

was introduced to negate the issue.

The Vulcan B.1 formally entered service when XA895 and XA898, the seventh and 10th production Vulcans, were delivered to 230 OCU in January 1957. Like the rest of the first 15, they had the Olympus 101 powerplant. By May 1957, 83 Squadron had formed and had begun receiving the B.1. XA904, the 16th off the line, was the first with the more powerful Olympus 104.

The early B.1s, used for various trials, had been finished in all over aluminium but those entering service were painted in high gloss anti-flash white. The B.1a saw minor changes to the standard Vulcan including the facility for in-flight refuelling, though the probes were not fitted at the time. The ECM equipment designed primarily for the B.2 was introduced and included an enlarged tail cone to accommodate it.

VULCAN B.1 XA895 230 OCU

One of the first production batch of Vulcan B.1s, XA895 was delivered in July 1956 to 230 OCU and was finished in all over aluminium.
It was later converted to B.1A configuration but following ECM trials with the A&AEE it was scrapped in September 1968.

While the B.1 was entering service, the design team turned their attention to improving the Vulcan further. This phase of development would see yet another wing form created. Known as the Phase 2 wing, it was introduced to eliminate the buffeting expected at high-altitude/high-speed with the introduction of the more powerful Olympus 201 and later 301 engines. These engines also necessitated a redesigned intake to allow for the higher airflow required. A range of modifications were also made in other areas, including the undercarriage, flying controls and new electronic counter-measures which required a redesigned tail.

83 Squadron received the first B.2 on December 23, 1960. The Vulcan was initially designed as a nuclear deterrent but the B.2 was the only type to be used in a conflict — during the Falklands War when flights of almost 6800 nautical miles were flown to attack the island.

The first of the five successful missions was flown by XM607 on the night of April 30/May 1 and hit the runway at Port Stanley. Due to the pressure placed on the Victor tanker fleet during the Falklands War, additional aircraft were needed. An interim solution was to convert six Vulcans to tankers. XM603 was used as a test frame for the tanker conversion programme at Woodford, and following this XH558, XH560, XH561, XJ825, XL445 and XM571 were selected for conversion.

The K.2 Vulcan could carry a total of 96,500lb of fuel. The hose drogue unit was housed in the tail but the ECM cone was insufficient so an inelegant 'dog box' was fitted underneath the rear fuselage to accommodate the excess equipment.

These six tankers served with 50 Squadron until the VC10s became fully operational and the Vulcan was no longer required. The squadron was disbanded in March 1984 and the Vulcan was officially retired from operational service.

This was not the end of the Vulcan's time with the RAF however – a pair being retained by the Vulcan Display Flight which continued to display the type until 1992. XL426 was first used for the display and later replaced by XH558, which by this time had been converted back to standard B.2 configuration. Following budget cuts even XH558 was retired by the RAF, but it was kept in flying condition and entered private ownership where it returned to flight and dominated air shows across the UK between 2007 and 2015.

This certainly helped keep the iconic delta wing bomber in the public eye and along with the Lightning it is generally regarded as one of the most impressive aircraft ever produced by the British aviation industry. Despite only 136 being built, the Vulcan left a lasting impression on all who saw and heard one fly.

Avro Vulcan

VARIANT	LENGTH	SPAN	HEIGHT	ENGINE
B.1	97FT 1IN/29.58M	99FT/30.17M	26FT 6IN/29.08M	4 X OLYMPUS 101
B.1A	99FT 11IN/30.45M	99FT/30.17M	26FT 6IN/29.08M	4 X OLYMPUS 101
B.2	99FT 11IN/30.45M	111FT/33.83M	27FT 2IN/8.28M	4 X OLYMPUS 201 OR 301
SR.2	99FT 11IN/30.45M	111FT/33.83M	27FT 2IN/8.28M	4 X OLYMPUS 201 OR 301
K.2	99FT 11IN/30.45M	111FT/33.83M	27FT 2IN/8.28M	4 X OLYMPUS 201 OR 301

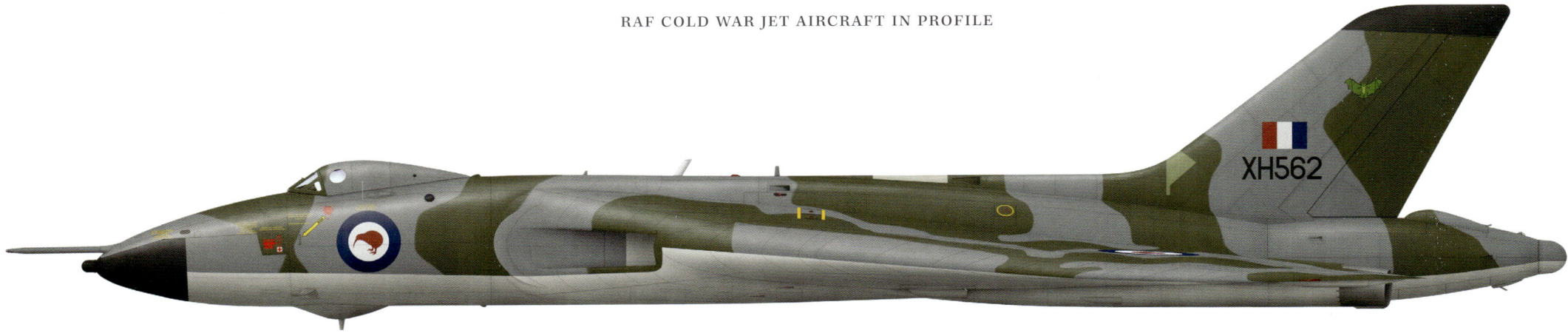

VULCAN B.2 XH562

While on a tour of New Zealand in 1972, XH562 was zapped at Ohakea. There is also a 75 Squadron RNZAF
badge on the nosewheel door. It ended up on the firedump at Catterick in 1982 and was finally scrapped
in 1984. Painted in medium sea grey and dark green with light aircraft grey underside.

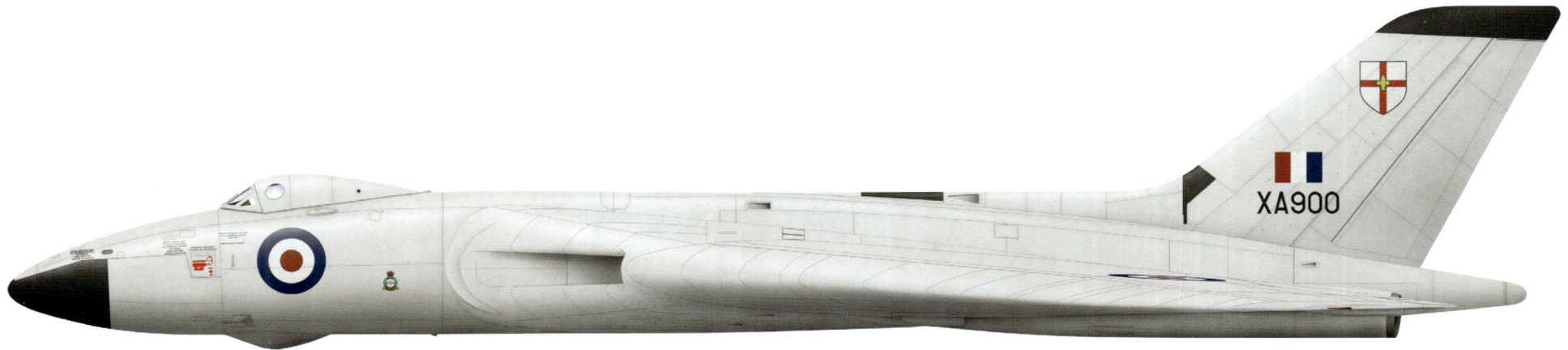

VULCAN B.1 XA900 230 OCU

Finished in all over White with standard roundels, XA900 served with 230 OCU and 11
Squadron. It was displayed at Cosford as last B.1 until it was scrapped in 1986.

VULCAN B.2 XJ781 12 SQUADRON

This aircraft was delivered to 83 Squadron in February 1961 and transferred to 12 Squadron the following year. While with Akrotiri Wing, XJ781 made a forced landing due to an undercarriage malfunction at Shiraz, Iran on May 23, 1973. It was scrapped by Iran.

VULCAN B.2 XL317 617 SQUADRON

Painted in all over gloss white with pale markings and squadron lightning bolts on the tail, XL317 was photographed carrying a Blue Steel training missile in 1963. The missile appears to be painted in PRU blue.

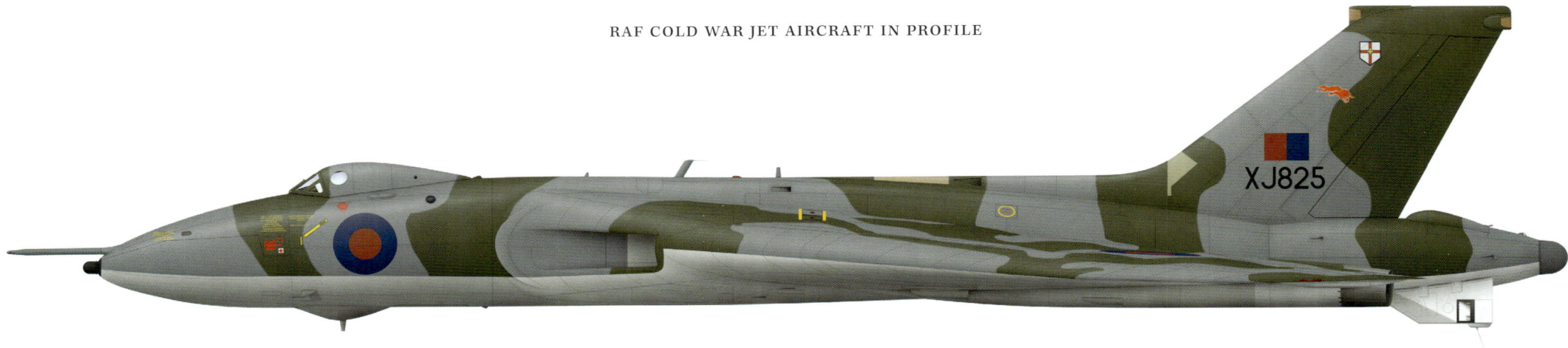

VULCAN K.2 XJ825 50 SQUADRON

Originally delivered to the RAF in July 1961, this aircraft was one of six allocated to tanker duties. It was converted in May 1982, struck off charge in 1984 and scrapped in 1992. It is shown here painted in medium sea grey and dark green upper surfaces, with light aircraft grey and white panels to the rear. There are high visibility tanker markings on the underside.

VULCAN B.2 XH558

As the first B.2 to enter service, XH558 was delivered to the RAF on August 1, 1960, and continued to fly for 55 years – up to October 28, 2015. Having been converted to K.2 configuration in 1982, two years later it was converted back and became the RAF display Vulcan. Once retired it was restored and displayed by the Vulcan to the Sky Trust. Painted in all over gloss dark green and dark sea grey.

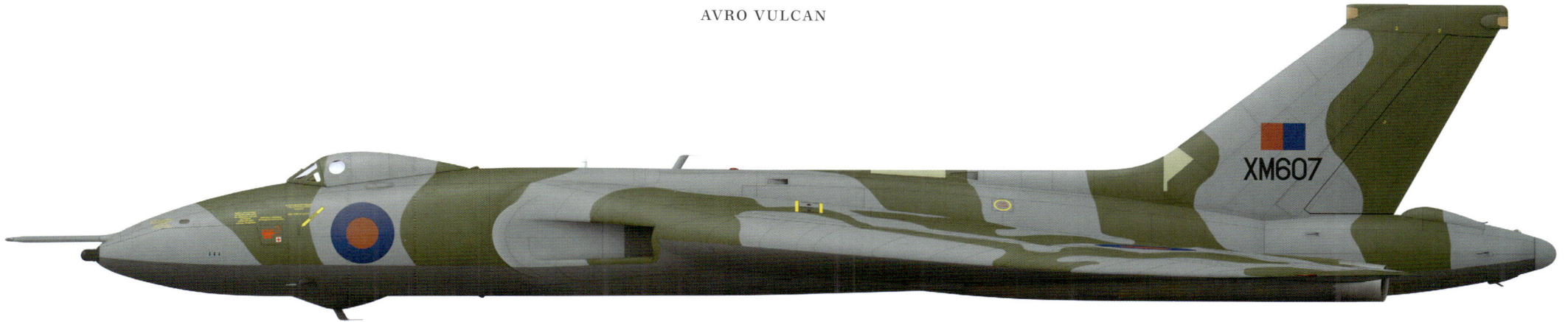

VULCAN B.2 XM607 44 SQUADRON

XM607 as it appear during the first of the Black Buck missions.

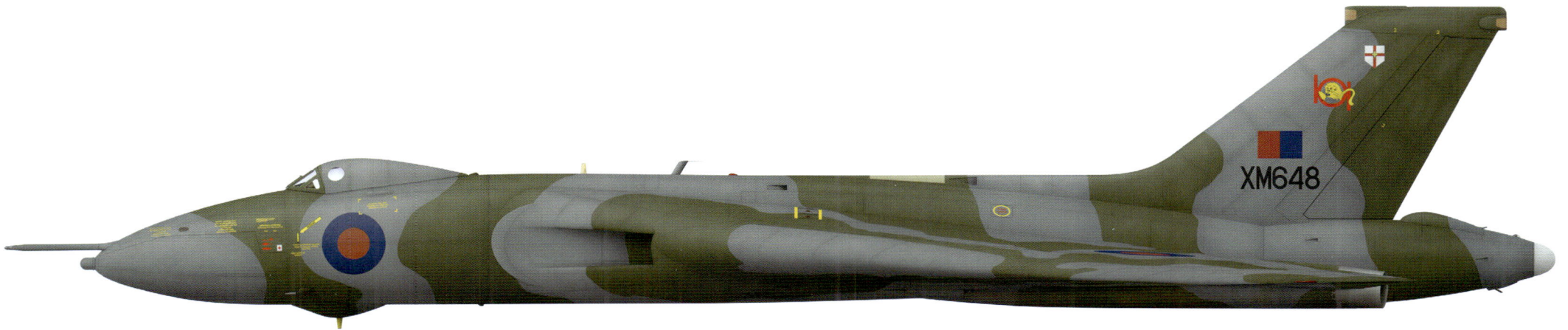

VULCAN B.2 XM648 101 SQUADRON

101 Squadron flew from Waddington to the USA for a series of exercises during the spring of
1982. This included XM648, which was based at McGuire AFB at the end of May.

VULCAN B.2 XL446 617 SQUADRON

During exercises in the US in 1979, XL446 received the attention of Strategic Air Command ground crew who applied the SAC shield to the nose. This was left in place for the Abingdon air show in September 1979.

VULCAN B.2 XM575

Delivered to 617 Squadron on May 22, 1963, XM575 participated in the final public Quick Reaction Alert display at RAF Finningley on September 19, 1981. It was later prepared for use during the Black Buck missions but never took part. XM575 was ferried to East Midlands Aeropark, Castle Donington on January 28, 1983, where it remains on display.

Vulcan K.2

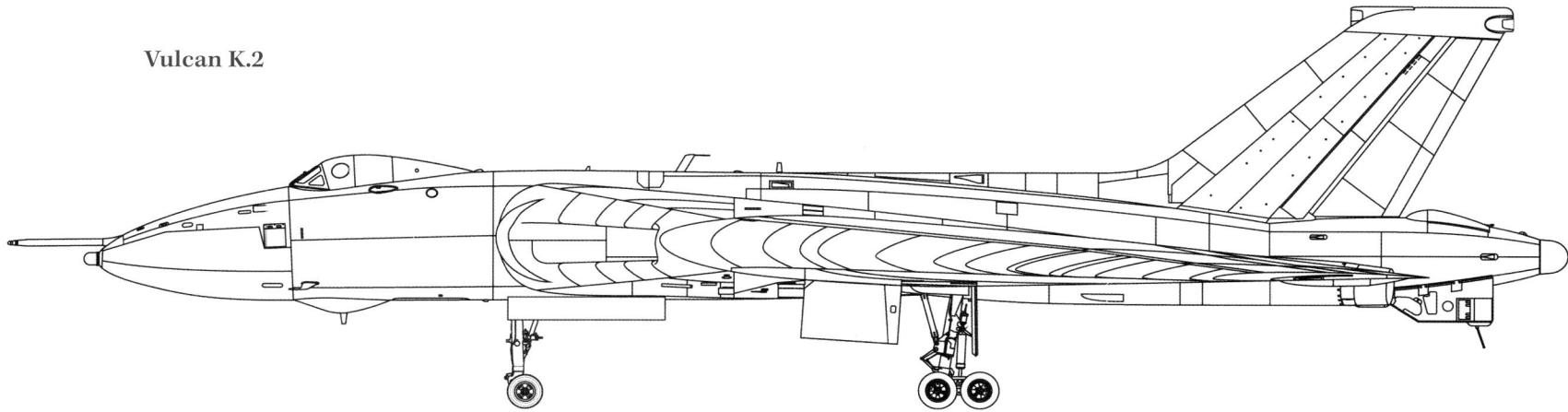

Vulcan B.1

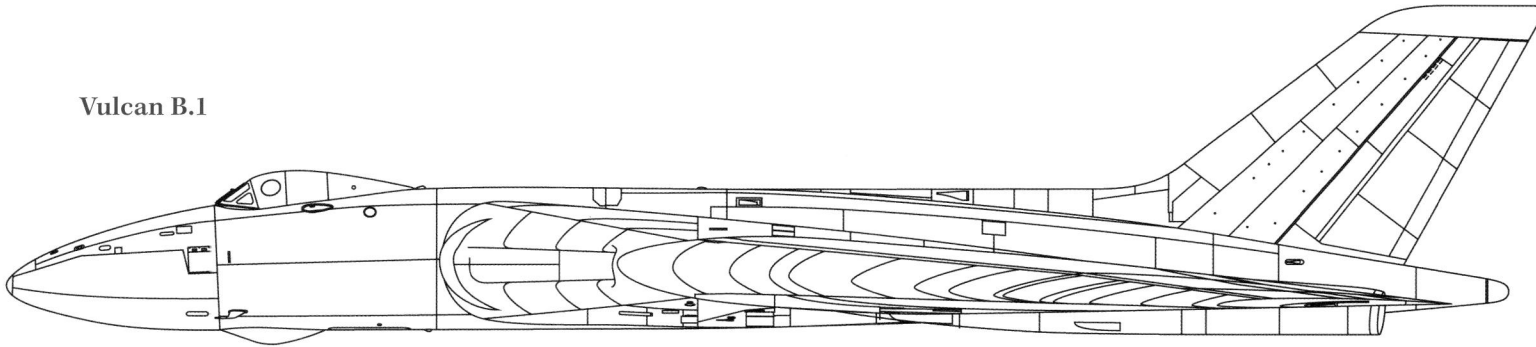

Blue Steel

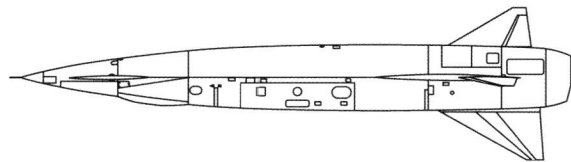

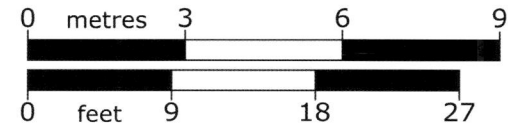

0 metres 3 6 9

0 feet 9 18 27

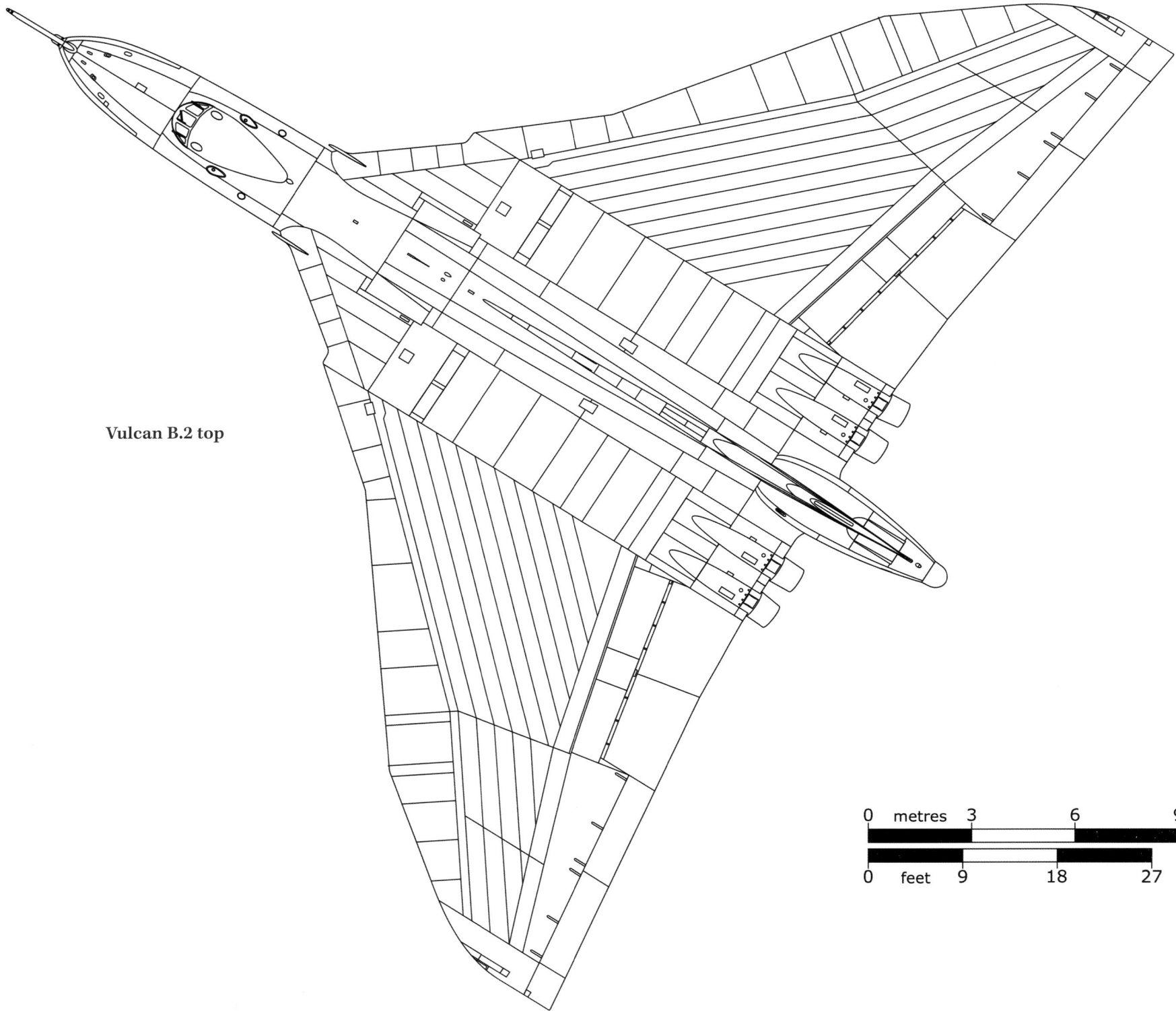

Vulcan B.2 top

0 metres 3   6   9

0 feet 9   18   27

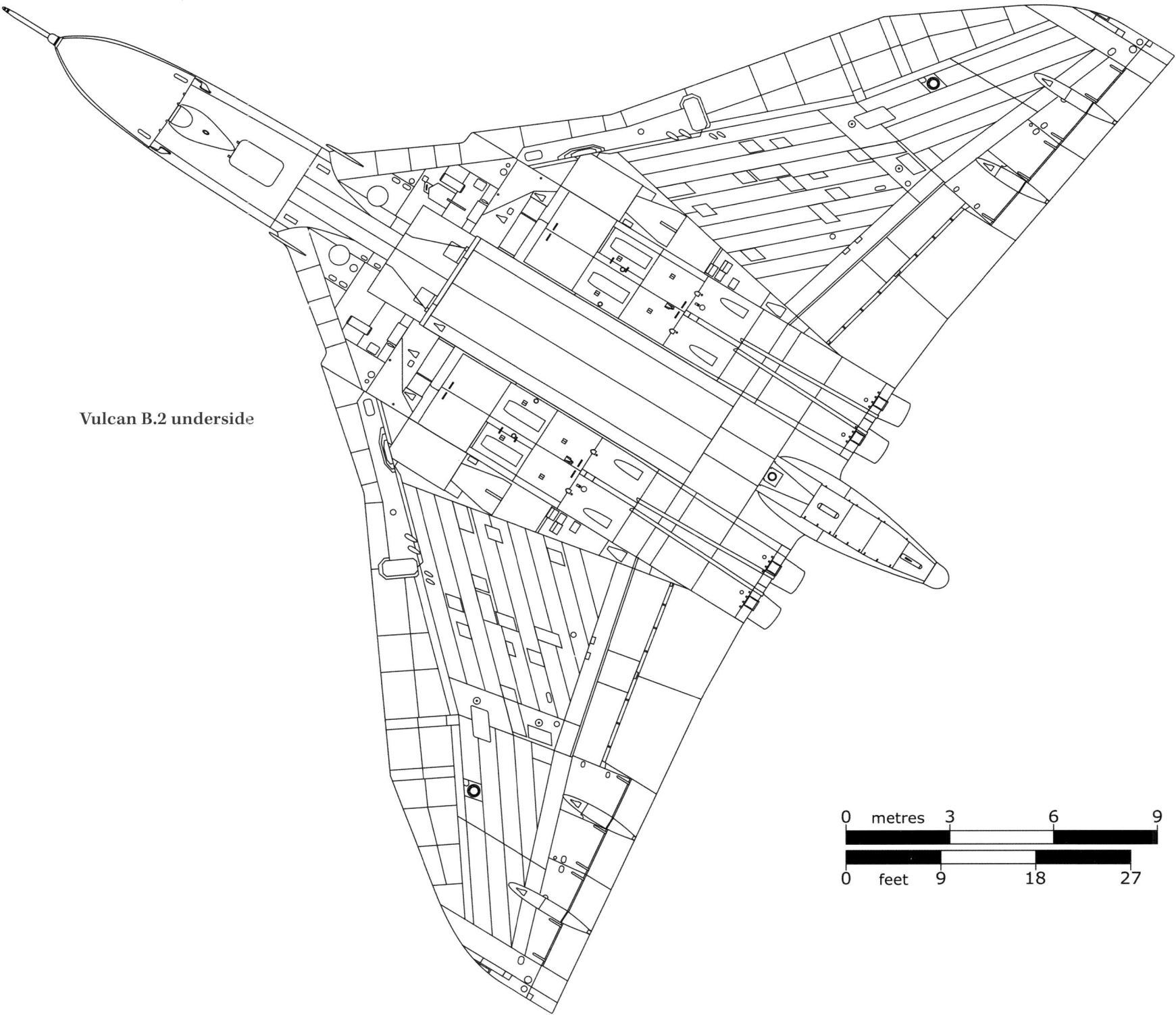

Vulcan B.2 underside

0 metres 3 6 9

0 feet 9 18 27

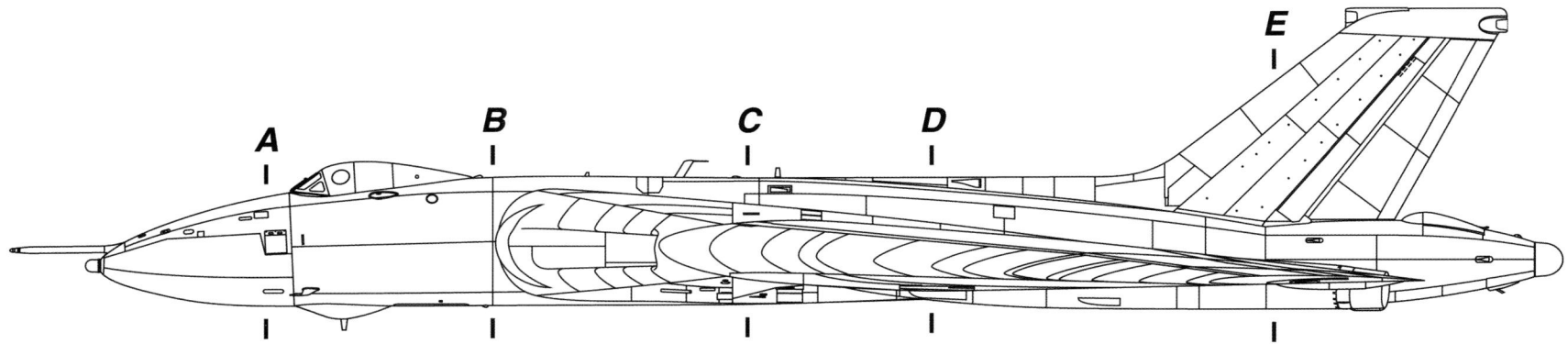

A   B   C   D   E

Vulcan B.2

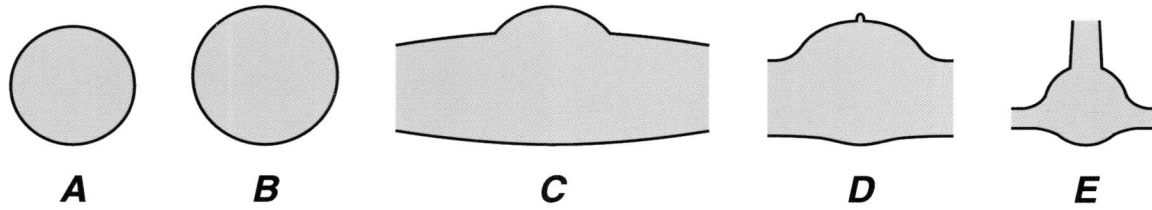

A   B   C   D   E

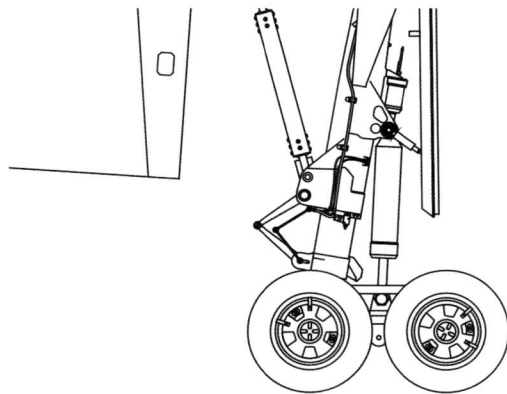

Main wheels

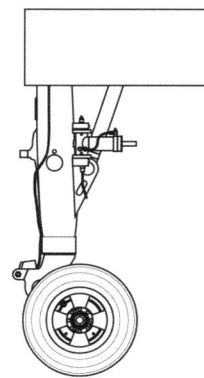

Nose wheel

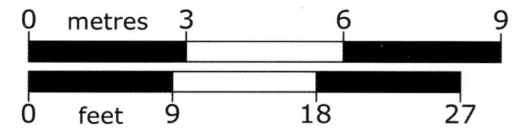

0   metres   3   6   9

0   feet   9   18   27

ENGLISH ELECTRIC LIGHTNING

The English Electric Lightning is perhaps the most iconic of all the British built jet fighters. Schoolboys dreamed of strapping in and experiencing the 16,000lb of thrust generated by two Rolls-Royce Avon engines while accelerating to Mach 2. The type entered service in 1959 and remained operational for nearly three decades.

The Lightning's origins can be traced back to 1948 and specification ER.103, which required a research aircraft that could fly at a minimum of Mach 1.4. This reputedly came about through lobbying by W. E. W. 'Teddy' Petter, head of the design team at English Electric and already responsible for the Canberra.

The outcome of this programme was the Fairey Delta 2 and the English Electric P.1. As a result of the proposal put forward by English Electric, the Air Ministry issued Specification F.23/49 which called for further development of the EECo P.1.

The original design of the P.1 included finlets fitted to the tips of the tail rather than a single fin due to concerns that a jettisoned canopy might destroy control surfaces, leading to a loss of stability and problems with ejection. This was soon rejected in favour of the more conventional tail fin. Other features were highly swept wings and vertically stacked twin engines, along with the large single intake in the nose.

Petter left for Folland in 1950 and responsibility for the project was passed to Freddie Page. Construction of the prototype, WG760, was completed and the P.1A was transported by road to Boscombe Down where it first flew on August 4, 1954, with Wg Cdr Roland Beamont at the controls.

During this flight it reached Mach 0.85. It became the first British-built aircraft to exceed Mach 1 in level flight a week later during only its third test flight. It was soon identified that the aircraft had

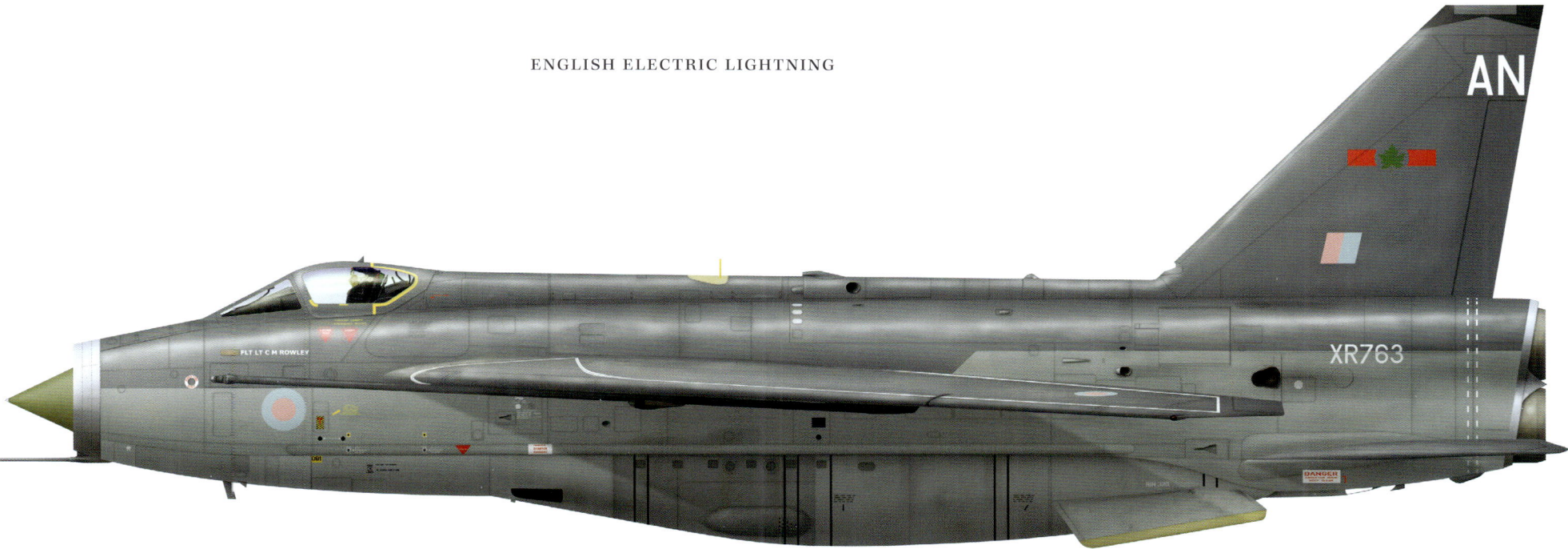

LIGHTNING F.6 XR763 5 SQUADRON

XR763 wears dark sea grey and medium sea grey on its upper surfaces with light aircraft grey undersides. The aircraft received damage during a live firing exercise and was written off at Akrotiri, Cyprus, on July 1, 1987. The pilot ejected safely.

an issue with fuel consumption however, exacerbated by small fuel tanks. To rectify this, a belly tank was added to the second P.1, WG763. The issue was never fully resolved and even in service a Lightning could burn through all of its fuel in under 18 minutes.

A further 21 production P.1s were built and used for trials, including some being sent to the first RAF Lightning unit – the Air Fighting Development Squadron at RAF Coltishall, Norfolk, where extensive testing was undertaken as the RAF prepared to declare the Lightning fit for service.

The F.1 was very similar to the production P.1B, having the Avon

200R fitted along with two 30mm Aden cannon. Externally it was virtually identical in appearance, apart from a slight increase in surface area of the tail. The belly tank now sported small fins too, a feature retained on all future Lightnings.

74 Squadron was the first to convert to the Lightning F.1 from the Hawker Hunter in July 1960. During this time the squadron was also based at RAF Coltishall alongside the AFDS. Unlike the Hunters, which had been camouflaged, the Lightings were delivered unpainted apart from standard markings. The only change 74 Sqn made was to paint the tail fin black with the squadron badge

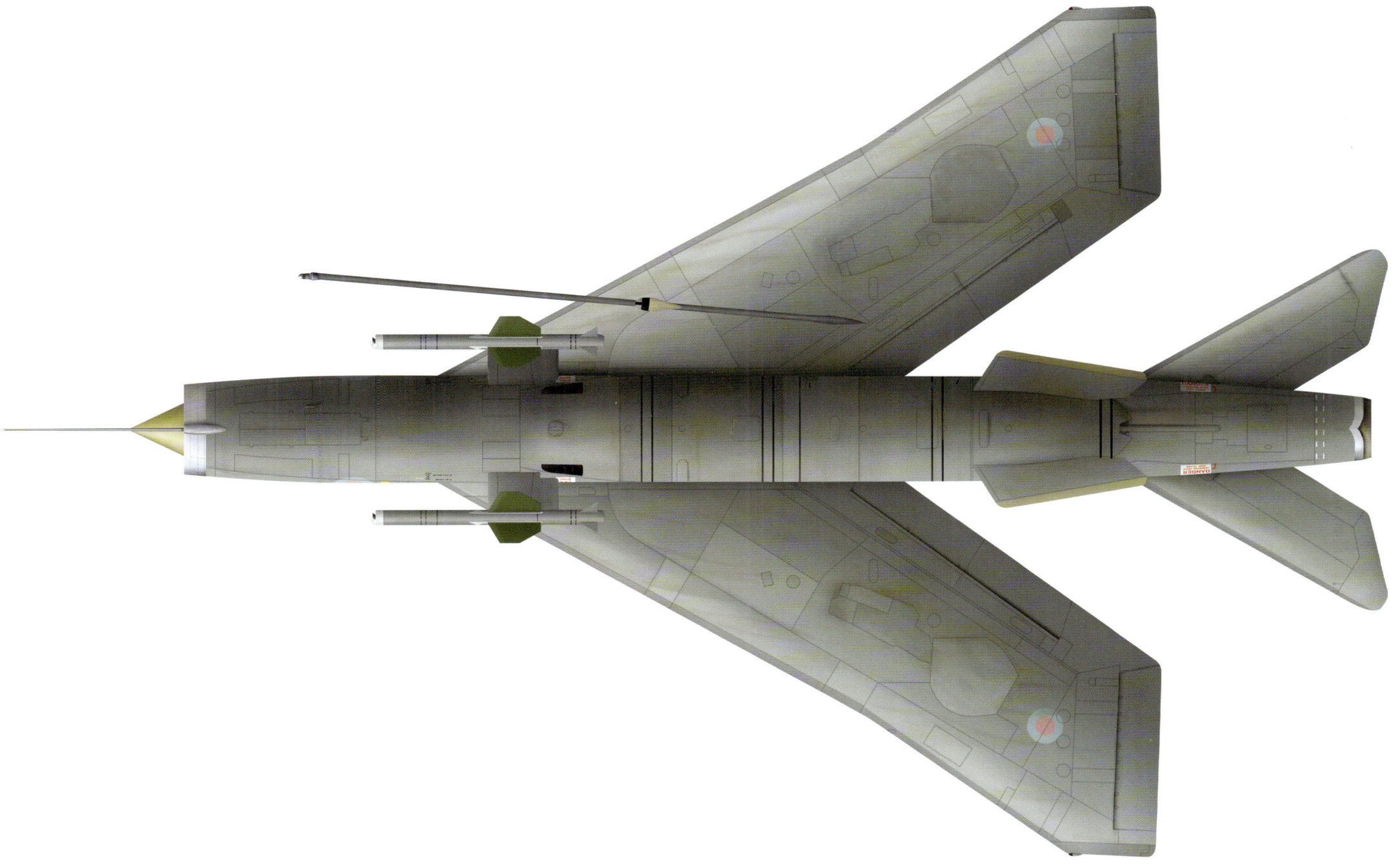

LIGHTNING F.2A XN784 19 SQUADRON

Built as an F.2, XN784 was later upgraded to F.2A standard while serving with 19 Squadron, RAF Germany in early 1969. During front line service it retained a natural metal finish with squadron markings. In retirement XN784 is on display at Baarlo, Holland, and wears a non-authentic camouflage scheme.

in a white circle and the squadron bars on the nose.

Once the F.1s had been completed, production of the F.1A commenced and deliveries to 56 and 111 Squadrons began, both being based at RAF Wattisham, Suffolk. The F.1A had a number of minor upgrades, the most significant being the Avon 210R along with the option to fit a refuelling probe under the port wing, increasing range significantly.

To the casual observer the F.2 looked identical to the F.1, the only difference being a small intake duct on the spine. Internally however there were a number of improvements, including nose wheel steering, OR.946 instrument suite, a liquid oxygen breathing system and a variable reheat system.

A total of 44 F.2s made it into service starting in late 1962 with 19 and 92 Squadrons at RAF Leconfield, Yorkshire. During 1965 these two squadrons were posted to Germany and they would be based at RAF Gütersloh for over a decade. With the introduction of the F.3 and F.6, the capabilities of the F.2 were starting to become dated.

From January 1968, the two squadrons began to receive the

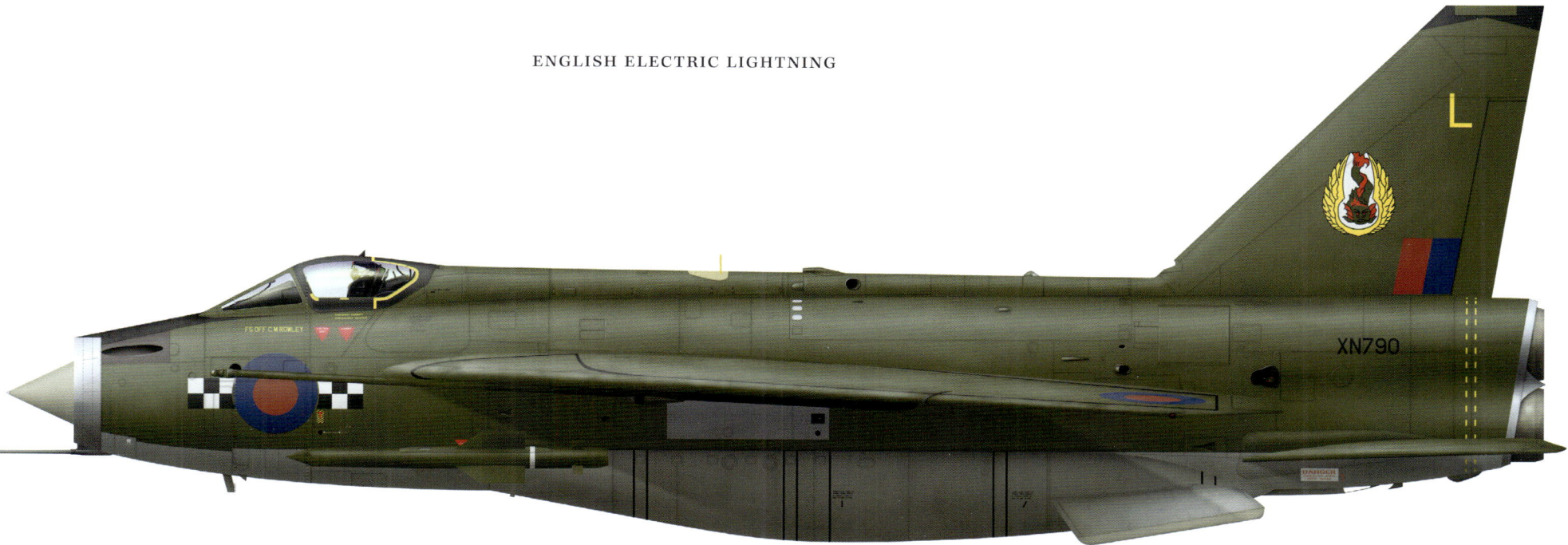

LIGHTNING F.2A XN790 19 SQUADRON

XN790 first served with 92 Squadron in NMF as an F.2. It was then converted to F.2A standard and transferred to 19 Squadron.
Based at RAF Gütersloh in 1975, XN790 was flown by Fg Off C. M. Rowley. Upper surfaces painted dark green over NMF.

upgraded F.2A. Many of the changes such as the enlarged belly tank (already included with the F.3) and Avon R211 engines gave improved performance and range, with the two 30mm Aden cannon retained.

The role of the F.3 was somewhat different to that of its predecessors. It was to become an interceptor with the capability for overseas deployment. To increase its range, the capacity of the ventral tank was increased to 560 gallons and the wings could now carry two 540 gallon overwing tanks. The wing leading edge was also modified with a cambered extension. Avon R301 engines were fitted and the top of the tail was squared off.

The F.3 could also now carry the Red Top missile and received the AI-23B radar. However, the 30mm Aden cannon were now removed. The final version of the Lightning was an upgrade of the F.3 with an increase in fuel capacity and completely revised ventral tank with significantly larger fins; there was also the capacity to fit two 30mm Aden cannon to the front of the tank.

The T.4 was based on the F.1 airframe with the nose section widened to accommodate two pilots in a side by side configuration. Wind tunnel tests had proven that a tandem layout would lead to a loss of directional stability. The dorsal spine was also enlarged to fit

LIGHTNING F.6 XR773 11 SQUADRON

This aircraft was first flown in February 1966 by Roland Beamont. While with 11 Squadron, WR773 wore
standard dark sea grey upper surfaces with light aircraft grey undersides; the pilot's name on the port side is Flt
Lt R. A. J. Heath. The aircraft also served with 74, 56 and 5 Squadrons and continued to fly once retired in South
Africa at Thunder City. While in civilian ownership the codes G-OPIB and later ZU-BEW were worn.

with the wider cockpit. Like the later F.1s, it had Avon 210R engines but the cannon were removed. The T.5 was based around the F.3 with the Avon 301R but was otherwise almost identical to the T.4.

The Lightning served with front line squadrons for 28 years and continued to perform well against many newer types such as the F-4 Phantom and Harrier GR.3 but limited range and firepower counted against the aircraft.

Squadrons started retiring their Lightnings in 1974 and the type was officially fully retired at the end of June 1988. However, this

was not the end of the Lightning and several continued to fly as targets at the Aberporth range against Buccaneers and Tornados while the Foxhunter radar was being developed. With the hours running out on the remaining airframes and the programme nearing completion, the aircraft were disposed of.

The last flight of a Lightning in British airspace was on January 21, 1993, when F.6 XS904 took off from Warton for the final time and was delivered to Bruntingthorpe where it is preserved with F.3 XR713 and F.6 XR728.

Unlike many other cold war jets, the Lightning was not an aircraft that could lend itself to a range of roles — the only exception being the trainer. It was a very specific design for the role and despite being regularly scrambled to intercept Soviet aircraft entering British airspace it was never required to engage in hostile action. It was a unique and iconic aircraft, with many examples surviving in museums.

English Electric Lightning

VARIANT	LENGTH	SPAN	HEIGHT	ENGINE
P.1A	49FT 8IN/15.14M	34FT 10IN/10.62M	17FT 3IN/5.26M	2 X SAPPHIRE SA.5
P.1B	55FT 3IN/16.23M	34FT 10IN/10.62M	19FT 5IN/5.92M	2 X AVON 200R
F.1	55FT 3IN/16.23M	34FT 10IN/10.62M	19FT 7IN/5.97M	2 X AVON 200R
F.1A	55FT 3IN/16.23M	34FT 10IN/10.62M	19FT 7IN/5.97M	2 X AVON 210R
F.2	55FT 3IN/16.23M	34FT 10IN/10.62M	19FT 7IN/5.97M	2 X AVON 210R2 OR 301R
F.2A	55FT 3IN/16.23M	34FT 10IN/10.62M	19FT 7IN/5.97M	2 X AVON 211R
F.3	55FT 3IN/16.23M	34FT 10IN/10.62M	19FT 7IN/5.97M	2 X AVON 301R
F.3A	55FT 3IN/16.23M	34FT 10IN/10.62M	19FT 7IN/5.97M	2 X AVON 301R
T.4	55FT 3IN/16.23M	34FT 10IN/10.62M	19FT 7IN/5.97M	2 X AVON 210R
T.5	55FT 3IN/16.23M	34FT 10IN/10.62M	19FT 7IN/5.97M	2 X AVON 301R
F.6	55FT 3IN/16.23M	34FT 10IN/10.62M	19FT 7IN/5.97M	2 X AVON 301R
F.53	55FT 3IN/16.23M	34FT 10IN/10.62M	19FT 7IN/5.97M	2 X AVON 302C
T.55	55FT 3IN/16.23M	34FT 10IN/10.62M	19FT 7IN/5.97M	2 X AVON 302C

LIGHTNING F.2 XN731 92 SQUADRON

XN731 was delivered in January 1962 and served with 92 Squadron. It
was converted to F.2A standard in early 1969.

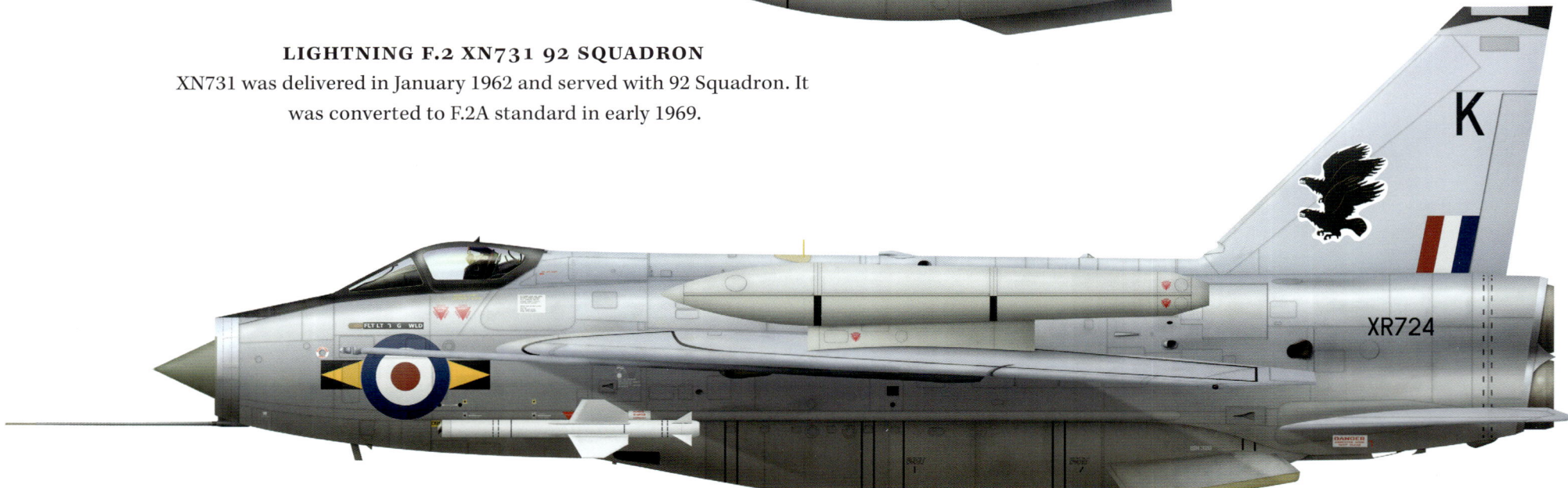

LIGHTNING F.6 XR724 11 SQUADRON

Originally built as an F.3, XR724 was converted and operated by 11 Squadron during the early
1970s. Later it was used as a chase aircraft for the Tornado programme, based at Warton.

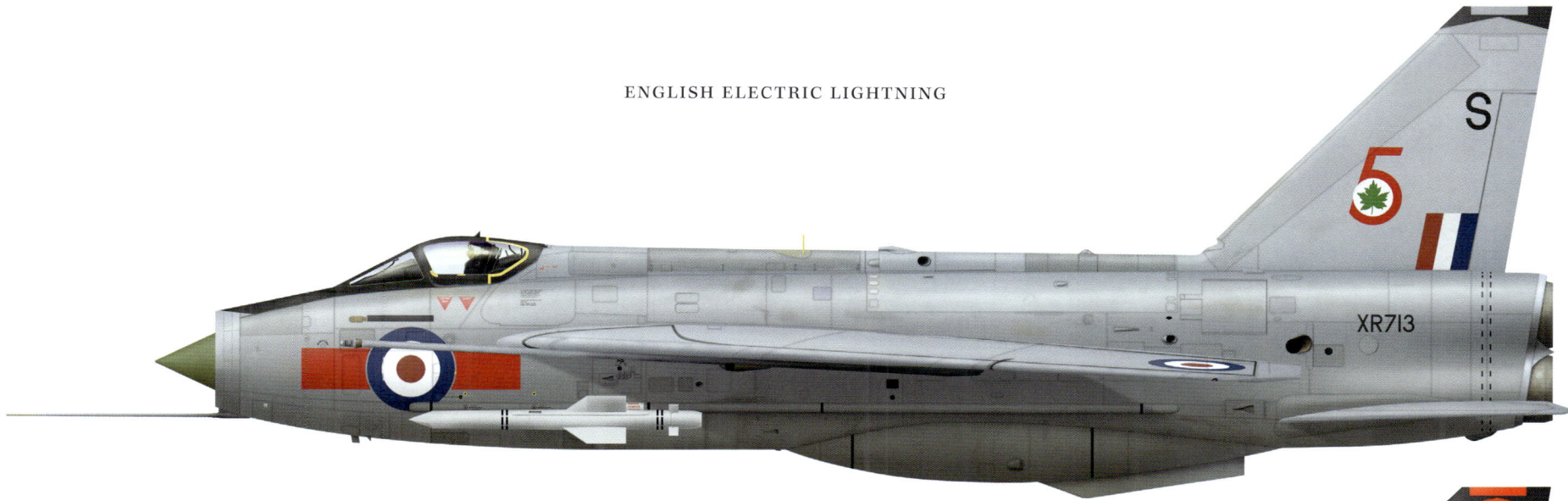

LIGHTNING F.3 XR713 5 SQUADRON

First flown on October 21, 1964, XR713 was delivered to 111 Squadron the following January. During the 1970s it was operated by 5 Squadron where it was coded S and then AR. It was later repainted in 111 Squadron markings when it became a mascot for the squadron at RAF Leuchars while operating the Tornado.

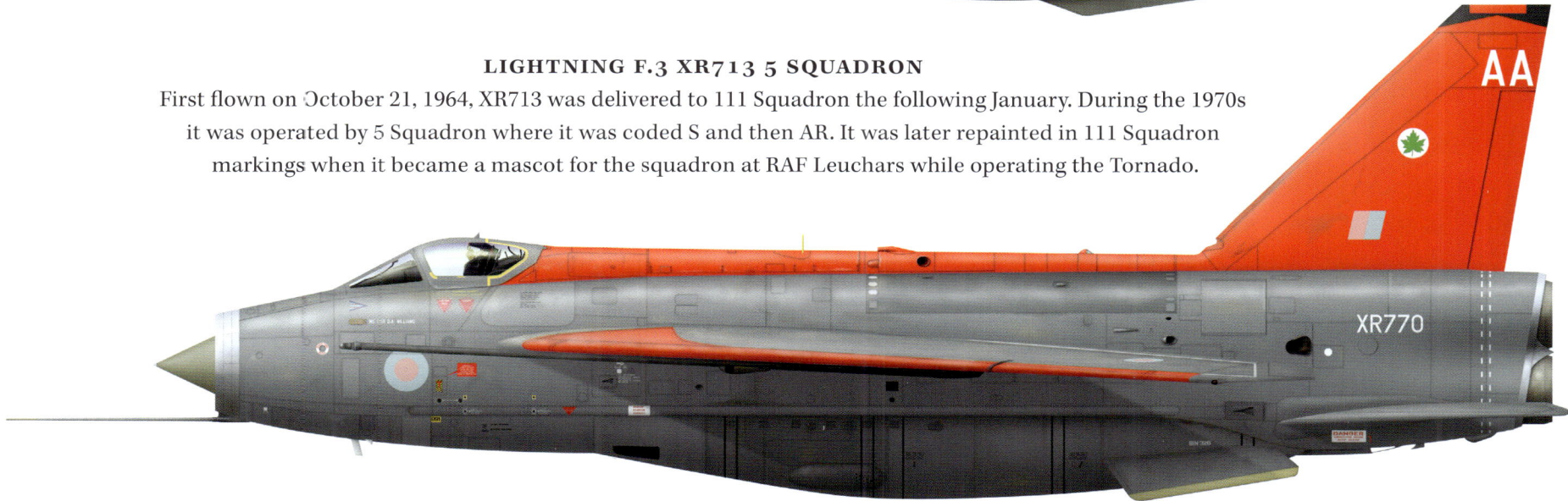

LIGHTNING F.6 XR770 5 SQUADRON

Following a first flight on December 16, 1966, the aircraft was displayed in a Saudi Arabian scheme at 1966 SBAC before entering service with 74 Squadron. It was later transferred to 5 Squadron, RAF Binbrook. Upon retirement the airframe ended up at the NATO Aircraft Museum, Grimsby. Restored, it is currently on display at the RAF Manston History Museum. Upper surfaces are dark sea grey.

LIGHTNING F.3 XP696 226 OCU

Delivered to 226 OCU in June 1970, spine and tail painted white, XP696
was used as the unit's display aircraft. Scrapped in October 1975.

LIGHTNING F.3 XP705 29 SQUADRON

Originally delivered to 74 Squadron, following time with 56 and 23 Squadrons XP705
was allocated to 29 Squadron in May 1968. It was ditched off the coast of Cyprus,
near RAF Akrotiri, after an engine fire on July 8, 1971. The pilot ejected.

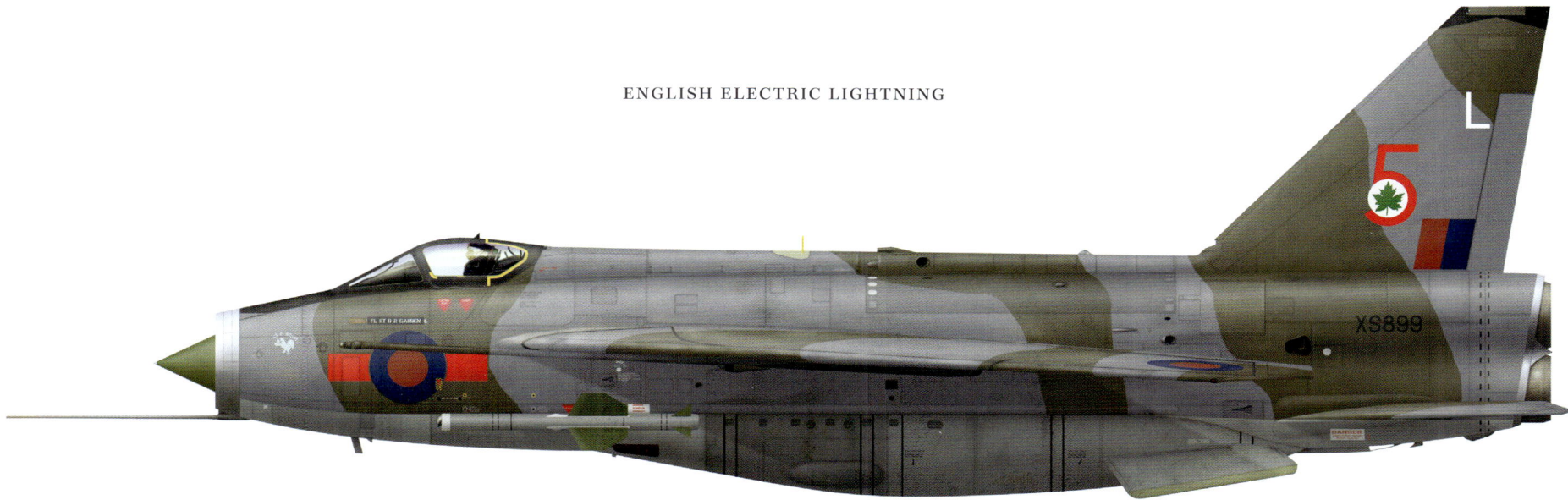

LIGHTNING F.6 XS899 5 SQUADRON

After a first flight on June 8, 1966, XS899 was delivered to 5 Squadron in January 1967. The aircraft served exclusively with that unit. It was painted in two tone camouflage with red bar and a 43 Squadron cock with boxing gloves on the nose (presumably a zap). During September 1977 it was flown by Flt Lt D. R. Carden from RAF Leuchars. While most of the airframe was scrapped, the cockpit has survived.

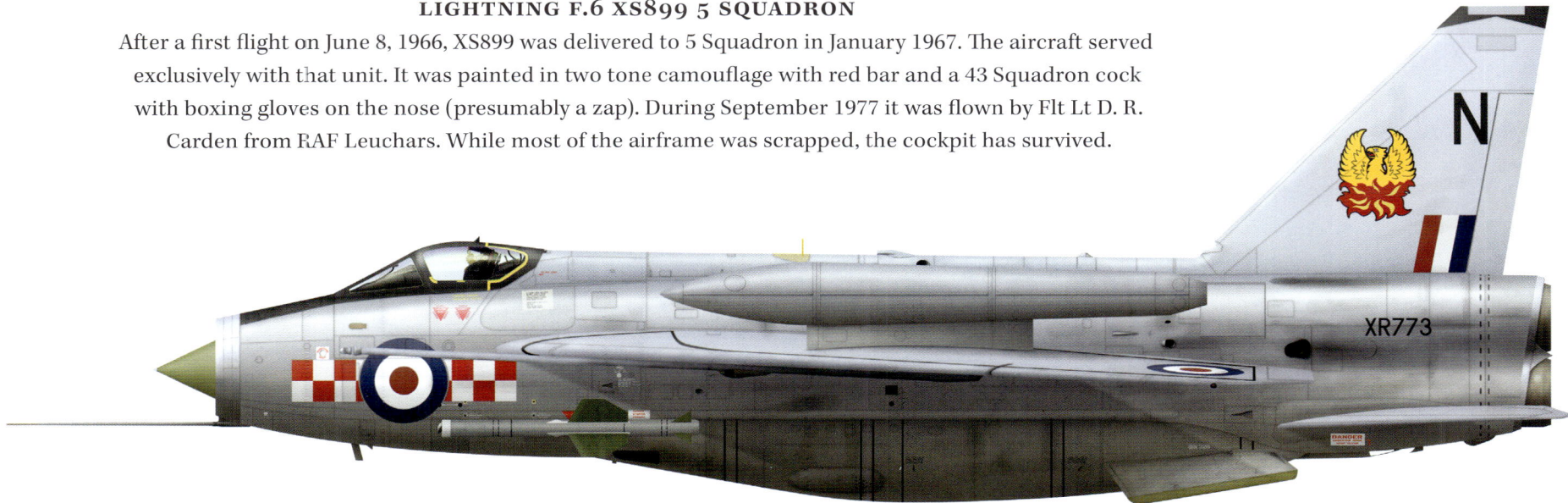

LIGHTNING F.6 XR773 56 SQUADRON

Wearing the earlier markings of 56 Squadron over a NMF, XR773 was also fitted with overwing tanks.

LIGHTNING F.2A XN782 92 SQUADRON

92 Squadron's Lightnings are possibly best known for their NMF scheme with the tail and spine painted
in bright blue. The unit had previously operated all over blue Hunters as the Blue Diamonds.

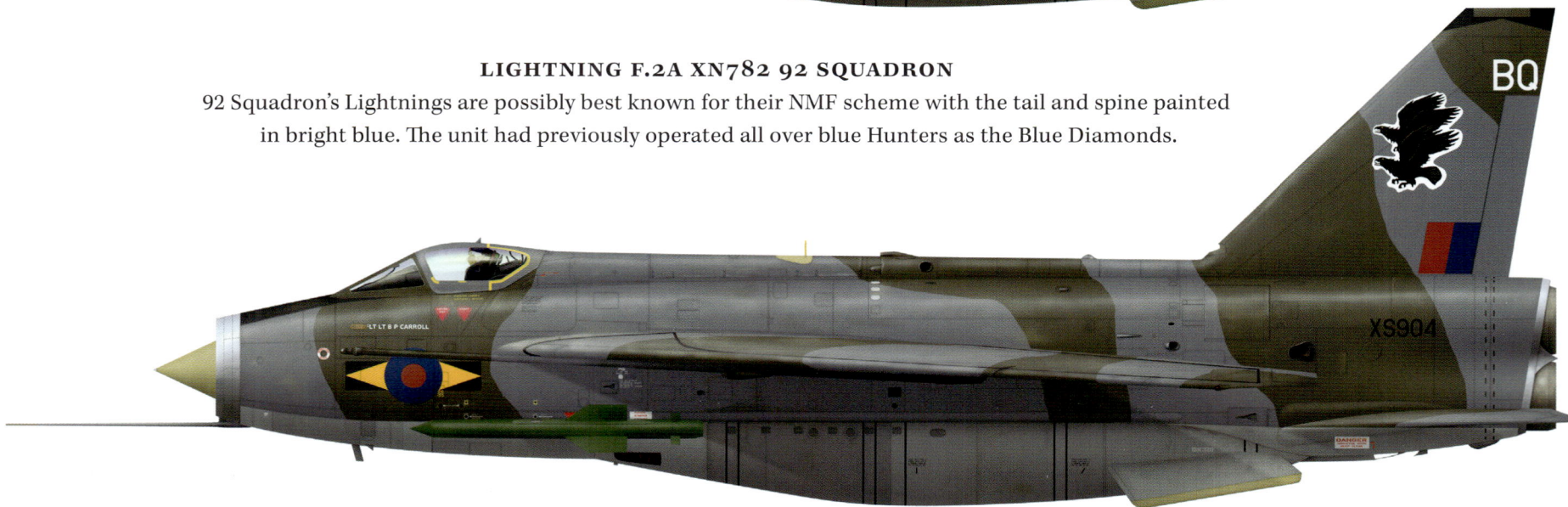

LIGHTNING F.6 XS904 11 SQUADRON

One of the most photographed Lightnings, XS904 served almost exclusively with 11 Squadron. Having retired from front line service, the
aircraft was retained by BAe for Tornado F.3 radar trials. Standard cold war two tone camouflage scheme with NMF undersides.

LIGHTNING F.2A XN778 92 SQUADRON

The standard scheme for later 92 Squadron Lightnings was dark green upper surfaces, with NMF retained on lower surfaces. Below the squadron badge on the tail of XN778 are two blue diamonds as a tribute to the display team. The aircraft was struck off charge in 1975 following a ground fire and used as a decoy. Finally scrapped in 1984.

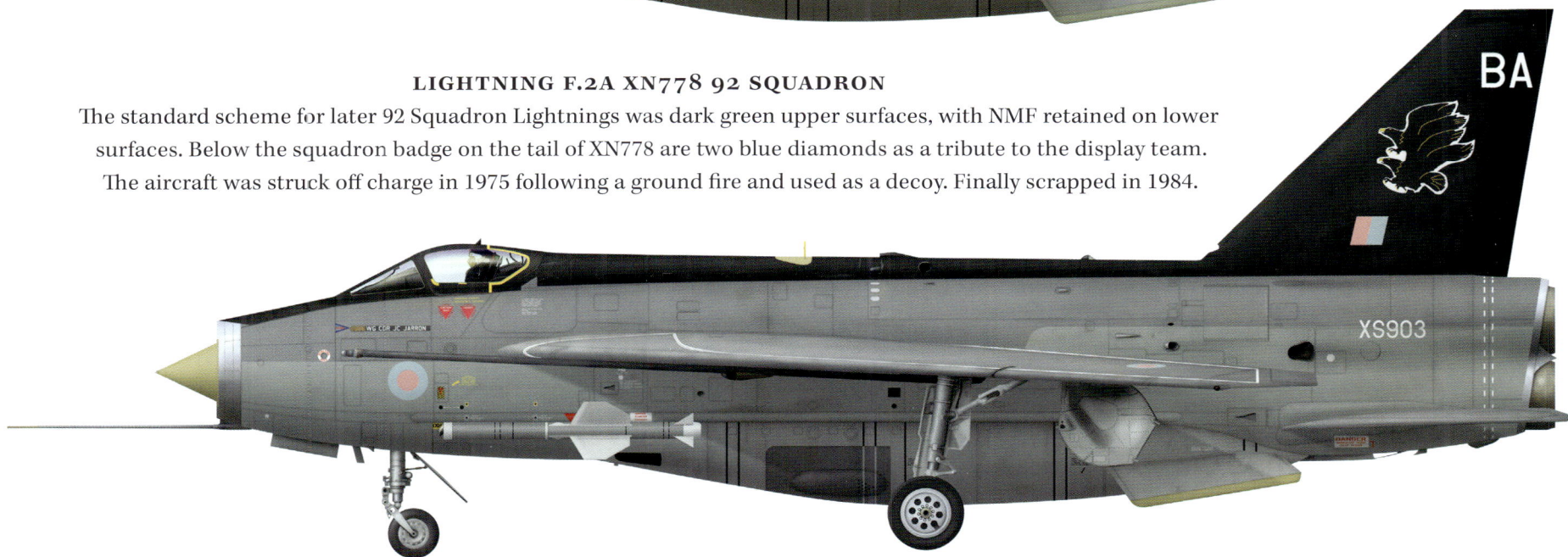

LIGHTNING F.6 XS903 11 SQUADRON

Delivered to 5 Squadron in August 1966, XS903 was displayed at the Paris Air Show the following year. It was transferred to 11 Squadron in 1980. Upon retirement it was flown to Elvington and displayed at the Yorkshire Aviation Museum.

LIGHTNING F.6 XS921 74 SQUADRON

XS921 has a distinctive black tail and squadron badge over NMF. The tail flash was picked out in yellow. While serving with 11 Squadron, the aircraft was written off following a loss of control over the North Sea. Flt Lt C. Penrice ejected and survived.

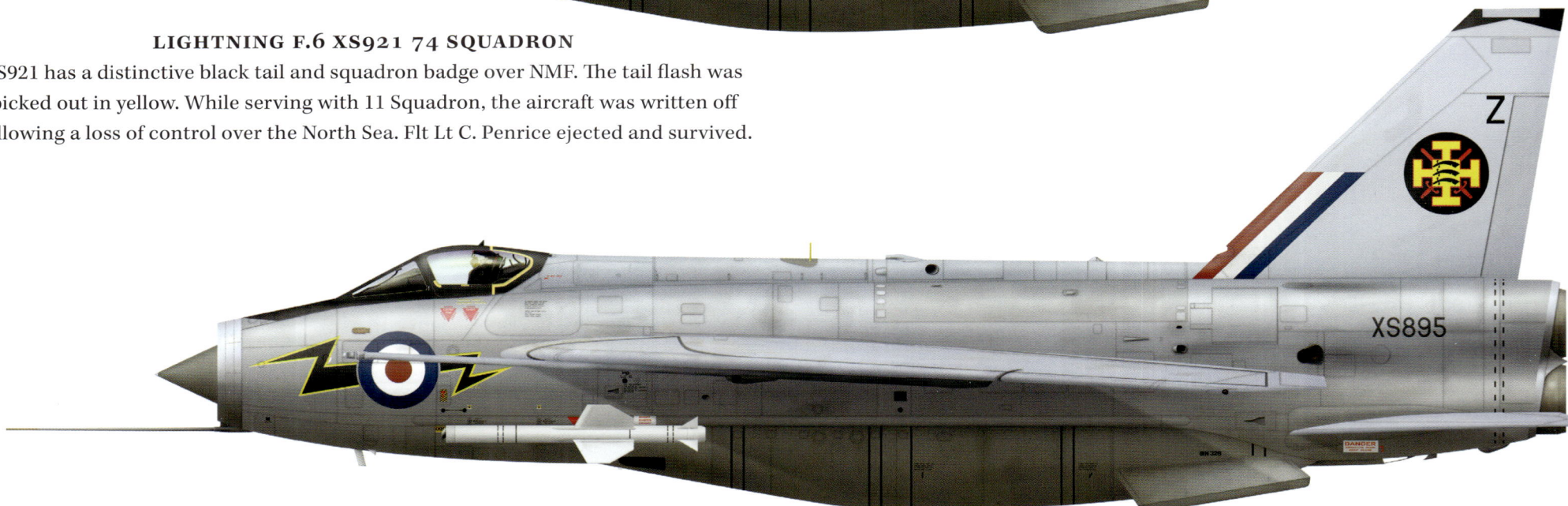

LIGHTNING F.6 XS895 111 SQUADRON

NMF with squadron markings and an extended tail flash made up F.6 XS895's 111 Squadron scheme. It also served with 5 and 11 Squadrons and the Lightning Training Flight.

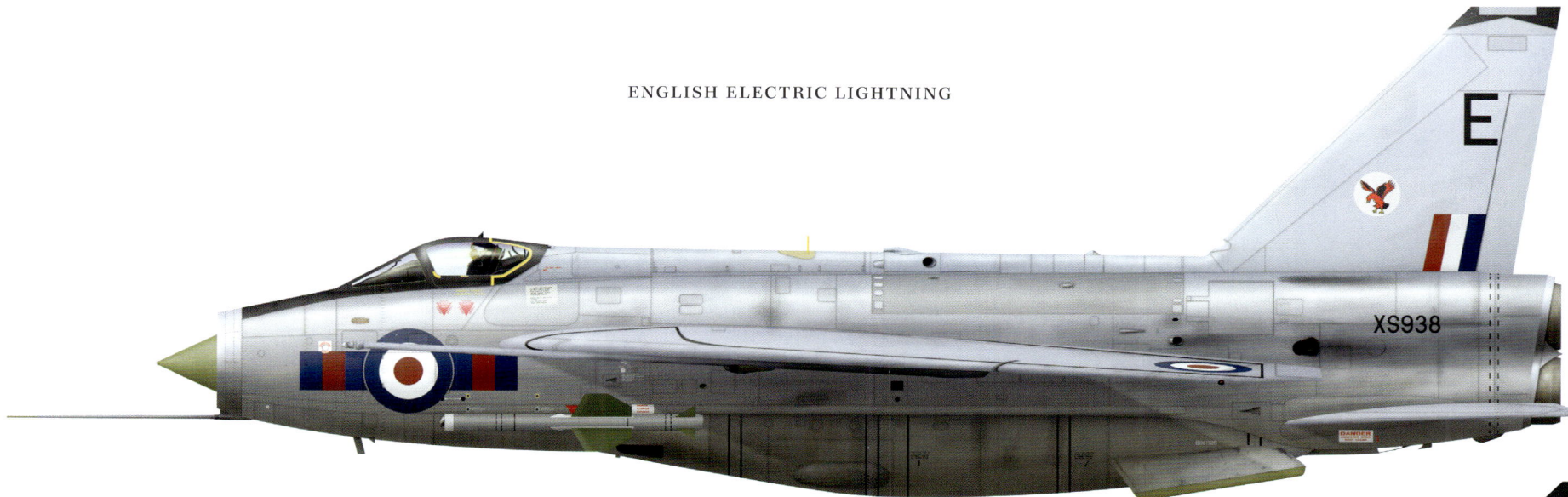

LIGHTNING F.6 XS938 23 SQUADRON

XS938 is shown here in standard early NMF scheme with squadron badge on tail and bar on fuselage. It was based at RAF Leuchars in the late 60s and early 70s.

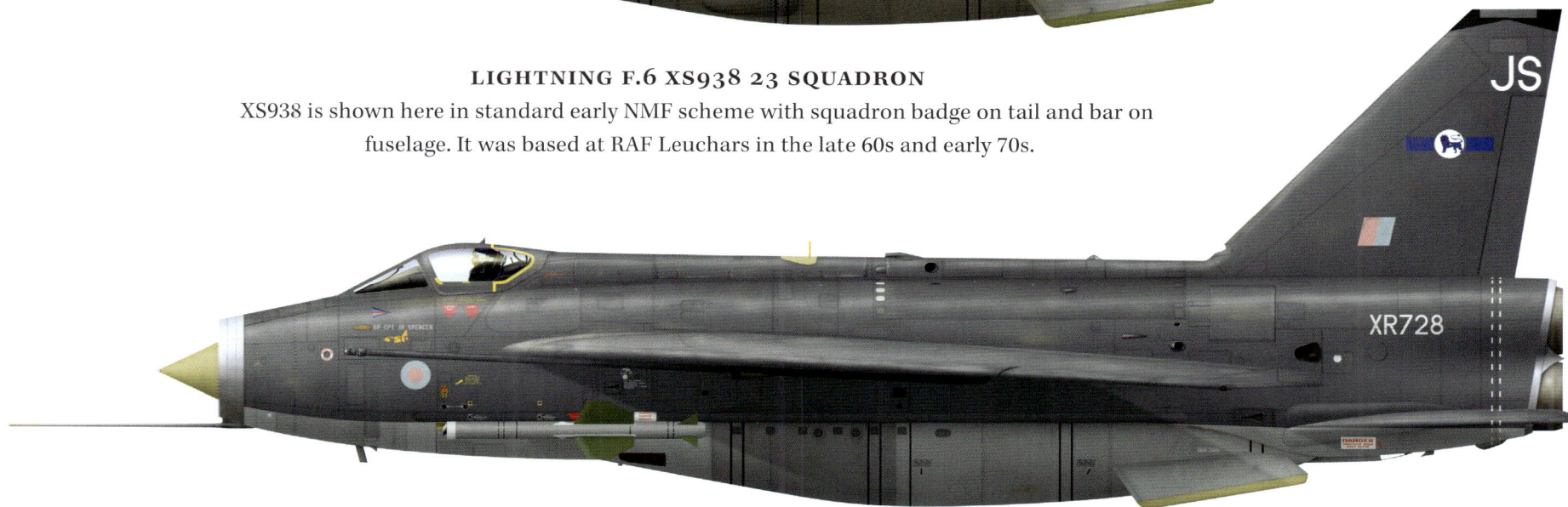

LIGHTNING F.6 XR728 LIGHTNING TRAINING FLIGHT

XR728 began life as an F.3 but was converted to F.6 standard before entering service with 23 Squadron in November 1967. It was then moved on to 5, 56 and 11 Squadrons. The aircraft ended its service career with the Lightning Training Flight and was the RAF Binbrook CO's personal aircraft.

LIGHTNING F.6 XR773 5 SQUADRON
Having been placed into temporary storage following a period with 11 Squadron, XR773 was allocated to 5 Squadron. It was scheduled for a camouflage scheme but following the application of the primer there was a delay. For a brief period in 1981, therefore, it flew in the primer colour.

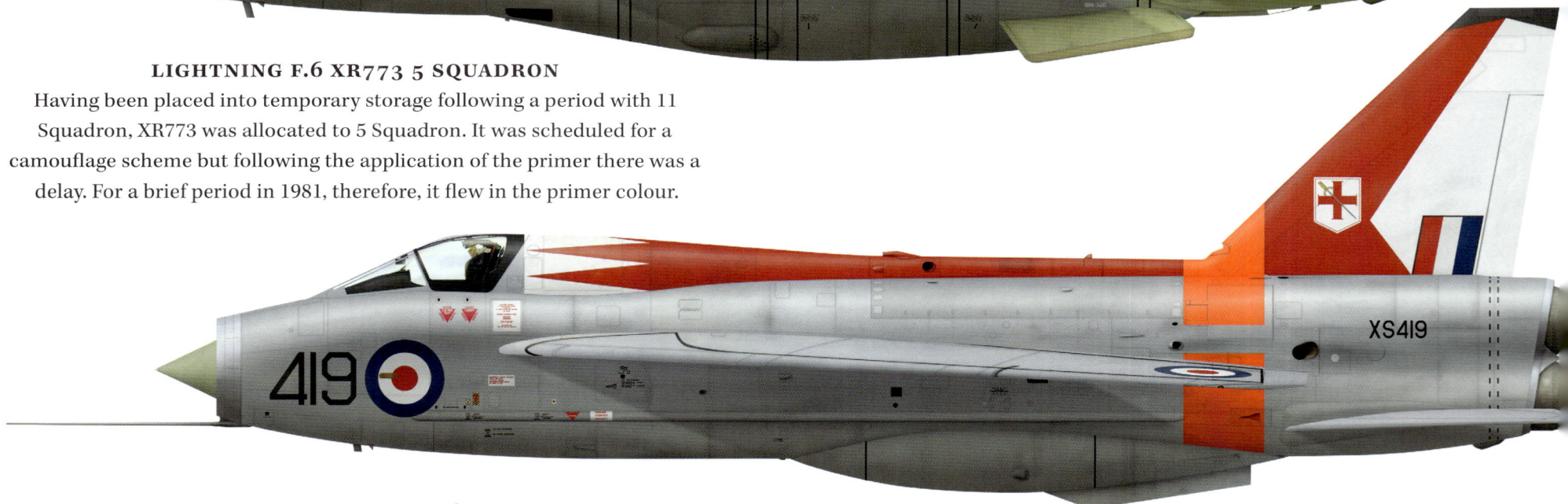

LIGHTNING T.5 XS419 226 OPERATIONAL CONVERSION UNIT
While not the first Lightning trainer, XS419 was the first to serve with an RAF unit when it was delivered to 226 OCU on April 20, 1965, and given these striking markings. It later served with the Lightning Training Flight before being scrapped in 1992.

LIGHTNING T.5 XS452 RAF AKROTIRI STATION FLIGHT

First flying in on June 30, 1965, XS452 was delivered to the OCU but was later allocated to Akrotiri where the pink tail and flamingo were added – the flamingo being on the RAF Akrotiri badge. It later served with the Lightning Training Flight and retired. However, XS452 was kept flying for several years in South Africa at Thunder City.

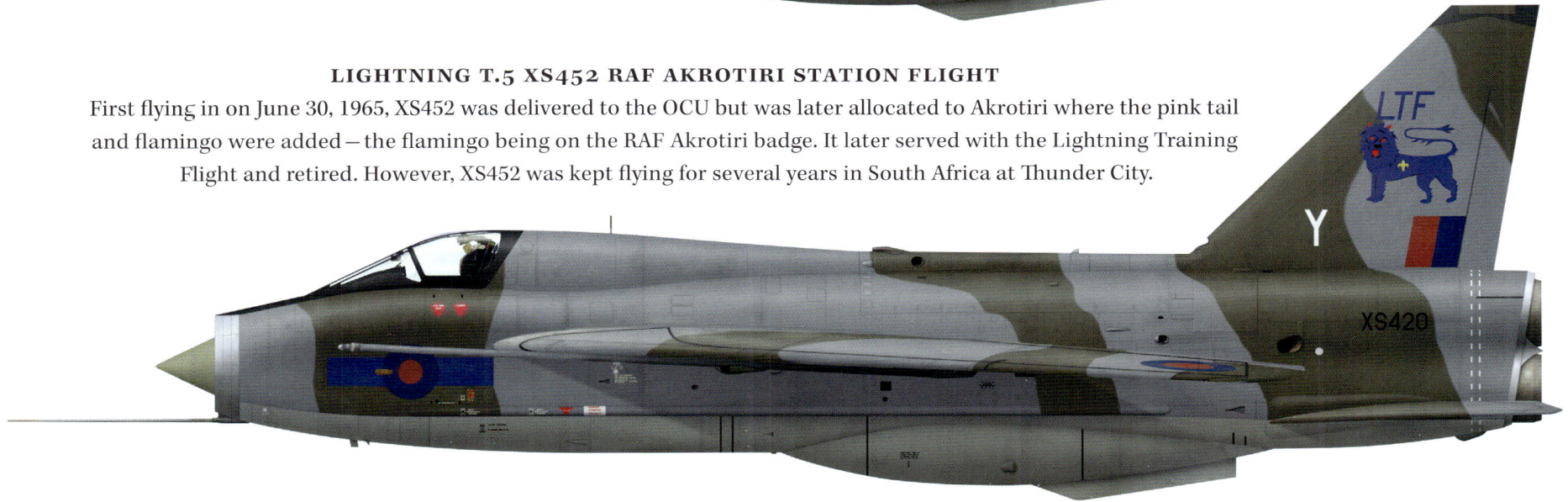

LIGHTNING T.5 XS420 LIGHTNING TRAINING FLIGHT

XS420 was operated by 226 OCU at Coltishall from its delivery in 1965 until 1983, when it was transferred to the LTF at Binbrook. By this time it had received the camouflage scheme. Following disposal, it was restored and the original scheme was reapplied. The aircraft was eventually placed on display at Farnborough.

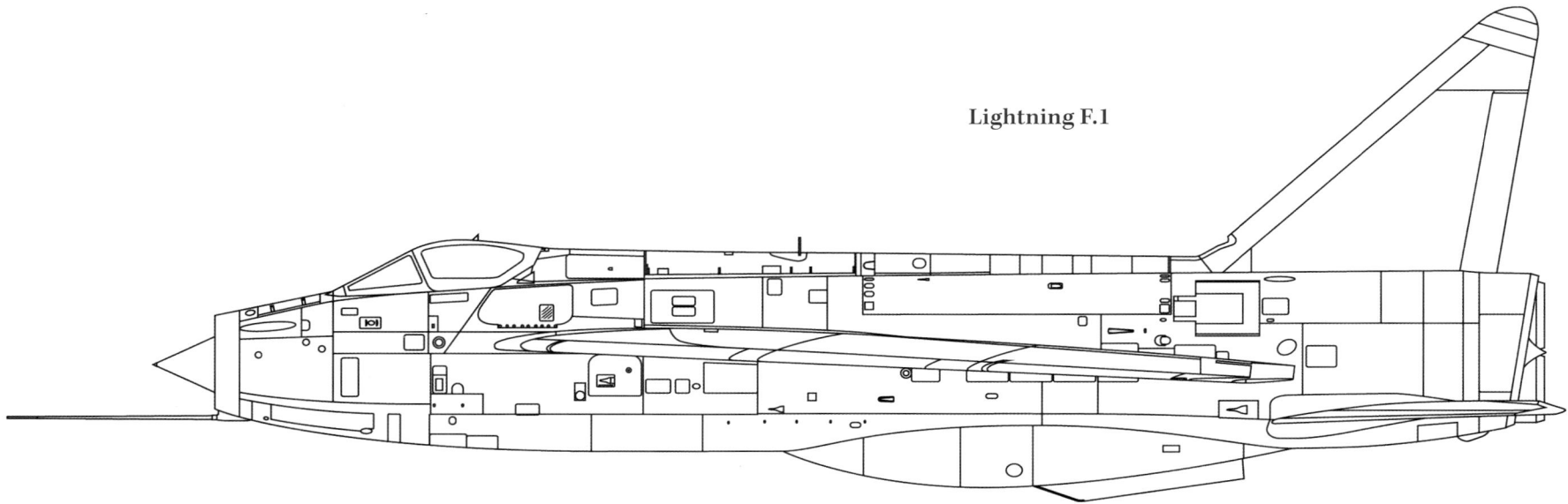

Lightning F.1

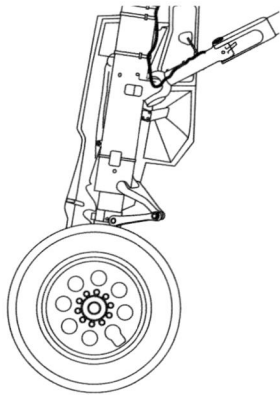

Main wheel

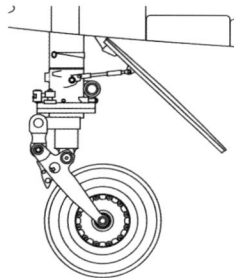

Nose wheel

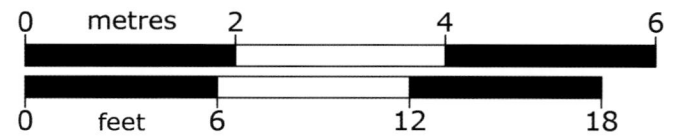

Lightning F.2A

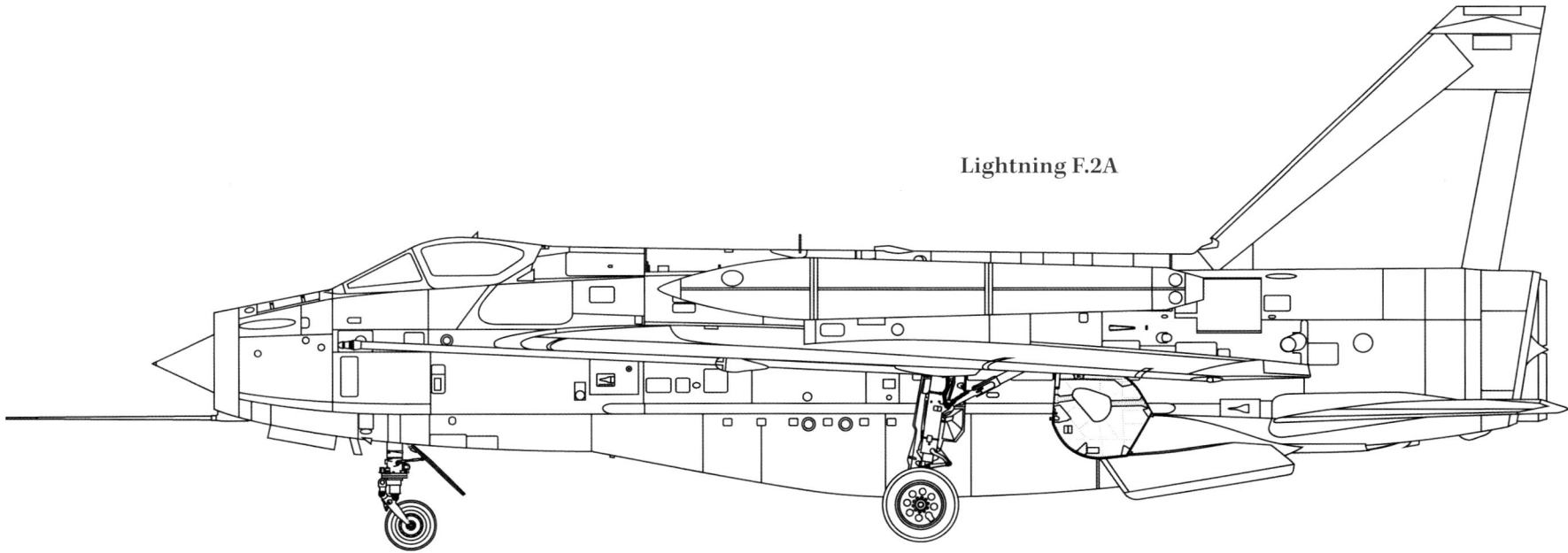

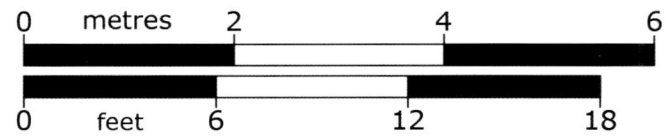

0 metres 2 4 6

0 feet 6 12 18

Lightning F.6 front

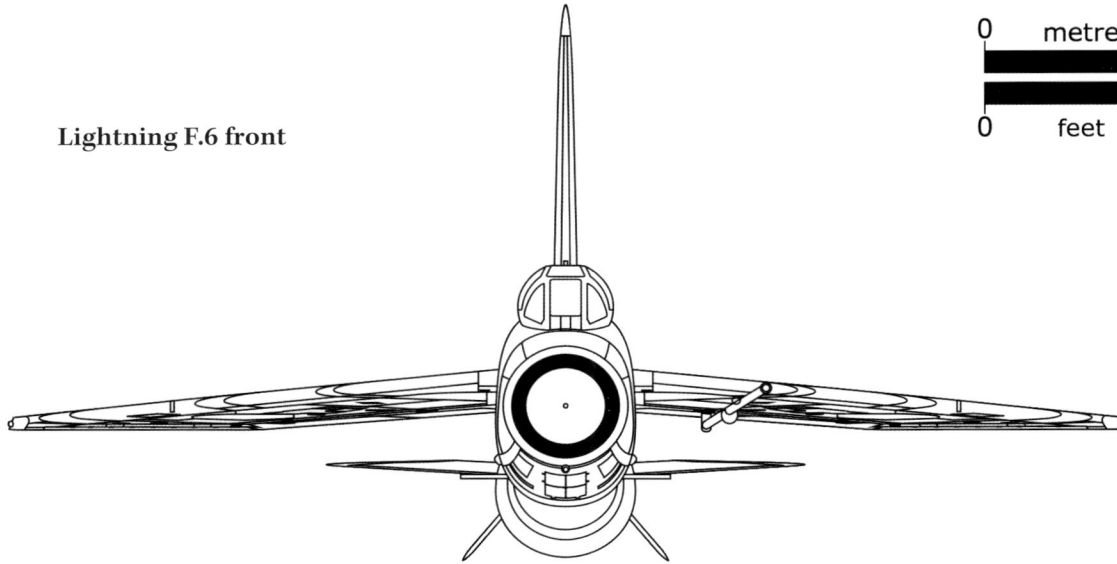

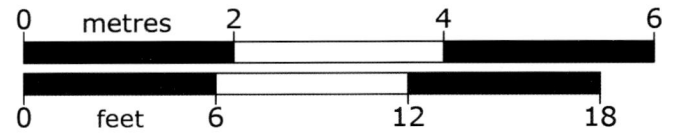

Lightning T.5

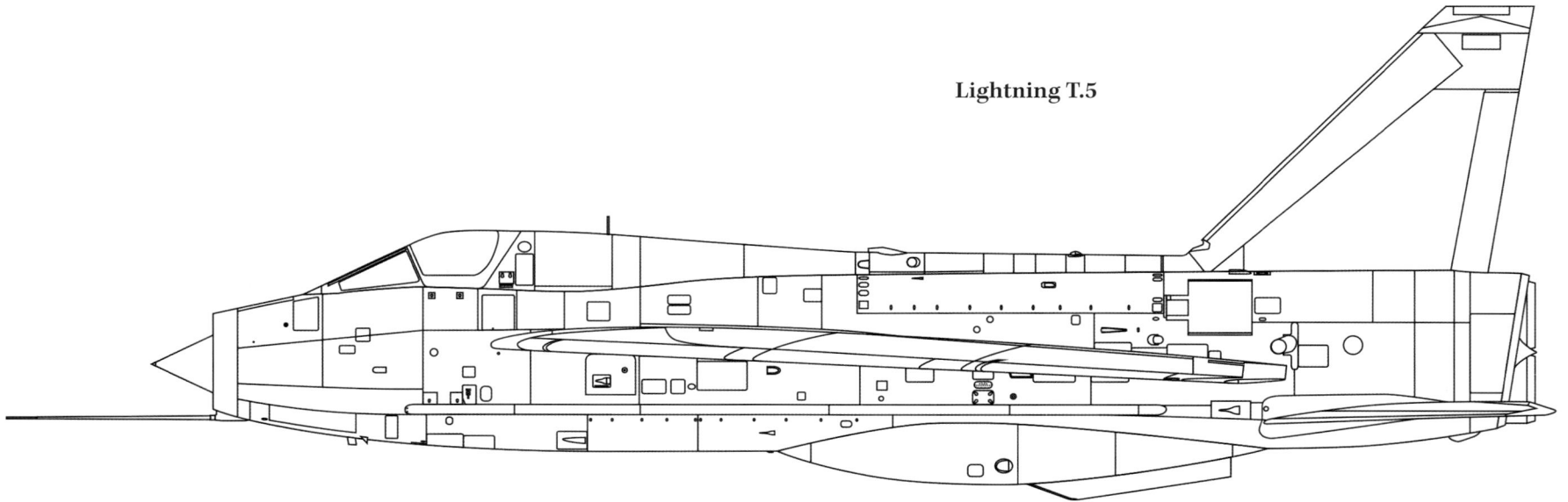

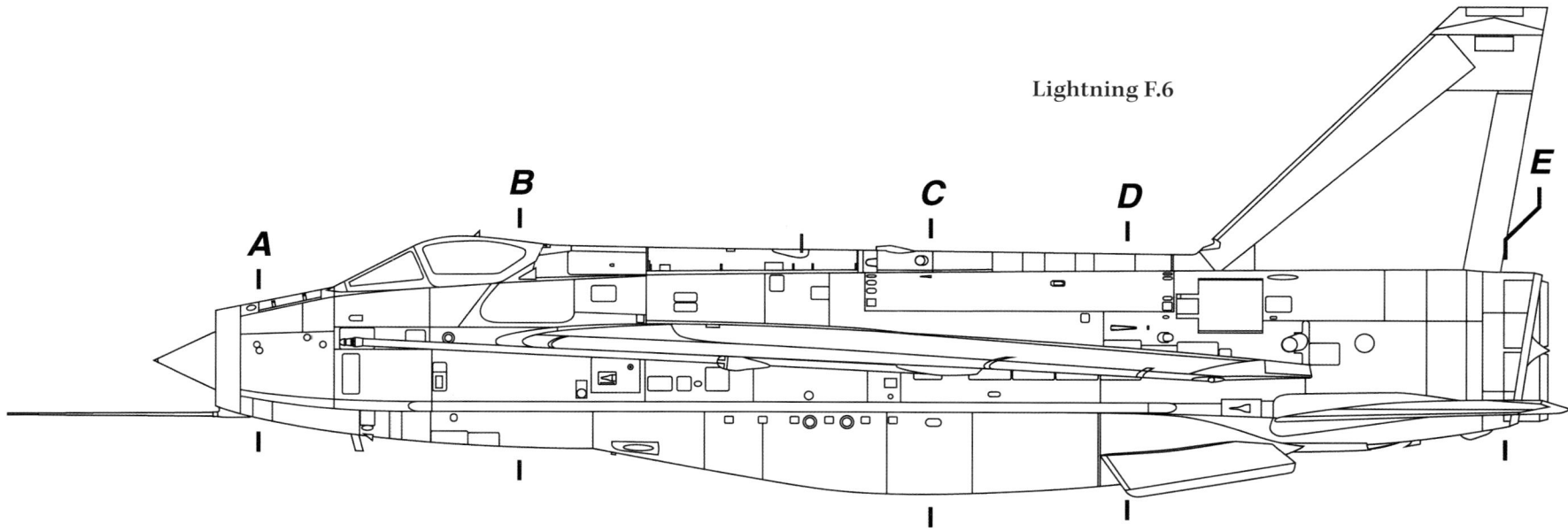

Lightning F.6

A   B   C   D   E

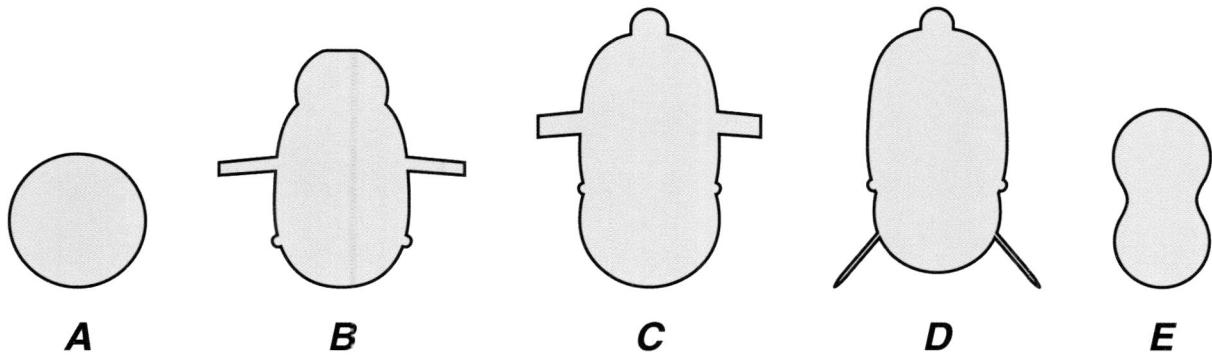

A   B   C   D   E

| 0 | metres | 2 | | 4 | | 6 |
| 0 | feet | 6 | | 12 | | 18 |

Lightning F.6 front

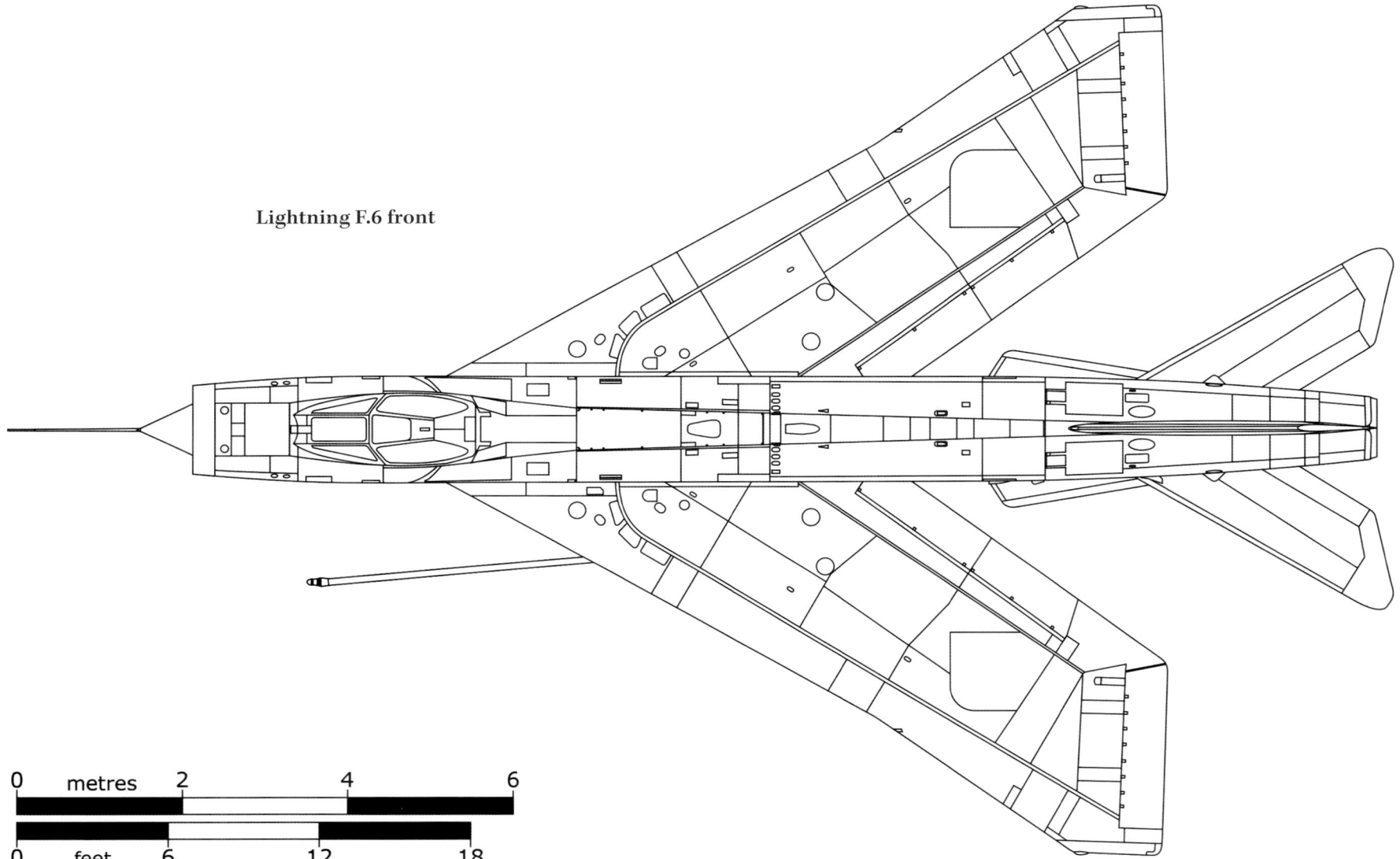

0 metres 2 4 6

0 feet 6 12 18

Lightning F.6 underside

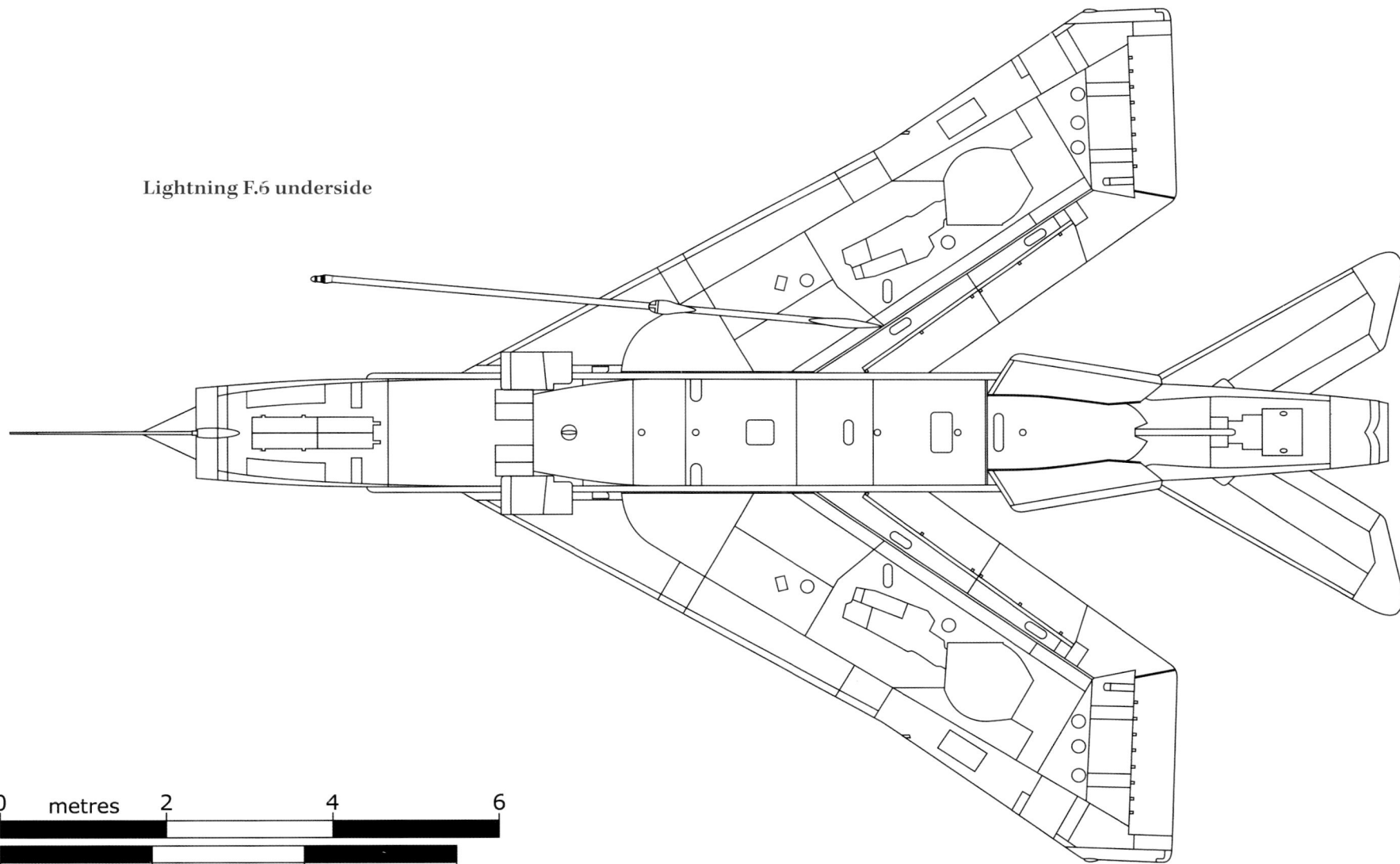

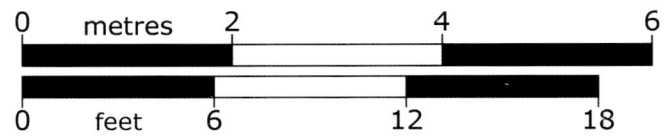

0   metres   2   4   6

0   feet   6   12   18

HAWKER SIDDELEY/BAE HARRIER

The Harrier is still considered a unique and highly versatile aircraft. It was designed to operate where no runway existed and could, if the need arose, take off vertically from a grass field. GR.5s even flew from the grass runway at Shuttleworth, Bedfordshire — a feat that a Lightning or Tornado might struggle to achieve. It may have been the Sea Harrier that first proved the capabilities of the type during the Falklands War, but the GR.3 also had a vital role and Harriers have been involved in several conflicts since.

The birth of the Harrier was a long and protracted affair involving several versions and nations before it finally entered service in 1969. At the height of the Battle of Britain the German bombing campaign switched from airfields to civilian targets in a move which is considered by many to have been the turning point in the fight. Even with damaged airfields, the Spitfires and Hurricanes of Fighter Command could still operate from grass strips which required minimal repairs. When the Second World War ended and the cold war escalated, however, the fighter aircraft used by NATO became bigger, more powerful and heavier — requiring longer and longer hard runways.

It was assumed by planners that a nuclear missile strike by the Soviets would take out as many of these airfields as possible. While some fighters like the Jaguar proved they could use the autobahns of West Germany as temporary runways, it was thought that the ideal solution would be a fast jet that could take off without using a runway at all.

During 1956, French aircraft designer Michel Wibault proposed a concept to the French Air Ministry where downward pointing exhausts gave a vertical take-off (VTO) capability, the thrust being

HARRIER GR.3 XW769 1 SQUADRON

The GR.3 was introduced in 1974 and an upgrade programme for the GR.1 was begun. By 1979 all aircraft had been converted. XW769 was written off in Belgium during July 1986. It is shown here painted in dark green and dark sea grey.

generated by four centrifugal blowers.

Around the same time, Bell began investigating VTO and experimenting with vectored thrust with the Model 65ATV. By combining the use of cold air and vectored thrust, the design team at the Bristol Engine Company headed by Sir Stanley Hooker came up with the BE 53 engine. This led directly to a new unit dubbed the Pegasus.

With an engine concept in hand, Bristol now needed an aircraft to go with it. Hooker approached Sir Sidney Camm and Hawker with the proposal. At the time Hawker was enjoying success with the Hunter and investing heavily in a new type known as the P.1121, but Camm had had a longstanding interest in the short take-off and landing (STOL) concept and work began on the Hawker P.1127 — a

privately funded venture which would lead to P.1127 prototypes XP831 and XP836.

During the design process, led by John Fozard, the layout slowly resolved itself into a configuration of two large intakes, two cold exhausts at the front and two hot at the rear. By July 15, 1960, XP831, the first P.1127, arrived at Hawker's Dunsfold facility for testing. Hover trials commenced on October 21 when it made a tethered hover lasting only a few seconds, rising to 1.5ft or 46cm, Bill Bedford conducting the historic flight with his leg in plaster. The first free hover followed on November 19.

As the P.1127's potential became apparent an order was placed for a further four prototypes. The more powerful Pegasus 2 was installed in these and an extensive flight testing programme was

HARRIER GR.3 XV752 1 SQUADRON
1 Sqn regularly went on exercise to Norway with the Harrier, commencing in September 1970. XV752
received a temporary whitewash snow camouflage over the dark green, which soon weathered.

initiated. In July 1961, XP836 made a conventional take off and transitioned to a hover.

During the trials, each of the six P.1127s was modified and altered in response to the trials data. In May 1962, nine more were ordered and with the lessons learned from trials changes were made in a number of areas.

These included the intake shape, fuselage lengthening, revised wings and fitment of the Pegasus 5. This version of the aircraft was officially named the Kestrel. By now interest had grown abroad and a Tripartite Evaluation Squadron was formed consisting of British, US and German test pilots.

The conclusion of the trials occurred at around the same time that the British Government requested the provision for four pylons for external stores. It may have still looked like a Kestrel but there were sufficient changes to warrant it being considered a new aircraft and XV276 was now known as the Harrier GR.1.

The Harrier had an opportunity to really show the press and public what it was capable of during the Daily Mail Transatlantic Air Race in May 1969. To commemorate the 50th anniversary of the first crossing of the Atlantic by Alcock and Brown, a race was held between the Post Office Tower, London, and the Empire State Building, New York, followed by a return trip. The Harrier took off from a coal yard by St Pancras station and landed at the Bristol Basin in a winning time of 6 hours 11 minutes. On the return leg a Navy Phantom won.

The inaugural flight of XV738, the first production GR.1, took

HARRIER GR.1 XV919 1 SQUADRON

XV919 was a 1 Squadron Harrier wearing the original scheme of dark sea grey and dark green camouflage with light aircraft grey undersides. While hovering it suffered an engine malfunction and made a heavy landing, receiving CAT4 damage in the process. Later repaired, it was converted to GR.3 standard.

place on December 28, 1967. By the end of 1968 a total of six had been completed. The Harrier Operational Conversion Unit was formed in January 1969 and RAF pilots began to familiarise themselves with the type. In April 1969, 1 Squadron began to receive the first of their Harriers and commence a 41-year association with the type.

As a trainer version had yet to be built, the training schedule for the 1 Squadron pilots was intensive, involving a helicopter course and a ground school course before a pilot could undertake a conventional flight. This was followed by the first short hovers. Naturally this new method of flying was not without mishaps and one Harrier missed the runway before landing inverted in a field of sprouts.

The following year the squadron began operating the Harrier in the environment it was designed for, taking off from farmers' fields around RAF Wittering and setting up bases in the surrounding woods.

1 Squadron was followed by 4 Squadron in June 1970, based at RAF Wildenrath, West Germany. 233 Operational Conversion Unit was formed at RAF Wittering and these were soon joined by 3 and 20 Squadrons. Due to the location of Wildenrath and its distance from the East German border, they were relocated to RAF Gütersloh which became the permanent home of the German Harriers.

Typical of cold war jets, the single seat version entered service before there was a trainer available. The order for the T.2 was placed

233

HARRIER GR.1 XV804 233 OCU

XV804 was with 233 OCU during 1975, having been delivered four years earlier. Converted to a GR.3, it later served with 4 Squadron in West Germany before sitting at North Luffenham for many years. The aircraft has since been restored.

in 1966 and involved extending the nose to create a tandem cockpit. The tail required lengthening due to the shift in the centre of gravity and with later versions the fin was made taller too. This design was also applied to the T.10, which was based on the second-generation Harrier.

The first operational deployment of the Harrier was to Belize in 1975. With the threat posed to the former colony of British Honduras, six aircraft were sent from 1 Squadron during Operation Nucha. 1417 Flight was formed and permanently based in Belize, remaining there until July 8, 1993.

With the development of the Pegasus 103, which delivered an extra 1000lb of thrust, and the installation of the Ferranti Laser Ranger and Marked Target Seeker (LRMTS) into a revised 'bottle'

nose, a new variant was created under the designation GR.3. The existing GR.1s all received the upgrade between 1973 and 1976 and a further 40 were built to the new standard.

While the Sea Harrier dominated the Falklands War, along with the few bombing missions of the Vulcans, the GR.3 also fulfilled a vital role – 1 Squadron was called upon to prepare for action. Suitable airframes were sourced from the UK squadrons with 10 being involved in the conflict, attacking ground targets. Three were lost as the result of ground fire and one in a landing accident but all the pilots survived.

The second generation Harrier was a US initiative to realise the full potential of the Harrier, creating a more powerful aircraft with greater weapons capacity. Originally this was to be a joint venture

HARRIER GR.3 ZD670 1417 FLIGHT

During 1975 there were concerns that Guatemala would invade neighbouring Belize, so 1 Squadron were sent out at short notice. The squadron was later replaced by 1417 Flight in 1980 which continued to fly the GR.3, including examples such as ZD670, until 1993.

but spending cuts in the 1975 Defence White Paper reduced the British involvement significantly.

Unlike the first generation Harriers, the new version was constructed using a range of composite materials and the nozzle shape was revised. Similar to the Sea Harrier, the cockpit was raised and the canopy size was increased for greater visibility. A new avionics system was also installed. The wings were expanded, allowing for four pylons per wing and thereby greatly increasing the weapons capacity of the Harrier. The outriggers were also moved inboard and Leading Edge Root Extensions (LERX) were fitted.

The new Pegasus 105, capable of delivering 21,750lb of thrust – 10,000lb more than the original found in the P.1127 – was fitted to the British version. This was designated the GR.5, an

order being placed for 60 (plus a further two for development) in 1981.

ZD318 was not ready to fly until April 30, 1985, and the RAF had to wait until April 1987 before deliveries to 233 OCU commenced. The next year 1 Squadron converted to the type, the other squadrons following as aircraft became available.

It may have been advanced compared to the first generation Harriers but there was still room for improvement with the GR.5. With the fitting of the Forward Looking Infra Red (FLIR) system, the new GR.7 had the ability to operate at night and in low light conditions. The absence of a radar meant it was not a truly night capable aircraft though.

Further improvements and the new Pegasus 107 saw the GR.7

become the GR.9, the final version of the RAF Harrier. These second generation Harriers saw active service, firstly with peace keeping forces in Kosovo, undertaking a number of strikes during March/April 1999. Then in February 2003 they were part of Operation Telic during the build up to the second Gulf War.

Ten GR.7s were dispatched to the region and remained there until late April. The longest deployment of the Harrier force was to Afghanistan in Operation Herrick, commencing in September 2004 and lasting until June 2009.

During an upgrade programme to the GR.9A, the Government announced, in a cost saving measure, that the entire Harrier fleet would be grounded at short notice and the airframes disposed of very cheaply to the US as spare parts. So on December 15, 2010, at a cold wet RAF Cottesmore, 16 Harriers plus a chase plane took off for a final flight. Upon return, ZG506, flown by Group Captain Gary Waterfall, waited until the other planes had landed, made a final bow to the crowd and touched down, bringing to an end the RAF's association with the formidable Harrier.

Hawker Siddeley/BAE Harrier

VARIANT	LENGTH	SPAN	HEIGHT	ENGINE
P.1127	41FT 2IN/12.55M	24FT 4IN/7.42M	10FT 9IN/3.28M	PEGASUS 2
KESTREL	22FT 10IN/12.8M	22FT 11IN/6.98M	10FT 9IN/3.28M	PEGASUS 5
GR.1	45FT 8IN/13.92M	25FT 3IN/7.7M	11FT 3IN/3.43M	PEGASUS 6 MK.101
GR.3	46FT 10IN/14.28M	25FT 3IN/7.7M	11FT 11IN/3.63M	PEGASUS 11 MK.103
FRS.1	47FT 7IN/14.5M	25FT 3IN/7.7M	12FT 2IN/3.71M	PEGASUS 11 MK.104
FA.2	46FT 6IN/14.2M	25FT 3IN/7.7M	12FT 2IN/3.71M	PEGASUS 11 MK.106
GR.5	46FT 4IN/14.12M	25FT 3IN/7.7M	11FT 8IN/3.56M	PEGASUS 11-21 MK.105
GR.7	46FT 4IN/14.12M	30FT 4IN/9.25M	11FT 8IN/3.56M	PEGASUS 11-21 MK.105
GR.9	46FT 4IN/14.12M	30FT 4IN/9.25M	11FT 8IN/3.56M	PEGASUS 11-21 MK.107
T.2	55FT 9.5IN/17.04M	25FT 3IN/7.7M	12FT/3.66M	PEGASUS 6 MK.101
T.4	57FT 2IN/17.42M	25FT 3IN/7.7M	13FT 8IN/4.17M	PEGASUS 11 MK.103
T.10	55FT 9IN/17M	25FT 3IN/7.7M	13FT 8IN/4.17M	PEGASUS 11-21 MK.105
T.12	55FT 9IN/17M	25FT 3IN/7.7M	13FT 8IN/4.17M	PEGASUS 11-21 MK.107

HARRIER GR.5 ZD349 3 SQUADRON

While still at RAF Gütersloh, West Germany, 3 Squadron replaced the GR.3 with the second generation GR.5. As a GR.7, ZD349 was being flown by Capt Brendan Hearney USMC on January 14, 1994, when it suffered engine failure after a bird strike and crashed near Aston Somerville, Cotswolds. Hearney died in the crash, having stayed with the aircraft to steer it away from homes. NATO IRR green and lichen green underside.

HARRIER GR.5 ZD409 1 SQUADRON

1 Squadron continued to deploy to Norway with the GR.5, applying temporary winter camouflage over the standard schemes worn by its aircraft. Several experimental patterns were applied.

1969 - 2010

ZG477

HARRIER GR.9A ZG477 1 SQUADRON

With the RAF Harrier fleet being retired on December 15, 2010, a number of
aircraft received special tails including 1 Squadron's ZG477.

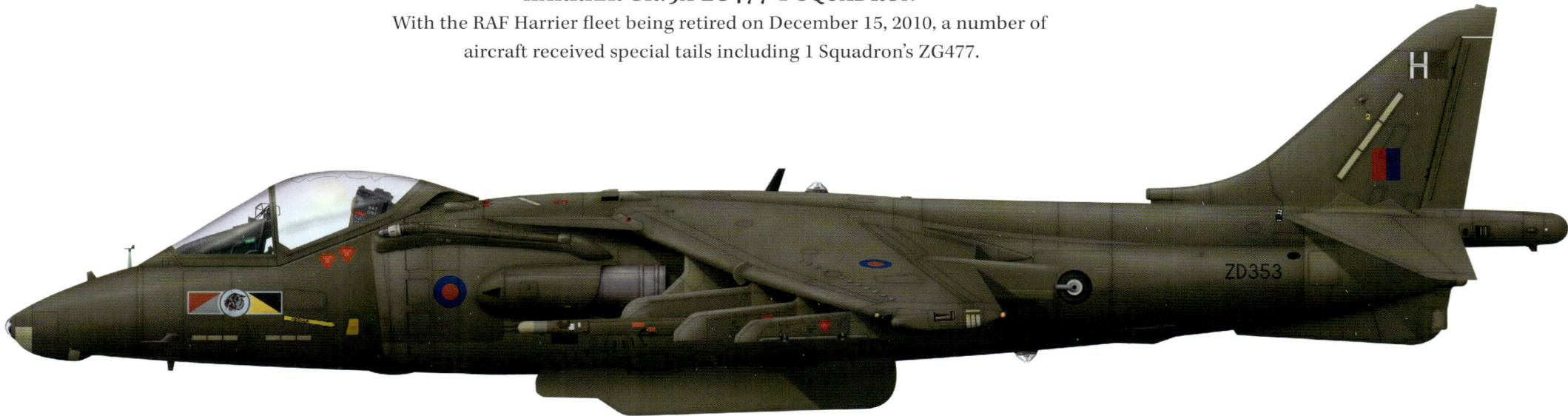

H

ZD353

HARRIER GR.5 ZD353 233 OCU

Based at RAF Wittering, ZD353 suffered a mid-air fire on June 29, 1991, and despite landing safely was subsequently written off.

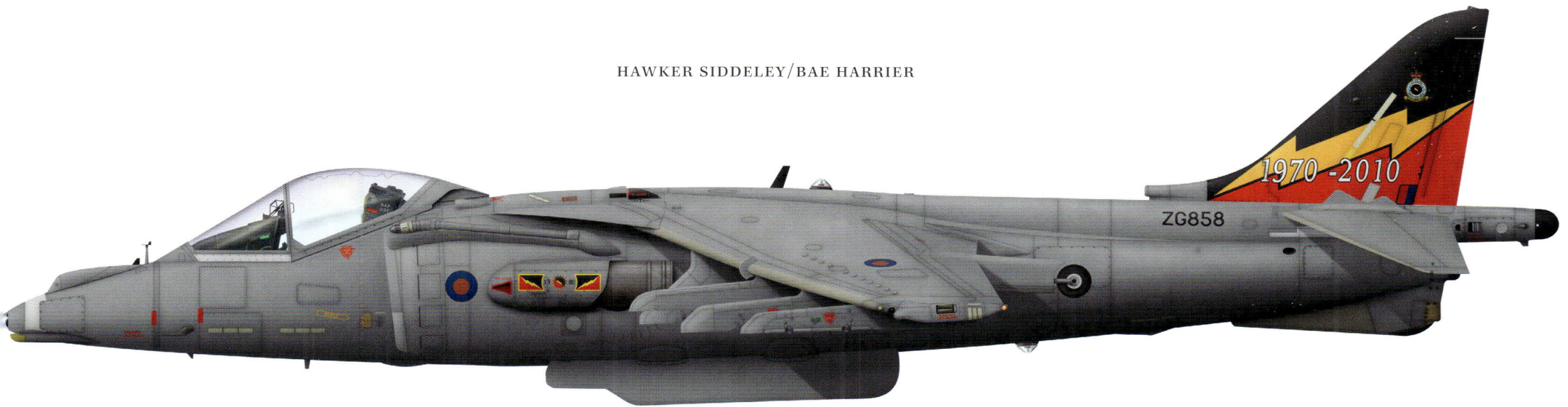

HARRIER GR.9 ZG858 4 SQUADRON

Similar to tail designs worn by earlier GR.3s, ZG858 commemorates 40 years of 4 Squadron's association with the Harrier.

HARRIER T.4A XW268 233 OCU

Built as a T.2, XW268 was converted to T.4 and later T.4A configuration. It served with 233 OCU from 1979 until 1983 when it was passed to the Royal Navy and converted to a T.4N. Currently at Norwich Aviation Museum.

HARRIER GR.9 ZD403 1 SQUADRON

As a tribute to Sgt Arthur Clowes' Hurricane P3395, his code JX-B and wasp were applied to the tail of ZD403. 1 Squadron have since applied the same markings to a Typhoon.

HARRIER T.2A XW926 3 SQUADRON

Built as a T.2A and delivered in May 1972, XW926 was later converted into a T.4. It was lost during a display when it collided with GR.3 XV795.

HARRIER GR.9 ZG478 41 SQUADRON

The RAF Test and Evaluation Squadron has operated a range of types including the Harrier, which had a special tail applied. ZG478 went on to have a heavy landing accident at Kandahar, Afghanistan, on May 14, 2009. The resulting fire severely damaged the 'Kandahar Kangaroo' but it has since been restored.

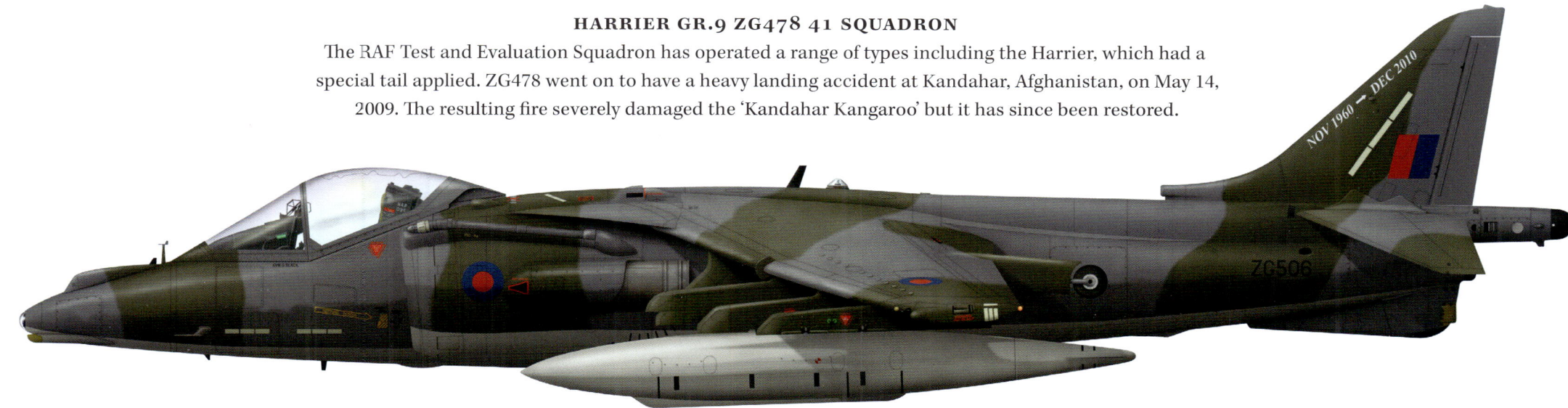

HARRIER GR.9 ZG506

As a homage to the GR.1 markings of 1969, ZG506 received a similar scheme. It was also the last RAF Harrier to fly when it touched down on December 15, 2010, flown by Group Captain Gary Waterfall, Joint Force Harrier Commander.

241

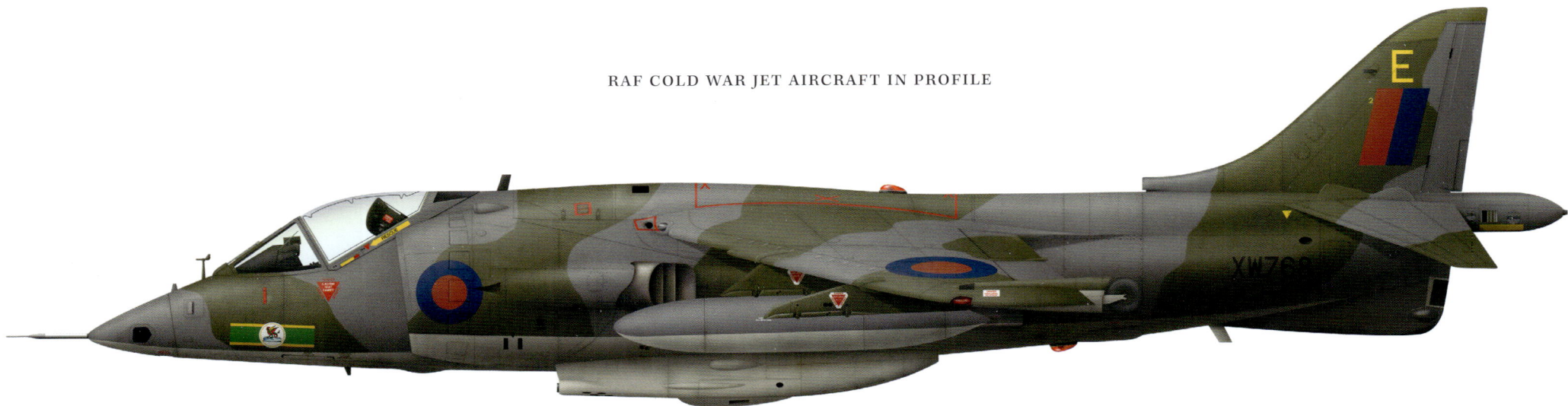

HARRIER GR.1 XW768 3 SQUADRON

Built as GR.1, XW768 served with both 20 and 3 Squadrons in West Germany during the 1970s before being converted to GR.3 standard. It was later flown to RAF Halton and used as an instructional airframe.

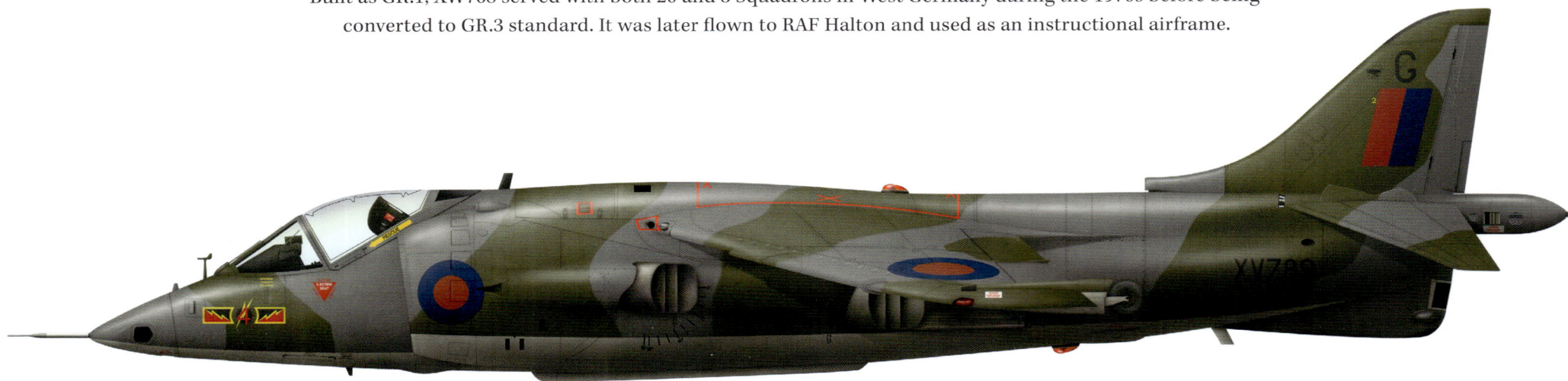

HARRIER GR.1 XV789 4 SQUADRON

XV789 first flew on March 26, 1970, and was delivered to 4 Squadron based in West Germany soon after. It was finished in the standard early Harrier scheme.

HARRIER GR.1 XW769 20 SQUADRON

This aircraft was operated by 20 Squadron, who used GR.1s and GR.3s while based at RAF Wildenrath, West Germany, between 1970 and 1977. They then converted to the Jaguar but the squadron would return to the Harrier in later years.

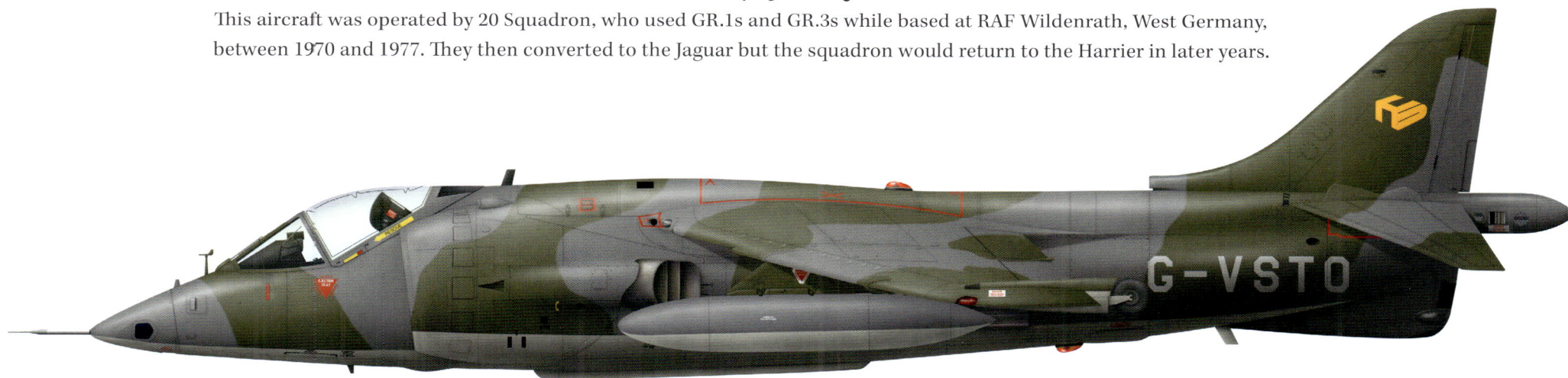

HARRIER GR.1 XV742 G-VSTO

Harrier XV742 was used as the company sales aircraft between July 7 and August 5, 1971, and put on the UK civil register while conducting displays in Europe. It was also briefly loaned to VMA-513 for evaluation. Later converted to GR.3 standard, it was written off on the Holbeach Range, Lincolnshire, on October 28, 1983, with the loss of pilot Flg Off J. R. Sewell.

HARRIER GR.3 XV760 3 SQUADRON

While based in West Germany some 3 Squadron aircraft temporarily wore a white tail fin during exercises in the summer of 1989 before the type was retired. XV760's nose was later converted to represent an FRS.1 for a museum exhibit.

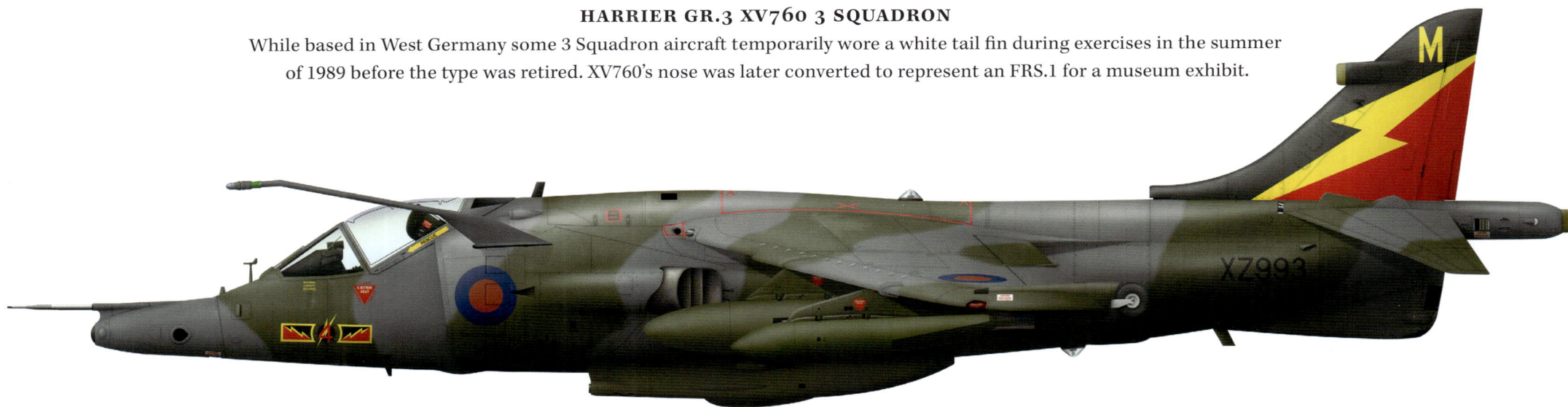

HARRIER GR.3 XZ993 4 SQUADRON

While operating the GR.3 at RAF Gütersloh, 4 Squadron painted several of their aircraft's tails with the squadron badge. The rest of XZ993 was painted in all over dark green and dark sea grey.

HARRIER GR.3 XW768 20 SQUADRON

Early GR.3s still wore the same scheme as the GR.1 with the light aircraft grey underside. This was phased out during the mid-1970s.

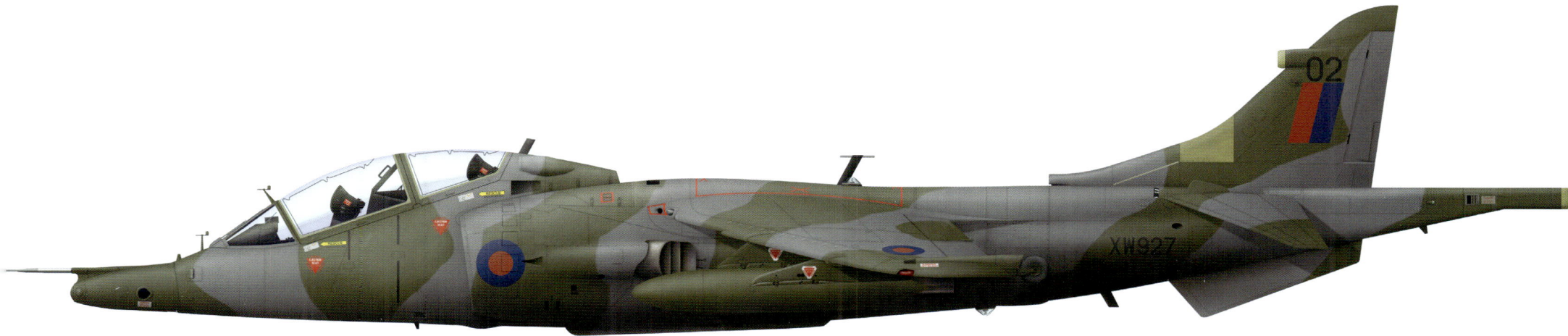

HARRIER T.4A XW927 GÜTERSLOH STATION FLIGHT

XW927 served with 233 OCU, 3 and 4 Squadrons, remaining in West Germany for the majority of its career. Heavily damaged during a landing at Gütersloh on February 7, 1992, it was not repaired due to the introduction of the T.8.

HARRIER GR.5 ZD318

The first Harrier GR.5 built, ZD318, made its first test flight on April 30, 1985, at Dunsfold before
it had visited the paint shop — the composite makeup of the rear fuselage being clearly evident.
Following retirement it was acquired by the Harrier Heritage Centre at Wittering.

HARRIER GR.5 ZD324

Flying for the first time on June 25, 1987, ZD324 was displayed at the Paris Air Show almost
immediately — hence the distinctive and unconventional 205 on the nose. Two years later, on October
31, 1997, while approaching Wittering the engine failed. The pilot successfully ejected.

HARRIER GR.7 ZD408 20 SQUADRON

Three of the Harriers involved in Operation Telic during May 2003, ZD408, ZG479 and ZG859,
had shark mouths applied and retained these upon return to the UK.

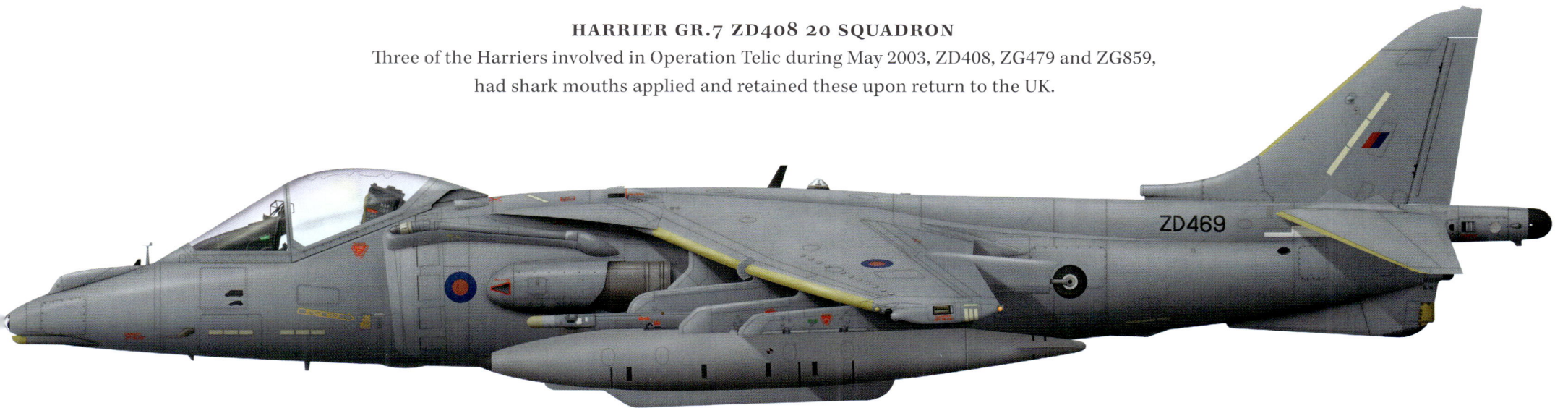

HARRIER GR.7 ZD469 'CHRISTINE'

Named after the car in the Stephen King book, ZD469 had a somewhat colourful career involving various incidents before being
written off during a rocket attack at Kanadahar on October 14, 2005. It was returned to the UK and eventually became the gate
guardian at Wittering. Even here, a car managed to leave the A1 and crash into it, a car 'kill' marking subsequently being added.

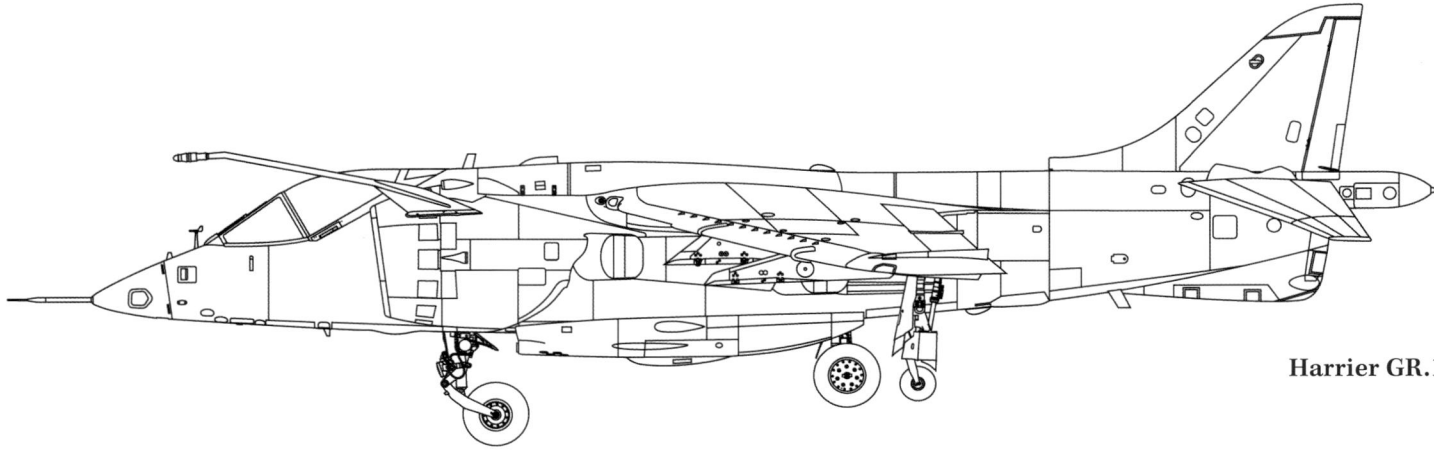

Harrier GR.1

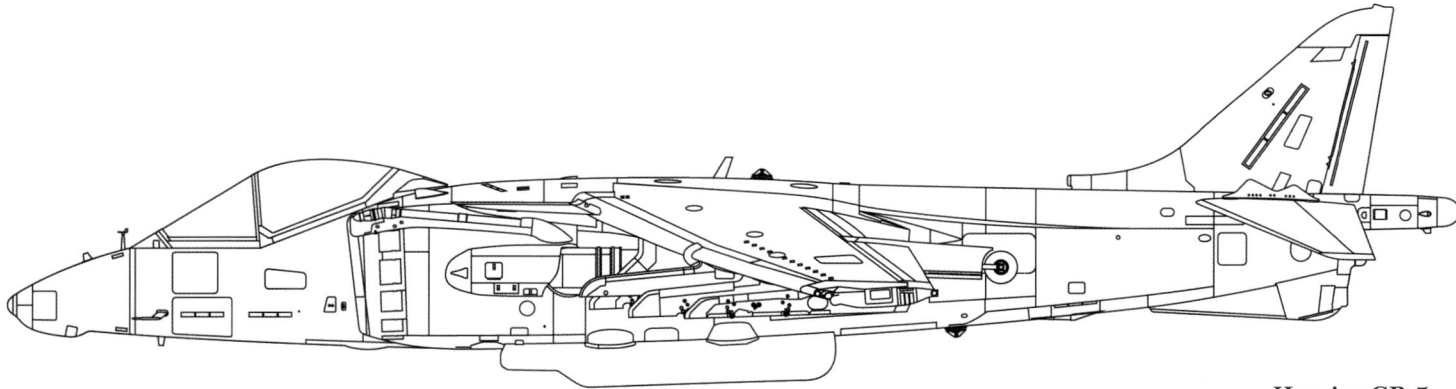

Harrier GR.5

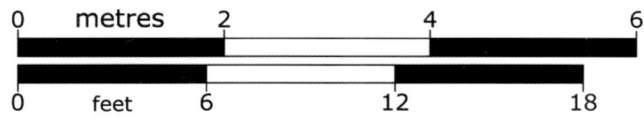

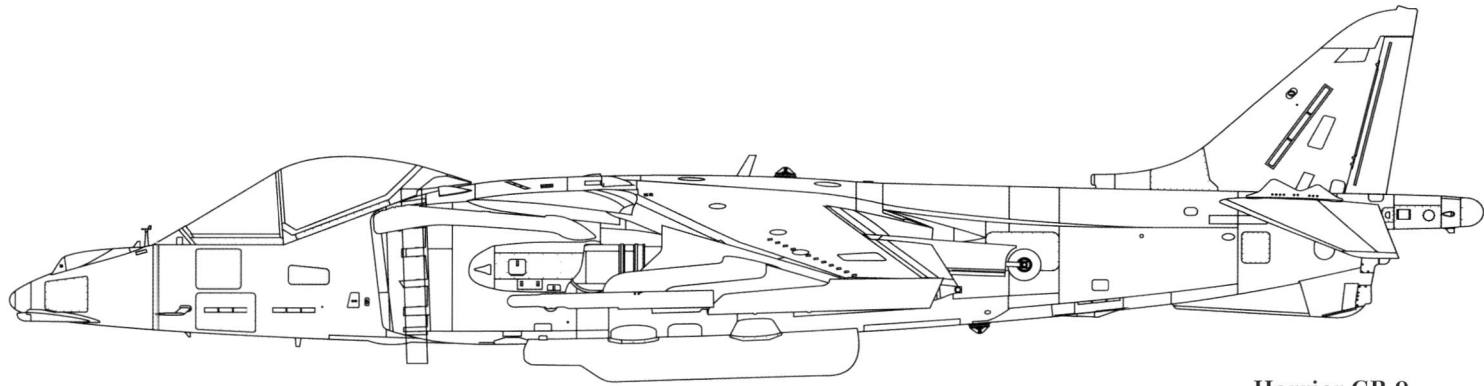

Harrier GR.9

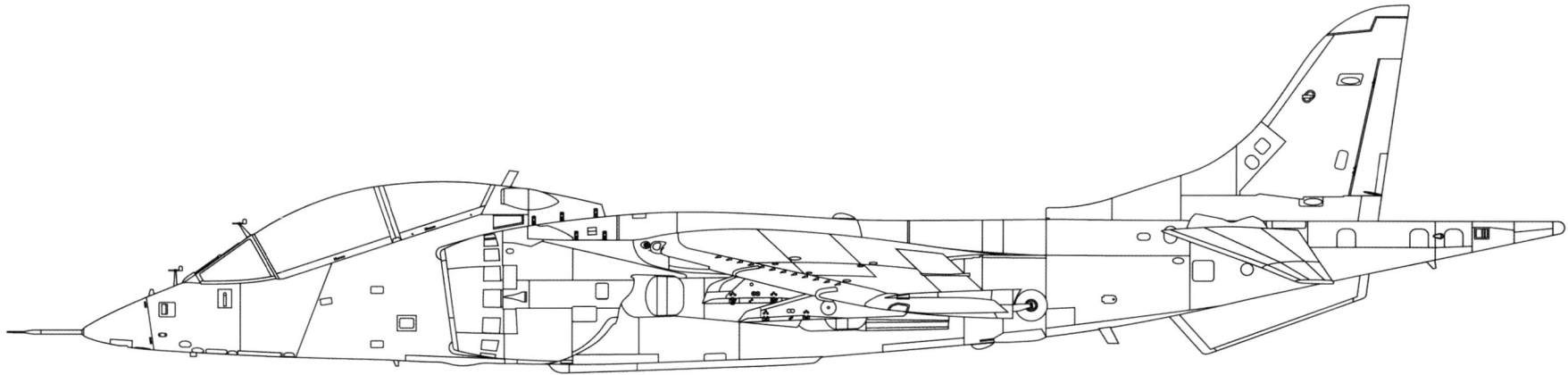

Harrier T.2

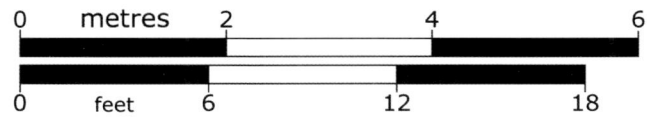

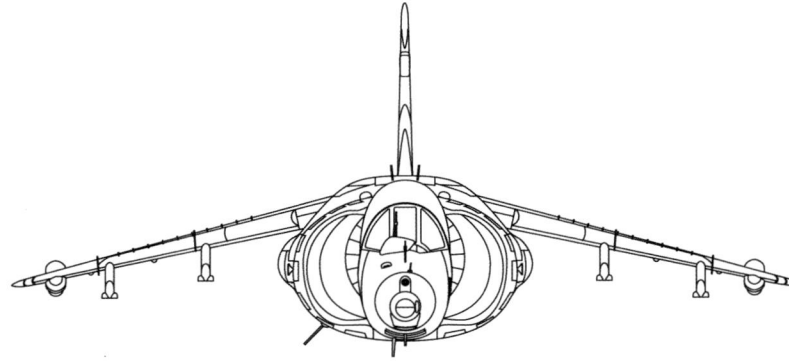

Harrier GR.3 front

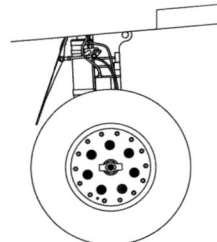

Main wheel

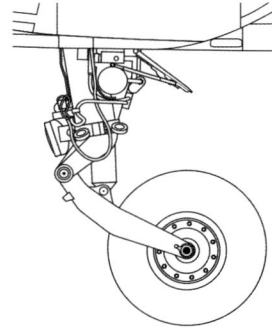

Nose wheel

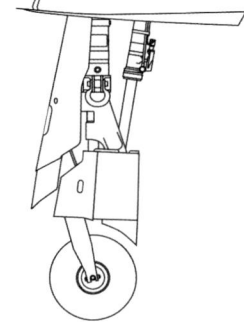

Outrigger

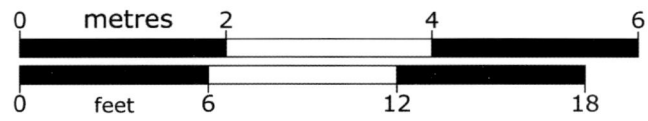

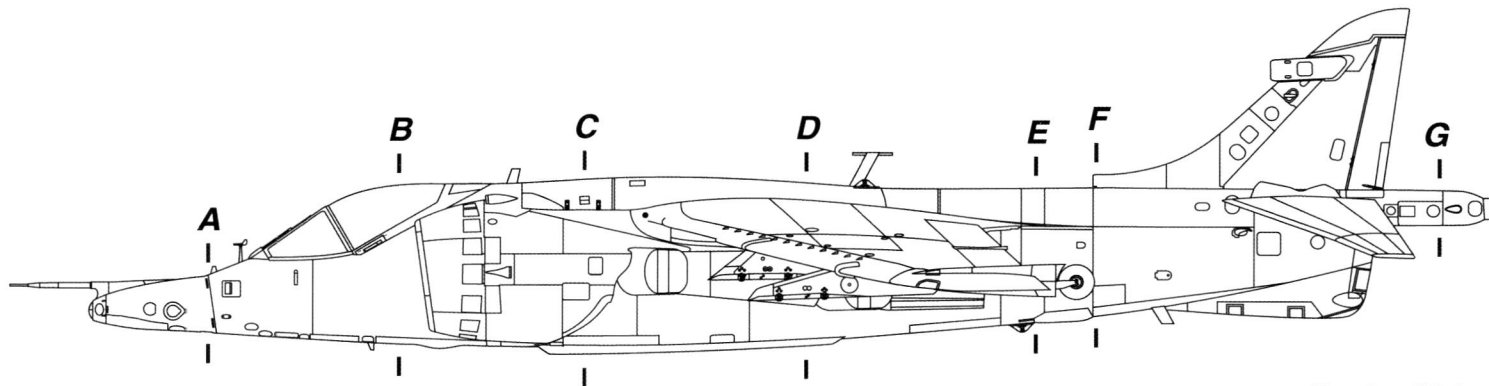

A B C D E F G

Harrier GR.3

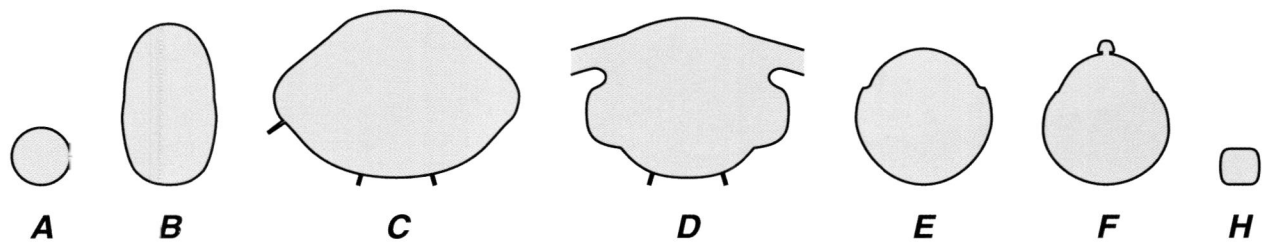

A   B   C   D   E   F   H

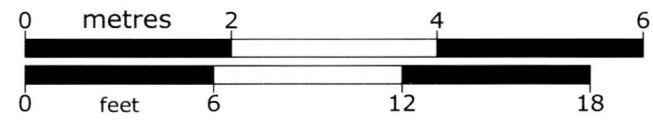

0   metres   2   4   6

0   feet   6   12   18

Harrier GR.3 top

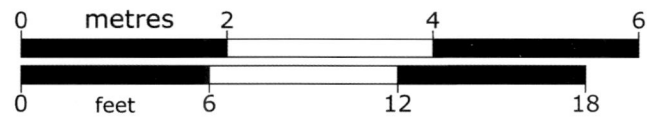

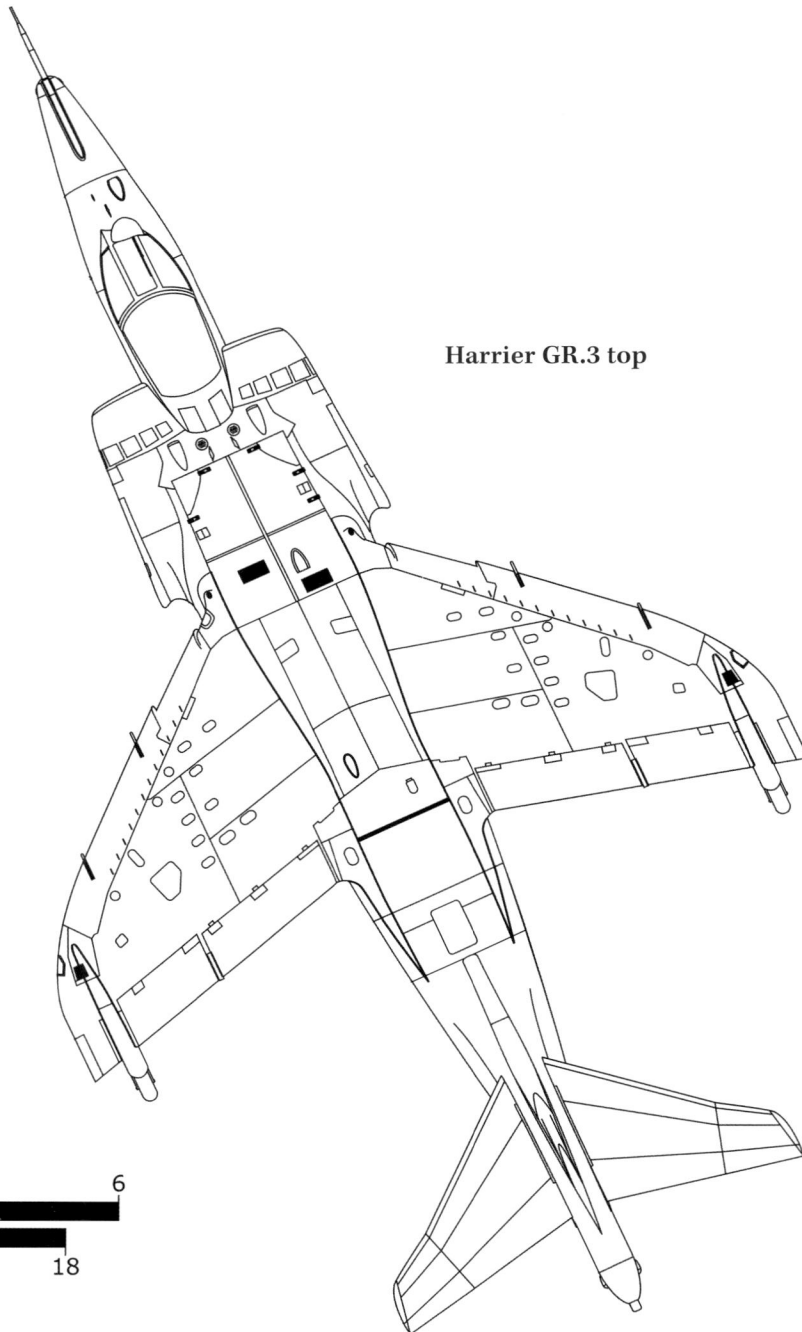

metres
0   2   4   6

feet
0   6   12   18

Harrier GR.3 underside

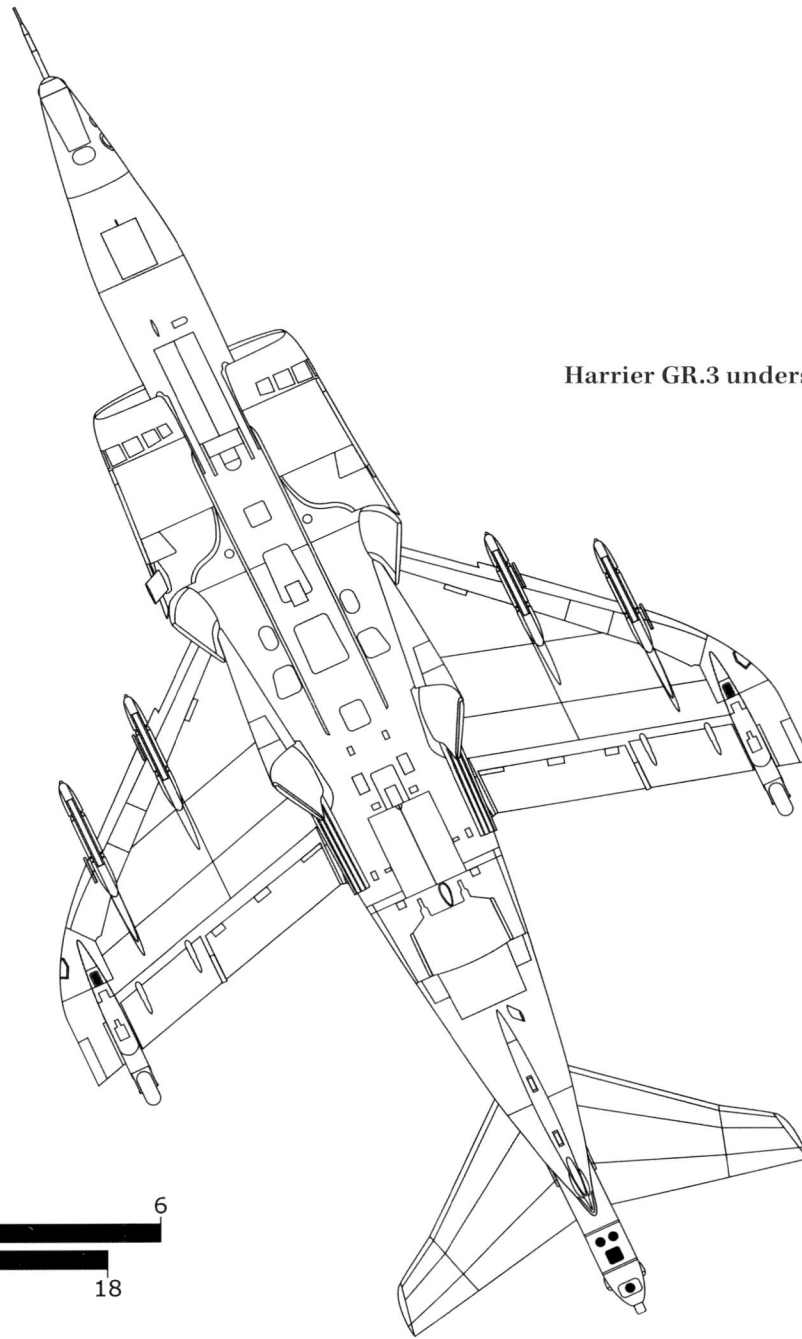

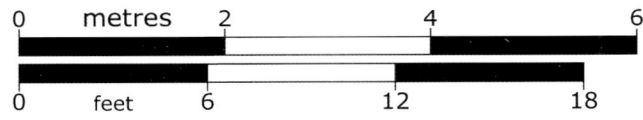

metres
0   2   4   6

feet
0   6   12   18

BLACKBURN BUCCANEER

It may have been born out of cold war necessity but the Buccaneer was never intended for RAF use, nor was it wanted by the RAF. The cancellation of the TSR2 and the failure of the F-111K to materialise, however, left the Buccaneer as the only option and it is what the RAF received.

During the early post-war years, the Soviet fleet saw the introduction of Sverdlov class cruisers which were perceived as a very serious threat by the Admiralty, being far superior to anything NATO was operating at that time. To neutralize this threat, an aircraft was required which could fly below enemy radar at a high enough speed for a surprise attack.

During a time when the RAF was still convinced that high-altitude bombing was the way forward, this displays remarkable foresight by the Admiralty—as the later switch to low level by the V force and requirements for the Jaguar were to prove. Specification M148T was issued in June 1952 and laid out the requirement for an aircraft that could fly under enemy radar at 200ft, with a range of over 400 nautical miles at 550 knots, while carrying a 4000lb payload of either conventional or nuclear weapons.

It also had to be able to detect enemy shipping with radar, have a wingspan of no more than 20ft and a length not in excess of 51ft when stored. This was quite a formidable set of specifications for a carrier based aircraft when the jet industry was still relatively young.

At that time, Blackburn was producing the Beverley piston engine transport but had been involved in the construction and testing of the Rolls-Royce Nene powered Handley Page HP.88 experimental aircraft. It had therefore gained some valuable experience in the field of jet aircraft design.

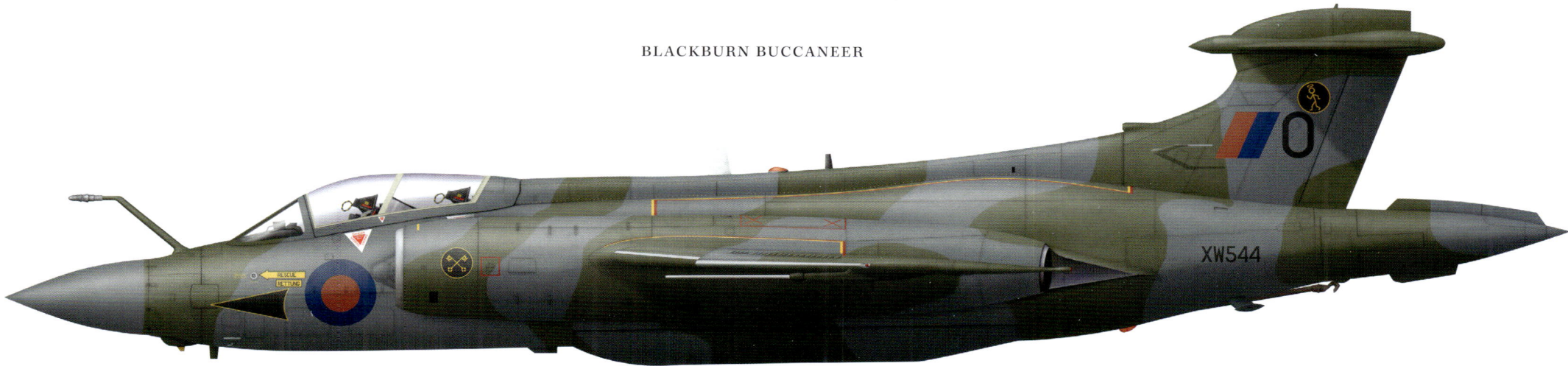

BUCCANEER S.2B XW544 16 SQUADRON
Having entered service with 15 Squadron, RAF Laarbruch, West Germany in June 1972, XW544 was
transferred to 16 Squadron in 1979. Following retirement in May 1985, it ended up at Bruntingthorpe as
a ground runner. It wears a standard RAF wraparound of dark sea grey and dark green.

The Blackburn tender for M148T, designated B-103 by the company, won the contract in 1955. Originally the Armstrong Siddeley Sapphire engine was to be used for the production model Buccaneer S.1, but it flew instead with two de Havilland Gyron Junior engines, these being a downscaled version of the Gyron, which was intended for use by the Hawker P.1121. These would later be replaced by the Rolls-Royce Spey in the S.2 and S.2B variants of the Buccaneer, with a larger intake required as part of the modification.

Blackburn had also begun experiments with boundary layer control to improve performance at low speeds. This involved bleeding high pressure air directly from the engines and blowing it across parts of the wing surfaces. Early results were very positive, the extra lift generated allowing for reduced take-off and landing

speeds which made a big difference to a carrier-based aircraft. It also had the advantage of a much smaller wing area, which would in turn be beneficial for low-level high-speed flight.

The boundary layer control system did lead to an increase in nose down pitching, but that was overcome by adding a blowing slit to the underside of the tailplane to compensate. The final key design feature, which led to the very distinctive Coke bottle look of the Buccaneer, was the application of the area rule. As an aircraft approaches the speed of sound shockwaves build up, particularly in the cross sectional area where the wings are. A convection of the fuselage can counter this and is a feature of many aircraft, but it is especially noticeable in the profile of the Buccaneer.

Most of the flight testing and early history of the Buccaneer

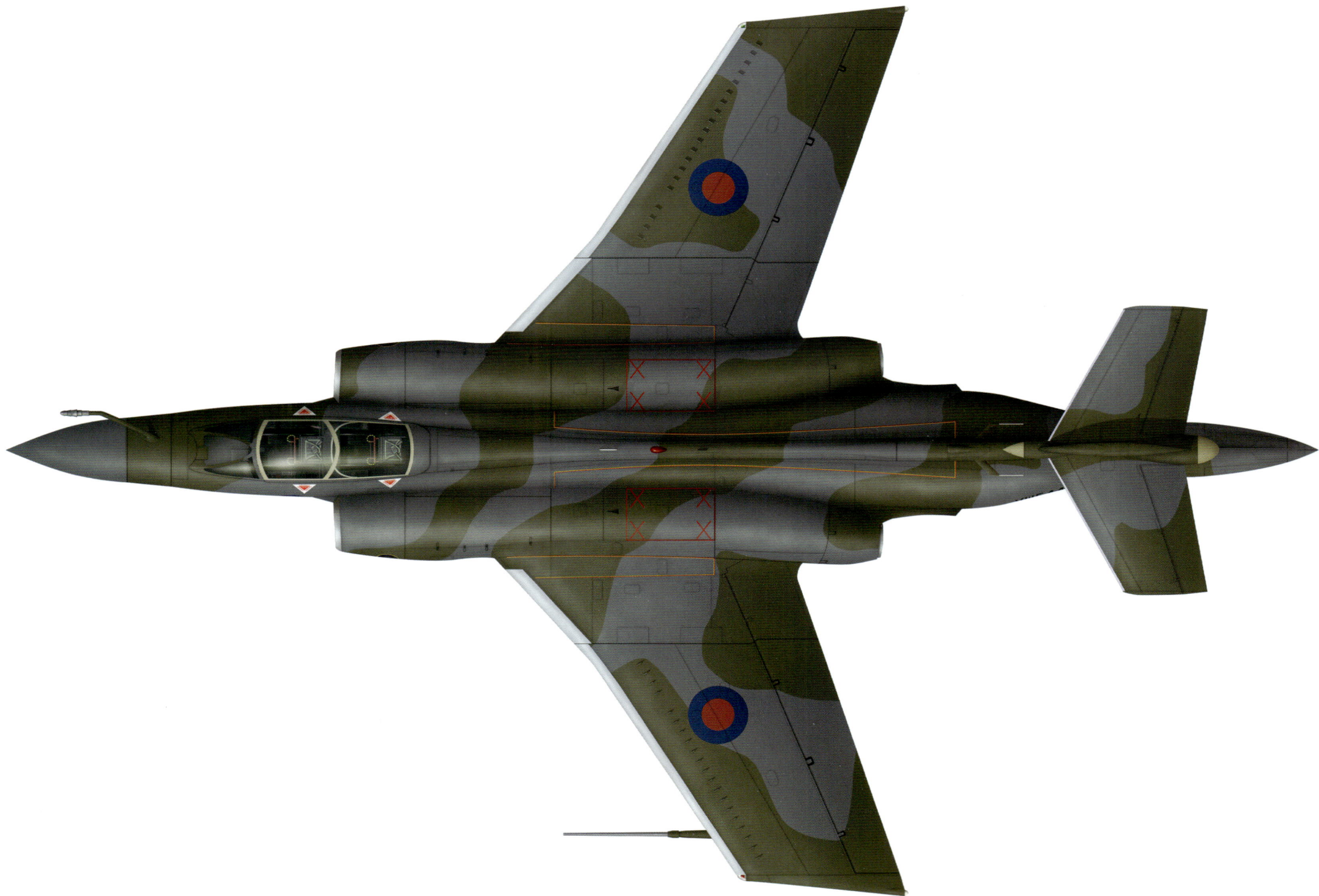

BUCCANEER S.1 XN923

Buccaneer S.1 XN923 was assigned to A&AEE in July 1962 for trials, having spent two months with 700Z flight. It was used exclusively for trials until struck off charge on May 17, 1974, and is currently on display at Gatwick Aviation Museum and ground running. Its scheme upon retirement was over all white with red radome and blue tail (possibly roundel blue).

was focused on preparing it for carrier operations and a role in naval squadrons, and it was not until July 1968 that the Ministry of Defence told the RAF it was getting the Buccaneer. An order was raised for 26 S.2s.

As the Royal Navy wound down its large carriers during the 1970s, the FAA Buccaneers were fed into RAF squadrons, providing a steady supply of additional aircraft to complement the new-delivery aircraft. The first of these, XV350, was delivered to 12 Squadron when it re-formed on October 1, 1969, at RAF Honington. At this time the RAF had not made the move to the low visibility roundel and all over camouflage, so early aircraft were finished in gloss dark green and dark sea grey with light aircraft grey, the roundels retaining their ring of white.

The first new purpose-built RAF Buccaneer flew in January 1970 and by the start of October there were sufficient aircraft to re-equip 15 Squadron. Shortly after re-forming, also at RAF Honington, they were moved to RAF Laarbruch, West Germany. 15 Squadron were joined by 16 Squadron in West Germany when they re-formed in January 1973.

The next summer, 208 Squadron joined 12 Squadron and 237 OCU at Honington. The final Buccaneer squadron was the short-lived 216 Squadron which was formed with the intention of being a Maritime Strike unit, however the Buccaneer fleet was grounded following a fatal accident at Red Flag, Nevada, in 1980. Subsequent inspections revealed that fatigue had caused the front spar to fail. Many aircraft were repaired but some were scrapped. As a result,

BUCCANEER S.2B XN976 208 SQUADRON

XN976 was the first S.2 received by the Royal Navy and was initially sent to Boscombe Down for trials. Following transfer to the RAF, it was upgraded to S.2B standard. In May 1991 it received a special seventh anniversary scheme of all over gloss black. The aircraft crashed on July 9, 1992.

216 Squadron never became operational due to a shortage of airframes and their aircraft were allocated to 12 Squadron instead.

Once the Buccaneer had been cleared to fly again, the squadrons relocated from RAF Honington to RAF Lossiemouth. As part of the UN intervention in Lebanon, some Buccaneers were tasked with supporting the British peacekeepers during Operation Pulsator. Six were based at RAF Akrotiri in the autumn of 1983 and two overflew Beirut in a show of force.

As the Tornado entered service, the Buccaneer's days as a strike aircraft were numbered, but in 1991 the aircraft was given the opportunity for a swansong. At just three days' notice, the remaining squadrons were tasked with preparing the Buccaneer for a laser designation role, using the Westinghouse AN/ASQ-23E laser pod, to support the Tornados during Operation Granby in the Gulf region.

An all over desert pink scheme was hastily applied and the 12 aircraft flew out to the Middle East. Once there, the conditions caused the paint scheme to fade and weather rapidly. Like other RAF aircraft involved in Granby, the Buccaneers all received nose art too.

Upon their return the remaining Buccaneers were to have their desert colours replaced with a new all over medium sea grey and camouflage grey scheme with revised national markings. This was a short-lived scheme as the type was officially retired on March 31, 1994. To commemorate the event, Buccaneers were painted up in the schemes of the RAF squadrons that had flown the type and one was painted in 809 NAS colours as a tribute to its naval origins.

Despite its performance and reputation, the Buccaneer was only exported to one country — South Africa — with Bristol Siddeley BS.605 rocket motors installed in the rear fuselage to aid take-off from high-altitude airfields. Even then, numbers were limited due to the fear that it could be used to keep apartheid in place.

Interest was also expressed by West Germany but the sale never went through. Since retirement, several Buccaneers have ended up being kept in serviceable condition. There are also airworthy examples in South Africa. For an aircraft that the RAF never wanted and only reluctantly accepted, it became much loved by all those involved and was missed when it was eventually retired.

Blackburn Buccaneer

VARIANT	LENGTH	SPAN	HEIGHT	ENGINE
S.1	63FT 5IN/19.33M	42FT 4IN/12.9M	16FT 3IN/4.95M	2 X GYRON JUNIOR DGJ.1
S.2 (SHORY WING)	63FT 5IN/19.33M	42FT 4IN/12.9M	16FT 3IN/4.95M	2 X RB.168-1A SPEY
S.2B (LONG WING)	63FT 5IN/19.33M	44FT/13.41M	16FT 3IN/4.95M	2 X RB.168-1A SPEY

BUCCANEER S.2B XV160 208 SQUADRON

Having initially served with the Royal Navy, XV160 was transferred to the RAF in 1970. In November 1977, while on exercise in Norway, a temporary white scheme was applied over the usual dark green. The underside remained light aircraft grey. XV160 crashed in September 1982, while off the coast of Sardinia.

BUCCANEER S.2B XW529 COLD WEATHER TRIALS

Delivered directly to A&AEE on September 29, 1970, XW529 was used for Martel trials and later Cold Weather Trials with an 'Explore Canada's Arctic, North West Territories' badge added to the starboard nose and tail. XW529 was eventually struck off charge in 1993 and finally scrapped in 1997.

BUCCANEER S.2A XT273 237 OCU

Constructed as an S.2, XT273 was converted to S.2A configuration while still with the Royal Navy. In June 1975 it was transferred to 237 OCU where this scheme was applied. At this stage the underside was still light aircraft grey but it wore the later style roundels.

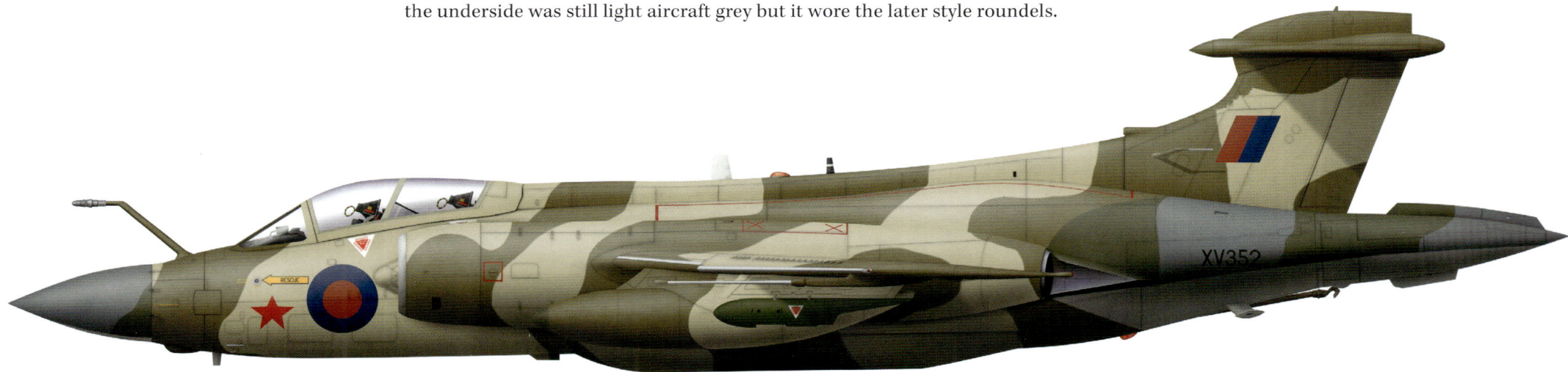

BUCCANEER S.2B XV352 208 SQUADRON

While taking part in the Red Flag exercise at Nellis AFB in August 1977, XV352 had a temporary scheme of dark earth and light stone applied over most areas except the nose and tail. The scheme was removed shortly after its return to RAF Honington.

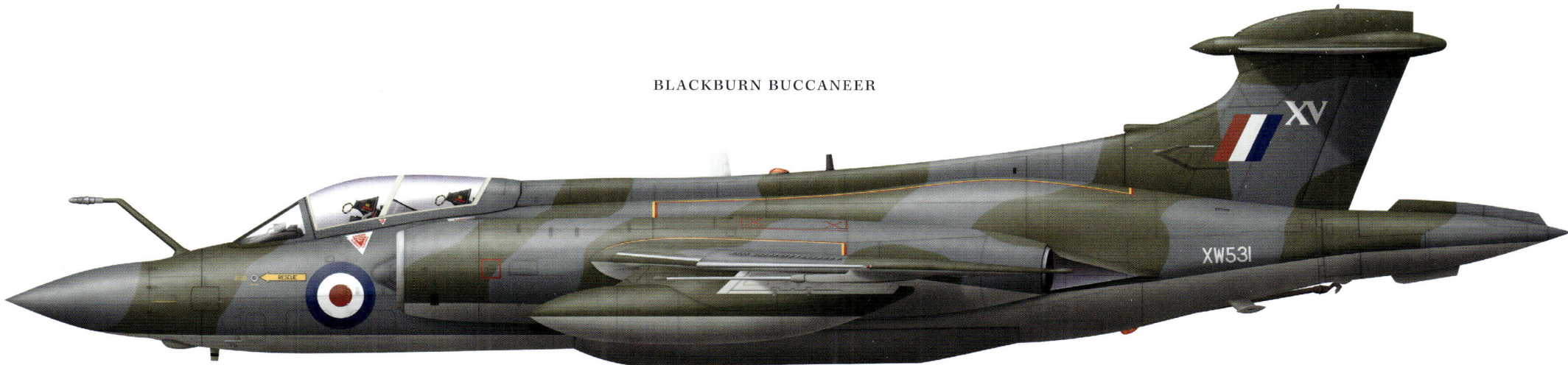

BUCCANEER S.2B XW531 15 SQUADRON

S.2B XW531 entered service in December 1970 with 15 Squadron at RAF Honington. It wore the early scheme of dark sea grey/dark green camouflage with light aircraft grey undersides. Early RAF Buccaneers wore a gloss scheme and also had red, white and blue roundels. XW531 crashed off the coast of Norway on October 29, 1976.

BUCCANEER S.2B XV863 OP GRANBY

XV863 was delivered to the Royal Navy in 1968 and saw active service in the Gulf War during Operation Granby. It remained there for just over a month in the Pavespike laser designation role. It wore the nose art Sea Witch Debbie and six mission symbols on the starboard side. A temporary scheme of desert pink was applied and this quickly weathered. After surviving many years in retirement, in early 2022 it was announced that XV863 had been sold for scrap.

BUCCANEER S.2B XW543 12 SQUADRON

Supplied to 15 Squadron at RAF Laarbuch, Germany, in May 1972, XW543 served with a
number of squadrons. It was repainted for the last time in all over medium sea grey in August
1990 with low visibility markings and two years later, in May 1992, it was scrapped.

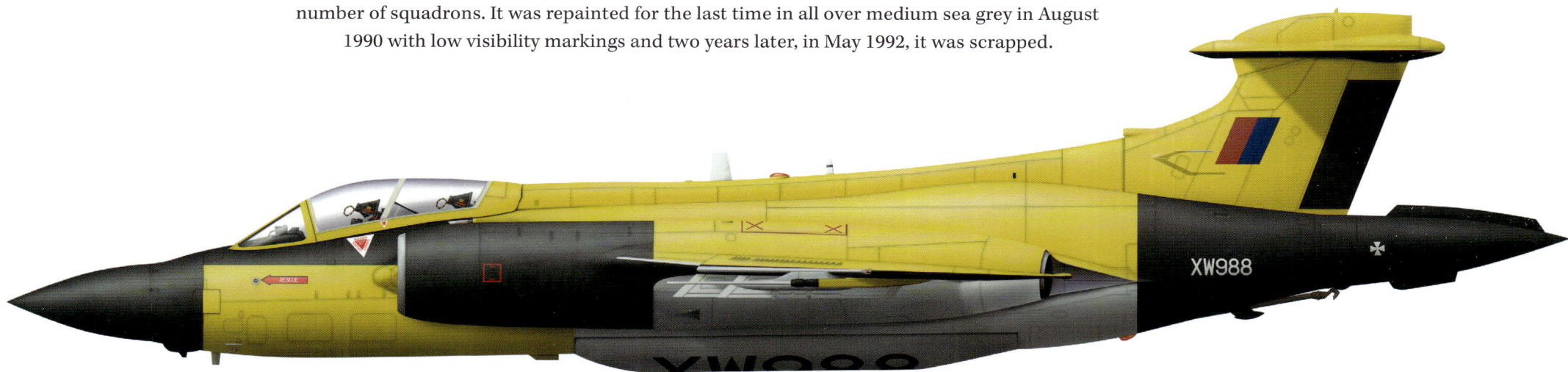

BUCCANEER S.2B XW988 A&AEE

Destined for the RAE from the outset, XW988 received a high visibility yellow, extra dark green and white scheme. When the initial drawing for
the scheme was supplied, someone had written the serial across the underside just for reference. However, this was applied to the full length
of the bomb bay and was retained. The aircraft was eventually sold to Thunder City in South Africa and has since been purchased by Hangar 51.

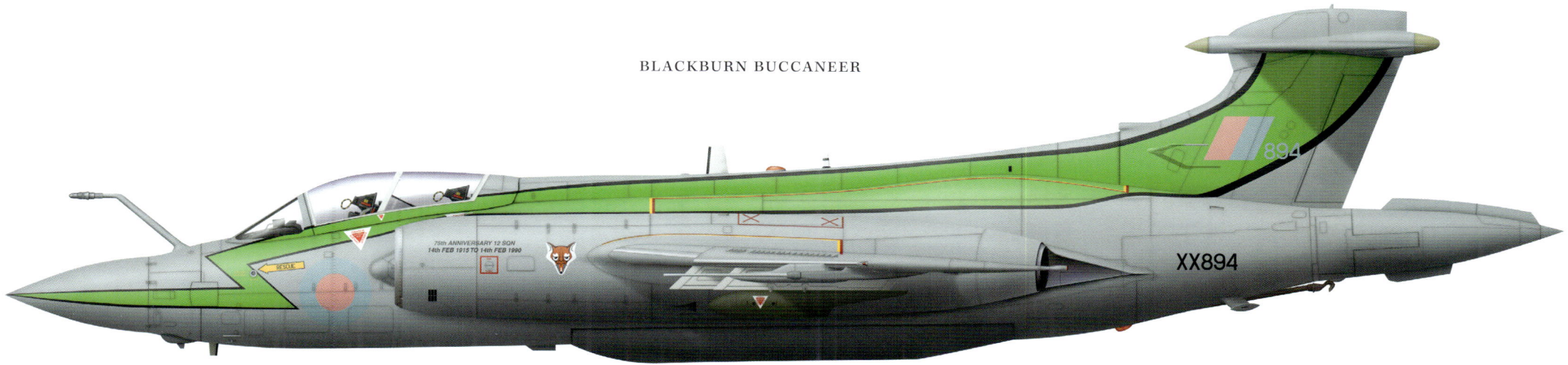

BUCCANEER S.2B XX894 12 SQUADRON

Wearing a scheme to commemorate the 75th anniversary of 12 Squadron, XX894 had a green
flash that was painted on top of the standard all-over medium sea grey.

BUCCANEER S.2B XX901 208 SQUADRON

Delivered to 208 Squadron on January 4, 1977, XX901 remained with them for a decade. As well as wearing 901 on the tail, it had a
temporary '3' during exercises. It later served in the Gulf during Operation Granby. Now on display at Yorkshire Air Museum, Elvington.

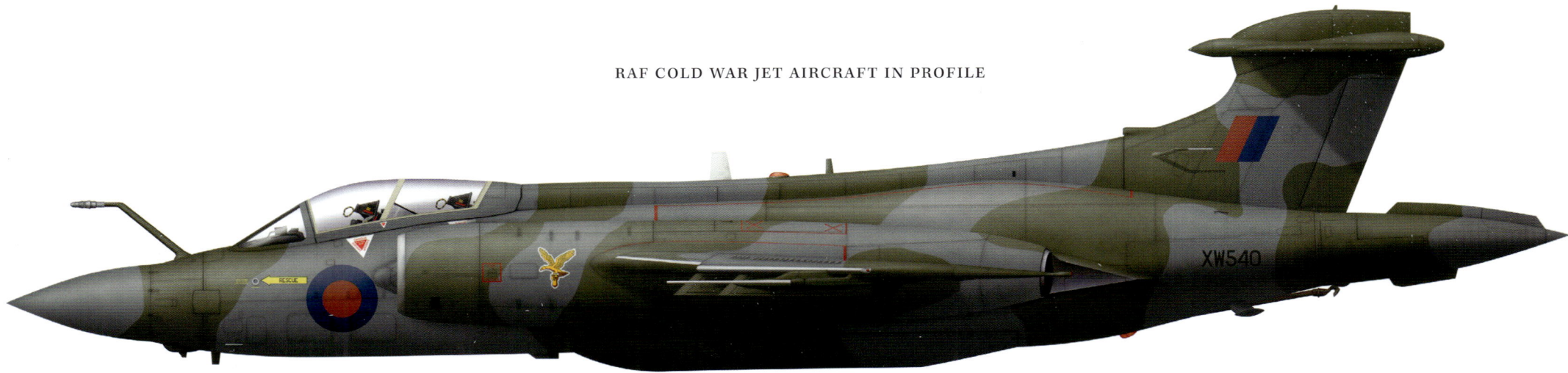

BUCCANEER S.2B XW540 216 SQUADRON

216 Squadron's association with the Buccaneer was brief, only having the type
for six months from July 1979 and never officially becoming operational. All their
aircraft including XW540 were subsequently passed to 12 Squadron.

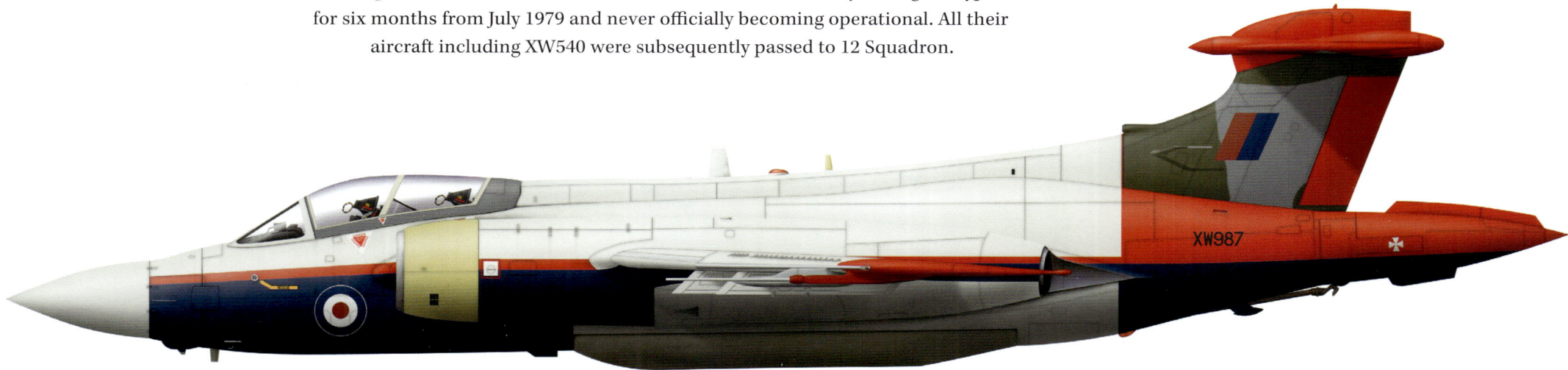

BUCCANEER S.2B XW987 A&AEE

XW987 was commissioned specifically for the RAE and originally painted in a high visibility scheme before being
repainted in a Raspberry Ripple scheme of signal red, white and Oxford blue (all gloss) in May 1982. Retired
in February 1995, it was sold to Thunder City, South Africa, and is now owned by Hangar 51.

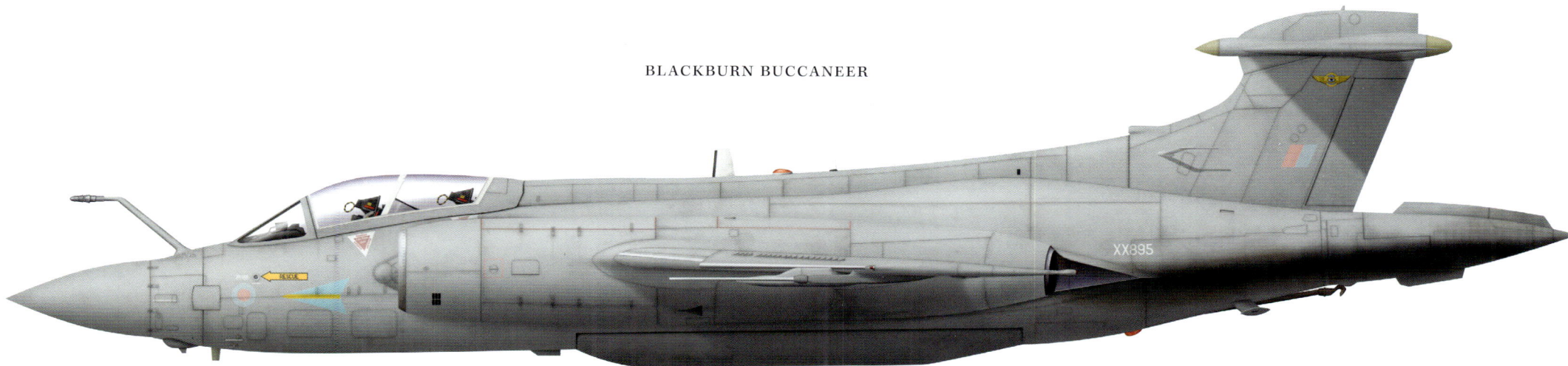

BUCCANEER S.2B XX895 208 SQUADRON

Wearing the late service low visibility markings of 208 Squadron, XX895 had previously
served in the Gulf War as Jaws/Lynn. Once retired, it was displayed in a bar in Woking and
now only the nose sections survives, once again wearing the Gulf War colours.

BUCCANEER S.2B XX899 'P' OPERATION GRANBY

XX899 was delivered directly to the RAF on September 29, 1976. After serving with 12 Squadron and 237 OCU, it was used during the first Gulf
War where the nose art 'Laser Lips Laura' was applied. The nose section has been restored and was loaned to Newark Air Museum in 2018.

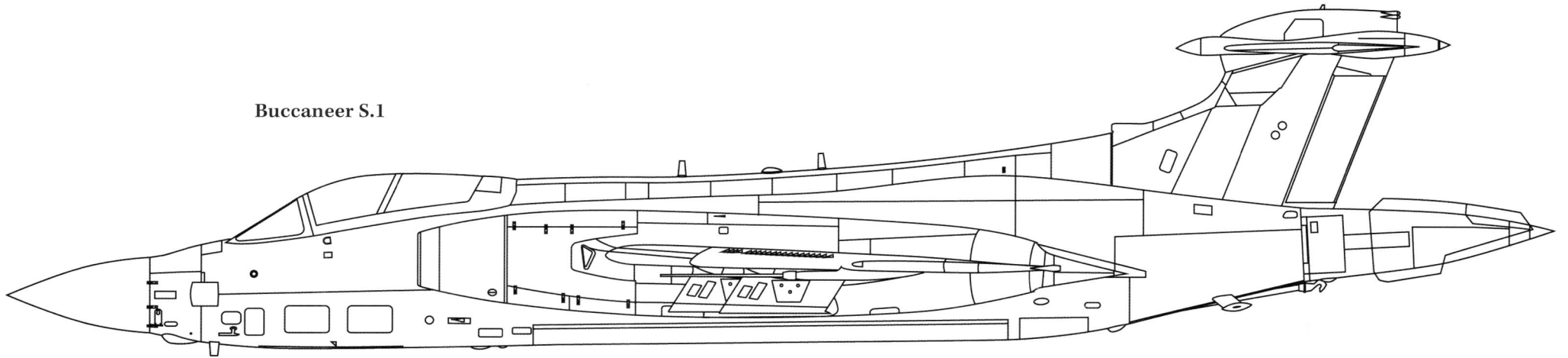

Buccaneer S.1

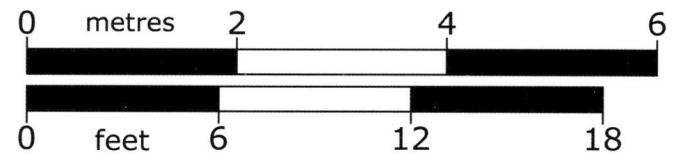

Buccaneer S.2B folded wings

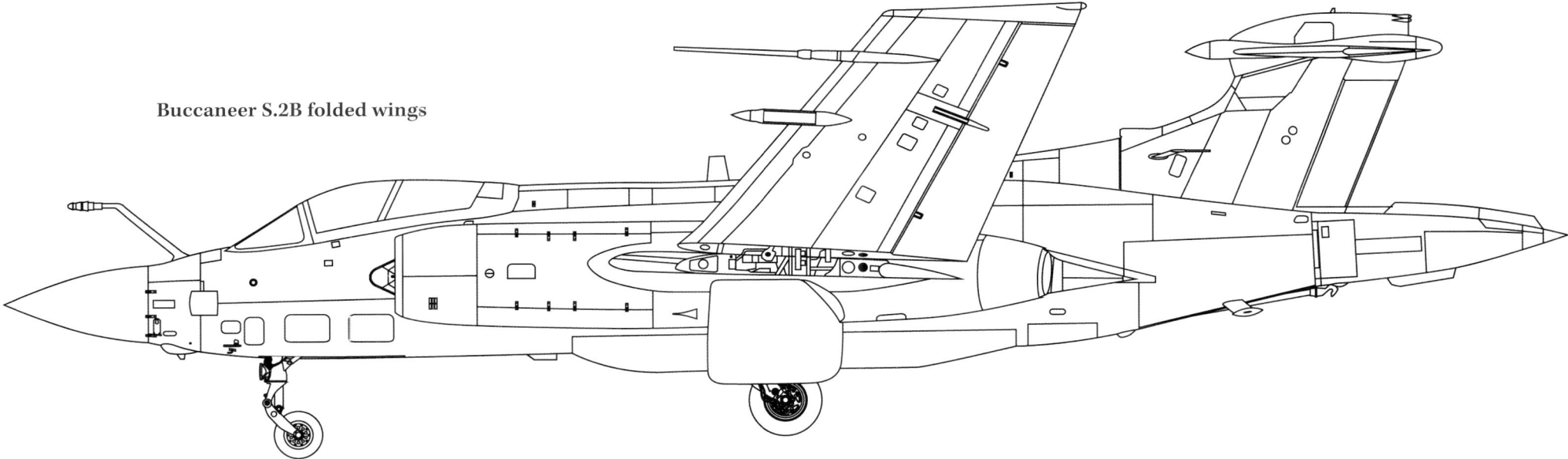

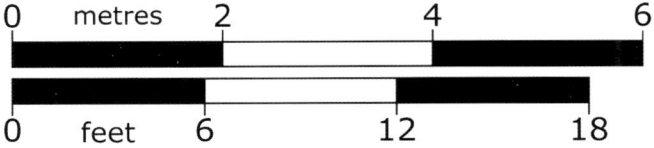

0   metres   2   4   6

0   feet   6   12   18

A

B

C

D

E

F

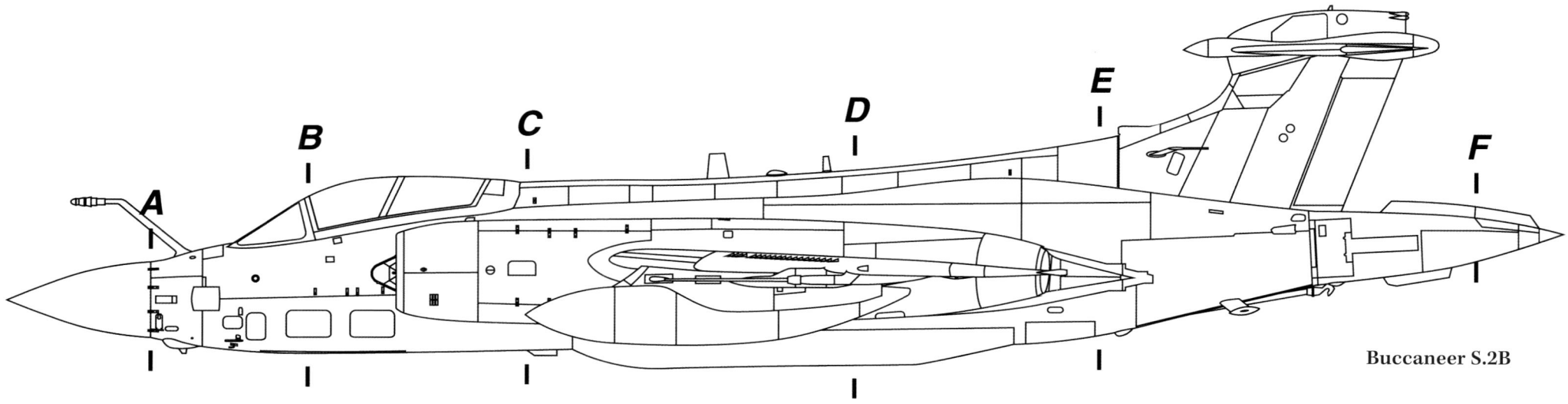

Buccaneer S.2B

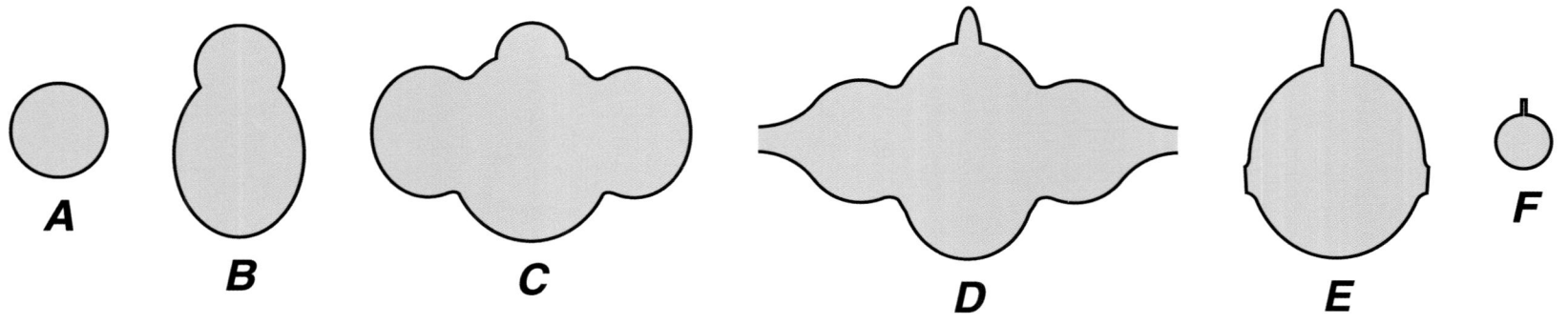

A

B

C

D

E

F

| 0 | metres | 2 | | 4 | | 6 |

| 0 | feet | 6 | | 12 | | 18 |

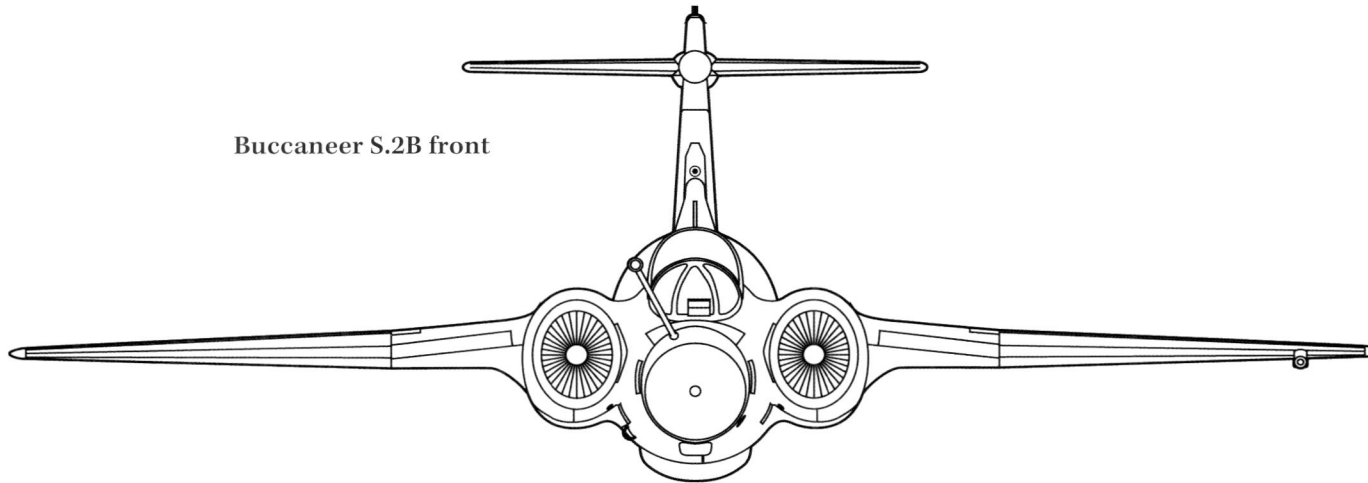

Buccaneer S.2B front

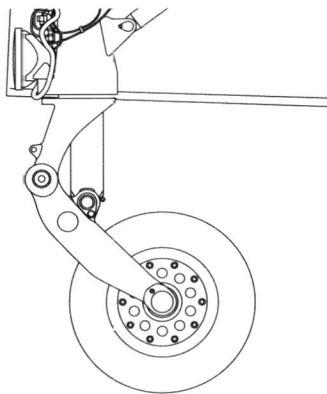

Nose wheel

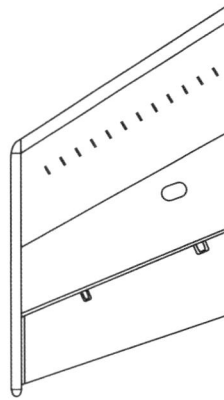

Scrap view alternative
wing tip

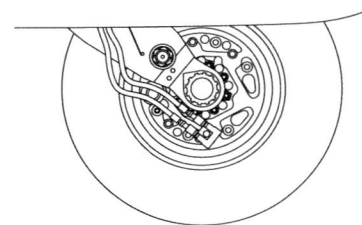

Main wheel

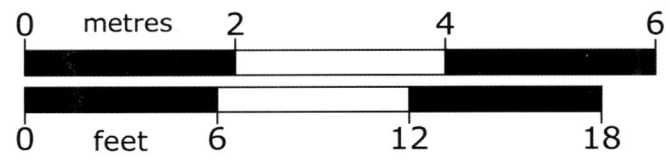

0 metres 2 4 6

0 feet 6 12 18

Buccaneer S.2B top

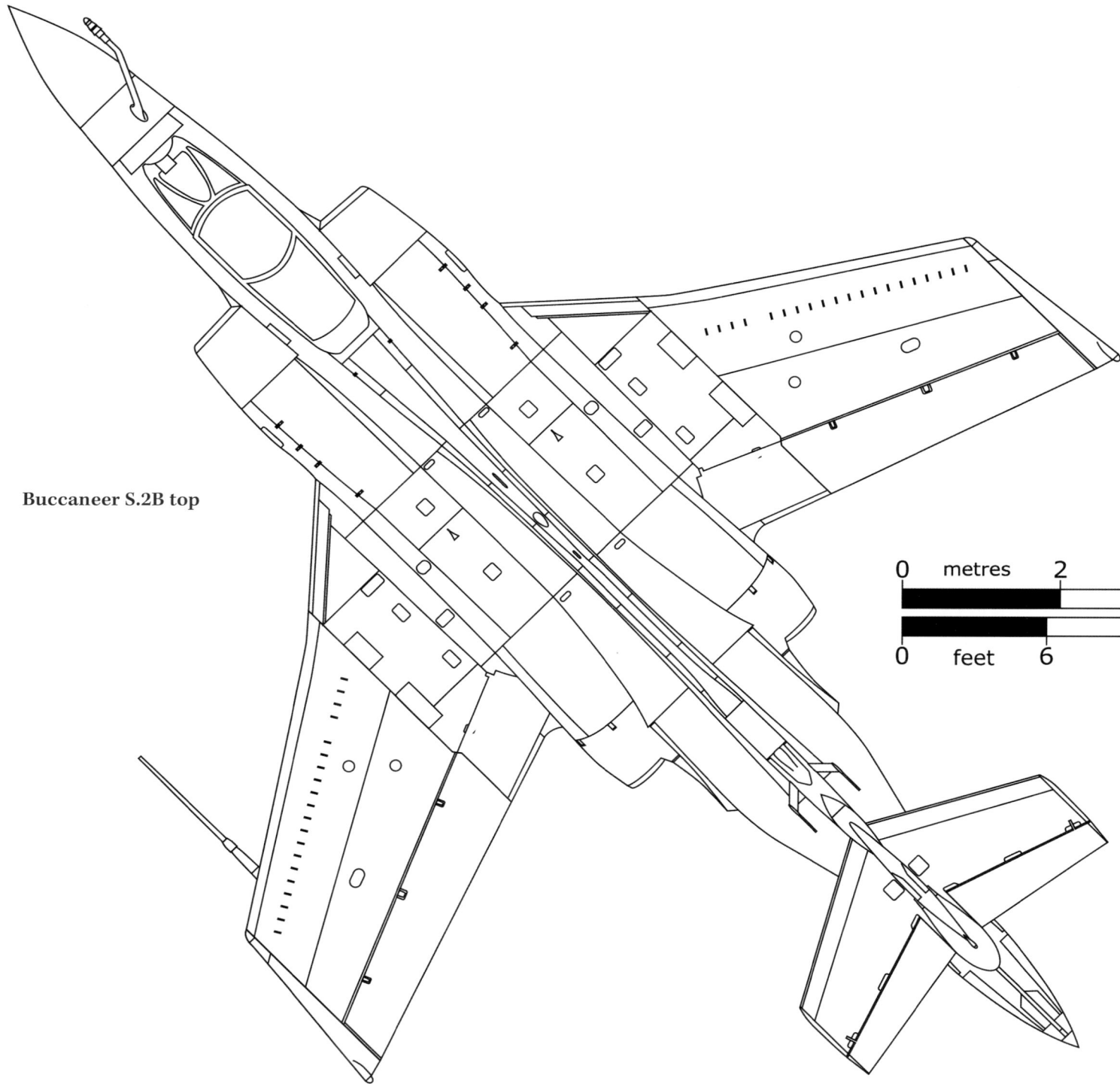

0 metres 2 4 6

0 feet 6 12 18

Buccaneer S.2B underside

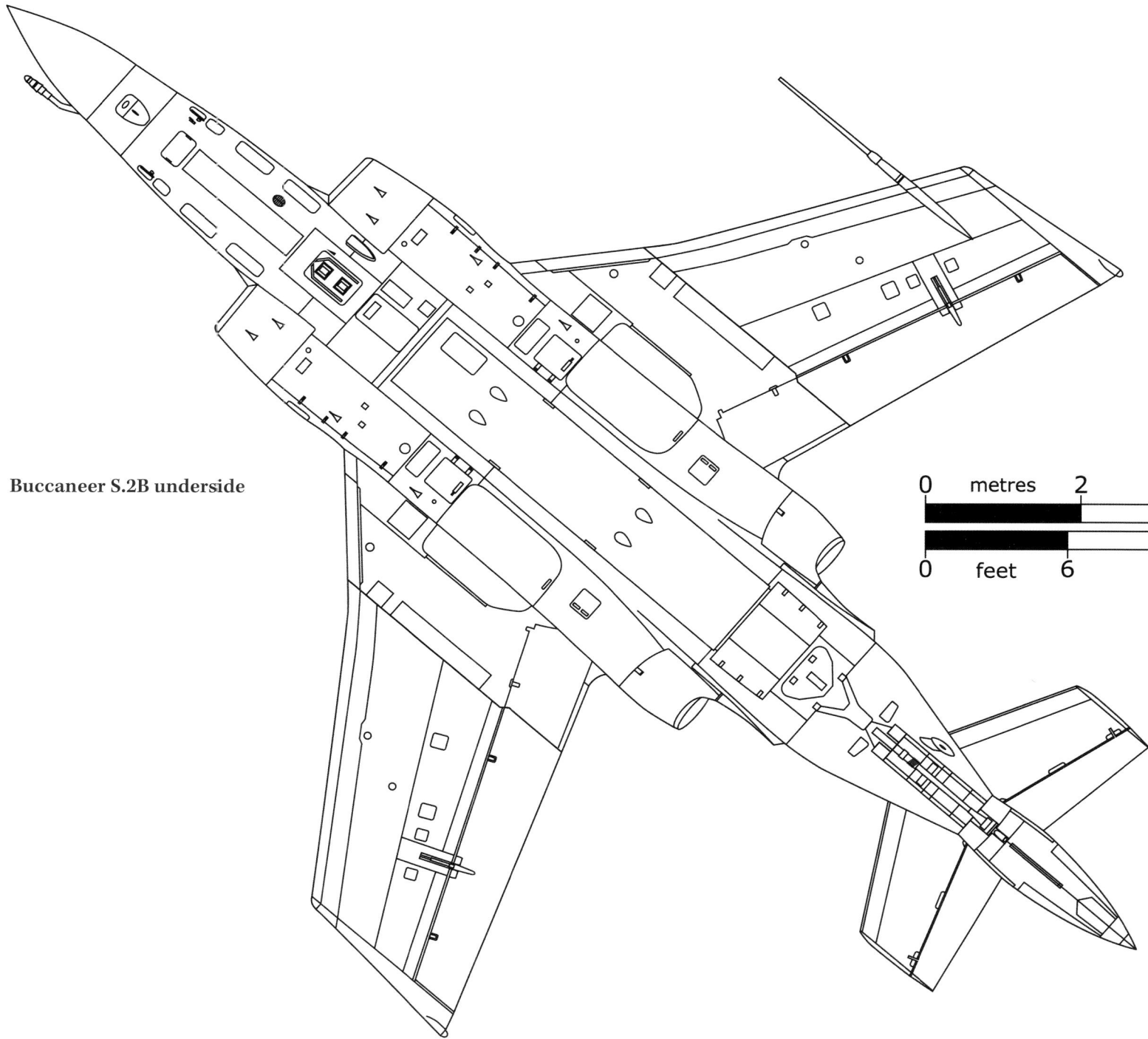

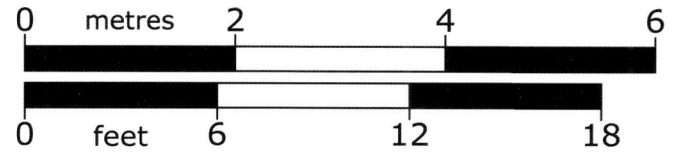

0   metres   2   4   6

0   feet   6   12   18

SEPECAT JAGUAR

The Jaguar was a direct result of cold war requirements, born out of the changing role of air defence and going against the practices that were developed and considered conventional by the Air Ministry. It was built as a low level ground-attack fighter fulfilling a range of roles and RAF Jaguar squadrons spent many years based in West Germany – but the only conflicts they were involved in were the first Gulf War of 1991 and Bosnia in 1995. In 31 years with the RAF the type served with distinction and was the last of the cold war warriors.

During the early 1960s both the British and French decided to replace their fast jet trainers – the Fouga Magister in France and the Hunter and Gnat in the UK. The French had already begun development of their intended Magister successor, the ECAT, which was intended as both a trainer and light attack aircraft.

Following cancellation of that project, aspects of the ECAT, along with parts of the cancelled British TSR2 programme, were fed into what would become the Jaguar. The two nations were both looking for an aircraft with similar requirements and in the climate of European cooperation and collaboration, which also led to the Gazelle and Concorde, the Anglo-French company SEPECAT (Société Européenne de Production de l'Avion d'École de Combat et d'Appui Tactique) was formed in 1965 by the British Aircraft Corporation and Breguet.

It was originally intended for the aircraft to be variable geometry and each nation agreed to purchase 150 with a two-seater variant being the preferred choice for the RAF and RN. Escalating costs became such a concern, however, that the French withdrew their initial order and altered their requirements.

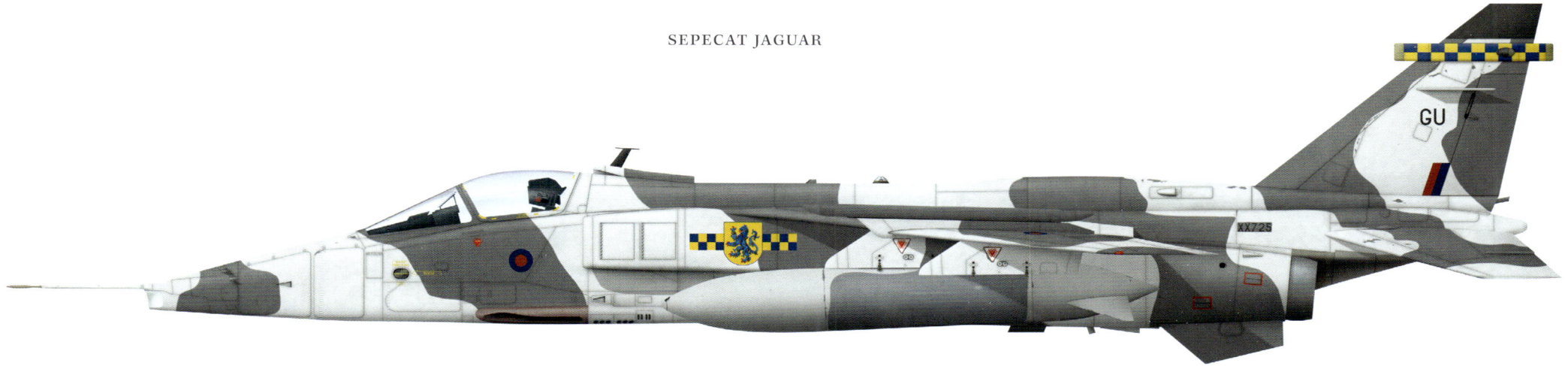

JAGUAR GR.3 XX725 54 SQUADRON

Jaguars were frequently deployed to Norway and several experimental schemes were applied. This late design, applied to XX725 during early 2005, was a temporary scheme of white over barley (camouflage grey) in a traditional camouflage pattern.

The British revised their order too, reducing the number of two-seaters and raising an order for a single seat strike variant. With Royal Navy interest rapidly waning, the aircraft would just be for the RAF, making up for the cancellation of other projects.

The name was only settled on a week before the project was due to be announced at the Paris Airshow in 1965, with permission to use it being sought from Jaguar cars. Design progressed at a steady pace and two years later at the 1967 Paris Air Show a wooden mock-up was displayed, though it suffered in heavy rain and started to sag.

Not only was a new aircraft developed but a new engine was also created to fit the Jaguar. Based on the Rolls-Royce RB.172, the Ardour was the result of a partnership between Turbomeca and Rolls-Royce. The project suffered many delays and the prototype was underpowered and suffered teething problems to such an extent that the first three airframes had been completed but only three engines had been built.

The Ardour was designed for low fuel consumption and to be able to cruise at low level but also high thrust needed to be available for take-off and to reach supersonic speeds. It did not help matters when Rolls-Royce filed for bankruptcy in 1971. Once it was completed, however, the Ardour proved to be a reliable engine, also being used in the Hawk and Goshawk.

Eventually engines were fitted to the Jaguar prototypes and taxiing trials commenced. These were followed on September 8, 1968, at Istres, France, with the first flight of a Jaguar taking place. Bernard Witt, Breguet's chief test pilot, was at the controls. He was impressed with the handling of the Jaguar and pleased with the incident-free flight. Over the next few months three more

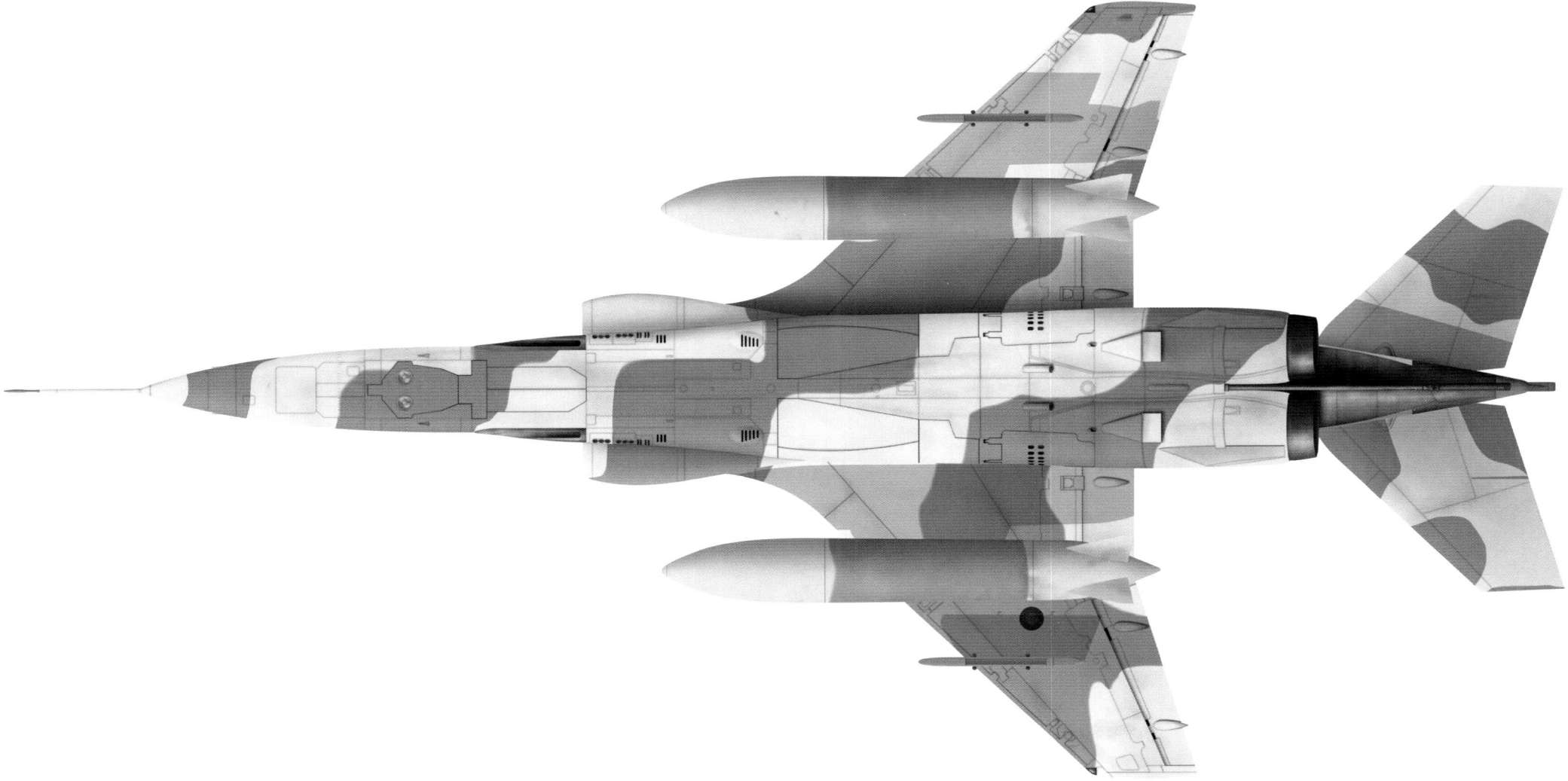

JAGUAR S06 XW560

XW560 was the first single seat British Jaguar, before LRMTS was fitted. It was lost in an engine fire in August
1972. The colours shown are gloss dark green, dark sea grey camouflage with light aircraft grey underside.

prototypes flew in France. Then the first British-built Jaguar S06 made its maiden flight from Warton, Lancashire, on October 12, 1969. Over the next few years an extensive testing programme took place with the six prototypes, two more being added.

The GR.1 was designed to be flexible and to evolve with the changing defence situation that was anticipated in the 70s and 80s. Key to this was the accuracy of the delivery system. A digital inertial navigation system, the Marconi-GEC 920ATC, was fitted along with the advanced Laser Ranger and Marked Target Seeker (LRMTS). As the Ardour 104 became available, the GR.1s were upgraded to accommodate it and it was fitted to new aircraft as they came off the production line.

Early in 1973 the French Air Force and RAF prepared to receive the type and commenced conversion. The first handover took place

at RAF Lossiemouth on May 30, 1973, to the Jaguar OCU; trials and training being initiated soon after. Deliveries of the GR.1 and T.2 continued throughout the year. The following year the Jaguar was ready to enter front line service, 54 Squadron officially receiving the GR.1 during a ceremony on June 5, 1974 (the OCU was numbered 226 at this time). Also present at the ceremony was a Jaguar in 6 Squadron markings, this one also being fitted with the LRMTS nose — which would be a distinguishing feature of RAF Jaguars.

Later in the year the Jaguar force relocated to RAF Coltishall, the station becoming the permanent home of the Jaguar fleet. The following spring the first two squadrons to be based in West Germany were formed, 14 Squadron forming in April and 17 Squadron in June. These were later followed by 2, 11 and 31 Squadrons also in West Germany. Finally 41 Squadron converted and 20 Squadron

JAGUAR GR.1 XZ361 2 SQUADRON

2 Squadron was equipped with Jaguars in 1976 while based at RAF Laarbruch in Germany. The squadron eventually replaced them with Tornados in January 1989. The aircraft is painted in all over dark green and dark sea grey.

exchanged their Harrier GR.3s for Jaguars (the squadron would later return to the Harrier when 233 OCU was renumbered).

Beginning in 1983, the existing navigation system was replaced with the Ferranti FIN 1064 and the type was redesignated the GR.1A. Subsequent minor upgrades saw the type become the GR.1B – though externally there were no noticeable differences. This was followed by yet more changes including the introduction of the Ardour 106 to the Jaguar 96 programme, resulting in the GR.3.

Both British and French Jaguars were deployed during the first Gulf War, Operation Granby, with 12 RAF Jaguars flying a total of 617 combat missions against a range of targets, including SAM and artillery sites. They also accounted for 15 ships of the Iraqi Navy. The aircraft and crews were drawn from 6, 41 and 54 Squadrons as well as 226 OCU, arriving in the Gulf during October 1990.

It was also intended for Jaguars to play an active role in Operation Telic, the second Gulf War, however there were deployment issues when Turkey withdrew permission to use its airfields. Between the two wars, the Jaguar was also used by the UN in the former Yugoslavia to attack Bosnian Serb targets and support Harrier GR.7s.

A trainer version was needed to convert pilots to the type, as with any advanced jet, but unlike other front line jets the Jaguar was originally intended to be a trainer until the requirements evolved. The French E and the RAF T.2 were closer than the A and GR.1 in design but the biggest difference was to the avionics system, the T.2 mirroring the GR.1. It was also fitted with only one Aden cannon.

The RAF wanted the T.2 to have a secondary function where it would be able to fly full combat missions should this prove necessary. Without a refuelling probe, its range was rather limited and its combat capability was so restricted that the circumstances would have had to be exceptionally dire for it to be used in anger. The T.4 resulted from the T.2 being upgraded as part of the Jaguar 96 programme and the aircraft received the same enhancements as the GR.3.

The Jaguar served with the RAF for more than 30 years and enjoyed a similar longevity with the French Air Force. It was also exported to Ecuador, India, Nigeria and Oman. A total of 543 were built with 165 GR.1s and 38 T.2s for the RAF. Due to defence cuts, the British Jaguars were retired with just five days' notice on April 30, 2007.

The Jaguar retired with distinction, having been involved in two conflicts and having spent many years in West Germany with the RAF. Many airframes survived and some have since been used at RAF Cosford as instructional ground trainers.

SEPECAT JAGUAR

VARIANT	LENGTH	SPAN	HEIGHT	ENGINE
S	55FT 2.5IN/16.83M	28FT 6IN/8.69M	16FT 10.5IN/5.14M	2 X ADOUR 102
GR.1A	55FT 2.5IN/16.83M	28FT 6IN/8.69M	16FT 10.5IN/5.14M	2 X ADOUR 102
T.2	57FT 6IN/17.53M	28FT 6IN/8.69M	16FT 10.5IN/5.14M	2 X ADOUR 104
GR.3	55FT 2.5IN/16.83M	28FT 6IN/8.69M	16FT 10.5IN/5.14M	2 X ADOUR 106
T.4	57FT 6IN/17.53M	28FT 6IN/8.69M	16FT 10.5IN/5.14M	2 X ADOUR 106
GA.11	45FT 11IN/14M	33FT 8IN/10.26M	13FT 2IN/4.01M	AVON 121

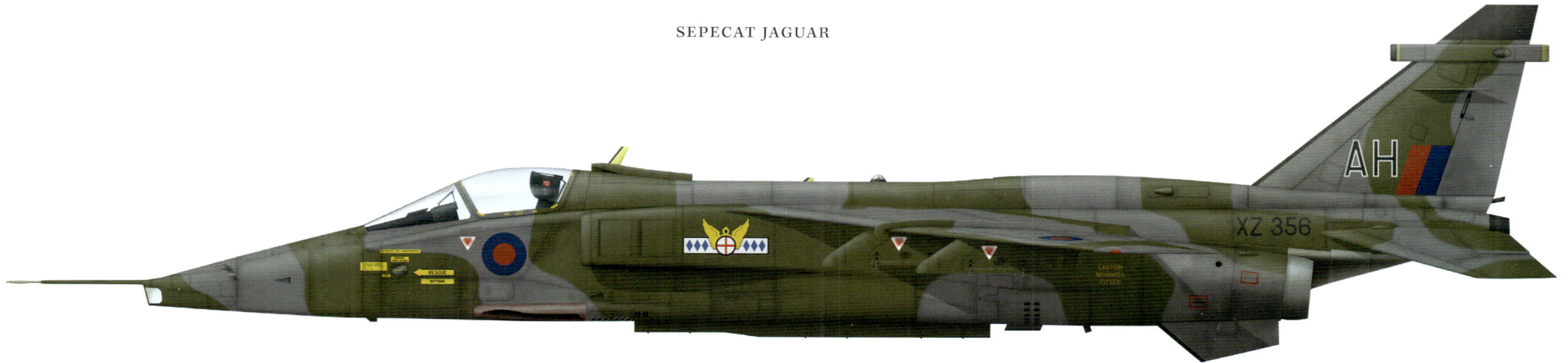

JAGUAR GR.1 XZ356 41 SQUADRON

The Jaguar was operated by 41 Squadron while based in RAF Bruggen, West Germany, from 1975. During this time their aircraft had a wraparound camouflage scheme. Delivered in 1976, XZ356 initially served with the unit before being transferred to 17 Squadron, then 20 Squadron. It then returned to 41 Squadron in time to participate in Operation Granby.

JAGUAR GR.1 XX821 17 SQUADRON

Having initially had a light aircraft grey underside in after their delivery in September 1975, 17 Squadron's Jaguars were later painted in all over dark sea grey with dark green upper surfaces. The squadron was re-equipped with the Tornado in 1985.

JAGUAR GR.1 XZ107 41 SQUADRON

Most schemes worn by the Jaguar were a variation on standard camouflage covering dark green, but a different approach to this scheme was taken with XZ107 during an exercise in April 1988. By the time the exercise had finished the paint had run and worn off over much of the airframe.

JAGUAR GR.1 XZ387 31 SQUADRON

31 Squadron remained in West Germany when it converted from the Phantom to Jaguar in 1976, its aircraft painted in typical wraparound scheme. The squadron also had eight WE.177 nuclear bombs which could be delivered by the Jaguar.

JAGUAR GR.1 XX116 16 SQUADRON

Between 1979 and 1984, XX116 was on loan to the Indian Air Force. In 1993 it was given this distinctive paint scheme with a huge 16 Squadron 'Saint' on the fin. For some years it was the air display mount of Flt Lt Andy Cubin and was last flown in 2005 before becoming a training aid at RAF Manston in Kent. In 2020 it was sent to Yorkshire-based restoration specialists Jet Art Aviation for restoration to its 'Black Cat' specification.

JAGUAR GR.1 XX818 20 SQUADRON

Between flying the early and late Harriers, 20 Sqn received 12 Jaguars in 1977 while at RAF Bruggen, West Germany. These were replaced with Tornados in 1984.

JAGUAR GR.1 XZ398 41 SQUADRON

Painted with a red tail and spine with white edging, XZ398 wore a 75 years anniversary scheme. The aircraft continued to fly with this scheme for several years before being repainted.

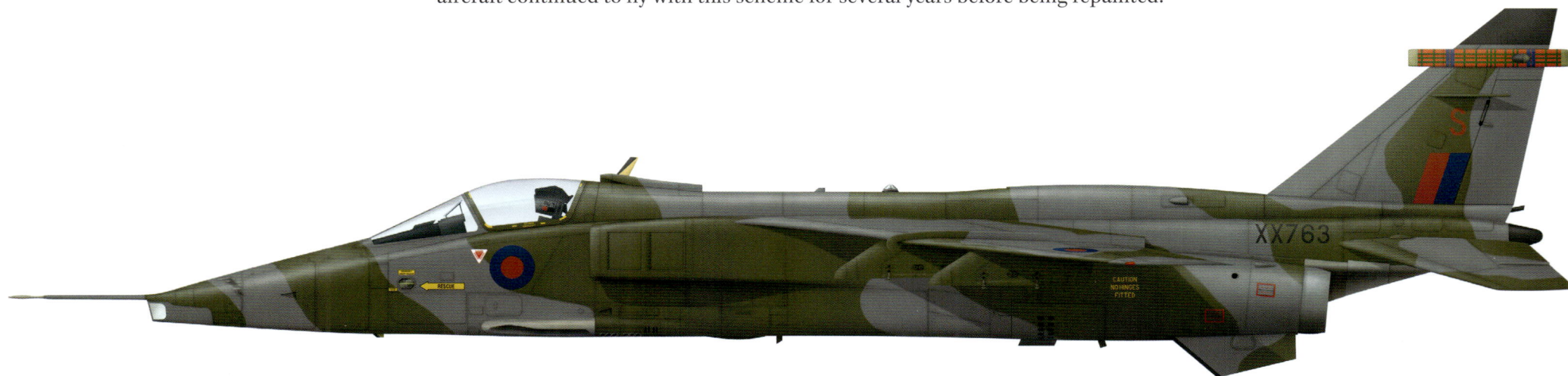

JAGUAR GR.1 XX763 226 OCU

Re-formed at RAF Lossiemouth in 1974 for conversion to the Jaguar, 226 OCU was also equipped with the WE.177 and would have been a front line squadron in the event of war.

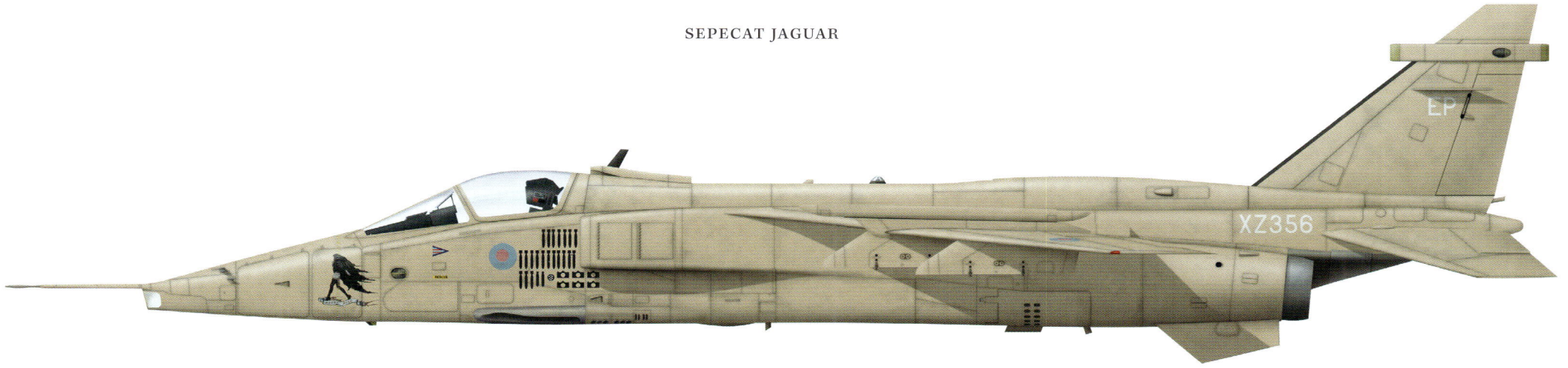

JAGUAR GR.1 XZ356 41 SQUADRON

XZ356 took part in Operation Granby wearing a desert scheme and 'Mary Rose' nose art. Today the aircraft survives in private ownership.

JAGUAR GR.1 XZ112 54 SQUADRON

Based at RAF Coltishall, 54 Squadron was one of the longest operating Jaguar squadrons (1974-2005).
XZ112 received a special blue tail and tank in 1991 for the squadron's 75th anniversary.

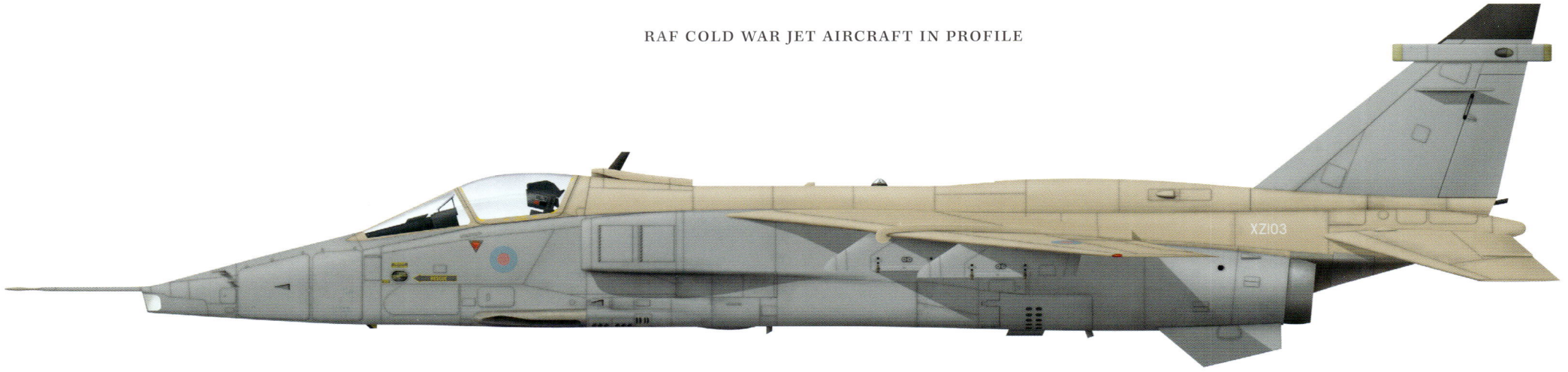

JAGUAR GR.1 XC XZ103
An experimental scheme was applied to XZ103, light aircraft grey with upper surfaces painted
desert pink, when it took part in trials during 2002 at China Lake, California.

: JAGUAR GR.1 XX733 14 SQUADRON
During Operation Granby, 6, 41 and 54 Squadrons supplied Jaguars. The aircraft were painted in desert pink, though this
rapidly faded in the hot and dry conditions. XX733 completed 39 missions, nose art being painted by Cpl Paul Robins.

JAGUAR GR.3 XX112 6 SQUADRON

Celebrating the 90th anniversary of 'The Flying Canopeners' in 2004, the tail of XX112
was painted light blue and bore the squadron's battle honours.

JAGUAR GR.3A XZ398 41 SQUADRON

Late Jaguars were painted in barley grey (now called camouflage grey), including XZ398, which was
again selected to commemorate a 41 Squadron anniversary, this time the 85th.

JAGUAR T.2 XX143 54 SQUADRON

54 Squadron also had trainers on strength such as this T.2 in wraparound camouflage. The
lion shield was on the nose and checks were on the intakes.

JAGUAR T.2 XX145 ETPS

Operated by the Empire Test Pilot School, XX145 wore the Raspberry Ripple scheme of the school.
Delivered in June 1974, XX145 was retired to Bruntingthorpe, Leicestershire, in April 2012.

JAGUAR T.4 XX847 6 SQUADRON

A typical if somewhat weathered scheme was applied to both 6 Squadron's fighters and trainers. XX847
was photographed in 2007 with a camouflaged external tank at RAF Coningsby.

JAGUAR T.4 XX846 16 SQUADRON

Jaguar schemes became increasingly patchwork as time wore on and XX846 flew for a brief period in December 2001
with an unpainted nose panel. The overall scheme was a mixture of camouflage grey and dark sea grey.

JAGUAR GR.1 XZ104 2 SQUADRON
While based at Laarbruch, Germany, 2 Squadron celebrated its 76th anniversary with a special tail scheme featuring the squadron crest. The squadron had moved to Germany late on during the Second World War and remained there until 1991.

JAGUAR GR.1 XZ115 41 SQUADRON
During September 1990, XX115 briefly wore an overall white scheme and was photographed while visiting 6 Squadron at Coltishall. It is thought to have been painted this way prior to a 41 Squadron winter deployment to Norway.

JAGUAR GR.3 XX725 BOSNIA

Jaguars were used as laser designators for Harriers in Bosnia during Operation Vulcan, September 1995. Some squadron and national markings were partially removed but it retained traces of 41 and 54 Squadrons.

JAGUAR GR.3A XX962

XX962 appeared in this scheme during Operation Vulcan in Bosnia. The lightning tally represents the missions flown.

JAGUAR GR.3 XX970 6 SQUADRON

Wearing a typical late scheme with squadron markings, this aircraft slowly became more weathered as it neared retirement — although in 2007 it was maintained in a relatively pristine condition. XX970 eventually found its way to Cosford.

JAGUAR T.2 XX141 CRANWELL

Delivered to the RAF in March 1974, XX141 was eventually retired as an operational aircraft and relegated to instructional airframe duties at Cranwell where it was painted gloss black. Today it is occasionally displayed at Cosford.

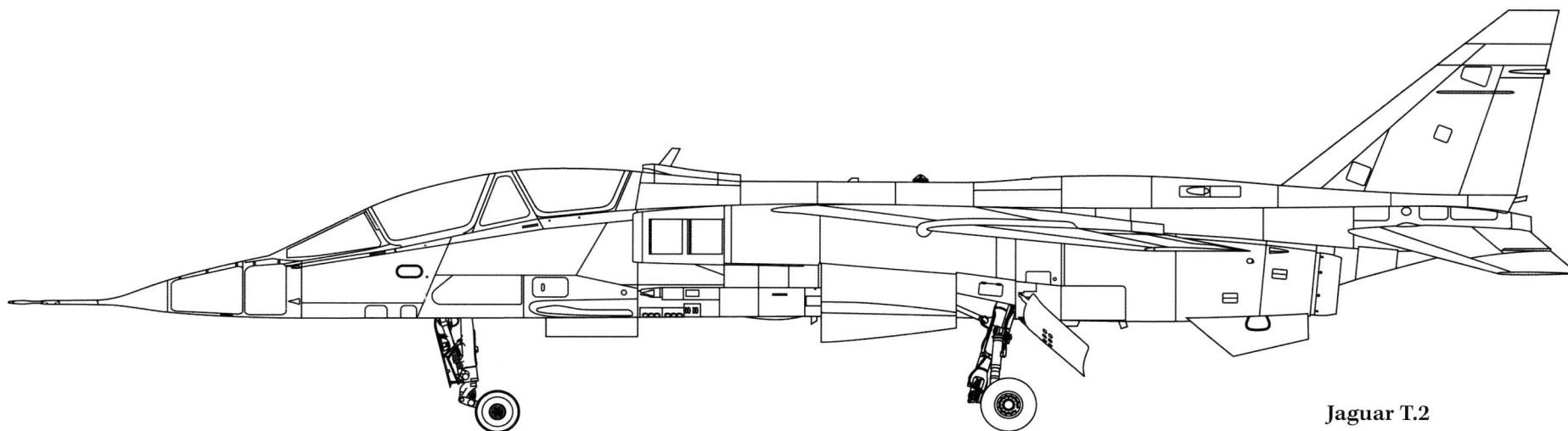

Jaguar T.2

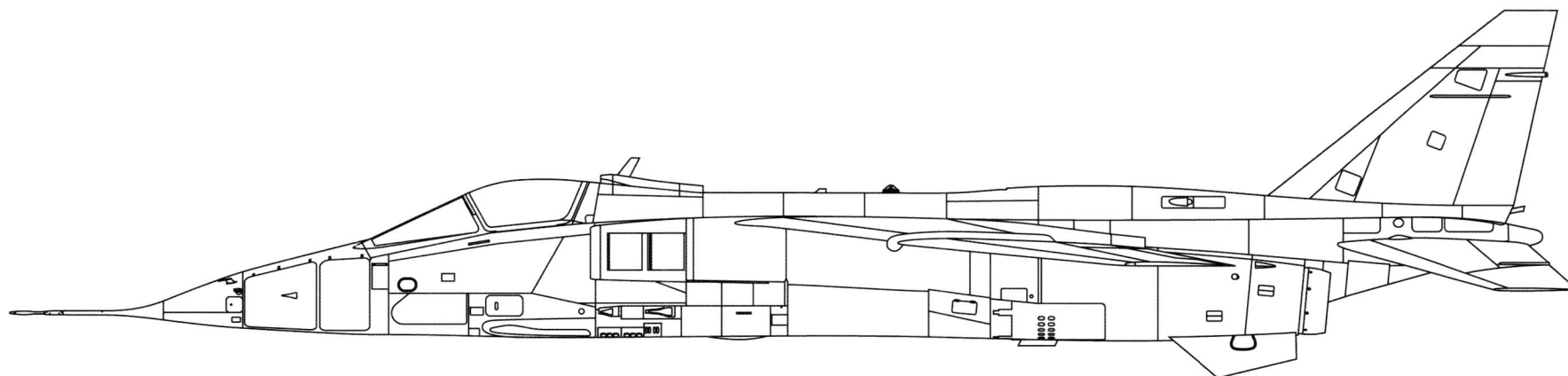

Jaguar S

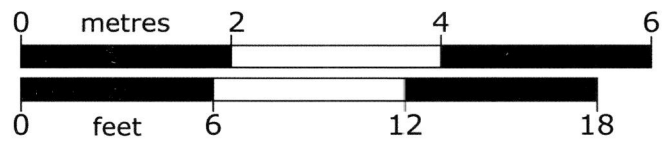

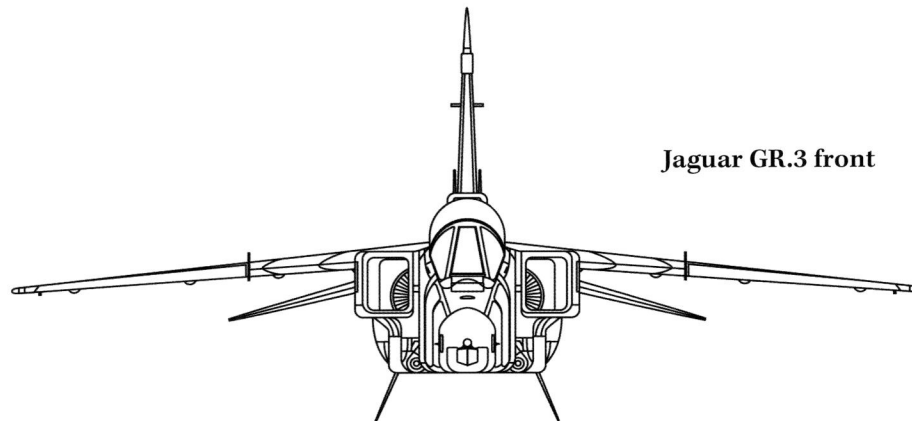

Jaguar GR.3 front

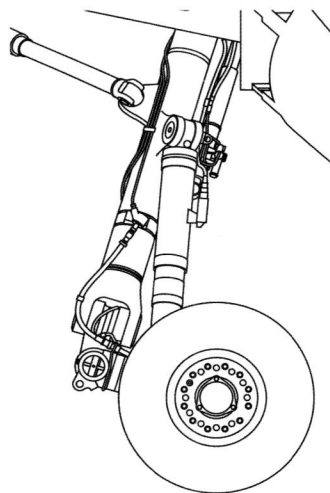

Main wheel

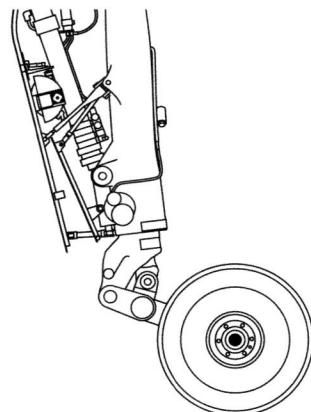

Nose wheel

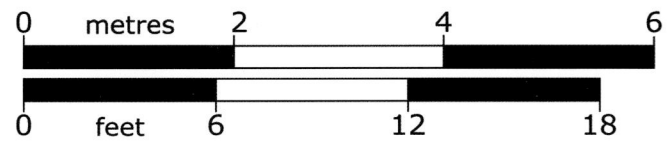

0	metres	2	4	6

0	feet	6	12	18

Jaguar GR.3

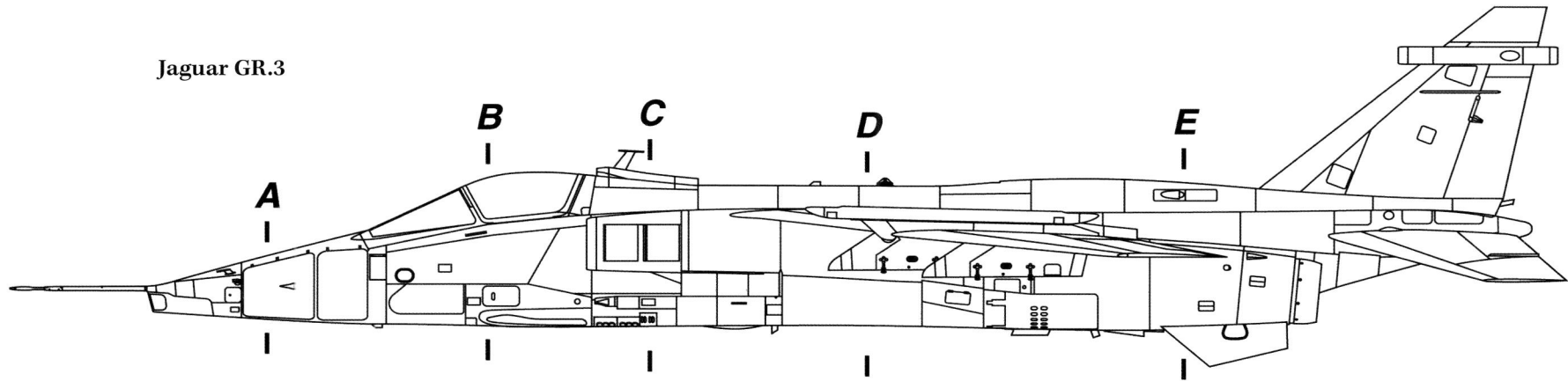

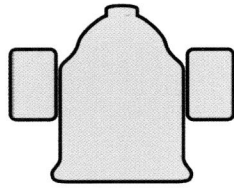

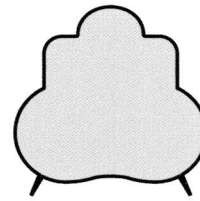

A   **B**   **C**   **D**   **E**

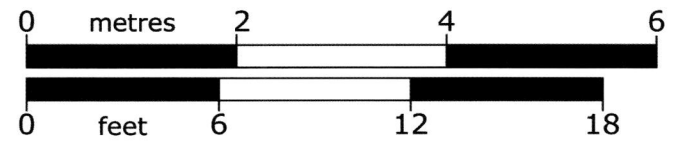

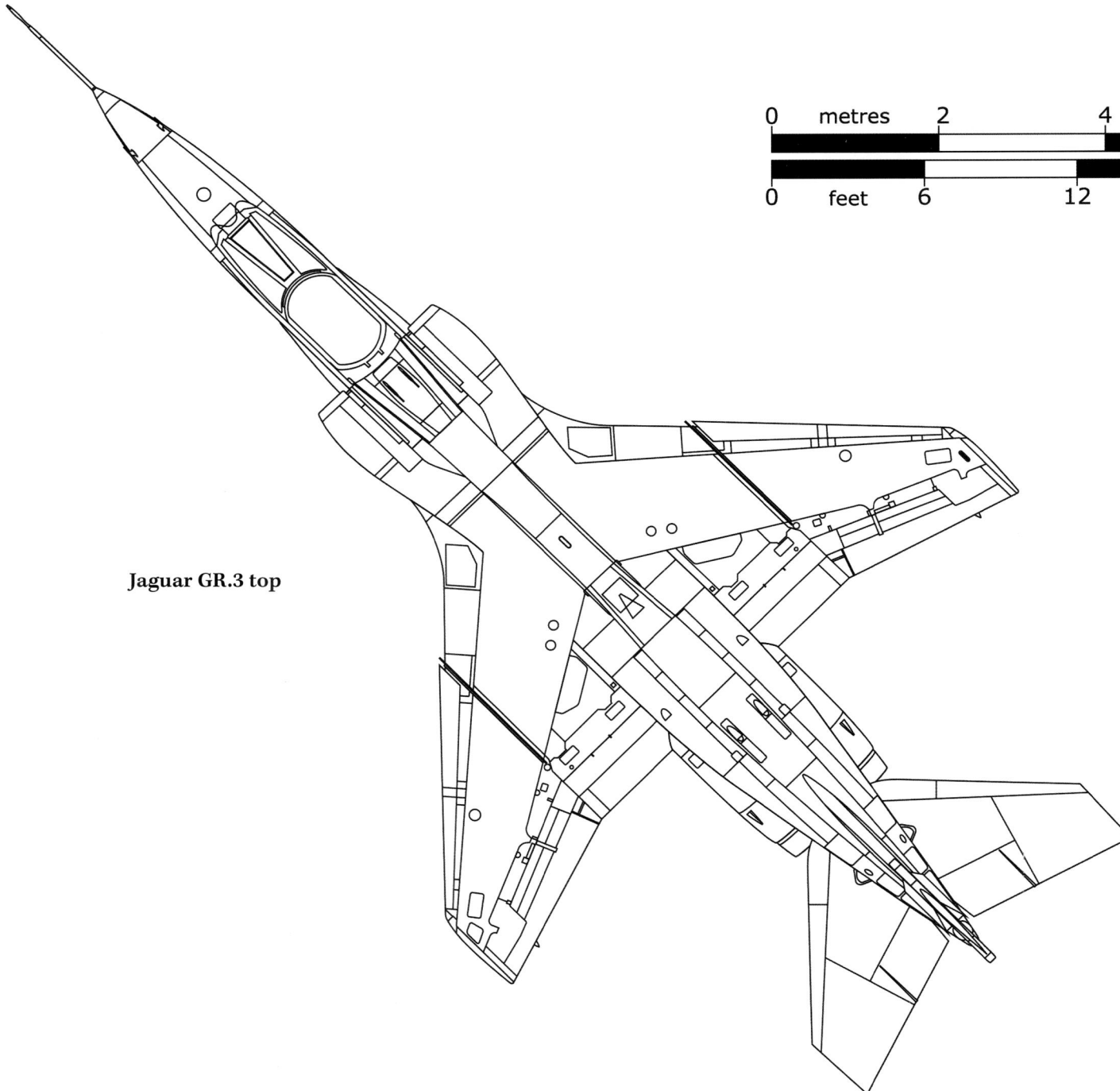

Jaguar GR.3 top

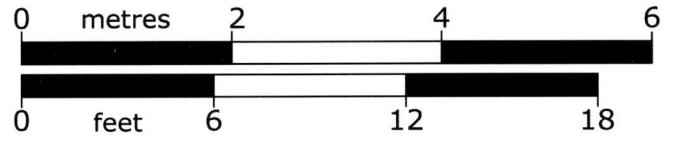

0   metres   2   4   6

0   feet   6   12   18

0   metres   2   4   6

0   feet   6   12   18

Jaguar GR.3 underside